MW00831479

Reviving Rationality

Reviving Rationality

Saving Cost-Benefit Analysis for the Sake of the Environment and Our Health

MICHAEL A. LIVERMORE
AND RICHARD L. REVESZ

OXFORD
UNIVERSITY PRESS

OXFORD
UNIVERSITY PRESS

Oxford University Press is a department of the University of Oxford. It furthers the University's objective of excellence in research, scholarship, and education by publishing worldwide. Oxford is a registered trade mark of Oxford University Press in the UK and certain other countries.

Published in the United States of America by Oxford University Press
198 Madison Avenue, New York, NY 10016, United States of America.

© Oxford University Press 2020

All rights reserved. No part of this publication may be reproduced, stored in a retrieval system, or transmitted, in any form or by any means, without the prior permission in writing of Oxford University Press, or as expressly permitted by law, by license, or under terms agreed with the appropriate reproduction rights organization. Inquiries concerning reproduction outside the scope of the above should be sent to the Rights Department, Oxford University Press, at the address above.

You must not circulate this work in any other form and you must impose this same condition on any acquirer.

Library of Congress Cataloging-in-Publication Data
Names: Livermore, Michael A., author. | Revesz, Richard L., 1958– author.
Title: Reviving rationality : saving cost-benefit analysis for the sake of the environment and our health / Michael A. Livermore and Richard L. Revesz.
Description: New York, NY : Oxford University Press, [2020] |
Includes index.
Identifiers: LCCN 2020018480 (print) | LCCN 2020018481 (ebook) |
ISBN 9780197539446 (hardback) | ISBN 9780197539460 (epub) |
ISBN 9780197539477
Subjects: LCSH: Trade regulation—United States. |
Trade regulation—United States—Cost effectiveness. |
Administrative agencies—United States—Decision making. |
Environmental law—United States—Cost effectiveness. |
Public health laws—United States—Cost effectiveness.
Classification: LCC KF1600 .L58 2020 (print) | LCC KF1600 (ebook) |
DDC 343.7307—dc23
LC record available at https://lccn.loc.gov/2020018480
LC ebook record available at https://lccn.loc.gov/2020018481

1 3 5 7 9 8 6 4 2

Printed by Sheridan Books, Inc., United States of America

For my students, who have taught me a great deal.—*ML*

For Vicki, for inspiring me and supporting my endeavors.—*RR*

Contents

Acknowledgments

This book is based in part on arguments that we have developed jointly, individually, and in collaboration with many others in prior work over a number of years. We gratefully acknowledge the contribution of our coauthors as well as others, such as research assistants and commenters, involved with these projects.[1] We are also grateful to our colleagues at the Institute for Policy Integrity at New York University School of Law. Their efforts to promote rationality in government decision making have made a real difference in the world, are a source of inspiration and intellectual engagement for us both, and have profoundly shaped the arguments in this book. We would like to especially thank Jonathan Adler, Caroline Cecot, Bethany Davis Noll, E. Donald Elliott, Denise Grab, Sally Katzen, Jack Lienke, Richard Morgenstern, Paul Noe, Jason Schwartz, Howard Shelanski, Derek Sylvan, W. Kip Viscusi, Wendy Wagner, Christopher Walker, Jonathan Wiener for their very valuable comments on earlier versions of this manuscript. Mae Bowen, Asha Brundage-Moore, Natasha Brunstein, Tim Duncheon, Nick Harper, Will Hughes, Ben Morris, Zoe Palenik, Cris Ray, Julia Ross, and Rachel Rothschild provided excellent research assistance. And we owe a special debt of gratitude to Ben Morris for working tirelessly with us through the latter stages of the project.

Introduction

In the summer of 2008, we published the book *Retaking Rationality: How Cost-Benefit Analysis Can Better Protect the Environment and Our Health*. At the time, the administration of George W. Bush was limping to the finish line after seven years during which the political system was focused intently on issues of terrorism and war. There remained no clear end in sight for US military engagements in Iraq and Afghanistan. Domestically, the country was at the brink of a financial crisis that would lead to the deepest economic downturn since the Great Depression.

Despite these circumstances, 2008 was also a time of optimism, especially in the realm of politics. The campaign of Barack Obama, in particular, capitalized on that feeling, with a strongly progressive policy program and matching rhetoric, first in his upstart challenge to Hillary Clinton for the Democratic nomination, and then in the general election. It is difficult to imagine that the poster of Obama by artist Shepard Fairey, which placed a stylized image of the candidate over the word "hope," would have achieved its iconic status in a more cynical time.

Our goal in writing *Retaking Rationality* was to intervene in what we believed was a stale debate between conservatives and progressives over the use of cost-benefit analysis in government decision making. Federal agencies have adopted thousands of rules to promote social goals like cleaning the air and reducing automobile fatalities. These rules have made important contributions to public well-being—for example, by saving lives that would otherwise have been lost—but they also require substantial investments from private parties. Cost-benefit analysis provides a formal means to compare positive and negative effects of new rules. In 1981, Ronald Reagan issued an executive order creating a new process of White House review of new rules and requiring agencies to conduct cost-benefit analyses of their regulatory proposals. The basic structure created by Reagan has stayed in place for four decades.

Perhaps unsurprisingly, given its genesis in a proudly anti-regulatory administration, progressives had spent the intervening years fighting against the use of cost-benefit analysis. Although there is clear intuitive value to examining the pros and cons of major government decisions, for complex regulatory decisions that routinely involve thousands of lives and billions of dollars, cost-benefit analysis is anything but simple and intuitive. Progressives' hostility to the technique

Reviving Rationality. Michael A. Livermore and Richard L. Revesz, Oxford University Press (2020). © Oxford University Press. DOI: 10.1093/oso/9780197539446.001.0001.

in part sprang from a fear that deep in the folds of jargon-laden reports, government officials under the sway of Big Business or partisan politicians would dismiss the benefits of protections for consumers, the environment, and public health, while inflating the costs.

In *Retaking Rationality*, we argued that although some of these fears were justified, the progressive opposition to cost-benefit analysis was ineffective and counterproductive. It was ineffective because cost-benefit analysis was not going anywhere. Early in his administration, Bill Clinton promulgated an executive order that continued forward the structure put in place by Reagan, thereby giving the technique a bipartisan imprimatur. And blanket opposition was counterproductive because, by ceding the conversation about how costs and benefits should be counted, progressives were allowing their political adversaries to shape the technique in an anti-regulatory direction.

After the publication of *Retaking Rationality*, we worked together to found the Institute for Policy Integrity, a think tank at the New York University School of Law. The mission of Policy Integrity is to improve the quality of government decision making through advocacy and scholarship in the fields of administrative law, economics, and public policy. Part of our goal in founding Policy Integrity was to work with progressive organizations to show them how cost-benefit analysis, done well, often supported strong protections for the environment, public health, and consumers. Over the years, Policy Integrity has collaborated with groups representing a diverse set of interests, participated in hundreds of regulatory and legal proceedings, issued in-depth reports on a wide range of issues, and facilitated a legal clinic that has trained scores of students.

A few months after Policy Integrity's founding, Barack Obama was elected. For the next eight years, we worked with the staff at the institute to push the administration to adopt more efficient rules and improve how it counted costs and benefits. When regulations were challenged in court, we weighed in with our views. From rules affecting safety in our nation's prisons to interstate air pollution, from a plan to expand offshore oil drilling to energy efficiency mandates for home appliances, Policy Integrity helped shape regulatory decisions across a wide range of issues by marshaling the types of cost-benefit arguments that progressive have sometimes eschewed.

As we will discuss in this book, the Obama administration was frequently inclined in the same direction that we were pushing: toward the use of rigorous cost-benefit analysis to identify and promote sound regulations that improved public well-being. Although we sometimes disagreed with the administration's decisions, we often found at least some sympathetic ears among both career public servants and political appointees.

Things have changed.

Policy Integrity is non-partisan and counts several Republicans (and former Republicans) among its core supporters. In our own recognition of the value of cost-benefit analysis and our embrace of regulatory tools long favored by economists—such as market-based mechanisms to reduce pollution—we have adopted views that, at one time, were much more widely accepted among Republicans than among Democrats. But in recent years, American politics shifted under our (and everyone else's) feet. Views once at the heartland of the Republican Party—such as enthusiasm for free trade—have been loudly denounced by a Republican president. And cost-benefit analysis, emissions trading, and other ideas that were hatched in economics departments and then embraced by Republican politicians have become verboten for many in the party, or have been twisted and deformed beyond recognition. When we wrote *Retaking Rationality* and founded Policy Integrity, it was to convince a skeptical progressive audience of the attractiveness of views that, in many ways, were Republican orthodoxy. Now, what is called cost-benefit analysis by a Republican administration is all but unrecognizable.

The declining prestige of cost-benefit analysis among Republican elites did not begin with the 2016 presidential election. For us, perhaps the most striking illustration of how strongly partisanship has reshaped views of cost-benefit analysis came during the 2012 campaign, when Republican presidential candidate Mitt Romney had this to say:

> Where standards are put in place to constrain the issuance of regulations— such as requiring the use of cost-benefit analysis—they tend to be vulnerable to manipulation and also disconnected from the central issue confronting our country today, namely, generating economic growth and creating jobs. The end result is an economy subject to the whims of unaccountable bureaucrats pursuing their own agendas.[1]

It was particularly telling that Romney—the former governor who had promoted a successful regional effort to create a cap-and-trade system for greenhouse gases; whose market-oriented health care reforms in his state served as the template for Obamacare; who had made a fortune in management consulting and private-equity investment—industries that rely heavily on economic models—would turn his back on the central tool of his former trades and what seemed to be his prior philosophy of governing.

This book is, accordingly, more frank in its recognition of the partisan dynamics that have shaped how cost-benefit analysis is used and abused, and it has a different intended audience. *Retaking Rationality* was addressed to progressives; here, we attempt to speak more generally to those affiliated with either party (or who have rejected both) who care about maintaining (or restoring) a system of protections for social priorities such as environmental quality and public health that is based on evidence, reasoned decision making, and a shared effort to improve public well-being.

People who are committed to preserving a system of rational regulation will not necessarily agree about any specific policy choice, and prior administrations have pursued quite different regulatory agendas when in office. The Clinton and Obama administrations placed relatively greater emphasis on addressing broadly shared risk such as pollution, while the administrations of Reagan, George H. W. Bush, and George W. Bush focused more on reducing burdens on business. But within this fairly large range, there were also important areas of agreement. Presidents of both parties recognized the value of keeping costs down for businesses; they also acknowledged that regulation is often necessary to pursue important social goals. Perhaps most important, the institutions that they built and the practices they adopted emphasized the place of evidence, analysis, and expertise in regulatory decision making.

There are many examples where analysis helped shape the decisions of prior administrations in what might seem like surprising ways. The Reagan administration continued and strengthened a phase-out of leaded gasoline.[2] George H. W. Bush worked with a Democratic Congress to overhaul and improve the nation's primary law on air quality protection, saving tens of thousands of lives that would have been lost each year from air pollution.[3] The Clinton and Obama administrations both embraced market-based mechanisms for cutting pollution, saving businesses billions while achieving their environmental goals.[4] The George W. Bush administration adopted controls on air pollution from power plants and more stringent fuel-economy standards for automobiles.[5] In each of these examples, ideological and interest-group opposition pushed in the opposite direction and was successfully resisted by a compelling, evidence-based case about how best to serve the public interest.

We do not want to paint an overly rosy or Pollyannaish picture of regulatory decision making over the past several decades. Rules were adopted that were far from perfect, and even counterproductive. At the same time, important social problems languished in the face of agency inaction. Well-funded and well-connected interest groups were frequently invited into the halls of power while the public watched from the outside. But, notwithstanding these shortcomings, in the push and pull of regulatory decision making, evidence, analysis, and expertise had a place at the table.

The message in this book is that, in abandoning these decades-long bipartisan practices, the Trump administration and its supporters risk undermining a fundamental set of norms in the American system of governance that have constrained and informed agency decision making for decades. In the process, they have promoted incoherent and harmful policies, demoralized the federal workforce, and provoked a backlash from courts. This experiment in abandoning the norms of good governance has been a disaster. There are legitimate debates to be had about regulatory policy. But the approach adopted by the Trump administration has been to ignore, without justification, norms and practices that were constructed through a slow and deliberative process by good-faith actors in both parties for decades. This unwise and frequently dishonest approach is at odds with the views of thinkers and politicians across the entire political spectrum and should be roundly rejected.

Going forward, leaders in both political parties have an important set of choices to make in the coming years about the place of evidence, analysis, and expertise in regulatory policymaking. For Democrats, the experience during the Trump administration has vindicated the analysis-based approach taken by the Obama administration, as rules that were adopted on the basis of sound evidence and careful reasoning have proven more difficult to undo.[6] Based on this lesson, it may seem obvious that the best course of action is to double-down on the Obama strategy by going even further to integrate cost-benefit analysis with a progressive regulatory agenda. Notwithstanding the strength of this argument, there continue to be progressive voices who oppose cost-benefit analysis as "a vehicle for corporate interests to attack common-sense safeguards" and argue that it should be abandoned entirely.[7]

For Republicans, the question is whether to continue down the path set by the Trump administration. Some in the Republican coalition have reacted with horror at this administration's approach to policymaking.[8] For those who believe in a principled, evidence-based conservative agenda concerning regulatory policy, the Trump administration's coupling of deregulation with a disregard for analysis and expertise is highly destructive. It is possible that the failures of the Trump administration will elevate these voices of dissent. However, so long as Donald Trump and his message continue to resonate with the Republican voter base, opposition to the Trump approach among party elites may remain muted and ineffective.

∗∗∗

This book proceeds in three parts. The four chapters in Part I provide context for understanding the anomalies of the Trump administration. In chapter 1, "Politics and Regulation," we describe the importance of agency decision making in modern society, and the need to balance the demands of democratic accountability with the sometimes countervailing desire to facilitate sound decision making. To help strike this balance, a system of guardrails has been developed by courts and executive officials in both parties that provides some scope for political influence over agencies while also establishing and enforcing limits on that influence and promoting norms of rationality and expertise. We then provide a preview of how the Trump administration has run into and weakened those guardrails by pursuing a regulatory agenda based on whim, caprice, and political expediency.

In chapter 2, "A Threatening Synthesis," we look to the recent past, when the Obama administration developed a unique approach to regulation that joined respect for cost-benefit analysis with a desire to aggressively pursue progressive policy goals. What resulted from these two impulses were protections in a wide range of domains that were frequently supported by strong justifications and backed by rigorous cost-benefit analysis. The playbook developed by the Obama administration to achieve its goals was deeply threatening to those groups that had supported cost-benefit analysis for instrumental reasons in the incorrect belief that it always pointed in an anti-regulatory direction.

Chapter 3, "Staying in Bounds," examines in more detail what it meant for the Obama administration to stay within the guardrails while pursuing its policy agenda. Some opponents of cost-benefit analysis have argued that it is infinitely malleable and can justify any policy. This critique is overblown—the reality is more complicated. The need to be transparent with data and assumptions, a long history of prior practice that provides a baseline for comparison, and the simple demand of honesty all act as constraints on how cost-benefit analysis is carried out. Over the course of the Obama administration, agencies generally hewed to those constraints and produced analyses that were consistent with a good faith effort to weigh costs and benefits in light of the best available evidence. We also discuss the ways in which the Obama administration's approach led to innovations in how cost-benefit analysis was conducted, and some of the challenges faced by the administration in applying the technique in new domains.

In chapter 4, "Retreating from Reason", we discuss the reaction of the Republican Party to the regulatory strategy of the Obama administration. After substantial losses in the 2008 election, rather than moving to the political center, many Republicans adopted a posture of intransigent opposition to the president, even when he was promoting policies or techniques that had been Republican orthodoxy. To counter the cost-benefit progressivism at the heart of the Obama regulatory approach, Republicans began to question the validity of cost-benefit analysis and adopted rhetorical poses, such as emphasizing the total number of regulations or accusing the administration of "killing" jobs and engaging in a "war on coal," that were largely divorced from the more impartial language of costs and benefits. We also discuss how the Trump administration then doubled down on this rhetoric and sought to "deconstruct" core government institutions by appointing incompetent senior political appointees and sidelining the White House office charged with overseeing agency cost-benefit analysis.

Part II of the book moves from institutions to substance, focusing on the specific ways in which the Trump administration has treated cost-benefit analysis as a charade, especially in the context of environmental and public health regulation. In chapter 5, "The Illusion of Costs without Benefits," we describe how an executive order at the beginning of the Trump administration broadcast its desire to focus exclusively on the costs of regulation, without attending to the benefits. We explain the fundamental irrationality of evaluating regulations in this way, and discuss how courts have responded by striking down regulatory rollbacks that fail to account for the benefits of the original protections.

Chapter 6, "Erasing Public Health Science," describes an attempt by the Environmental Protection Agency (EPA) to disregard public health science that demonstrates the link between certain types of air pollution and premature mortality. Under the guise of increasing regulatory "transparency," the Trump EPA has proposed to exclude well-conducted, peer-reviewed studies—especially those that are based on epidemiological data—from consideration in its cost-benefit analyses.

In chapter 7, "Resurrecting Discredited Models," we discuss efforts by the Trump EPA to reject the long-standing scientific consensus that, for population-level environmental risks, there is no known safe level for many types of pollutants. If the agency is successful in bringing life back to these outdated "threshold" models, especially for important air pollutants such as particulate matter, it would instantly hide the substantial number of premature deaths that are avoided through stringent air quality regulations.

Chapter 8, "Ignoring Indirect Benefits", describes how the Trump EPA has departed from decades of prior practice to treat the indirect effects of regulation as though they do not exist, at least when those effects are politically inconvenient. The most important context for this move is a proposal to withdraw the legal underpinnings of a rule to reduce mercury pollution from power plants. That rule, adopted during the Obama administration, saved thousands of lives each year when industry adopted pollution control technologies to come into compliance. The Trump EPA has proposed to entirely ignore those effects on the grounds that they do not result directly from a reduction in mercury exposure. However, when indirect benefits can be used to justify deregulation—as the agency purports to be the case in an effort to roll back emissions standards for automobiles—the Trump EPA is happy to embrace them.

Chapter 9, "Trivializing Climate Change," describes how the Trump administration has downplayed the costs associated with climate change. The "social cost of carbon" is a concept developed by, among others, Nobel-prize winning economist William Nordhaus to provide a monetary estimate of the harms that result from greenhouse gas emissions. The best existing estimate of the social cost of carbon was developed by an interagency working group during the Obama administration. Shortly after taking office, Trump withdrew that estimate in an executive order, and agencies have attempted to radically lower the estimated benefits of reducing greenhouse gases by severely discounting effects on future generations and entirely ignoring all climate harms outside of US borders.

Chapter 10, "Manipulating Transfers," discusses how the administration is willing to pluck benefits out of thin air when it helps create the appearance of a cost-benefit justification for efforts to transfer resources away from disfavored groups and toward the politically connected. Two actions that sharply demonstrate this willingness involve an effort to change how royalty rates are set for companies engaged in fossil fuel extraction on federal land; and an effort to rescind a rule adopted during the Obama administration to protect student borrowers who have been defrauded. In the royalty rule, the Interior Department characterized a transfer of funds *from* the US treasury to fossil fuel companies as a benefit to industry which justified the rule; while in the student loan context the Education Department treated money transferred from student borrowers *to* the US treasury as a benefit. This flatly contradictory treatment is perhaps the ultimate exercise in manipulating cost-benefit analysis for the sake of political convenience.

Part III concludes the book and offers some of our thoughts on how cost-benefit analysis might be saved. Chapter 11, "Future Directions," charts the options that are available to both parties. There are two diametrically opposed conclusions that could be drawn about the value of cost-benefit analysis from experiences during the Obama and Trump administrations. One is that cost-benefit analysis has shown its merit. For groups in the Democratic Party coalition, the Obama administration's ability to pursue a progressive regulatory agenda while adhering to cost-benefit analysis not only achieved success during Obama's term in office, but it also protected rules that were targeted for rollbacks after Democrats left the White House. For those affiliated with the Republican Party, the ability of cost-benefit analysis to channel the energies of the Obama administration toward actions with net benefits, and the Trump administration's losses in court and inability to achieve consistent and long-lasting regulatory policy change may illustrate the risks of abandoning long-standing norms governing regulatory decision making. If these are the lessons learned, then there is hope that the Trump administration will come to be seen as a strange aberration in its departure from the prior, bipartisan consensus concerning cost-benefit analysis.

But the other conclusion that some may draw from the Obama and Trump administrations is that cost-benefit analysis is an unnecessary constraint that hinders the ability of powerful constituencies to achieve their policy goals and that it should either be openly abandoned or publicly maintained but ignored in practice. The Trump style of governing has won many supporters within the

Republican Party, who may view court losses as a temporary setback that can be overcome with the appointment of more sympathetic judges. For Democrats, a new argument is available for those who oppose the use of cost-benefit analysis: if the Republicans won't play by the rules, why should we?

In the final chapter, "Improving the Guardrails," we set out an agenda for reforming cost-benefit analysis and regulatory review, assuming that there will continue to be some political constituency that seeks to build on, rather than abandon, the system of guardrails described in the book. Most urgently, we argue that course set by the Trump administration be reversed, and the place of evidence, expertise, and analysis be reestablished in agency decision making, based on the practice of administrations of both parties prior to January 20, 2017. Beyond that important step, future administrations should push forward by improving the practice of cost-benefit analysis. We have three recommendations. First, we urge a renewed emphasis on program evaluation and evidence-based policymaking that goes beyond efforts at retrospective review in earlier administrations. Second, we argue for the development of more systematic methods of considering difficult-to-quantify regulatory effects. Finally, we argue for a consistent and harmonized approach to taking account of the distribution of regulatory costs and benefits.

***

Retaking Rationality went to press when the outcome of the 2008 presidential election was still unknown. Notwithstanding that uncertainty, some things were clear, and one of them was the stable bipartisan tradition of embracing cost-benefit analysis and preserving a role for expertise and evidence in regulatory decision making. Whatever happened on Tuesday, November 4, 2008, this basic structure seemed secure, and our goal was to encourage the progressive community to engage with, rather than deny, that reality.

This book goes to press during a time of far greater uncertainty. The failures of the Trump administration that we document occurred or were mostly underway before 2020 when, at the dawn of the decade, the novel coronavirus that would lead to a global pandemic began its spread. Governments around the world have strugged with this extraordinary challenge. But the inadequacies of the federal response in the United States demonstrate with grave severity the consequences of the Trump administration's long-standing rejection of expertise, analysis, and evidence. At the time of this writing, well over one hundred thousand people have died in the United States, and public health experts predict that many more deaths are likely in the coming months.

The outcome of the 2020 election is also unknown, and whatever voters decide, the future of regulatory decision making in the United States is far less clear than it once was. Expertise, evidence, and analysis have fallen out of favor in the White House. The bipartisan consensus on cost-benefit analysis has been severely destabilized, and it is difficult to predict whether it will be rebuilt. What seems most likely is that there will be a continued conversation in both political parties about the place of cost-benefit analysis, and more generally about the role of expertise and evidence in politics and public policy, for some time. These questions are likely to loom large for future administrations for the foreseeable future.

Accordingly, the message of this book is not one of unmitigated optimism. Certainly, in 2008, we would not have predicted the current unwelcome state of affairs. But human beings and human institutions are capable of resilience and flexibility, and politics can be noble as well as petty. The failures of the Trump administration are manifest, and should be obvious to honest observers in both political parties. The value of the path taken by the Obama administration, which balanced the policy demands of its core constituencies with an emphasis on careful analysis, has been thrown into sharp relief. We certainly have hope that reason will yet prevail and that the last four years will come to be seen as a temporary departure from an arc bending toward rationality.

Charlottesville, Virginia
New York City, New York
July 2020

PART I
GUARDRAILS

1

Politics and Regulation

One of the defining features of politics in the contemporary United States is the central role played by the actions, or inactions, of federal administrative agencies. One might expect that Congress, with its ability to write law and its power to tax and spend, would be the preeminent policymaking venue in US political life. But the complex nature of many policy problems, coupled with the limited ability of Congress to act, has frequently led to statutes that delegate to specialist agencies the task of translating broad policy mandates into fine-tuned regulations.

Both activists and the broader public look to regulatory agencies for answers to society's most pressing and contested issues, from climate change and workplace safety to immigration and public health. Industry groups, for their part, cry foul over "job-killing regulations," pressure agencies to delay new rules, and muster courts, Congress, and presidents to stop or roll back regulatory protections. In the early years of twenty-first century America, regulation has become a central—if not *the* central—forum where power, politics, and policy meet.

The push and pull of supply and demand help explain why regulations have come to play such an important role in US policymaking. On the demand side, the American people look to the US government for effective policy on a wide range of issues. People want clean air, stable financial markets, and safe food, workplaces, roads, and airplanes. In contemporary society, there is a wide range of risks to people's well-being that can be addressed with wise policy, and the American public reasonably looks to government to provide that policy.

It is extremely difficult to meet this demand through legislation alone. The sheer volume and detail of legislation that would be required to respond to the policy needs of the public—and the expertise needed to craft this type of legislation—would overwhelm even a very effective legislature. And the US Constitution did not create a nimble legislature: a two-chamber Congress and presidential veto mean that well-positioned special interests can block popular legislation. Layered on top of this already cumbersome structure are further norms, rules, and practices—such as the filibuster in the Senate, which creates a de facto supermajority requirement for legislation to move to a vote—that give rise to even more friction. These structural impediments have been exacerbated by a new form of hyper-partisanship that makes compromise extremely difficult. When structural barriers combine with oppositional partisan politics, the result is frequent legislative gridlock.

Reviving Rationality. Michael A. Livermore and Richard L. Revesz, Oxford University Press (2020). © Oxford University Press. DOI: 10.1093/oso/9780197539446.001.0001.

Congress's limitations, however, do not reduce demand for policy, and so administrative agencies have taken on an increasingly important role. With their expertise and relatively streamlined policymaking processes, agencies are able to act on issues in ways that are difficult for Congress, either because it lacks the relevant expertise or is mired in partisan gridlock. Even when Congress is able to act, it cannot craft legislation with the necessary detail or that anticipates every new circumstance, and so a great deal of discretionary power is still left to agencies. The result of the relative scarcity of legislation, and the broad delegation in the statutes that do exist, is that agencies have considerable policymaking powers.

Administrative agencies are now, and have been for decades, the primary producers of the rules that structure commerce and regulate risk. A few examples illustrate the point: the Environmental Protection Agency (EPA) writes rules that clean the air and water, saving tens of thousands of lives every year; the Securities and Exchange Commission and a range of other agencies protect the integrity of financial markets; the Department of Transportation requires safer, more fuel-efficient cars; the Department of Homeland Security identifies risks at the nation's ports; and the Food and Drug Administration regulates what new drugs come to market. All of these agencies operate under authority delegated to them by Congress through statutes, but they act under broad mandates and have considerable discretion to decide whether, when, and how to exercise their powers. But, although administrative agencies are where much of the policymaking happens, that does not mean politicians are content to take a backseat to professional civil servants. As power has shifted to agencies, political actors in the White House and Congress have invested more of their efforts in exerting influence over agency rulemaking by enhancing oversight and increasing the number of political appointees at the senior levels of agency management.[1]

In a democratic society, some amount of agency responsiveness to political pressure is healthy. Agency officials are not elected, and so the need to respond to demands from politicians who are put in office by voters helps ensure some level of democratic accountability.[2] But agencies are also called upon to make judgments on questions that are highly technical and difficult for the lay public or even professional politicians to understand. Accordingly, agencies largely derive their legitimacy from reputations for impartiality and expertise.[3] Those reputations are put at risk when the line between appropriate political responsiveness and partisan meddling is crossed too regularly.

Since its beginnings in January 2017, the Trump administration has found few boundaries that it was not willing to cross. Most relevant for administrative agencies and the policies they make, the Trump administration has walked away from a decades-long bipartisan consensus that placed cost-benefit analysis at the heart of regulatory decision making.[4] Prior Republican and Democratic administrations had different visions on many regulatory issues, but there was a shared understanding that the overall goal of the regulatory system should be to maximize the well-being of the American public. They might have assessed benefits and costs somewhat differently, but they agreed on the enterprise. That focus on overall well-being was implemented through the requirement that agencies make a reasonable effort to anticipate and consider the consequences of their regulatory decisions through a formal analysis of costs and benefits.

The Trump administration has paid lip service to that approach but engaged in methodological trickery to pursue an agenda driven by interest group pressure, personal relationships, and ideological whim. Rather than use cost-benefit analysis to inform and improve agency decision making, the Trump administration openly manipulates the technique to provide thin post hoc rationalizations for its decisions. The results have included haphazard and incoherent policy, social division, failure in the courts, a demoralized federal workforce, and a loss of faith in government's ability to respond to the pressing problems facing American society.

The reason that the Trump administration's approach to regulation is dangerous is not because of attempts by political appointees to influence agency decision making. Political oversight of agencies is a normal and expected part of the contemporary presidency. The problem is that the administration has rejected the system of norms, conventions, and practices that have evolved over the past several decades to channel that political influence.[5] These guardrails have been constructed by leaders from both parties to secure the legitimacy of agency action by balancing politics with the impartial exercise of government power. By forsaking them, the Trump administration has not only rendered itself ineffectual at pursuing its own goals, but it has also threatened to undermine the integrity of the entire regulatory system and all of the social values—from clear air to a functioning economy—that this system protects.

Divided Government and the Institutions
of Regulatory Politics

In the mid-twentieth century, there was a widespread belief that agencies acted like "transmission belts" that simply conveyed the policy preferences of Congress into practical implementation.[6] The idea at the time was that agency decision makers were simply impartial and neutral experts who *administered* the laws rather than exercising political power. This idea was relatively easy to maintain in part because, for a while, the United States was effectively a single-party state, with the New Deal Democrats largely dominating the entire apparatus of government, from the presidency and Congress to agencies and the judiciary.

The notion of agencies as transmission belts broke down with the decline of the New Deal coalition, and especially with the election of Richard Nixon in 1968. Nixon's election ushered in a decades-long period of divided government in which Republicans had almost exclusive control over the White House while the Democrats continued to dominate Congress. The 1968 election also coincided with a new shift in the emphasis of policymaking at the national level, from the types of economic management associated with the New Deal toward a concern with the regulation of risks that arose from diffuse sources across the economy, such as environmental pollution, workplace hazards, and dangerous consumer products. The new demand for risk regulation led to a spate of lawmaking throughout the 1970s at a time when Democratic lawmakers were increasingly skeptical about how their laws would be implemented by Republican administrations.

The period of divided government, which lasted from Nixon's election through the end of George H. W. Bush's single term, crystallized a set of disagreements over regulatory policy between the two major parties that reflected the differing interests, values, and views of their respective constituencies.

During this time, the Democratic Party remained the party of labor, despite the waning power of unions. The new public interest groups representing consumers and environmentalists also gravitated toward the Democratic Party, as did civil rights organizations. This constellation of interests pushed for risk regulation legislation in the late 1960s and 1970s, and sought to have these laws implemented as aggressively as possible.

There was a great deal of cross-aisle consensus in some areas, such as environmental protection, but the Republican Party, with its traditional relationship to business owners and managers, did sometimes cast a more skeptical eye on regulation. For example, President Nixon established the EPA through an executive order and signed the Clean Air Act into law,[7] but he also vetoed the Clean Water Act, arguing that its "laudable intent is outweighed by its unconscionable . . . price tag."[8] The law was ultimately adopted only because there was sufficient bipartisan support for the bill in Congress to override his veto.[9]

As the period of divided government continued, the positions of the two parties on regulatory issues became more distinct. In the early years, both parties were more diverse, with more liberal northern Republicans and more conservative southern Democrats still holding influence within their parties. But after the Democratic Party embraced the civil rights movement under President Johnson, white Southerners quickly began migrating into the Republican Party, and Northerners gravitated to the Democratic Party, leaving the parties more ideologically uniform.[10] As partisanship more clearly lined up with ideology, the Democrats firmly embraced a protection-oriented agenda. The Republicans, in contrast, coalesced around a "regulatory reform" agenda.[11] This agenda represented a diversity of views but shared an overall skepticism toward the existing regulatory system. More moderate reformers favored achieving social goals with more flexible approaches—for example, by replacing command-and-control style rules that required firms to comply with specific pollution-control mandates with market-oriented approaches such as pollution fees or cap-and-trade programs. More extreme versions of the regulatory reform agenda were articulated by skeptics and libertarians who viewed any government intervention in the private sector as suspect.

The Nixon presidency also coincided with a loss of New Deal optimism about the capacity and impartiality of agencies, which was part of a broader loss of faith in social institutions after the failures of the Vietnam War and Watergate and the social unrest of the 1960s. New fears emerged that agencies would abandon their public interest mandates and instead become captured by powerful special interests. This new capture theory was taken up by political scientists and economists and popularized across the political spectrum by figures as diverse as William Niskanen (founder of the conservative Cato Institute) and Ralph Nader (the liberal consumer advocate). But, although left and right agreed about the risk of capture, they disagreed about who was doing the capturing, and to what effect. For Niskanen and other like-minded figures, it was the bureaucracy itself (egged on by the new public interest groups) that was the threat.[12] They were concerned that agency managers would adopt an "empire building" mindset that justified ever more costly and unnecessary intrusions into the private sector. On the left, Nader and others worried that wealthy and powerful special interest groups, representing Big Business, would influence agencies to forgo stringent protection for the environment, workers, and consumers.[13]

Despite these increasingly divergent views over regulatory policy, and the lack of united party control over Congress and the White House, the period of divided government was not characterized by unending gridlock and stalemate. Rather, because both parties understood that they faced a relatively stable dynamic, they found room to compromise with each other. Major bipartisan legislation still passed Congress, agency rulemakings proceeded at a regular pace, and a general equilibrium was attained in which the two parties managed to arrive at a middle ground on most policy issues.

That stable dynamic did not imply that the parties, and the institutions in their hands, did not compete with each other over policy. In addition to bargaining over legislation and the budget, Congress and the White House engaged in an arms race to build out their respective institutional capacity to oversee, and influence, the work of administrative agencies. For Congress, that meant increasing the sophistication of its staff, holding hearings, building relations with agency personnel, selectively feeding information to the media, and, in the Senate, using confirmation power to influence political appointees.

For the president that meant constructing what is sometimes referred to as the "presidential bureaucracy."[14] This staff, primarily located in the White House and directly accountable to the president, is distinct from the larger federal bureaucracy that is sprawled across hundreds of departments, agencies, and offices. Nixon engaged in particularly extensive efforts to wrest decisions from agencies that were staffed by civil-service protected professionals largely hired during the terms of his Democratic predecessors. Nixon deeply mistrusted the professional staff at agencies, believing (likely at least sometimes correctly) that they opposed and even actively subverted his agenda.

For purposes of controlling regulatory decisions, perhaps the most important institutional innovation within the presidential bureaucracy came at the beginning of the Reagan administration, with the creation of the system of regulatory review overseen by the Office of Information and Regulatory Affairs (OIRA), within the Office of Management and Budget in the White House.[15] OIRA remains relatively obscure and little known among the broader public, but for four decades it has played an extremely important role. Executive Order 12,291, issued by Reagan less than a month after he took office in 1981, required that agencies conduct a cost-benefit analysis of all major rulemakings and submit their proposed rules to OIRA for review.[16] This relatively simple-sounding procedure inserted the White House directly into the regulatory process and established cost-benefit analysis as the substantive standard that was intended to guide agency decision making.

Courts also played a role in shifting power between the two political branches during the period of divided government. In the early years—from roughly 1968 to 1980—the judiciary was still dominated by New Deal Democrats, and courts asserted their authority to review agency decisions in a much more muscular fashion.[17] They made it easier for regulatory beneficiaries—typically constituents of the Democratic Party—to gain access to courts, and began imposing more onerous procedural requirements on agency decision making. This approach to judicial review worked hand-in-glove with new procedural and analytic requirements that were imposed on agencies by Congress, which included transparency requirements under the Freedom of Information Act and duties to consider the environmental consequences of agency action under the National Environmental Policy Act. The attitude of the courts in this period is nicely characterized by Truman appointee J. Skelly Wright in a 1971 decision for the United States Court of Appeals for the District of Columbia Circuit that articulated a role for courts "to see that important legislative purposes, heralded in the halls of Congress, are not lost or misdirected in the vast hallways of the federal bureaucracy."[18] At the time of this opinion, the country was entering a long period when the "halls of Congress" would be dominated by Democrats, while the "hallways" of the federal bureaucracy" would be overseen by Republican presidents.

As time wore on, and Republican-appointed judges replaced the New Deal Democrats as the dominant force on the judiciary, a different attitude took hold, one that was friendlier to agency discretion under the watchful eye of Republican presidents.[19] An important turning point was *Vermont Yankee Nuclear Power Corp v. NRDC*, a 1979 decision involving a challenge by an environmental organization to a new nuclear power plant. That decision, authored by Justice William Rehnquist—a Nixon appointee later elevated to Chief Justice by Ronald Reagan—sharply upbraided the likes of Judge Wright for expanding procedural requirements to the point of the "Kafkaesque" and creating too much room for courts to impose their policy views (which were often relatively liberal) on agencies that were tied to Republican presidents.[20] For Rehnquist, the role of review was "to insure a fully informed and well-considered decision, not necessarily a decision the judges of the Court of Appeals . . . would have reached had they been members of the decisionmaking unit of the agency."[21]

During this timeframe, the Court also decided *Chevron v. NRDC*, which granted considerable discretion to agency interpretations of statutory text.[22] The *Chevron* rule was a favorite of Justice Antonin Scalia, a conservative justice who was closely aligned with the deregulatory views of the Republican Party.[23] Justice Scalia was admirably frank about his view of why it was wise for conservative judges to embrace agency discretion at a time when the Republican Party reliably occupied the White House. Writing in the conservative magazine *Reason*, prior to his appointment, Scalia had this to say:

> At a time when the GOP has gained control of the executive branch with an evident mandate for fundamental change in domestic policies . . . every curtailment of desirable agency discretion obstructs (principally) the departure from a Democrat-produced, pro-regulatory status quo. . . .
>
> Executive-enfeebling measures . . . do not specifically deter regulation. What they deter is change. Imposed upon a regulation-prone executive, they will on balance slow the increase of regulation; but imposed upon an executive that is seeking to dissolve the encrusted regulation of past decades, they will impede the dissolution. Regulatory reformers who do not recognize this fact, and who continue to support the unmodified proposals of the past as though the fundamental game had not been altered, will be scoring points for the other team.[24]

By the time George H. W. Bush took office, the administrative institutions of divided government were firmly in place. After decades of growth, the presidential bureaucracy was well-poised to oversee the activities of administrative agencies, with OIRA review and cost-benefit analysis as the centerpiece. The Republican Party had a well-established regulatory reform agenda, which the first Bush administration sought to advance with another (somewhat ceremonial) layer of review conducted by its Council on Competitiveness, which was chaired by Vice President Dan Quayle. The regime of *Chevron* deference had been established, and its most ardent defender, Justice Scalia, had become a dominant voice on the Court. The still-Democratic Congress continued to use its oversight power to push in favor of more stringent protections—for example, by holding hearings critical of agency inaction. Public interest groups and regulated industry both cultivated effective channels within the institutions most closely aligned with their interests.

The George H. W. Bush administration also oversaw the last substantial over-haul of one of the major pollution control statutes, the Clean Air Act Amendments of 1990. That legislation, which garnered bipartisan support in both the House and the Senate, created a new market-based mechanism to control sulfur dioxide emissions from power plants as well as an effective technology-based approach to regulating hazardous air pollutants, plus new deadlines and enhanced penalties for parts of the country that fail to attain air quality standards. The amendments reflected the kind of compromise that was still possible during the period of divided government, with Democrats in Congress pushing for more stringent standards and the Republican president pushing for market-based approaches to reducing pollution. Programs implemented under this legislation saved many tens of thousands of lives and delivered hundreds of billions of dollars' worth of net benefits to the American public.

Although it was not clear at the time, the George H. W. Bush administra-tion represented the final culmination of the political system that had reigned for over two decades, with a stable equilibrium of divided government under a Republican White House and Democratic Congress. Bush's 1992 defeat, and Newt Gingrich's rise to power in the House two years later, would set the stage for a new system, characterized by ideological polarization, weak party in-frastructure, and wild volatility in control over the levers of executive and legislative power.

Cabining Political Influence

When President Clinton took office, it was not clear what his election meant for the future of US politics. Some optimistic Democrats hoped that with a popular young president who represented a generational change of the guard, a new pe-riod of Democratic Party dominance might begin—if not as deep as after the New Deal election, then perhaps approximating the Kennedy-Johnson years. Republicans looked to the more recent example of Jimmy Carter and anticipated another quick return home for a southern governor turned president. But both Democratic hopes for a semi-permanent majority and Republican hopes of a

one-term presidency proved false. In reality, Clinton's election ushered in a period of volatility, with Congress and the White House changing hands in every
possible configuration over the coming years. This new situation of oscillating
control over the political branches was accompanied by increasing polarization
and the gradual "hollowing out" of the official party organizations, whose function was slowly replaced by a loose coalition of donors, media personalities, and
ideological activists with strong views but little loyalty to party institutions.[25]

Although few saw the coming "era of partisan volatility,"[26] Clinton's election
undoubtedly presented an opportunity for substantial changes in the normal
operating patterns in Washington, DC. Since a strong presidential bureaucracy
had come to be closely associated with Republican presidents and the related
agenda of regulatory reform, many constituencies within the Democratic Party
coalition, including public interest advocacy groups, urged the new president to
dismantle those institutions, focusing especially on the role of OIRA. Clinton
ignored that advice and instead strengthened the system of presidential review
and turned it to somewhat different purposes.

One centerpiece of the Clinton approach was his Executive Order 12,866.[27]
Building on the basic structure of Reagan's Executive Order 12,291, the Clinton
Order continued the practice of requiring agencies to conduct cost-benefit
analyses of their regulations and subjecting those analyses to OIRA review.
However, the Clinton Order did include several substantive and process reforms.
One of the major criticisms of the practice of OIRA review under Reagan and
George H. W. Bush had been its secrecy, and the Clinton Order included several
provisions to make OIRA review more transparent.[28] The Clinton Order also
responded to concerns that the Reagan Order focused too much on effects that
could easily be quantified by placing greater emphasis on "qualitative measures
of costs and benefits," and stating, as one of its "Principles of Regulation" that,
"Each agency shall assess both the costs and the benefits of the intended regulation and, *recognizing that some costs and benefits are difficult to quantify*, propose
or adopt a regulation only upon a reasoned determination that the benefits of the
intended regulation justify its costs."[29]

Years before her appointment to the Supreme Court, Elena Kagan described
the interaction between executive review and partisan control of the White
House in a law review article that she wrote after her stint in Clinton's Domestic
Policy Council:

> Where once presidential supervision had worked to dilute or delay regulatory
> initiatives, it served in the Clinton years as part of a distinctly activist and pro-
> regulatory governing agenda. Where once presidential supervision had tended
> to favor politically conservative positions, it generally operated during the
> Clinton Presidency as a mechanism to achieve progressive goals. Or expressed

in the terms most sympathetic to all these Presidents (and therefore most contestable), if Reagan and Bush showed that presidential supervision could thwart regulators intent on regulating no matter what the cost, Clinton showed that presidential supervision could jolt into action bureaucrats suffering from bureaucratic inertia in the face of unmet needs and challenges.[30]

At their core, Kagan's argument and Scalia's share a basic premise, which is that institutions or practices, such as judicial deference or regulatory review, that enhance presidential power, do not map onto standard liberal/conservative or pro-/anti-regulatory ideological dimensions. Everything depends on who holds the White House: during the prolonged period of divided government, when Republicans held the White House, presidential power advanced a broadly anti-regulatory agenda. Kagan's argument is that the situation was symmetrical: with a Democrat in the White House, presidential power could be put to use to advance Democratic policy priorities, especially after the Gingrich revolution in 1994 placed Congress in Republican hands, which largely shut down legislation as a viable policy path.

The two decades after Clinton's election featured multiple iterations of every possible party alignment in the political branches, with both Democratic and Republican presidents facing both friendly and hostile Congresses. What emerged were two distinctive but also related visions of the regulatory system. Under George W. Bush, the White House largely continued on the path that had been set during the Republican presidencies starting with Nixon, which involved using the instruments of presidential oversight to pursue some version of the regulatory reform agenda. More moderate voices within the party acknowledged the value of the underlying goals of the regulatory system, but questioned the methods, focusing especially on what they saw as the heavy hand of the government in command-and-control-style rules. On the more extreme end were the libertarians with their emphasis on economic rights, and government skeptics who viewed even moderate regulations as initiating a slippery slide into tyranny. Successful governance during Republican presidencies involved striking a balance between the more moderate and extreme voices within the party.

First under President Clinton and then under President Obama, Democratic administrations forged a distinctive identity on regulatory issues. To some degree, the Clinton/Obama approach borrowed some of the regulatory reform ideas that circulated among more moderate Republicans during the 1980s and 1990s—ideas that included the use of cost-benefit analysis to evaluate rules and the use of more flexible, market-based instruments to achieve regulatory goals. But the Democratic administrations also had to balance voices from the left on regulatory issues, which tended to be both more focused on using government policy to reduce risks and less concerned with costs imposed on large businesses.

These dynamics between the two parties established a kind of "Overton Window" on regulatory policies.[31] Named for Joseph P. Overton, who was senior vice president at a free-market think tank in Michigan, the idea of an Overton Window is that there is a certain range of views that are considered acceptable in public discourse, with ideas toward the center of the window forming the basis for policy reforms. For those who find themselves at the fringes of the Overton Window (as Overton himself did), the goal of advocacy is to shift the window so that ideas once considered radical become widely accepted. A recent example of a shift in the Overton Window has occurred on the issues of marriage equality and marijuana legalization: ideas that were once relegated to advocates outside the mainstream have become broadly accepted over the course of the past two decades.

The Overton Window on regulatory issues remained relatively stable during the periods that lasted from 1968 to 2016, first during prolonged divided government (Nixon to George H. W. Bush) and then during the more recent time of partisan volatility (Clinton to Obama). On the right side of the window was a regulatory reform agenda that sought more stringent cost-benefit analysis, greater use of regulatory review to reduce the stock of existing regulation, elimination to a large extent of command-and-control rules in favor of market mechanisms, and light-touch regulatory approaches (such as voluntary programs) whenever possible. On the left side of the window was a more traditional regulatory approach that sought fewer constraints on agencies; expansion of the regulatory system to cover more risks; and more directive, mandatory rules.

The area of overlap between the parties is well characterized by the governing documents that have been adopted and applied by both parties to interpret the requirements of OIRA review and cost-benefit analysis over the years. Reagan's Executive Order 12,291 established the basic structure of review, and the substantive standard. Clinton's Order 12,866 carried forward that structure, with important reforms to improve transparency and expand the types of considerations that are relevant for analysis. George W. Bush kept the Clinton Order in place and added his own foundational document: Circular A-4, a memorandum issued by the Office of Management and Budget to provide guidance for agencies on how to conduct cost-benefit analysis. Circular A-4 includes a number of technical details, but the general approach is to build on the principles outlined in Clinton's Executive Order 12,866. For example, Circular A-4 urges agencies to engage in quantitative analysis where possible but also recognizes that "economic efficiency [may not be] the only or the overriding public policy objective" and "it will not always be possible to express in monetary units all of the important benefits and costs [of a rule]."[32]

Of course, the regulatory Overton Window does not capture the entire spectrum of views but instead reflects the broad consensus among elites within the two political parties. Many Democratic constituencies, such as labor unions and environmentalists, argued that cost-benefit analysis should be abandoned altogether, while libertarians and free-market advocates urged for a radically scaled-back role for government and a reinvigoration of the idea of economic rights. But, in general, these more radical ideas did not succeed in broadly shifting the policy landscape.

Even with a relatively stable Overton Window on regulatory issues, as the White House continued to change hands after Clinton's election, there was some degree of oscillation in regulatory approaches as Democratic and Republican administrations both sought to implement their different visions. Sometimes this led to waste: regulatory programs that were initiated by one administration were abandoned by another and then taken up again later. Reversals on regulatory policy, which inject uncertainty into the economy and make it difficult to achieve regulatory goals, impose costs with few benefits—for a given set of regulatory goals, a consistent approach over time is generally better than one that wildly swings with the changing fortunes of the political parties.

At the same time, however, there were institutions and practices that played a stabilizing role, mitigating the problem of wild policy swings. Perhaps the two most important were OIRA and the courts. There are several reasons that OIRA has been a stabilizing force.[33] OIRA is a generalist institution, meaning that it is not affiliated with any particular interest group or party constituency. For this reason, it is more difficult for special interests to capture OIRA than it is for them to capture issue-oriented agencies. For example, it makes sense for the pharmaceutical industry to focus its lobbying and relationship building efforts on the Food and Drug Administration, where it is a dominant player, rather than at OIRA where it is one of many. OIRA administrators under both parties also have historically tended to come from academia rather than advocacy groups or industry trade associations. Finally, OIRA review is based on the methodology of cost-benefit analysis, which, in the past, has been relatively stable across administrations, comprehensive, and technocratic.[34] All of these features of cost-benefit analysis orient OIRA review toward greater stability between administrations.

OIRA's influence can serve as a counterbalance to strong constituencies during both Republican and Democratic administrations.[35] After his time as George W. Bush's OIRA administrator, John Graham described instances when "OIRA served as a crucial advocate of several lifesaving regulations that, in the absence of OIRA's support, might not have survived White House oversight in a pro-business Republican administration."[36] Graham argues that OIRA's intervention was particularly important in support of two major rules to limit air pollution, which collectively saved tens of thousands of lives, as well as a rule to increase automobile fuel economy that saved consumers many billions of dollars. During

Cass Sunstein's tenure as OIRA administrator under Obama, he helped resist an EPA rule that would have substantially increased the stringency of air quality standards for ground level ozone (known as smog).[37] Environmentalists—a core Democratic constituency who had been advocating for years for the more stringent standard—were outraged by the administration's decision. League of Conservation Voters' president Gene Karpinski said at the time that the ozone decision was "the worst thing a Democratic president had ever done on our issues. Period."[38]

Although the views of OIRA administrators like Cass Sunstein and John Graham on regulatory issues tended to be more similar to each other than those of average political appointees in Democratic and Republican administrations (respectively), that does not mean that there was no difference in the regulatory policies that they pursued. In a study on OIRA's cost-benefit analyses under administrations of different political parties, Art Fraas and Richard Morgenstern at Resources for the Future found that there were important differences in emphasis, even if many of the underlying methods were similar. For example, Fraas and Morgenstern found that Republican administrations tended to be more focused on the downsides of regulation, such as harm to the international competitiveness of US business or the cumulative effects of many rules, while Democratic administrations placed more emphasis on ensuring that regulatory benefits were properly counted—for example, by relying on the field of behavioral economics to identify new classes of benefits or developing methods to account for unquantified benefits.[39] The overall impression from Fraas and Morgenstern's study is of OIRA overseeing a fairly constrained Overton Window, with Republican and Democratic administrations agreeing on a foundational approach of counting costs and benefits and using regulation to improve the aggregate well-being of the American public, but with different emphases and some disagreement on specific methodological issues.

Judicial review of agency actions also tended to have a moderating influence. As discussed above, under the *Chevron* doctrine, courts are supposed to defer to agencies when the agencies make reasonable interpretations of their governing statutes. But courts do not defer completely, and they also have an obligation under the Administrative Procedure Act to ensure that agency decisions are not "arbitrary and capricious." In practice, courts regularly strike down agency rules for improper or inadequately explained decisions.[40] The practice of probing judicial review places power in the hands of judges who are appointed for life and therefore are no longer accountable to the political process. Both parties have used their time in the White House to fill judicial vacancies, so the judiciary includes both Republican and Democratic appointees. The need to secure Senate confirmation may sometimes also tilt appointments in a moderate direction during periods of divided government. Because agencies know that their important decisions are likely to be litigated before judges from both parties who no longer need serve any particular political master, they adopt less extreme positions.

At the highest level, the US Supreme Court has dealt setbacks for presidents of both parties on regulatory issues. For example, the Court struck down a major initiative of the Clinton-era Food and Drug Administration to regulate tobacco, finding that the agency had overstepped its regulatory authority,[41] but it also found that the George W. Bush administration's refusal to regulate greenhouse gas emissions violated the Clean Air Act.[42] The Obama administration found its own regulatory hurdles on the Court, for example, a decision—authored by Justice Scalia—that the agency had to consider the costs of limiting mercury pollution from electricity generators prior to initiating the regulatory process.[43]

But focusing on the Supreme Court alone misses much of the real work of the courts in overseeing administrative agencies—many major rules are litigated in the federal courts, but only a very few are ultimately taken all the way to the Supreme Court. The federal appellate courts also tend to be less obviously political than the Supreme Court, deciding many more cases where the law is clearer and the ideological stakes less obvious. In more run-of-the-mill cases involving agency regulations, the appellate courts—and especially the DC Circuit, where many of these cases are litigated—play an important role in moderating agencies and encouraging them toward the consensus path.

One important example of this influence came during the George W. Bush administration rulemaking by the Department of Transportation to improve fuel-economy standards for automobiles. For a generation, these standards had been flatlined, so the Bush administration's move was a useful step in the right direction. Environmental groups, however, argued that the administration had not gone far enough, and in particular they criticized the agency for failing to count the climate benefits that were associated with anticipated greenhouse gas reductions from the rule. The Bush administration argued that these benefits were so uncertain that they couldn't be counted.

In *Center for Biological Diversity v. National Highway Traffic Safety Administration*, the United States Court of Appeals for the Ninth Circuit held that the Bush administration had inappropriately put a "thumb on the scale" by failing to count climate benefits in its cost-benefit analysis of the rule.[44] The court acknowledged that there was some uncertainty about the dollar value of these benefits, but it also held that their value was definitely "not zero," which is how they were treated by the agency. Because of the inadequate cost-benefit analysis, the court remanded the rule back to the agency for further consideration. In writing about the case, John Graham (George W. Bush's OIRA administrator) noted that the court's reasoning on "the need to include a monetized value of carbon dioxide in the benefit calculation" was "consistent with OIRA's views."[45]

The Obama administration faced its own cost-benefit-analysis-related setbacks in the appellate courts. One came after an effort by the Securities and Exchange Commission to increase the influence of shareholders in the management decisions of publicly held corporations in the aftermath of the 2008 financial crisis.[46] The Securities and Exchange Commission's Proxy Access Rule operated by making it easier for outsider board-of-director candidates to win seats on the board. A challenge to the rule was brought before the DC Circuit, and in *Business Roundtable v. Securities and Exchange Commission*, the court found that the agency "inconsistently and opportunistically framed the costs and benefits of the rule; failed adequately to quantify the certain costs or to explain why those costs could not be quantified; neglected to support its predictive judgments; contradicted itself; and failed to respond to substantial problems raised by commenters."[47] The rule was struck down. The cost-benefit logic of this opinion and its similarity to the kinds of limits often imposed by OIRA was not incidental: the authoring judge in *Business Roundtable* was Douglas Ginsburg, who was an OIRA administrator during the Ronald Reagan administration before being appointed to the DC Circuit.

During the period of partisan volatility inaugurated by the election of Bill Clinton in 1992, the parties developed distinct approaches to regulatory policymaking. But those differences were cabined within a relatively narrow policymaking space. Although political considerations and ideological views were accepted to play some role in shaping policy, there was nonetheless a broadly shared consensus that the goal of the regulatory system was to improve public well-being. That general consensus was coupled with the practice of carrying out relatively rigorous and methodologically consistent cost-benefit analysis of major rulemakings. In addition, during administrations of both parties, stabilizing institutions such as OIRA and the courts were accepted as playing the important role of preserving norms of rational and impartial decision making that acted as guardrails and oriented agencies toward the middle of the road.

The results were far from perfect. Policy sometimes oscillated erratically between administrations; imperfect rules were adopted, and regulations that should have been fast-tracked languished in bureaucratic holding patterns; political considerations shuffled benefits to favored constituencies while disfavored groups were shut out; civil servants at agencies sometimes became too close to the industries they were charged with overseeing, leading to lax rules and inadequate enforcement. All of this meant that benefits that should have been delivered to the public were not, and costs that could have been avoided were nonetheless imposed.

But, despite its failings, the system of guardrails operated well enough in achieving a reasonable balance of two sometimes conflicting goals of modern agencies: facilitating democratic legitimacy by rendering agencies accountable to elected officials; and making sound policy choices that improve social well-being. Accountability to elected officials helps ground agency decision making in the popular political process, but it also opens the door to partisanship, favoritism, demagoguery, and group conflict. Informed decision making, by contrast, tends to place power in the hands of experts operating within professional worlds that are cut off from public accountability. The guardrails balanced these two tendencies by giving political officials a substantial amount of scope to influence policy while ensuring that expertise, reasoned decision making, and legal limits constrained the more immoderate tendencies in both parties. What resulted was a period of relative stability, where—despite the volatility in partisan control over the political branches—industry and the American public more generally could count on a considerable degree of consistency and continuity between administrations. But despite its advantages, changes were on the horizon that would fundamentally challenge this system.

Kicking at the Guardrails

With the election of Donald Trump in 2016, the settled dynamics governing administrative governance have broken down. Under Trump, OIRA has largely lost either the desire or ability to effectively perform its oversight role, and cost-benefit analysis has been subject to flagrant manipulation.[48] The process of judicial nomination and confirmation has become further polarized, potentially threatening the independence and legitimacy of the judiciary and undermining the ability (and perhaps desire) of judges to provide a neutral external check on agencies.[49] Other stabilizing institutions, from external peer review consultants to career civil service professionals at agencies, have been politicized or attacked. Counterproductive institutional changes, such as a requirement that agencies engage in two deregulatory efforts for every new regulation, have sowed confusion and incoherence. Enforcement of existing rules has slacked, and the failure to conform to even basic legal requirements of agency decision making has led to delays and losses in court. Cronyism has dictated the appointment of senior political officials. All of this has resulted in a crisis in the system of regulatory governance.

This crisis was precipitated by the final breakdown in party control of the process that nominates presidential candidates, a system that had been under increasing stress for decades. For much of the twentieth century, party elites controlled their party's decisions of which candidates to nominate for office, especially at the national level during presidential elections.[50] After the Democratic Party's infamous fiasco at the its 1968 convention in Chicago,[51] however, it adopted a series of reforms to its nomination process, to place more power in the hands of voters, in particular by giving greater weight to primary elections.[52] The Republican Party followed suit a few years later, and although both sets of reforms did create paths for less conventional candidates—specifically Jimmy Carter in 1976 and Ronald Reagan in 1980—insiders continued to play a central role. Even with a primary process that ostensibly gave voters considerable input during the nomination process, party activists were able to work within the party system to both direct campaign resources and control messaging to maintain a considerable degree of influence over the process.[53] In a widely read book, *The Party Decides: Presidential Nominations Before and After Reform,* published in 2008, a team of political scientists argued that despite the post-1968 reforms, the real presidential nomination contest was not for primary votes but instead for the high-profile endorsements that dominate the "invisible primary."[54] Based on analysis through the 2000 election, *The Party Decides* team showed how insider favorites were able to defeat outside candidates, even those with popular positions and biographies.[55]

Not long after its publication, the nomination of Barack Obama over Hillary Clinton suggested that *The Party Decides* model may have lost some of its predictive power. Although Obama had some support within the party, Clinton was the clear favorite of party insiders, and she was able to collect endorsements from a wide range of figures across the party's core constituencies.[56] Obama's victory demonstrated that a relative outsider could pull off a challenge against even a firmly entrenched and widely supported insider candidate.

But if Obama's nomination suggested a deviation from the model, the nomination of Donald Trump as the Republican nominee eight years later was a full-scale repudiation.[57] Unlike other successful prior candidates, Trump was shunned by the party establishment, and lined up very few endorsements in advance of the Republican primaries.[58] Not only did party elites withhold their endorsements, establishment figures were quite active in their condemnations. For example, fellow candidate Rick Perry had this to say:

> Let no one be mistaken Donald Trump's candidacy is a cancer on conservatism and it must be clearly diagnosed, excised, and discarded. It cannot be pacified or ignored for it will destroy a set of principles that has lifted more people out of poverty than any force in the history of the civilized world.[59]

The lack of enthusiasm for Donald Trump within Republican officialdom was no accident: he took a wrecking ball to Republican policy and political orthodoxy that had structured the party for decades. On policy, he was a free-trade skeptic in a party that traditionally pushed to lower trade barriers; a vociferous opponent of immigration in a party that sought to expand its base among Latino voters; and a critic of foreign military intervention in a party tied to the Iraq War. In terms of political style, his departures were, if anything, even more extreme: one would be hard pressed to identify a political figure who more harshly contrasted with the folksy "compassionate conservative" style of George W. Bush; the war hero stature of John McCain; or the straight-laced family values persona of Mitt Romney.

Despite his historically low standing among party insiders, Trump captured the nomination. His victory over party elites doubtless had numerous sources,[60] but it was certainly fueled by a changing media and social media landscape as well as legal changes that have reduced the influence of the official party apparatus.[61] With Trump, the long-simmering potential for the post-1968 changes to the presidential nomination process to wipe out insiders' influence was finally realized.

After this historic victory over party elites, Trump faced a difficult choice that essentially pitted his ability to govern effectively against his outsider tendencies. When presidents take office, they face the enormous problem of exerting control over the vast and sprawling federal bureaucracy. The federal government employs 2.7 million civilians who are divided into an array of agencies with unique histories, conflicting and overlapping missions and priorities, and distinct policy preferences and cultures. The relationship between presidents and their administrations has often been characterized by political scientists and other students of the presidency as raising a "principal-agent" problem: it is impossible for the president to be aware of most of the work that goes on in the federal government, and effectively monitoring and supervising that work is out of the question.[62] The way that presidents respond to this challenge sets the course for their administrations.

As political scientist Terry Moe noted in the 1980s, presidents use two strategies to control the executive branch: politicizing the top-tier management at agencies and centralizing decisions in the White House.[63] To pursue either, the president needs to appoint a large group of loyal and competent personnel. These days, that means finding roughly 3,000–4,000 trustworthy staff who are capable of managing complex agencies while implementing a shared policy agenda.[64]

In the past, parties have helped presidents meet this challenge. Contemporary parties are diffused networks of donors, politicians, think tanks, interest groups, campaign consultants, academics, state and local officials, congressional staff, and lobbyists. Many of the core group are professionals: lawyers, public relations people, managers, economists, or policy wonks. These people can be thought of as "partisan technocrats" who share a rough ideological perspective, have long-standing working relationships with each other and party constituencies, and possess deep knowledge about policy and how government works. When presidents move into the White House, they historically have drawn heavily on this group to fill positions around government and exert control over the bureaucracy.

Upon taking office, Trump faced a kind of Hobson's choice. He could have governed like a traditional Republican and drawn on the party network for political appointees. But that would have meant essentially turning over the government to the establishment that he had just defeated. Instead, he attempted to strike out on his own, trying to personally solve the problem of loyalty and competence without party support.

After abandoning party orthodoxy and vanquishing party elites during the 2016 election, and then shunning the partisan technocrats needed to effectively govern after taking office, Trump's next move was to kick at the guardrails that constrain agency decision making. In Part II of this book, we document the ways in which the Trump administration has treated the practice of cost-benefit analysis—a methodology that evolved through decades of painstaking effort by civil servants and political appointees of both parties—like a charade. Other steps have included the reduction of OIRA to a shadow of its former role and the appointment of senior political appointees who are a strange mix of incompetent and actively hostile to their agencies' missions (both discussed in chapter 4). These steps to dismantle procedural and institutional constraints on regulatory policymaking have had a range of serious negative consequences, for the Trump administration, for agencies, and for the American public.

For the administration, the failure to conform to established regulatory practices has resulted in an embarrassing string of legal defeats. As discussed above, courts play a role in enforcing some of the most important guardrails on regulatory policymaking. Many of the guardrails—such as cost-benefit analyses, OIRA review, or input from civil servants—operate within the executive branch and therefore can be circumvented by a hostile administration. Courts, on the other hand, are an external check that is not as easily thwarted. As it turns out, the administration's strategy of ignoring the guardrails has so far seriously backfired in court. According to one measure, as of July 2019, the Trump administration has lost nearly 90 percent of regulatory cases.[65] This win rate of around 10 percent is a stunningly poor track record, particularly when compared to a typical administration, which wins 70 percent of challenges to its regulatory actions.[66] The reasons for many of these losses include improper interpretation of statutes, the failure to conform to procedural requirements (like giving the public an opportunity to comment on proposed rules), and issuing decisions that are based on inadequate analysis.

As a consequence of its extraordinary failure in the courts, the administration—at least so far—has had an extremely difficult time making regulatory policy changes with a lasting impact. The failure to adopt new protections and a general slackening of enforcement mean that some temporary deregulatory effects have been achieved during the administration itself, but lasting change ultimately means that regulatory changes (including deregulations) must survive judicial scrutiny. However, it is unclear whether a sustained effort to reshape the judiciary might erode even this final backstop. The appointment of young, highly ideological judges has been one area where the Trump administration has worked reasonably well with co-partisans in Congress.[67] There has been a mixed track record in these appointments in terms of experience and qualifications for lifetime appointment to the bench: some of the new judges are highly credentialed, experienced, and well-respected, if clearly conservative; for others, ideological purity appears to have been an overriding consideration.[68]

For agencies, the Trump administration's refusal to abide by well-established norms has undermined morale and hastened the departure of experienced personnel.[69] Only months after the turnover in administrations, civil servants began reporting low morale and a decline in the ability of agencies to fulfill their missions.[70] Within a year, reports arose of morale so low that "some [agency] employees said they were suffering from increased anxiety and depression that has complicated their personal relationships and even led to heavier drinking."[71] Jeffrey David Cox, the president of the country's largest federal employee union, referred to the Trump administration as "the worst," going back as far as Ronald Reagan, due to effects on morale at agencies.[72] Agency employees report being subject to poor decision-making procedures, obfuscation and lack of communication, and hostile messages from political appointees.[73] Some agencies, such as the State Department and the EPA, have been particularly hard hit.[74]

The Trump administration's disregard of the established guardrails has led it to career into destructive territory by engaging in a wide range of actions that flagrantly undermine the American public's well-being. There are many examples, but some of the most significant include undermining a clean air rule that is expected to save tens of thousands of lives; attempting to shovel billions of dollars to prop up dirty and outdated coal-fired power plants by increasing electricity rates for regular consumers; and rolling back vehicle emissions standards that improve air quality, reduce greenhouse gas emissions, and save drivers billions of dollars at the tank. If successful, these efforts would impose enormous costs on the American public, and, in many cases, even the industries that the Trump administration purports to protect have objected to measures they see as going too far.[75] Even where these efforts have failed, either as a result of internal dissent or due to court losses, they impose opportunity costs, as all of the useful initiatives that a competent, good-faith administration might have pursued are forgone.

***

In the contemporary political environment, agencies play an extremely important policy-making role in American society. Given the complexity of many regulatory challenges, a polarized political environment that facilitates legislative gridlock, and continued demand from the public for polices that address the many important risks of modern life, the central role of agencies is unlikely to diminish any time soon. To balance the demands of democratic accountability with the need to ensure expertise-informed, impartial administration of the law, a system of guardrails has grown over the past several decades—enforced by courts and institutions within the executive branch—that gives a degree of freedom for political officials to influence agency policy while also cabining that freedom through norms designed to facilitate expert input and promote rational decision making.[76]

When the Trump administration began kicking at the guardrails that had constrained agency decision making for decades, it effected a clear break with the prior system. Institutions and practices cultivated by administrations of both parties were abandoned, disregarded, or treated as a sham. As a consequence, this administration has faced backlash in courts and internally, interfering with its ability to fulfill its own policy goals; it has eroded the institutions of good government and severely undermined morale at major agencies such as the EPA; and it has imposed substantial costs on the American public.

But, notwithstanding the radical nature of this administration's departure from the past, this attitude did not spring, wholly formed, from the minds of Donald Trump and his senior advisors. Rather, its roots can at least partially be found in the Republican reaction to the Obama administration. After the 2008 election, Republican Party leadership—presumably responding to signals from organized constituencies as well as base voters—adopted a position of absolute opposition to the president and his party, even when that meant attacking traditional Republican views on issues such as market-based mechanisms for pollution control and cost-benefit analysis. This oppositional dynamic set the stage for the moves made by the Trump administration.

In the next chapter, we turn to the use of cost-benefit analysis under the Obama administration. By demonstrating that cost-benefit analysis often favors strong regulation, the Obama administration drove a wedge between two traditional constituencies for the technique: those who see cost-benefit analysis as a tool to shape regulation to best promote public well-being; and those who favor its use only because they believe that it will lead to less regulation. For those in the latter, instrumental category, the experience under Obama confounded expectations, raising doubts about the value of their old allegiances.

2

A Threatening Synthesis

In the summer of 2008, the outcome of the upcoming presidential election was far from clear. Barack Obama had successfully challenged Hillary Clinton for the Democratic Party's nomination, leading to a skilled but still relatively untested candidate at the top of the ticket. At the same time, the deep unpopularity of the outgoing George W. Bush administration was a serious drag on the candidacy of Republican nominee John McCain and pointed to a likely change of parties in the White House. The unfolding financial crisis—illustrated by the rapid collapse of Lehman Brothers—also injected considerable uncertainty into the race.

Although the outcome of the election was unknown, the direction of certain policies for the next four years was clearer. Despite their differences, both candidates acknowledged the reality and importance of climate change. McCain had been one of the chief champions of climate legislation in the Senate, and Obama was a proponent of immediate steps to cut greenhouse gas emissions. Both recognized the need for health care reform and embraced market-oriented solutions. And neither contender intended to break with the long-standing orthodoxy concerning the importance of careful deliberation over costs and benefits as part of the regulatory process. As a Republican, McCain inherited that position from his predecessors. For his part, Obama seemed likely to hew to the course set by the Clinton administration of adopting cost-benefit analysis and turning it toward more progressive ends rather than attempting to reject it altogether.

No one would have predicted it at the time, but Obama's election on November 4, 2008, would ultimately lead to a breakdown in the bipartisan consensus over the role of cost-benefit analysis in regulatory decision making. Despite objections from certain constituencies, Obama placed cost-benefit analysis at the very center of his administration's governing philosophy. He also pursued an aggressive agenda of new regulatory protections for public health, consumers, and the environment. His time in office demonstrated in powerful terms that cost-benefit analysis need not be associated with an anti-regulatory agenda. It also closely associated cost-benefit analysis with the Democratic Party, its policy objectives, and with President Obama specifically. In the increasingly heated partisan environment of American politics, the closer the Democratic Party leaned toward cost-benefit analysis, the more mistrustful Republicans grew of the technique.

Reviving Rationality. Michael A. Livermore and Richard L. Revesz, Oxford University Press (2020). © Oxford University Press. DOI: 10.1093/oso/9780197539446.001.0001.

The Cost-Benefit Rivals

As discussed earlier, balancing the requirements of loyalty and competence in making personnel decisions is one of the most difficult challenges that presidents face, especially when they first assume office.[1] But it is also the point where presidents put their most lasting stamp on their administrations, making decisions that will affect a host of choices on nearly every conceivable policy and political dimension. This reality was reflected in a motto adopted by the Reagan transition team: "people are policy."[2]

President Obama famously respected Abraham Lincoln's approach of filling his cabinet with a "team of rivals"—a group of opinionated, high-powered political figures who did not always agree with each other but who could be counted on to express their frank opinions, even when they conflicted with the president's own views.[3] He made that inclination especially clear in some of his early appointments, most notably when he selected his rival for the Democratic Party nomination, Hillary Clinton, to serve as secretary of state.

The team of rivals approach also helped President Obama implement cost-benefit progressivism through regulatory policy. In deciding on personnel for important regulatory posts, the administration drew from representatives of traditionally opposing camps concerning the value of cost-benefit analysis. In the push-and-pull between these different perspectives, the administration was ultimately able to implement an agenda that spanned a strong ideological divide within the Democratic Party.

To understand the origins of this divide, it is useful to take a brief detour several decades in the past, when the terms of the political debate over cost-benefit analysis were first set. During the late 1970s, a troubled US economy was characterized by inflation, unemployment, and oil shortages. Conservative thinkers at the time—who included Murray L. Weidenbaum, William A. Niskanen, James C. Miller III, and Christopher DeMuth—drew a link between these economic problems and overly intrusive government regulation.[4] Associated with academic institutions as well as think tanks such as Cato and the American Enterprise Institute, these scholars offered both their diagnosis of the causes of economic malaise—over-regulation—and a treatment: their program of regulatory reform.

Weidenbaum, for example, who conducted one of the first studies of the aggregate costs imposed by regulation on the US economy,[5] argued that deregulation was needed to spur economic growth, and blamed over-regulation on the influence of "self-styled representative[s] of the Public Interest, who [have] succeeded so frequently in identifying [their] personal prejudices with the national well-being."[6] Niskanen introduced the theory of the "empire-building" bureaucrat who sought to maximize the budget and mandate of his or her office, regardless of the costs imposed on society.[7] Miller argued that cost-benefit analysis was needed to dial back overzealous environmental regulators,[8] while DeMuth took aim at the "splurge of new health, safety, and environmental laws" that he argued were "hostile toward traditional business values and paternalistic toward the consumer."[9]

The regulatory reform agenda offered by these scholars centered around deregulation. But they also typically recognized that some regulation of the free market was necessary. So they proposed ways to separate the bad regulations from the good. One idea was to create something called a "regulatory budget" that would constrain the costs that agencies could impose on private actors.[10] This idea was largely dropped at the time, perhaps in part due to the difficulty of establishing a sensible budget.[11] A more successful idea, attributable to Weidenbaum among others, was the use of cost-benefit analysis to screen regulations.

The 1970s recession gave unusual salience to these scholars' ideas, and they helped shape the conversation during the 1980 presidential election, with regulatory reform included as important planks in both of the major party platforms.[12] The Republican Party, in particular, focused on regulation as a key cause of economic difficulty, declaring a "war on government overregulation."[13] In a colloquy on regulation during the second presidential debate, which commentators have flagged as a key turning point in the race,[14] President Reagan summarized his position:

> I am suggesting that there are literally thousands of unnecessary regulations that invade every facet of business, and indeed, very much of our personal lives, that are unnecessary; that Government can do without; that have added $130 billion to the cost of production in this country; and that are contributing their part to inflation. And I would like to see us a little more free, as we once were.[15]

Discussing his opposition to proposed national air quality regulations while he was California governor, Reagan provided the following characterization of the actions of the EPA:

> The Federal Government tried to impose on the State of California—not a law, but regulations—that would have made it impossible to drive an automobile within the city limits of any California city, or to have a place to put it if you did drive it against their regulations. It would have destroyed the economy of California . . .

One week after this debate, Reagan won the presidency in a landslide election. In accordance with its "people are policy" strategy, Reagan tapped the cadre of conservative scholars instrumental in defining the regulatory reform agenda for leading positions in the administration: with Weidenbaum as the first chairman of Reagan's Council of Economic Advisers (CEA), Niskanen as a member of the CEA, Miller as the first OIRA chief, and DeMuth as the second. With this group in place, Reagan quickly went on to "assert[] vigorous centralized control over the regulatory process"[16] through regulatory review and cost-benefit analysis.

Groups like environmental organizations and labor unions began to criticize Reagan's new structure almost immediately, amid fears of regulatory delays and a deregulatory bent.[17] One technique was to criticize cost-benefit analysis in starkly moral terms, with union leaders arguing that it "prices out human life"[18] and environmentalists condemning the methodology as "basically fraudulent" because it "ignores ethical and moral choices."[19] Some Democratic politicians picked up these arguments: for example, Representative Henry Waxman, a major voice for environmental issues in the House for many years, argued that cost-benefit analysis was "dangerous" because "we don't know how to measure the true cost of health or disease."[20] This basic political dynamic put many Democratic constituencies on a decades-long path of aggressive opposition to cost-benefit analysis.

But opposition to cost-benefit analysis was not universal among those who favored strong protections for public health and the environment. For example, although many environmental groups were skeptical, some environmental economists argued that cost-benefit analysis could show the value of more stringent environmental regulation.[21] In addition, throughout the 1980s and 1990s, a growing intellectual movement emerged that attempted to deploy concepts typically associated with conservatives in a more progressive direction.[22]

The political analogue to this intellectual movement was the New Democrat movement, which was a reaction to Republican dominance in presidential elections and an attempt to remake the Democratic Party coalition to generate better electoral outcomes.[23] In the mid-1980s, the Democratic Leadership Council (DLC) was formed by party operative Al From and a group of politicians to promote a revised policy agenda for the Democratic Party that borrowed heavily from Republican Party orthodoxy on some issues—such as trade, taxation and spending, welfare and crime control—while maintaining more liberal positions on social issues.

The DLC's influence in Democratic politics was cemented when Bill Clinton, shortly after leaving his post as the organization's chair, captured the party's presidential nomination in 1992. The policy agenda of the Clinton administration closely tracked the priorities of the DLC, and his maintenance of cost-benefit analysis and regulatory review was consistent with this overall position. During the Clinton years, progressive groups largely maintained their hostility toward cost-benefit analysis. This antipathy for the technique was sufficiently ingrained that groups even rebuffed requests by Clinton's OIRA administrator Sally Katzen to engage them in conversation about how cost-benefit analysis should be carried out.[24]

Barack Obama's primary campaign gained substantial support from Democratic Party constituencies that disagreed with the course set out by the DLC. The DLC had supported the Iraq War, as did Hillary Clinton, and her link to the unpopular war became a major distinction between Obama and Clinton over the course of the primary. Progressive activists—many of whom had long opposed the use of cost-benefit analysis to evaluate regulation—provided donations, volunteers, and energy for the Obama campaign, both during his long-shot primary victory over Clinton and in the general election.

When taking office in 2009, it may have seemed to many that President Obama faced the impossible task of bringing together two camps within the Democratic Party that had irreconcilable demands. One approach might have been to choose sides: perhaps by jettisoning the DLC wing of the party in favor of the progressive wing that had provided so much support for his candidacy. But Obama instead adopted the team-of-rivals strategy, nicely illustrated in the context of cost-benefit analysis with the appointment of Cass Sunstein to head OIRA and another academic—Lisa Heinzerling—as the EPA's associate administrator in charge of the Office of Policy, which has been characterized as a "mini-OMB" within the agency.[25]

As legal scholars, Sunstein and Heinzerling could not have staked out positions that were further apart on the issue of cost-benefit analysis. Sunstein had spent the bulk of his career at the University of Chicago, alongside law-and-economics figures such as Richard Posner (who was appointed by Ronald Reagan as a judge on the United States Court of Appeals for the Seventh Circuit), and ultimately adopted a moderate, DLC-friendly position in support of cost-benefit analysis. Heinzerling, by contrast, aligned with the progressive opposition: she was a leading figure in the founding of the Center for Progressive Reform (CPR), a group of legal academics who engage in advocacy in favor of more stringent regulatory protections on a range of issues, many of whom reject cost-benefit analysis.

Two books from these legal academics tell the story of the divide within the Democratic Party over cost-benefit analysis.[26] Sunstein's *Risk and Reason* lays out the argument for weighing costs and benefits when setting regulatory policy. Sunstein identifies several cases that he believed illustrate improper government reactions to risk based on the quick emotional-driven judgments of the public and policymakers. He argues that sometimes, as in the case of indoor air pollution or obesity, people naturally underestimate risks, leading to an inadequate policy response, while in other cases—such as exposure to chemicals from toxic waste dumps—people overestimate the risks, leading to government overreaction. The solution for Sunstein is a slower, more rational deliberative process that is informed by careful weighing of costs and benefits. Sunstein sees government cost-benefit analysis as the cool-headed counterpart that can help tame a policymaking process that is too often driven by hotheaded responses.

Heinzerling's book, *Priceless* (co-authored with heterodox economist Frank Ackerman) argues for the opposite position. For Heinzerling, cost-benefit is far from the cool, dispassionate tool described by Sunstein. Instead, in her view, cost-benefit analysis smuggles in controversial assumptions—such as the comparability of morally important goods such as health with less morally significant goods like consumer satisfaction—under a veneer of scientific objectivity. As practiced in the United States, cost-benefit analysis places all regulatory effects on a common dollar-denominated scale, a process that Heinzerling argues is reductionist and disrespectful. Heinzerling also criticizes certain techniques in cost-benefit analysis, such as discounting future costs and benefits to current dollars, which she believes inadequately values future generations.

But, although Sunstein and Heinzerling could not disagree more about the merits of cost-benefit analysis, they were able to work in the same administration toward a shared set of goals. Sunstein met Barack Obama during their time together at the University of Chicago, where Obama spent time teaching constitutional law and writing his first book, *Dreams from My Father*, while he served as a state senator in Illinois. Sunstein was an early supporter of Obama's presidential ambitions. After Obama's victory, Sunstein was appointed to head OIRA, arguably the most important regulatory position in government. In the late years of the George W. Bush presidency, Heinzerling burnished her advocacy credentials as one of the main lawyers for the environmental community in *Massachusetts v. EPA*, the case in which the Supreme Court held that the EPA had the authority to regulate greenhouse gases under the Clean Air Act. After serving on the Obama transition team committee on environmental agencies, Heinzerling first took up a role as a special counselor at the EPA before leading the agency's Office of Policy. In that role, she oversaw the National Center for Environmental Economics, the main shop at the EPA in charge of developing the agency's guidelines for cost-benefit analysis and of supervising the analysis used to support individual regulations.

The essential fact that bridged the gap between the DLC moderates and CPR-style progressives is that cost-benefit analysis often supports stringent protections for the environment, public health, and other social values. Where cost-benefit analysis and the progressive policy agenda point in the same direction—which is often the case—then there is no difficulty in finding common ground between people as ideologically diverse as Sunstein and Heinzerling.

In his writings on legal theory, Sunstein came up with a name for his time of compromise: "incompletely theorized agreements."[27] The idea is that, in law and politics, it is often difficult to agree on fundamentals, but often much easier to agree on a course of action. So don't bother arguing about *why* and instead focus on *what* and *how*: "[We] need not agree on fundamental principle. . . . When [we] disagree on an abstraction, [we] move to a level of greater particularity."[28] Working successfully in the Obama administration meant focusing on the particular and the practical—what rules to support and how—rather than on fundamental principles such as whether all costs and benefits could be placed on a common scale.

President Obama's Executive Order 13,563 reflected the "incompletely theorized agreements" approach to compromise. Shortly after the beginning of the Obama administration, the president circulated a memorandum directing the Office of Management and Budget to develop recommendations for a "new Executive Order on Federal regulatory review" that

> offer suggestions for the relationship between OIRA and the agencies; provide guidance on disclosure and transparency; encourage public participation in agency regulatory processes; offer suggestions on the role of cost-benefit analysis; address the role of distributional considerations, fairness, and concern for the interests of future generations; identify methods of ensuring that regulatory review does not produce undue delay; clarify the role of the behavioral sciences in formulating regulatory policy; and identify the best tools for achieving public goals through the regulatory process.[29]

The ambitious executive order anticipated in the memorandum never arrived.[30] Instead, Obama issued Executive Order 13,563, which "reaffirm[ed]" Clinton's Executive Order 12,866 with relatively minor modifications, such as emphasizing that agencies were permitted to "consider (and discuss qualitatively) values that are difficult or impossible to quantify, including equity, human dignity, fairness, and distributive impacts."[31] The larger reform effort was perhaps abandoned in part due to the difficulty of arriving at agreement—even among senior political appointees—on first principles. Rather than engage in internal struggles about how best to "address the role of distributional considerations, fairness, and concern for the interests of future generations" in the abstract, the Obama administration decided to focus on concrete policy reforms, using the institutional setup and substantive standards that it inherited from prior administrations.

This compromise played out in a series of major rulemakings in which the Obama administration took progressive stances to advance Democratic Party policy priorities, such as environmental protection, while relying on mainstream approaches to cost-benefit analysis to examine, and ultimately justify, these rules. In this way, the Obama presidency developed a Democratic approach to regulatory policy that reconciled the demands of party constituencies with the guardrails around regulatory policy that had evolved under previous administrations.

The Playbook

The election in 2008 placed the Democratic Party in a stronger position than it had been since at least 1992, with control of the White House, a substantial majority in the House, and, briefly, a filibuster-proof majority in the Senate. After Obama's inauguration on January 20, 2009, the new Congress quickly embarked on a busy legislative calendar, perhaps sensing that that its ability to move Democratic priorities in Congress would be ephemeral. Major legislation followed in one of the most productive legislative sessions in decades. The most important bills included the Lilly Ledbetter Fair Pay Act, the American Recovery and Reinvestment Act (i.e., the stimulus package), the Patient Protection and Affordable Care Act (which came to be known as Obamacare), and the Dodd-Frank Wall Street Reform and Consumer Protection Act.

There were also substantial failures that demonstrated the limits of intraparty agreement, and the strength of interparty hostility. Perhaps most striking was the failure of the 111th Congress to adopt climate legislation, despite decades of advocacy by a core Democratic constituency and the active support of President Obama. The story of the failure of the Waxman-Markey climate bill—which passed the House in a close vote but died in the Senate—is long and complex and involves much of the political intrigue, missteps, and dirty tricks that accompany any legislation, successful or not.[32] But opposition to the American Clean Energy and Security Act (as it was officially called) also presaged the new partisan dynamic that would affect the shape of regulatory policy in the coming years.

The Waxman-Markey bill was largely based on the recommendations from a diverse group of stakeholders called the US Climate Action Partnership (USCAP). That organization was a coalition that included both the major national environmental organizations, such as the Natural Resources Defense Council and the Environmental Defense Fund, as well as major corporations including BP America, DuPont, Duke Energy, and General Electric. The core of the USCAP approach was a cap-and-trade program modeled on the sulfur dioxide trading program to combat acid rain that was established as part of the 1990 Clean Air Act Amendments. That trading program was the result of a compromise between more conservative, market-oriented interests in the George H. W. Bush White House and environmentalists and their supporters in Congress who sought stronger protections. It was an example of the old style of compromise that was possible during the era of divided government, when relative stability in the balance of power between the parties created a consistent negotiating dynamic that facilitated bipartisan lawmaking. The subsequent decades of the implementation of the sulfur-dioxide trading program also showed it to be a significant success, dramatically cutting emissions and associated health and environmental harms at relatively low cost.

The USCAP approach attempted to replicate this compromise in the context of greenhouse gas emissions. Ultimately, this strategy failed in the face of strident Republican opposition. In the House, moderate Republicans had been losing ground for decades, and very few of the old-guard of environmentally friendly Republicans were left. Nevertheless, with a strong Democratic majority and the leadership of majority leader Nancy Pelosi, the Waxman-Markey bill passed the House with strong support from Democrats and nearly universal opposition from Republicans.[33] The Senate, with its filibuster tradition and larger number of Democrats from coal-dependent states, is where the bill died. Republican minority leader Mitch McConnell had announced a strategy of absolute opposition to the Democratic majority, including on issues where compromise might seem possible. Even John McCain—who had been a major supporter of climate legislation and cap-and-trade in the past—voted against the Senate version of the Waxman-Markey bill, helping to seal its fate.[34]

With legislative gridlock on some issues even under unified Democratic control, and later on an end to legislative productivity with the 2010 Republican takeover of the House, the Obama administration took what had become the well-worn path of prior administrations and looked to agencies and regulation as an alternative pathway to achieve its policy goals. To do so, it used a playbook that it had begun to put in place in the early days of the administration.

Developing the Playbook: Cutting Greenhouse Gas Emissions from Cars

On environmental issues, the administration's most important first step was a rulemaking that established nationwide limits on greenhouse gas emissions from the transportation sector. The proposed rule was announced by President Obama in May 2009—just a few months after his inauguration—and came in response to the Supreme Court's decision in *Massachusetts v. EPA*. That decision, which established the legal basis for greenhouse gas regulation under the Clean Air Act, dealt with pollution from automobiles specifically. The Court held that the EPA had to either move forward with regulating greenhouse gas emissions from cars or give scientific reasons for not doing so. The Bush administration had stalled compliance with the Court's ruling in its waning days, kicking the can to the next president. When Obama came into office, the EPA was ready to respond to *Massachusetts v. EPA*.

Controlling greenhouse gas emissions from automobiles presents a number of political and bureaucratic complexities.[35] From a technological perspective, a promising option is to improve vehicle fuel economy.[36] For some other forms of pollution from cars, devices such as catalytic converters or regulations on fuel content can be used to reduce emissions. Catalytic converters work by chemically transforming more harmful substances (e.g., hydrocarbons) into less harmful emissions (e.g., carbon dioxide and water). The phasing out of lead as a gasoline additive and rules requiring low-sulfur content in fuels reduce emissions of those two compounds. These alternative approaches are not available for carbon dioxide emissions, so reducing emissions requires that less gasoline be consumed.[37]

Bureaucratically, controlling greenhouse gas emissions from cars, without creating a mishmash of different conflicting standards, requires a coordinated program to harmonize rules among the three different institutions with concurrent jurisdiction over cars: the EPA, the Department of Transportation, and the state of California. This overlapping regulatory authority came with a clash of cultures, with the EPA running major pollution control programs across many industries, the Department of Transportation mostly focused on the demands of consumers and manufacturers in a single industry, and California's particularly aggressive approach to regulating automobile pollution.[38]

There were also many external pressures on the administration. After their victory in *Massachusetts v. EPA*, environmentalists were eager for the Obama administration to show that it was serious about tackling greenhouse gas emissions from automobiles. At the same time, the 2008 financial crisis had also placed the US auto manufacturing industry into a tailspin, with GM and Chrysler looking to the US government for multi-billion-dollar bailouts. Getting the automakers back on their feet was a major policy priority, and so imposing costly new environmental protections was a difficult political lift.

In reconciling this clash of pressures and interests, the Obama administration developed a playbook that would come to characterize its approach to regulation. One page of the playbook drew from progressive optimism that government policy could be a force for good, correcting failures in markets and nudging private behavior in a direction that improves human well-being. This page was supported by the constituencies of the Democratic Party, such as environmentalists, that looked to Obama for renewed policymaking energy, and figures like Heinzerling in the administration. The other page recognized the limits of government and the need for careful planning to avoid harmful unintended consequences, drawing lessons from the political and policy successes of the regulatory reform movement. This page was supported by more moderate constituencies within the party and represented in the administration by Sunstein, among others.

When applied to the vehicle greenhouse gas standard, the playbook generated a timeline of increasingly stringent standards, a range of flexibility measures for industry to reduce disruption and compliance costs, and a rigorous cost-benefit analysis that demonstrated massive anticipated net benefits. The primary costs associated with the rule were increased purchase prices for cars that include enhanced fuel-saving technologies. An important component of the rule was that it was carefully designed so that the safety of vehicles was not compromised. John Graham, the OIRA administrator under George W. Bush, played an important role in his academic career studying the potential trade-off between safety and fuel economy.[39] Recognizing and responding to this potential trade-off was an example of the Obama administration's willingness to stay within the guardrails around regulatory decision making that had evolved over the course of prior administrations.

There were two main categories of benefits from the vehicle greenhouse gas standard.[40] The first involved reductions in air pollution. The target pollutant was carbon dioxide, the most important greenhouse gas. In addition to reductions in these emissions, the rule also resulted in fewer emissions of other pollutants, such as superfine particulate matter, that have localized health consequences. The second major category of benefits were fuel savings for consumers. More fuel-efficient cars mean that less fuel is burned (reducing pollution) but also that less fuel is purchased, which saves consumers money. By 2030, the annual monetary value of the environmental and health benefits of the rule were estimated to be over $10 billion dollars, while American consumers were expected to reap nearly $80 billion in fuel savings. The projected compliance costs of the rule in the same year were comparatively modest at nearly $16 billion.[41] Thus, the rule was extremely attractive from a cost-benefit perspective.

Politically and as a matter of policy, the vehicle greenhouse gas standard was an outstanding success. The major US car manufacturers were in a conciliatory mood due to the need for a bailout from the federal government in the wake of the 2008 financial crisis, and they also feared that California could adopt standards unilaterally, leading to multiple conflicting sets of rules. The car companies endorsed the rule, allowing it to move forward without an industry-backed court challenge.[42] Environmentalists were also pleased with the outcome and chalked up an important victory toward their goal of decarbonizing the US economy. The EPA, Department of Transportation, and California regulators all worked closely together and developed a joint rulemaking that led to coordinated standards, helping secure the backing of the car makers, who prized regulatory certainty. US consumers saved billions of dollars, lives were saved from decreased exposure to harmful pollutants, and millions of tons of greenhouse gas emissions were avoided.

In conducting the cost-benefit analysis of the vehicle greenhouse gas standard, the agencies faced a number of questions.[43] As mentioned earlier, some experts in the past raised concerns about a trade-off between safety and fuel economy, and regulators had to figure out how to address this issue in the rule. Placing a monetary value on the benefits of greenhouse gas emissions reductions also required developing a rigorous methodology, and considerable effort was expended by the administration to derive a defensible number. Another relevant economic question concerns the phenomenon referred to as the "energy paradox," which describes consumers who are unwilling to make investments in fuel efficiency that pay off in the long term. An additional phenomenon is the "rebound effect" where increased fuel economy reduces the cost of driving, which increases vehicle miles traveled, partially offsetting the pollution control benefits of the rule. The agencies spent considerable time in examining and discussing these and similar questions, tailoring the rulemaking where possible to increase net benefits, and carefully calculating costs and benefits in light of these effects.

A Picture of Cost-Benefit Progressivism

Over the course of President Obama's two terms, agencies applied this same playbook in a variety of regulatory contexts, and in the process they created a clear picture of what *cost-benefit progressivism*—the combination of progressive policy goals and cost-benefit analysis—looked like in practice. In the background of the picture was a tendency to hew fairly closely to traditional ways of understanding the role of regulation in a market economy. Under a mainstream economic model that has dominated for decades—and which remained central to how the Obama administration pursued regulation—the choices made by individuals in the marketplace are generally understood to result in outcomes that maximize collective well-being. This way of thinking about markets is related to Adam Smith's concept of the "invisible hand" as well as the defense of markets offered by more recent libertarian-oriented economists such as Friedrich von Hayek and Milton Friedman. The basic gist of the argument is that whenever people enter into voluntary transactions with each other, it is because they believe that they will each be better off as a consequence of those transactions. When all welfare-improving transactions are made, this is referred to as a Pareto optimal outcome (after Italian economist Vilfredo Pareto) because, by definition, it is impossible to make anyone better off without making someone else worse off. A perfectly functioning market should generate a Pareto optimal outcome.

But, of course, markets do not always function perfectly. And so the traditional economic model creates a justification for government intervention: to correct for conditions where markets "fail" and therefore do not deliver efficient results. The goal of cost-benefit analysis in this model is to identify those market failures as well as the regulatory interventions that are well-suited to address them. This notion that the private market serves as a default, supplemented by regulation when necessary to correct for market failures, has informed the development of cost-benefit analysis since the Reagan administration and remained central to the approach adopted by the Obama administration. To the extent that cost-benefit progressivism departed from past practice in this area, it was by its willingness to pursue the kinds of regulations that were justified by cost-benefit analysis, even in the face of concerted political opposition.

In the foreground of the picture of cost-benefit progressivism painted by the Obama administration were efforts to expand the notion of "market failures" based on recent advances in fields such as behavioral economics. For some rules, traditional economic analysis provided an extremely strong foundation for regulation, and the link between progressive policy goals and cost-benefit analysis was sturdy. In other regulatory contexts, the Obama administration was cutting a more controversial path and had to work harder to provide a solid defense for its decisions. But despite some setbacks and challenges, the track record of the administration in constructing a workable synthesis that was both grounded in the foundations of cost-benefit analysis while also looking forward toward new developments was generally successful.

The Threat

The Obama administration's success in navigating within the existing guardrails, while pushing bold policy initiatives, undermined long-standing assumptions shared by both conservatives and liberals about the interaction of cost-benefit analysis and strong regulatory protections.

As discussed above, the early advocates in the Republican Party for cost-benefit analysis consistently argued that it would be a mechanism to rein in overzealous regulators.[44] Similar arguments continued to be made by prominent figures in the coming decades. One influential example was an analysis conducted by John F. Morrall III, an economist at the Office of Management and Budget, that compared the estimated costs of federal regulations with their benefits, finding some striking results, such as a rule that spent nearly $70 billion per life saved.[45] Similar types of analyses were carried out by John Graham during his time as an academic at Harvard University[46] and Robert Hahn, an economist who directed the AEI-Brookings Joint Center and served on the Council of Economic Advisers during the George H. W. Bush administration.[47]

One example of the degree of consensus over the anti-regulatory inclination of cost-benefit analysis was the positions of parties and groups in the case

Whitman v. American Trucking, which litigated the question of whether the EPA could take costs into consideration when setting the National Ambient Air Quality Standards (NAAQS).[48] In that case, the EPA argued that the Clean Air Act prohibited cost consideration, while the challengers—who favored more lax regulation—argued the agency could have, and should have, considered costs. A number of parties filed *amicus* briefs in that case, and among those, not a single industrial group or trade association argued that cost-benefit analysis should be prohibited, and not a single environmental group argued that cost-benefit analysis should be allowed.[49] In his opinion for the majority, largely agreeing with the EPA's interpretation of the act, Justice Scalia maintained the same assumption that cost considerations would lead to less stringent standards.[50]

The irony of this widely shared assumption is that it is wrong. As it turns out, regulation of air quality has very clear and relatively easily monetized benefits, and stringent standards are highly justified from a cost-benefit perspective. Although the judgment in *American Trucking* prohibited the EPA from considering costs when setting the NAAQS,[51] the agency nonetheless conducts cost-benefit analysis for information purposes.[52] All of the NAAQS currently in force have substantial net benefits.[53] What is more, the cost-benefit analysis conducted by the EPA shows that the cost-blind standards selected by the agency were *weaker* than the standards that would be chosen using cost-benefit analysis.[54] Everyone—from the leading environmental organizations and trade associations to the ideologically diverse justices on the Supreme Court—operated under the view that cost considerations would lead to weaker NAAQS. In fact, the opposite is true.

Experience with the NAAQS shows how shared assumptions about cost-benefit analysis in that context can be completely backward. Experience during the Obama administration across a wide variety of agencies in many different regulatory contexts upended the traditional assumptions far more comprehensively. The synthesis of reliance on cost-benefit analysis and the pursuit of an aggressive regulatory agenda may go a long way toward helping to explain why some prior advocates of cost-benefit analysis—who largely understood the technique as pushing in an anti-regulatory direction—would come to question the technique during Obama's administration.

When strong regulations pass a cost-benefit test, proponents of cost-benefit analysis who came to their view under the assumption that it would largely lead in deregulatory direction face a choice: either embrace a more expansive understanding of cost-benefit analysis in which it promotes sound regulatory decision making but does not necessarily lead to less regulation; or drop cost-benefit analysis. As noted by conservative legal scholar Alexander Volokh, if cost-benefit analysis can be used successfully to justify regulation, advocates of regulation "who have been historically suspicious of cost-benefit analysis" may embrace the technique. But he goes on to note:

> [There is] a corollary for free-market advocates who are hostile to regulation. Free-market advocates have mostly gone along with cost-benefit analysis because of a belief that it would serve as a brake on regulation. [But if] cost-benefit analysis, neutrally applied, can easily be proregulatory[,] perhaps natural-rights libertarians should reconsider their tolerance of cost-benefit analysis and focus more on making their case for deregulation in moral terms.[55]

Although some proponents of cost-benefit analysis have maintained their confidence in the technique, others have followed the path urged by Volokh. Once it became clear that cost-benefit analysis could no longer be counted on to generate anti-regulatory effects, many of the technique's traditional allies chose to ditch the tool.

***

Upon taking office, President Obama adopted a team of rivals approach to balancing the demands of different constituencies within the Democratic Party, and he used that approach to bring together the centrist, economically oriented wing of the party with more liberal, regulation-oriented constituencies. The playbook used by the Obama administration in a variety of different regulatory contexts was based on a synthesis between cost-benefit analysis and a progressive policy agenda. Deploying this playbook, the administration showed how cost-benefit analysis could help identify and justify a raft of new protections for values as diverse as environmental health and prison safety. That playbook was highly successful in promoting new protections that massively benefited the American public. But its very success threatened powerful interests—regulated industry—that had embraced cost-benefit analysis for instrumental reasons in the belief that it would always point in the direction of less regulation.

Before turning to this reaction, it is worth considering in greater detail how the Obama administration managed to promote its regulatory goals while adhering to established norms. This experience helps illustrate exactly why the synthesis achieved by the Obama administration was so threatening. By staying within existing guardrails, new regulations adopted under Obama directly undermined the views of those advocates of cost-benefit analysis who believed that the technique naturally led to deregulation. This forced those earlier friends of cost-benefit analysis to consider their priorities: Did they care more about careful analysis to ensure that regulations generated net benefits, or was their priority deregulation, regardless of the social consequences?

The Obama administration also demonstrated how it is possible to achieve policy goals while staying within the confines of cost-benefit analysis. The system of guardrails that was constructed by prior administrations over the past several decades was not intended to eliminate policy discretion at agencies or in the White House. Rather, it struck a balance between the appropriate exercise of political influence over regulatory policy and the need to protect values—such as expertise, impartiality, and legality—that are cornerstones of the legitimacy of administrative agencies. When the policy goals of political officials are reasonably aligned with the public interest, and those officials are willing to listen to evidence and tailor their policies accordingly, there need be no conflict between democratic accountability for agencies through political oversight and evidence-based regulatory decision making.

3

Staying in Bounds

From its beginning, the Obama administration broadcast its approach of pursuing an aggressive regulatory agenda while retaining a central place for cost-benefit analysis. This synthesis did not always sit well with every constituency within the Democratic party, but it was remarkably successful in mitigating intraparty conflict while moving forward with major rulemakings. When challenged in court, many of these rules were upheld, and have proven difficult for the Trump administration to reverse, exactly because they were supported by rigorous analysis.

Over the course of its eight years, the administration pursued rulemakings on a large number of subjects, from greenhouse gas emissions to health care, from safety features in automobiles to the stability of financial markets. In developing these policies, the agencies made many policy choices that gave rise to fierce opposition—some based on partisan or ideological grounds, but often from interest groups unhappy with the extent or distribution of costs and benefits. On many issues, there were legitimate grounds for disagreement and the administration had to select from among plausible policy alternatives.

In keeping with the practices of prior administrations, although political considerations and the demands of party constituencies no doubt influenced the direction of policy, so too did evidence, analysis, and expertise. There is every indication that the president and senior political officials at the White House and agencies did not view their decisions as simply the raw exercise of power. Rather, many officials appeared to respect the system of governance that they inherited, with its established methods for incorporating analysis and evidence into regulatory decision making. Their personal policy preferences and perspectives were tempered by these long-standing practices, which ultimately led to better decision making.

Constraints

Critics of cost-benefit analysis have long argued that the technique is too easily subject to manipulation. These critics claim that although regulation that is supported by cost-benefit analysis gives the impression of objectivity and genuine deliberation, this impression is an illusion. Rather, the argument goes,

Reviving Rationality. Michael A. Livermore and Richard L. Revesz, Oxford University Press (2020). © Oxford University Press. DOI: 10.1093/oso/9780197539446.001.0001.

regulatory decisions are fundamentally political in nature, and the long, detailed, and technical cost-benefit analyses that accompany regulations are nothing more than jargon-laden exercises in post hoc rationalization that obscure more than illuminate.

In support of this claim, the critics often point to difficult empirical questions and value-laden methodological choices that can be found in cost-benefit analyses of complex regulations. On the empirical side, agencies must often assess the effects of regulation when there is considerable uncertainty about the underlying risks and associated pathways. For example, to conduct a full cost-benefit analysis of a Transportation Security Administration screening requirement for air travelers, regulators must determine how the additional screening will affect the risk of a terrorist attack—a very difficult risk to estimate. Similar uncertainty abounds in many regulatory contexts, from potentially carcinogenic pesticides and prison safety to dangerous workplaces and the stability of financial markets. In some cases, existing data or methods make it very difficult or impossible to provide quantitative estimates for some regulatory effects, leading to non-quantified costs or benefits.

On the methodological side, some of the choices that must be made in cost-benefit analysis have dimensions that are not purely empirical. For example, when costs and benefits occur over time, analysts must choose a discount rate to apply to the future. Over sufficiently long time horizons, this discount rate can raise question about intergenerational responsibility.[1] Regulators estimate people's preferences over mortality risk reduction to value life-saving regulation, but face the question of whether to use an average value or make adjustments for differences between people based on their risk tolerance or the budget constraints they face.[2]

Other skeptics acknowledge that cost-benefit analysis can, in principle, inform regulatory decision making but question whether it does so in practice—often pointing to genuine shortcomings in the analyses that are actually produced by agencies.[3] Sometimes, agencies fail to consider an adequate range of alternatives and simply compare their preferred approach to the status quo.[4] Benefits and costs that could, in principle, be quantified and monetized sometimes are not.[5] Agencies face finite resources and must make choices about how extensive an analysis to carry out and where to focus their efforts. These choices often mean that the analyses that are produced are less useful to regulatory decision makers and the public than they could, in principle, be.

There are further complications. Agencies are not always free to use cost-benefit analysis as they see fit. Every time an agency regulates, it is pursuant to some power that is established in statute. Those statutes often describe the factors that agencies are to consider when regulating. Sometimes, these factors are fairly expansive or statutory silence gives agencies a considerable amount of discretion.

In those cases, agencies are tasked by Clinton's Executive Order 12,866 to ensure that costs and benefits are considered in a comprehensive manner and that regulations seek to maximize net benefits. However, there are cases in which courts have interpreted some statutes to prohibit certain considerations. One important example is the National Ambient Air Quality Standards (NAAQS): as discussed in chapter 2, the Supreme Court has held that the EPA cannot consider costs when setting those standards. In such cases, agencies may conduct a cost-benefit analysis and report the results to the public, but they cannot use it as the basis for their decisions.

Relatedly, there are sometimes legitimate values that bear on regulatory decisions that are not captured in the standard methods of cost-benefit analysis. Values that are typically outside of cost-benefit analysis include anti-discrimination, human dignity, libertarian autonomy, social justice, and fair distribution. Very few argue that these values are not important. But there is no generally accepted methodology for either incorporating them into cost-benefit analysis or explicitly weighing them against cost-benefit considerations.

Given these practical realities, it is foolhardy to argue that cost-benefit analysis is a fully deterministic methodology that always gives clear answers concerning how best to regulate. But it does not follow that the technique is infinitely malleable.

There are at least three important constraints on the ability of agencies to manipulate cost-benefit analysis: transparency, consistency, and honesty. In terms of transparency, cost-benefit analysis requires agencies to disclose and explain how they arrived at their conclusions. This means that all of the empirical data, models, and methodological choices are explicitly stated and subject to scrutiny and critique. If agencies ignore data, use flawed models, or make outlandish methodological choices, they can be held to account, by the public, Congress, and the courts.

Consistency is a related source of constraint. Because prior analyses are part of the public record, the choices in any new analysis can be compared to those made in the past. Inconsistencies with prior practice naturally give rise to a demand for justification. Although there are sometimes legitimate reasons that an agency might depart from a prior practice, that agency should be able to give a reason for the departure, and those reasons can be subject to scrutiny.

The final source of constraints is honesty. James Madison famously wrote, "If men were angels, no government would be necessary. If angels were to govern men, neither external nor internal controls on government would be necessary."[6] Although Madison makes an important point, it is also unwise to discount human decency altogether when considering the functioning of government institutions. Cost-benefit analysis creates a context in which many different people must work together on a collective product. In large and diverse groups, maintaining a widespread conspiracy to manipulate the results is difficult. It may be impossible to collect the necessary human capital together without running the risk of incorporating a few honest people onto the team. And even the threat of potential whistleblowers may be sufficient to keep everyone else in line.

The tension between the indeterminacy of cost-benefit analysis and the risk of manipulation can be understood in terms of the degree of flexibility that agencies have, in light of the constraints of transparency, consistency, and accountability. At one extreme, it is possible to imagine a best possible interpretation of cost-benefit analysis in which all empirical questions and methodological choices were settled by a perfectly knowledgeable and impartial analysts in light of existing guidelines (such as Executive Order 12,866 and Circular A-4), prior practice, and the broader purposes of cost-benefit analysis in the US system of government.[7] Under such conditions, there might be determinate answers to the question of how best to carry out cost-benefit analysis for a given regulatory decision.

But even in this extremely optimistic scenario, cost-benefit analysis might not provide a definitive answer to the question of how best to regulate. For example, there might be important categories of values that do not fit in the cost-benefit framework, or costs and benefits that cannot reasonably be quantified. In these cases, subsidiary forms of economic analysis might be relevant, such as break-even analysis.[8] But even when analysis is informed by such techniques, there may be an irreducible role for judgment that cannot be directly integrated into the cost-benefit calculus.

At the other extreme, it is possible to imagine an analyst who seeks only to provide the thinnest fig leaf to clothe the naked exercise of power. Such an analyst would have to be entirely unconstrained by the demands of transparency, consistency, and honesty, and would be willing to boldly make absurd assumptions, depart from prior practice without justification, and intentionally obfuscate reality. In such situations, cost-benefit analysis would not provide any *internal* constraint. But it may ultimately subject such an unscrupulous regulator to external forms of accountability, such as a challenge in court.

Somewhere in between is the actual practice of cost-benefit analysis, where there are choices to be made, and some of them are likely to be controversial. This category is defined by a genuine attempt to engage in a good faith examination of costs and benefits, building on the tradition of cost-benefit analysis established by prior administrations. Although it falls far short of a deterministic methodology, such a good faith effort creates real boundaries on how cost-benefit analysis can properly be carried out.

In the remainder of this chapter, we argue that the Obama administration pursued its regulatory agenda within those boundaries. That does not mean that every decision that it made—either in terms of regulatory policy or in terms of cost-benefit analysis—was the best one that it could have. Rather, it means that the choices made by agencies under Obama were consistent with a good faith effort to weigh costs and benefits in line with the goals described in Reagan's Executive Order 12,291, Clinton's Executive Order 12,866, the George W. Bush-era Circular A-4, and Obama's own Executive Order 13,563. Where agencies departed from past practice or made controversial choices, they offered sound reasons for doing so. The analytic shortcomings that can be found in Obama-era analyses were generally no worse than in prior administrations—and often agencies improved on their earlier efforts.

Respect for the constraints of cost-benefit analysis does not imply an aversion to innovation, and the Obama administration also pushed the practice forward in important ways. As we discuss in more detail in the following sections, there are a number of different types of justifications for regulation, all stemming from different ways in which private markets can fail to generate socially desirable outcomes. Some market failures fit more comfortably with existing techniques and data; others require new methods or empirical estimates. Where existing techniques were adequate, the Obama administration worked to refine them. But agencies also took important—though sometimes imperfect—steps to use cost-benefit analysis to inform decision making in a broader set of regulatory contexts.

Justifying Regulation

One of the most basic principles that undergirds the process of cost-benefit analysis is the need to justify regulatory interventions. The assumed default is private conduct and free markets, with government limitations on individual choices only under special circumstances. The language of Clinton's Executive Order 12,866 states this principle as follows:

> Federal agencies should promulgate only such regulations as are required by law, are necessary to interpret the law, or are made necessary by compelling public need, such as material failures of private markets to protect or improve the health and safety of the public, the environment, or the well-being of the American people.[9]

The "material failures of private markets" referenced in the Clinton order can take several forms. The most basic market failures, firmly accepted by even the most hard-nosed neoclassical economists, are related to the notion of an "externality." Stated simply, an externality occurs when a transaction within the marketplace (say, the buying and selling of electricity) has effects that occur through pathways that are outside the marketplace (for example, through pollution from a coal-fired power plant). Those "external" effects are not accounted for by transacting parties—the sellers and purchasers of electricity—and therefore are not priced to take into account the external damages.[10] Absent some legal regime to "internalize" the pollution costs, neither the electricity generator nor the consumer will have any incentive to account for those effects when making decisions, leading to the inefficient result of too much pollution.

Cost-benefit analysis has often been used to identify regulations that correct this type of market failures. Because externality related market failures fit well with the theoretical foundations of cost-benefit analysis, it should come as no surprise that it is relatively easy to stay within the bounds of traditional cost-benefit analysis for rules that address these types of problems. Environmental rules are one example of a context where externalities can justify regulation. There is a market failure whenever pollution is released that causes environmental or health harms and the polluters do not face the costs of their actions.[11] Pollution control is a case where the market on its own simply will not generate efficient results, and some government intervention is needed.[12]

Several major environmental rulemakings during the Obama administration perfectly illustrate this point. Perhaps the most straightforward case was an EPA rule to cut down on pollution that travels among states, called the Cross-State Air Pollution Rule. This rule addressed interstate externalities that are created by the fact that air pollution has a nasty habit of ignoring jurisdictional boundaries.

One of the peculiar features of the Clean Air Act is that its centerpiece regulatory regime—a set of ambient standards (the NAAQS) and State Implementation Plans—largely addresses pollution at the local level. Although the statute also includes provisions focused on interstate air pollution, the EPA struggled for decades to figure out how to best control pollution that is "exported" from one state to another. The lack of controls on interstate air pollution was so severe that one of the ways in which states improved local air quality was by encouraging polluters to build tall towers that released the pollution hundreds of feet in the air, where the wind could carry it over to the next jurisdiction.[13] During this time, downwind jurisdictions, whose air was polluted by upwind neighbor states, had to impose very costly local controls to come into compliance with national air quality standards, and sometimes they could not comply even after taking very expensive steps.

The Obama administration's Cross-State Air Pollution Rule addressed this problem by creating limitations at the state level for how much pollution could be exported across state lines. This rule was an update to an earlier rule by the George W. Bush administration—called the Clean Air Interstate Rule—that attempted to address the same problem but that was struck down in court in part because it allowed too much trading of emission allowances among states.[14]

The Cross-State Air Pollution Rule cured this problem by reducing the amount of the interstate trading of emissions that was allowed, while still implementing a market-based approach as far as the statute would allow.[15] The rule set each state's limits based on the cost of reducing pollution in that state.

The cost-benefit analysis supporting the Cross-State Air Pollution Rule showed truly massive net benefits, with over $100 billion in annual benefits expected on expenditures of less than $1 billion annually.[16] Almost all of the monetized benefits are due to reductions in premature mortality associated with decreased exposure to particulate matter pollution: the number of lives saved from the rule was estimated to range between 13,000 and 34,000 per year.

Large net benefits do not, of course, guarantee that everyone will be happy with the outcome, and industry sued to overturn the rule. Somewhat paradoxically, industry's argument was that the EPA could not consider costs when setting pollution limits: traditionally, industry pushes the agency to consider costs, and it is environmentalists who are wary of inserting cost consideration into environmental decision making. In the opening paragraph of the ruling upholding the regulation, Justice Ginsburg, writing for a majority of the Supreme Court, noted that interstate externalities provide a classic context for federal environmental regulation:

> These cases concern the efforts of Congress and the Environmental Protection Agency to cope with a complex problem: air pollution emitted in one State, but causing harm in other States. Left unregulated, the emitting or upwind State reaps the benefits of the economic activity causing the pollution without bearing all the costs. Conversely, downwind States to which the pollution travels are unable to achieve clean air because of the influx of out-of-state pollution they lack authority to control. To tackle the problem, Congress included a Good Neighbor Provision in the Clean Air Act.[17]

Another Obama-era environmental rulemaking with massive net benefits was the Mercury and Air Toxics Standards (MATS), which imposed strict new limits on the release of toxic pollutants from coal-fired power plants. The targets of the rule were certain toxic emissions, including mercury, which can bioaccumulate and have a range of negative health effects, such as damage to neurological development and lost cognitive capacity. Cutting these emissions is expected to have substantial direct public benefits.[18] In addition, the EPA calculated the value of "co-benefits," or indirect benefits, arising from the rule: the technologies used to control mercury and other toxic emissions would also cut particulate matter pollution, saving thousands of lives every year.[19] Ultimately, the estimated value of these benefits were between $37 and $90 billion dollars per year, vastly exceedingly the rule's roughly $10 billion in compliance costs.[20]

Like the Cross-State Air Pollution Rule, regulated industry challenged the rule in court, again resulting in a Supreme Court decision. That litigation turned on the question of when during the course of developing the regulation the EPA had to consider the costs and benefits of the rule. The statutory provision under the Clean Air Act that gave the EPA the authority to regulate required the agency to make a threshold determination that such regulations were "appropriate and necessary" in light of a study of public health risks. The agency's position was that Congress did not want it to consider costs at the threshold stage but that costs entered into the equation later, when it set the actual regulatory standards. Challengers to the rule argued that costs needed to be accounted for in the "appropriate and necessary" determination, and they were ultimately successful before the Supreme Court. Justice Scalia, writing on behalf of the five conservative justices, determined that it was unreasonable not to examine costs at the threshold stage, even if costs were considered later.[21]

The rule was remanded to the agency, but the underlying reality of the massive net benefits of the MATS Rule meant that the agency could easily move forward, simply shifting when it considered costs and benefits.[22] The rule was put into place toward the end of the Obama administration, and by that time, industry had already largely complied by installing the required pollution control technology. As we will discuss in chapter 8, the Trump administration is now taking steps to undermine the MATS rule, even though industry has already made the necessary investments.

Other Obama-era environmental rules with substantial projected net benefits included several rules to tighten the NAAQS.[23] New rules to strengthen standards for nitrogen dioxide, sulfur dioxide, and particulate matter showed considerable net benefits for the American public, including a substantial number of lives saved.

The most controversial of the NAAQS decisions during the Obama presidency concerned updated standards for ground-level ozone. Although ozone in the stratosphere is beneficial—because it absorbs ultraviolet radiation—near to the ground ozone is known as "smog" and has a range of negative respiratory health effects. During the George W. Bush administration, the EPA updated the ground-level ozone standard to make it more stringent,[24] but many environmental groups argued that the agency had not gone far enough.[25] Obama's first EPA administrator, Lisa Jackson, pledged to revisit the Bush-era decision, and in 2010 proposed a more stringent standard.[26] Regulated industry unleashed a vigorous campaign of opposition to the new rule.

One of the main arguments raised by industry is that the costs of the rule were too high. The industry analysis—released by the National Association of Manufacturers—in support of these claims provides a nice demonstration of what it means to cross the boundaries around reasonable, good faith efforts to weigh costs and benefits. Extrapolating from a list of pollution control technologies provided by the EPA, the industry analysis concluded that they were insufficient to meet the new standard. The analysis then added an additional data point, based on the cost of emissions reductions achieved in the Cash-for-Clunkers program. The problem is that Cash-for-Clunkers was an Obama-era car buyback initiative designed to stimulate the economy, not clean the air in a cost-effective manner. The program was not, and would never have been, implemented for its air quality benefits because there are less expensive ways to cut down on emissions. Using the Cash-for-Clunkers program as a benchmark led to a radically skewed overestimate of the costs of the proposed ozone standard that were untethered from both economic and political reality.[27]

Despite the poor quality of the National Association of Manufacturers analysis, it received considerable news coverage.[28] The more reasonable cost-benefit analysis carried out by the EPA, however, also found that the new ozone standard would have net costs—although nowhere near as extreme as the estimates trumpeted by industry.[29] Ultimately, President Obama quashed the effort to revise the Bush-era standard.[30] One of the rationales cited by the White House was the regulatory uncertainty that would be created in light of a requirement to again revisit the standard within a couple of years.[31]

But the ozone saga did not end there. During Obama's second term, the agency again evaluated the public health science of ozone and also reexamined the costs and benefits of more stringent standards in light of updated data on pollution control technology, existing air quality levels, and new forecasts of the emissions changes necessary to meet the standards. The new analysis found that increasing the stringency of the ozone standard would generate net benefits.[32] Ultimately, the agency adopted more stringent standards.

The ozone saga illustrates the more general point. Air pollution is a classic externality that private markets cannot be expected to correct on their own. For this reason, air quality regulations often have net benefits. The industry analysis that purported to show massive and disruptive costs from the new standard was based on absurd assumptions. Although the initial cost-benefit analysis of the 2010 proposal by the EPA showed that it would have net costs, after more extensive review, the more stringent NAAQS were estimated to have net benefits.

Unquantified Environmental Benefits

In several additional environmental protections that the EPA adopted to address classic market failures, the agency did not provide a monetary estimate of important categories of expected benefits. These included a rule to reduce the environmental damage caused by cooling intake structures at power plants,[33] a rule governing the storage of hazardous coal ash,[34] and a rule that limited the harmful effects of mountaintop-removal mining.[35] In these rules, the primary benefits were discussed in a qualitative, narrative manner, rather than given a quantitative monetary value that could be directly compared to costs.

In an important respect, the administration's willingness to move forward with these rules on the basis of its judgment about the scale of unquantified benefits was an important vindication of long-standing requirements that unquantified benefits be given due consideration.[36] Since Clinton's Executive Order 12,866, agencies have been directed to take account of unquantified costs and benefits, but as a practical reality, effects that were reflected in the quantitative cost-benefit analysis were often given greater weight. From the perspective of increasingly public well-being, this greater weight on costs and benefit that are expressed in quantitative terms is irrational—the fact that an effect defines quantification does not mean that it is not important.

One approach to dealing with unquantified costs or benefits is to quantify more of the regulatory effects. Although the Obama administration took an innovative approach to improving cost-benefit analysis in some areas (which we discuss later in this chapter), it was also averse in other respects. In particular, there were specific areas where it could have pushed forward techniques to quantitatively value regulatory effects that are frequently left unquantified, but it decided not to. This conservative approach kept the administration well within the traditional bounds of cost-benefit analysis but was also a lost opportunity to improve the technique.

Perhaps the most important example of methodological timidity in an Obama-era analysis concerned the rule on cooling intake structures. Electricity-generating power plants produce a considerable amount of heat and, without adequate cooling mechanisms, would break down. The typical cooling structure draws water from a nearby source and circulates that water through the facility. One of the negative environmental impacts from these structures is that they "remove[] and kill[] hundreds of billions of aquatic organisms from waters of the United States each year, including plankton (small aquatic animals, including fish eggs and larvae), fish, crustaceans, shellfish, sea turtles, marine mammals, and many other forms of aquatic life."[37] The Clean Water Act empowers the agency to set standards for cooling intake structures to limit their environmental impact. The standards that the agency set were anticipated to cost between $275 and $297 million per year, with *quantified* benefits of between $29 and $33 million. But the agency also noted that "this estimate of benefits omits important categories of benefits that [the] EPA expects the rule will achieve."[38] Specifically, the agency valued the benefits to marine life only in terms of commercial and recreational catches and did not quantify the value that the public otherwise places on reduced damage to aquatic life.

Oddly, the agency actually conducted a stated preference survey to estimate the non-market benefits of the rule but decided not to use that information to inform the final rulemaking.[39] The agency also did not select the most stringent alternative that it considered—which would have required more extensive retrofitting of existing facilities. Were the non-market benefits of the rule to have been quantified, the more stringent alternative would have looked much more attractive from a cost-benefit perspective.

The agency's hesitancy to use stated preference studies in this context is out of step with the mainstream in environmental economics. Although extracting prices from the market is the most straightforward valuation mechanism, it is well known that regulations can have effects on non-market goods, and stated preference studies are a reasonable approach to valuating these effects. There is a considerable literature on how to use stated preferences to elicit information from people about non-use values—such as the value placed on preserving aquatic life that will not be commercially or recreationally harvested.[40] Although these techniques have some critics,[41] their use to inform government decision making has long been supported by the leading experts in the area.[42] Circular A-4 also recognizes the value of these types of studies, although with some reservations.[43] The EPA's failure to rely on its stated preferences study in the cooling water intake structure rule is an example of the Obama administration's hesitancy to use even a moderately controversial cost-benefit analysis technique, even when it would have helped justify stronger protections.

Climate Change

Regulation to address pollution that has local or regional externalities is a very comfortable fit with traditional cost-benefit analysis, and rules of this sort have been successfully examined using cost-benefit analysis for decades. That comfortable fit does not mean that there were never any methodological challenges. For example, the primary benefit of many regulations is reduction in mortality risk. In the early days of cost-benefit analysis, there were questions about how best to go about placing a monetary value on these benefits.[44] Over time, however, agencies have settled on an approach that is based on the studies of people's willingness to pay to avoid similar risks as consumers or in the workplace.[45] The "value of statistical life" that is derived from these studies has become a mainstay of contemporary cost-benefit analysis and is used across agencies for rules that save lives.

In recent years, the challenge of addressing climate change has created the need to develop a way to estimate the benefits associated with greenhouse gas emissions reduction. Just as agencies developed the value of statistical life to carry out cost-benefit analysis of life-saving rules, the new generation of regulations that reduce greenhouse gas emissions has spurred agencies to develop new valuation techniques to carry out cost-benefit analysis in this new context.

Climate change is an externality like other forms of pollution—market actors that consume fossil fuels do not pay the costs that they impose on society by increasing climate risks. These risks are also global in nature and are not contained within any national jurisdiction: greenhouse gas emissions anywhere have effects everywhere. The most important greenhouse gas—carbon dioxide—is also extremely long-lived in the environment, so a release of emissions today will continue to have warming effects for many generations.

The Obama administration's climate strategy unfolded along multiple fronts. Globally, the administration pursued international negotiations to hammer out a treaty with binding emissions limits. The United Nations Framework Convention on Climate Change, adopted in 1992, established a multi-year process of negotiation that was intended to be carried out through a series of rounds (called Conferences of the Parties or COPs), with ever more specific and aggressive agreements being developed over time.[46] The Obama administration set its sights on the COP that was held in Copenhagen, Denmark, in December 2009. The administration's approach was to push climate legislation in the US Congress while negotiating an agreement at the international level at the same time, with the overall goal of a new global climate change regime that dovetailed with the domestic policy adopted at home. As discussed earlier, united Republican opposition along with Democratic defections sank hopes of domestic legislation. In Copenhagen, the administration's hopes were again dashed as countries could only agree on a weak document—called the Copenhagen Accord—that lacked any substantive binding commitments.[47]

The other front on the campaign was regulatory. The vehicle greenhouse gas rule discussed in chapter 2 was the first step, making important gains on cutting emissions in the transportation sector and establishing the legal, scientific, and economic footing for future rules. Legally, the vehicle greenhouse gas standard was the first in which the EPA issued an "endangerment finding" for greenhouse gas emissions under the Clean Air Act.[48] This finding serves as the trigger for subsequent regulatory efforts and was based on the massive scientific consensus concerning the relationship between greenhouse gas emissions and climate change. The core of the finding is that there is sufficient evidence to conclude that burning fossil fuels "cause[s] or contribute[s] to air pollution which may reasonably be anticipated to endanger public health or welfare."[49]

Economically, the administration needed a way to place a monetary value on the benefits associated with reducing climate change risks. In *Center for Biological Diversity v. National Highway Traffic Safety Administration*, the United States Court of Appeals for the Ninth Circuit struck down the George W. Bush administration's decision not to place a value on the greenhouse gas reduction benefits of new fuel-economy standards.[50] The Obama administration had no desire to repeat this mistake but faced the challenge of putting together a defensible number that would stand up to scrutiny by the public and courts and allow multiple different agencies to apply a consistent number. The White House convened an Interagency Working Group on the Social Cost of Greenhouse Gases made up of representatives from across the government, and chaired by Sunstein and Michael Greenstone, an environmental economist who took leave from his appointment at MIT to serve as chief economist for the Council of Economic Advisers.

After months of data collection, analysis, and debate, the Interagency Working Group arrived at a range of estimates focused on a central estimate that captured the global damages to agricultural productivity, human health, property, and other climate-sensitive sectors caused by each additional ton of carbon dioxide emissions; the range of estimates also offered a high-impact estimate that reflected the risk of lower-probability but higher-impact catastrophic outcomes.[51] The Interagency Working Group updated its estimates several times, most recently in 2016. The most recent central estimate calculates that a ton of carbon dioxide released in the year 2020 will cause about $52 in climate damages (converted to 2019 dollars); the high-impact estimate for year 2020 is about $152 per ton (in 2019$).[52] The social cost of carbon also increases over time, so that by year 2050, a ton of emissions will have a projected central estimate of $85 in climate costs (in 2019$).[53] The analysis of the social cost of carbon used for the vehicle greenhouse gas standard was a harmonized, off-the-shelf estimate that the administration could rely on for any decision with consequences for greenhouse gas emissions.

After the success of the initial vehicle emissions standard, a subsequent rule required more aggressive improvements in fuel economy for future model years, culminating in a fleet average for automobiles of over fifty miles per gallon for model year 2025.[54] The EPA also expanded coverage to medium- and heavy-duty trucks.[55] Together, these rules were projected to generate many billions of dollars in fuel savings while avoiding hundreds of millions of tons of greenhouse gas emissions.

The administration also turned to emissions beyond transportation, most importantly the electricity-generating sector. The centerpiece of the administration's regulatory approach to cutting greenhouse gas emissions from existing power plants was its Clean Power Plan. The Obama administration began work on the rule in earnest during the second term with a proposed rule issued in June 2014 and the final rule the following summer.[56] The national goal of the rule was to reduce emissions of carbon dioxide from the power sector by 32 percent below the 2005 level by 2030. These reductions were to be achieved through a set of state plans, with the EPA setting statewide emissions guidelines based on factors such as renewable energy potential and electricity demand. States were given substantial flexibility in how they met the new requirements, including through market-based mechanisms and existing interstate cooperative agreements such as the Regional Greenhouse Gas Initiative in the Northeast. The benefits of the rule included reductions in greenhouse gases (valued by the social cost of carbon), as well as a range of health co-benefits that would result from switching to cleaner fuel sources. The EPA estimated that the rule would begin generating modest net benefits in the early years of implementation ($1–2 billion in 2020), with net benefits increasing as emissions declined, ultimately reaching $26–45 billion per year in 2030.[57]

In part because of its late start, the Obama administration finalized the Clean Power Plan only a year and a half before the end of its term, and subsequent litigation tied the rule up in court. In a particularly unusual twist, in the months leading up to the 2016 election, the Supreme Court took the extraordinary step of overriding the decision by the United States Court of Appeals for the District of Columbia Circuit not to stay the rule pending litigation.[58] This move halted implementation of the rule as the case made its way through the courts. With Donald Trump's 2016 victory, the fate of the Clean Power Plan was cast into severe doubt. His administration has now significantly rolled back the rule's requirements, and we will see how this effort plays out in court.

In its approach to climate change regulation, the Obama administration adopted important innovations—most notably, developing a value for the social cost of carbon—but took an approach to innovation well within the heartland of mainstream economics. If anything, the approach that it adopted was quite conservative and resulted in an underestimate of the harms associated with climate change.[59] For its model of climate damages, the Interagency Working Group selected only the most widely used models, such as the DICE (Dynamic Integrated Climate-Economy) model, developed by the economist William Nordhaus—who would go on to win the Nobel prize in economics for his work "integrating climate change into long-run macroeconomic analysis."[60] There are large number of damages that are omitted from these models, including those that arise from forced migration, social and political conflict, and violence; weather variability and extreme weather events; and potential shocks to economic growth.[61] The models that underly the social cost of carbon also assume that the value of ecosystem services will stay the same, even though basic economic principles imply that they will become more valuable as climate disruption makes them more scarce.[62] Current estimates of the social cost of carbon also assume a constant discount rate for future climate harms. But given uncertainty about the extent of damages and the correct discount rate and the long time horizons involved, a more economically rational approach is to use a declining rate that places far more weight on the long-term future.[63]

Despite these shortcomings, the Obama-era social cost of carbon remains the best existing estimate of the marginal damages of greenhouse gas emissions.[64] As we discuss in chapter 9, the Trump administration has moved to undermine this number to obscure the damages associated with climate change. But the Obama administration's efforts to stay firmly within the boundaries of standard cost-benefit analysis methodologies also led to a social cost of carbon that likely understates the true extent of climate damages. Improved models that incorporate more accurate damage functions and account for factors such as discount rate uncertainty and the likely future scarcity of environmental goods would lead to a higher value that better reflects the true costs of climate inaction.

Behavioral Economics

Traditional market failures such as externalities are not the only justification for government regulation. In recent years, leading scholars in law, economics, and psychology have coalesced around an understanding of a second category of market failures that occur because *homo sapiens* (that is, actual humans making real decisions in the marketplace) differ from the *homo economicus* of economic models (which assume the existence of perfectly rational, fully informed humans dispassionately making decisions to maximize their welfare). Thus, an additional class of regulation finds its justification outside of the most standard neoclassical economic framework by incorporating a more nuanced (and in many ways more realistic) understanding of human behavior. This revolution in *behavioral economics* was led by researchers such as Daniel Kahneman, Amos Tversky, and Richard Thaler and has been embraced by many legal academics, perhaps most prominently Cass Sunstein, who took this behavioral economic perspective with him to his position in the Obama administration.[65]

The logic behind Adam Smith's invisible hand is that voluntary transactions are, essentially by definition, beneficial to both parties. This logic underlies the default of private market transactions that is reflected in Clinton's Executive Order 12,866 and the US practice of cost-benefit analysis. This idea is also fairly intuitive: why would someone voluntarily agree to do something that is not in his or her best interest? The work of Kahneman, Tversky, Thaler, and others in the behavioral economics field help answer that question.[66] It may be as simple as a mistake, as when a person thinks a fancy new gadget will lead to lots of satisfaction, but really it just causes frustration and gets abandoned in the attic. People are sometimes myopic, often have a difficult time making judgments that involve probabilities, can suffer from deficits of willpower, and are influenced by irrelevant information. These and other behavioral quirks can lead to situations in which people engage in voluntary transactions that are not optimal from the perspective of their own long-term well-being.[67]

Regulations that have behavioral economic justification at their root recognize these limitations in human judgment and use government intervention in the marketplace as a corrective. Some of these limitations are almost universally recognized as beneficial. Very few people think that it would be a good idea to sell heroin over the counter at the drugstore, even though some people might voluntarily choose to buy it. This is an example of a government policy that is justified on behavioral grounds: addiction is well known to cause people to make decisions that are not in their best interest.[68] But other behaviorally based regulations are more controversial. For example, when Michael Bloomberg was mayor of New York City, his administration pursued a policy of banning very large servings of high-calorie soft drinks at establishments like movie theaters.[69] The ban sparked serious opposition.[70] For some, this measure was emblematic of an intrusive "nanny state" that interfered with individual freedom of choice.[71]

Because behavioral economics is relatively new, and behavioral justifications for regulation are generally more controversial than ones grounded on externalities, they may fit somewhat less comfortably within the cost-benefit analysis framework. This is in part a limitation of the methodology in its current form: as more information about the interaction of human decision making and government regulation develops, the information base for conducting cost-benefit analysis of these types of regulations will grow. The Obama administration took several important steps in this direction and generally had success in applying its cost-benefit progressive playbook to these rules.

Energy efficiency is an area of public policy where behavioral economics has useful insights. The vehicle greenhouse gas standard adopted by the Obama administration is one example. Pollution from automobiles is an externality, and so regulation is warranted based purely on traditional market failure grounds. But the air pollution benefits of the rule were only a part of the total picture—the rule also resulted in large fuel savings for consumers.[72] For every dollar increase in the price of cars that was anticipated from the rulemaking, consumers were anticipated to save three dollars in fuel costs over the life of the vehicle.[73] But this raises the question of why, if car buyers benefit from driving more fuel-efficient cars, they weren't already demanding that manufacturers produce them.

In the rulemaking for the vehicle greenhouse gas standard, the Obama administration took this question very seriously. It devoted a considerable amount of space in its rule to reviewing the decades-long literature documenting the "energy paradox"—a tendency for consumers to underpay for energy efficiency.[74] It also commissioned a review of econometric studies of the value that consumers place on fuel economy,[75] and it assessed whether the fuel-economy benefits were likely to materialize.[76] Ultimately, it found adequate justification for its valuation approach, but only after having conducted a serious review of the relevant literature and arguments.[77] This decision was in keeping with the practice in prior administrations when valuing energy efficiency.[78]

Another area in which behavioral research has had an effect on regulation is consumer finance. In the waning years of the George W. Bush administration, in a relatively rare example of bipartisan lawmaking during the era of partisan volatility, Congress passed the Pension Protection Act of 2006.[79] One of the main provisions of the bill builds on an insight from behavioral economics showing that, oftentimes, people tend to be biased toward the status quo and so they stick with the "default" choice in many contexts. For example, whether the decision to become an organ donor when applying for or renewing a drivers' license is structured as an "opt-in"—with a default of *no*—or an "opt-out"—with a default of *yes*—can have major effects on the rate of donation. In countries that treat the decision as an opt-out, many more people agree to be organ donors.[80] Similar dynamics are at play in other contexts, including retirement savings. The Pension Protection Act provided incentives for employers to treat 401(k) enrollments as an "opt-out" by automatically enrolling employees in these plans.[81] This type of light-touch regulatory approach had bipartisan support: one of the major advocates for the law was Peter Orszag, who went on to become the director of the Office of Management and Budget in the Obama administration.

Another example of a similar behavioral approach to consumer finance taken during the Obama administration was a 2009 rule by the Federal Reserve that prohibited banks from charging overdraft fees on debit accounts without garnering the prior consent of consumers for overdraft service.[82] This opt-in approach set the default of *no*. Under a traditional economic model, this type of change in a default wouldn't have much of an effect, but in practice the opt-in rule led to a substantially lower uptake of these services.[83] Industry trade associations oppose additional measures to restrict overdraft fees, in part arguing that the overdrafts and associated fees reflect the rational choices of bank consumers to use their checking accounts as a source of short-term credit.[84] Estimating the costs and benefits of the opt-in rule—which does seem to affect behavior—is difficult in part because such "rational" overdrafts are hard to separate from those that result from behavioral quirks.[85] Although the rules as they stand are relatively popular and are not actively opposed even by regulated industry, they lack the solid foundations that would be provided by more rigorous assessment of costs and benefits.

Because agencies have only recently been more explicit in adopting behavioral economics rationales for regulation, the evidence base for these rules and the cost-benefit analysis methodology to estimate their effects is considerably more limited than in the context of traditional market failure. As demonstrated by the vehicle greenhouse gas standards, solid cost-benefit analyses can still be done. Nevertheless, as evidenced by the prior examples, evaluating rules with important behavioral economic elements using cost-benefit analysis can be more challenging. The Obama administration made progress in this area, but more work remains.

Protecting the Stability of Financial Markets

Perhaps the most substantial challenge faced by the Obama administration in applying cost-benefit analysis to a major regulatory priority concerned rules to improve the stability of financial markets and institutions in the wake of the Great Recession. There was and remains a considerable amount of debate about the economic bases of such rules and their consistency with the cost-benefit framework. At the same time, the 2008 financial collapse cast doubt on the view that financial markets are able to self-regulate effectively.[86] The combination of political urgency in the post–Great Recession period and the unsettled state of economic theory created a challenging environment for financial regulatory agencies. The Obama administration undertook a number of important regulatory initiatives directed at financial stability. But integrating these initiatives with the traditional framework of cost-benefit analysis was more difficult than incorporating rules addressing classic externalities or even those that relied on behavioral economics for their justification.

Rules that protect the stability of financial markets have a different relationship to the notion of market failures than many other regulations. Both the traditional market failure and the behavioral economic rationales for regulation assume a relatively well-functioning, competitive marketplace. Problems arise when effects occur outside the marketplace, or where biases, heuristics, or other behavioral quirks lead consumers astray, but the market itself is assumed to work well. Relaxing these assumptions leads to a third way in which Adam Smith's invisible hand can end up impeding social well-being, through distortions associated with economic structure. There are a variety of ways in which economic structure can affect the marketplace, but three issues in particular have played a significant role in regulatory decision making: monopoly power; systemic risk; and concerns about the interface of economic and political power.

Economic structure has animated government action in the United States for well over a century, and views concerning the problems generated by market concentration has evolved considerably over that time.[87] Within mainstream economics, the most widely accepted concern with market concentration is that monopolies can use their positions to extract wealth from consumers and, to do so, will inflate prices by artificially limiting supply.[88] This consumer-based concern has led to a variety of efforts to ban certain business practices that drive down competition (such as price-fixing cartels) or to impose quality-of-service, anti-discrimination, and ratemaking requirements on companies when they operate in markets that naturally tend toward concentration. An example of the latter regulatory case is electricity transmission: it does not make sense to have two different concurrent electricity transmission grids, but if only one company owns the grid, there is a legitimate concern that it will use this position to siphon off excess profits for itself, with consumers suffering in the process. This dilemma is the reason that electricity markets are so heavily regulated, with an alphabet soup of agencies at the federal and state levels governing everything from rates, to investments, to grid stability.[89]

Although there is a fair amount of agreement that consumer welfare can be threatened by market concentration in general, there is much more disagreement in practice: for example, whether various practices of credit card companies are anti-competitive in ways that harm consumers.[90] The structure of US antitrust law, and the complexity of these cases, has generally driven US competition law to the back burner, and like its predecessors, the Obama administration did not make antitrust a top priority. At the same time, there has been a push over the past several decades toward the dismantling of the agencies that oversee naturally concentrated industries.[91] Indeed, a major initiative to deregulate the electricity sector—a classic example of a natural monopoly—was undertaken during the Clinton administration.[92]

In the wake of the 2008 financial crisis, a second type of concern about economic structure emerged related to systemic risks to the financial sector posed by various firms and practices. One example were regulations that placed additional capital requirements on banks that are found to be "systematically important" to the global financial system, with the goal of reducing the risk that financial decisions at a few companies could have disastrous effects for the global economy.[93] Another regulation intended to protect the financial stability of banks is the Volcker Rule, which limits the types of speculative investments that can be made by banking institutions.[94] Regulation of individual financial choices can also be justified in terms of systemic risks. One of the root causes of the 2008 financial crisis was the interaction of a housing bubble and a range of complex, related financial products held by major banks and other investors. When the housing bubble collapsed, it pushed the entire global financial system to the brink.[95] As one part of a broader effort to avoid a repeat, the Consumer Financial Protection Bureau (CFPB) published a rule that implemented portions of the Dodd-Frank Act, setting a number of requirements on mortgage lenders to ensure that they adequately vetted potential borrowers for their ability to pay. [96]

Although in some ways, the types of systemic risks that agencies sought to address in the regulation of "too big to fail" financial firms and consumer products linked to the financial crash are similar to traditional market failures, they are not an entirely comfortable fit with the traditional paradigm of cost-benefit analysis. As the Obama administration began to roll out financial regulation in these areas, a substantial academic debate broke out concerning whether cost-benefit analysis was appropriate at all in this context. Critics charged that cost-benefit analysis would be more likely to "camouflage" regulatory decision making than "discipline" agencies, while others argued that there is "no reason to think that it is always or usually impossible for financial regulators to conduct cost-benefit analysis."[97]

One part of the challenge is conceptual. Systemic risks are different from classic externalities like pollution, which floats along from one place to another, entirely outside the system of commerce and exchange that defines the market.[98] These types of externalities are market failures that provide a prima facie case for government intervention.[99] Systemic risks build up *within* financial markets andrisks are communicated entirely through market channels. Because the risk occurs in and is spread through markets, people operating within those markets have the incentive and opportunity to trade against, and therefore reduce, that risk. The incentives might be insufficient to avoid inefficient risks at the systemic level, but the nature of the relevant market failures is often more complex than a simple pollution-like externality that is entirely outside the market.[100]

The logic of behavioral economics is also a somewhat uncomfortable fit with systemic risks that could be identified and mitigated by financial firms. Large and sophisticated financial firms do not appear to be obvious candidates for the kind of heuristics, biases, and other quirks that affect personal decision making.[101] If some financial firms were subject to these kinds of decision-making failures, there would be opportunities for more rational traders to take advantage of this situation and pump them for money. A major bank or hedge fund that was subject to the kind of psychological phenomenon that has been well studied in the behavioral economics literature (such as loss aversion or framing effects) would face considerable pressure in the hyper-competitive environment of financial markets.[102]

Even if these conceptual issues were ironed out, there are serious empirical challenges to incorporating systemic risk into cost-benefit analysis. The underlying problem—serious financial disruption—is (thankfully) extremely rare. For this reason, the relationship between any particular institutional structure or financial practice and overall risk is difficult to establish. Because the underlying causal mechanisms are so difficult to understand, and market behavior updates in light of both prior experience and government action, regulators may find themselves focusing on issues that led to a previous problem (which market actors may have already figured out) while unanticipated risks accumulate elsewhere.[103]

The Obama administration faced considerable challenges in integrating financial risk regulation in the cost-benefit framework and, accordingly, moved somewhat tentatively. For the capital requirements on systematically important financial institutions and the Volker Rule, no quantitative cost-benefit analyses were offered.[104] Instead, the agencies discussed and quantified some of the costs but benefits were treated in a qualitative manner.[105] The CFPB likewise presented qualitative arguments in favor of the benefits of limits on mortgage lending that were based on concerns about the ability of borrowers or even sophisticated financial institutions to understand the complex mortgage-related financial products, evidence of myopia or other behavioral issues that might distort consumer decision making, and a concern about systemic risk.[106]

Although stable financial markets are broadly recognized to contribute to well-being, cost-benefit analyses of rules to limit risks in this area run into a number of challenges. Qualitative discussion of costs and benefits, which was the common practice under the Obama administration, is a useful step in helping to clarify the stakes of these decisions. But more can be done to build the theoretical and empirical foundation for informed regulatory policymaking in this area.[107]

In addition to monopoly power and systemic risk, a third concern related to economic structure arises from worries about the concentration of economic power in the hands of a few. Although dormant for some time, this concern has been periodically raised throughout US history: it was dominant for the trustbusters in the Progressive Era around the turn of the twentieth century, and it also emerged in the 1970s amid fear that government regulators would become "captured" by Big Business. The 2008 financial crisis and greater attention to rising inequality (briefly embodied by the Occupy Wall Street movement) has led to renewed attention to this line of thought.[108]

Despite its long history, the concentration-of-power rationale remains somewhat vague and underspecified, which makes it a poor fit with cost-benefit analysis in its current form. The problem is perhaps best illustrated by the failure of the Security and Exchange Commission's proxy access rule. That rule governed access to proxy materials that allow shareholders who do not attend annual meetings to vote through proxies. Since the governing board controls these materials and generally circulates proxy materials for board-backed director candidates, it is difficult for potential outside directors to gather the necessary votes. Proxy access rules would open up the process by making it easier for outsiders to be included in the distribution of proxy materials. In keeping with the economic structure argument in favor of regulation, part of the idea behind proxy access is to reallocate power over large publicly held US corporations.[109] Critics argue that the rule would lead to counterproductive and expensive campaigns for director seats that would not improve firm performance. The issue of proxy access is highly controversial, and the Securities and Exchange Commission has made multiple attempts to regulate in this area, starting in 1942, without success.[110]

As discussed in chapter 1, this rule was struck down in the DC Circuit in *Business Roundtable v. Securities and Exchange Commission*, largely based on the court's reading of the agency's cost-benefit analysis. Writing for a unanimous majority, Judge Douglas Ginsburg took the agency to task for underestimating the costs that would be incurred in director campaigns and overestimating the benefits of the rule. The court also faulted the agency for downplaying the costs of the rule based on existing state law obligations, stating that "this type of reasoning, which fails to view a cost at the margin, is illogical and, in an economic analysis, unacceptable." Finally, the court criticized the Securities and Exchange Commission for failing to consider how particularly large shareholders, and specifically union and state pension funds, might use proxy access "as leverage to gain concessions, such as additional benefits for unionized employees, unrelated to shareholder value."[111] Overall, the court found the agency's analysis to be inadequate and struck down the rule, which the agency then shelved indefinitely.[112]

Another example of a rule that was at least partially justified on economic power grounds was the Federal Communication Commission's "net neutrality" regulation of internet service providers (ISPs). Fundamentally, the net neutrality rule limited the ability of ISPs to discriminate between different types of content or content providers, mandating that the internet act as an open-access platform available to all. Opponents of the rule argued that it stifled investment and made it difficult for ISPs to manage their networks in ways that maximized capacity for all users.

In its 2015 Protecting and Promoting the Open Internet Rule, the Federal Communication Commission provided a range of justifications for its net neutrality policy. Among these, the agency emphasized its finding that "the Internet's openness is critical to its ability to serve as a platform for speech and civic engagement" and concerns that ISPs act as "gatekeepers" between end-users and providers of content,[113] a role that allows them to "block access altogether . . . target competitors . . . [and] extract unfair tolls."[114] The Federal Communication Commission described this gatekeeping role as creating the "incentive and ability to limit openness,"[115] which is particularly troubling in light of the "the economic, social, and civic benefits of an open Internet."[116] The regulation itself was not accompanied by a formal accounting of costs and benefits. This was perhaps in part because of current limitations in the methodology of cost-benefit analysis to quantify the kinds of benefits that the rule sought to achieve, or perhaps because, as an independent agency, the Federal

Communication Commission was not subject to regulatory review by OIRA.[117] The Federal Communication Commission's effort to require net neutrality faced numerous court challenges and was ultimately reversed by the Trump administration.[118]

Appeals to economic structure as a justification for government intervention in the marketplace extend back to the dawn of the US administrative state in the late nineteenth century. However, despite this lengthy history, there has been relatively little effort to translate regulatory effects in this context into the readily quantifiable terms that are amenable to inclusion in cost-benefit analysis. It was only during the latter portion of the Obama administration, after setbacks in court, that agencies began to build out the institutional apparatus needed to tackle the thorny conceptual and empirical challenges that arise when applying cost-benefit analysis in this area.[119] Additional investments in analytic capacity as well as developments in data analysis and economic modeling are needed to improve the capacity of agencies to use cost-benefit analysis to evaluate regulations that attempt to address problems arising from economic structure.

Equity, Human Dignity, Fairness, and Distribution

The progressive policy agenda of the Obama administration extended beyond simply improving economic efficiency. Other concerns included the distribution of wealth and risk across society and the dignity of people who have been subject to past discrimination. Obama's Executive Order 13,563 carved out a special place for these considerations by explicitly empowering agencies to "consider (and discuss qualitatively) values that are difficult or impossible to quantify, including equity, human dignity, fairness, and distributive impacts."[120] Many actions of the Obama administration can be understood as promoting these values, including rules governing the extension of health insurance under Obamacare, regulations of federal prisons to reduce incidence of sexual assaults, and the Deferred Action for Childhood Arrivals (DACA) policy limiting immigration enforcement for a class of undocumented workers.

As indicated in Executive Order 13,563, there are substantial challenges to incorporating values like dignity and fair distribution into cost-benefit analysis, at least in its current form.[121] In different contexts, the Obama administration took a variety of approaches to the question of whether and how to engage in cost-benefit analysis of decisions where these values played an important role.

In some contexts, the administration did not use cost-benefit analysis. For example, DACA was an exercise of enforcement discretion, which is not typically accompanied by a balancing of costs and benefits. As part of making the case for DACA to the public, the administration could have carried out a cost-benefit analysis, but one of the challenges of doing so would be the need to decide the question of who has "standing" in such an analysis, and in particular how to treat the benefits that flow to those eligible for relief under the policy. In the context of climate change regulation, Ted Gayer and W. Kip Viscusi have argued that only costs and benefits that flow to US citizens should count in cost-benefit analysis.[122] Applying the Gayer-Viscusi approach to DACA would exclude a large category of benefits.[123] Because DACA was an enforcement decision rather than a rulemaking, the administration did not have to confront this controversial question.

In other cases, the administration made limited attempts to apply cost-benefit analysis but did not fully address the difficult-to-value effects. For example, the Department of Health and Human Services (HHS) carried out a regulatory impact analysis of several rules to implement the Affordable Care Act, including establishing exchanges and setting standards for employers and insurance companies.[124] The categories of benefits described by the agency included improvements of clinical outcomes and financial security for Obamacare beneficiaries. Costs included the compliance costs for states, employers, and insurance companies. The agency did not attempt to provide a quantitative estimate of the net benefits of the rules or alternatives, and it did not address or attempt to evaluate the very large distributional consequences of the rules and related transfers under Obamacare.

In theory, it is possible to incorporate distributional effects directly into cost-benefit analysis, through tools such as equity-weighting.[125] The basic idea is that there is a diminishing marginal utility of consumption, and so a transfer from a relatively wealthy person to a relatively poor person results in an increase in aggregate utility. This transfer is not potentially Pareto efficient, because the well-off person cannot be compensated for the wealth loss, but nevertheless total utility improves.[126] In addition, some ways of understanding the notion of social well-being place greater emphasis on utility enjoyed by the least well off.[127]

Some countries engage in forms of distributional analysis that treat these kinds of transfers as regulatory benefits,[128] and Clinton's Executive Order 12,866 explicitly refers to "distributive impacts" as a class of regulatory effects that ought to be considered.[129] Nevertheless, in the United States, there is considerable debate over whether this kind of analysis is appropriate and if so, how it should be done. A classic objection is that agency regulation should focus on efficiency (increasing the "size of the pie") while Congress's role is to address distribution through the tax-and-transfer system. The strength of this argument derives from the claim that, in general, whatever beneficial redistribution occurs through the regulatory system could be achieved at lower total social cost by taxing the wealthy and using those funds to provide resources to the less fortunate.[130] Others argue that Congress has failed in this task, and so redistribution through the regulatory system is the only available alternative, and they also argue that some regulatory effects, such as health risks, cannot be redistributed through taxes and transfers.[131]

Even if there was agreement over the need to do distributional analysis, there are many specific questions to be answered, such as whether such analysis should be done on a rule-by-rule basis or more holistically, and how to differentially weight costs and benefits that affect the rich and the poor. In the face of these normative and technical controversies, the Obama administration did not adopt any rigorous approach to incorporating (or not) distributional effects into its cost-benefit analysis.

In some contexts, the administration made strenuous efforts to express difficult-to-value regulatory benefits in monetary terms, even when doing so courted controversy. Perhaps the best illustration of this approach was a rule by the Department of Justice to implement a provision of the Prison Rape Elimination Act (PREA). The law, somewhat contradictorily, established zero tolerance for sexual assaults in the nation's prisons, but also mandated that the Department of Justice impose no "substantial costs" on regulated facilities.[132] Under one interpretation, the "substantial costs" limitation could have eviscerated the agency's rulemaking power, as steps to cut down on sexual assaults will tend to impose some costs. However, substantial costs can also be understood in terms consistent with a cost-benefit test. The agency chose something closer to the second interpretation, conducting an analysis of costs and benefits while also examining the costs of the rule compared to the total national expenditures on prison operations.[133] To carry out this analysis, the agency placed a monetary value on lower rates of sexual assaults, based in part on surveys of people's willingness to pay to reduce this risk.[134] For some, this effort to quantify and monetize regulatory benefits went too far. Writing after departing from her position at the Obama administration, Lisa Heinzerling characterized the decision as "bizarre and unfortunate," questioning whether the Obama administration wished to leave "a legacy that holds that any human encounter, no matter how violent and coerced, can be treated as just another day at the market."[135]

Overall, the Obama administration's attempts to apply cost-benefit analysis to regulations that implicated values such as equity, distribution, or dignity helped illustrate the difficulty of the task. Obama's executive order frankly acknowledged this difficulty and attempted to create space for agencies to consider these values in a qualitative fashion. This approach is consistent with the practice of cost-benefit analysis, at least as far back as Clinton's Executive Order 12,866. Part of staying within the bounds of cost-benefit analysis is to recognized the limits of existing methodologies and not allow those limits to be paralyzing.

***

Although there is room for the exercise of discretion when carrying out cost-benefit analysis, there are also important constraints. Agencies must transparently disclose their assumptions, models, and data. The long track record of cost-benefit analyses provides a baseline for comparison. When an agency departs from prior practice, it should be able to give a reasonable explanation for why it chose to do so. In addition, simple honesty helps serve as a check for an agency official who might wish to flagrantly manipulate the technique for political ends.

During the two terms of the Obama administration, agencies pursued a number of ambitious regulatory initiatives. Some of these, which sought to address classic externalities such as air and water pollution, were a comfortable fit with traditional cost-benefit analysis. But even some of these cases require continued methodological innovation, and the social cost of carbon is an example of an important contribution made by the Obama administration to the practice of cost-benefit analysis. But agencies were also sometimes fairly tentative in pushing forward the methodology. The social cost of carbon developed under Obama includes several conservative assumptions, and agencies sometimes declined to use even moderately controversial tools to provide quantitative estimates for the benefits of rules that protect non-market environmental values.

Behavioral economics was another area where the Obama administration made important, but limited, strides in fitting cost-benefit analysis to new situations. The field of economics has largely moved past a model of human behavior that assumes a simple, rational utility-maximizing agent in favor of a more psychologically realistic understanding. But it is not enough to wave an analytic hand in the direction of human limitations—rigorous cost-benefit analysis requires that, where possible, the behavioral economic consequences of rules be understood based on well-established psychological phenomena that have been subjected to substantial empirical study. In regulations such as the vehicle greenhouse gas standard, the Obama administration demonstrated how behavioral economics can fit within the cost-benefit framework.

Rules to protect the stability of financial markets and regulations that affect values such as equity, dignity, fairness, and distribution raise considerable challenges for cost-benefit analysis. As during prior administrations, agencies under Obama struggled to find the best approach to engage in rigorous, formal cost-benefit analysis while also giving due consideration to these values. Importantly, the Obama administration was not paralyzed by these challenges but pushed forward with rules even in cases where important categories of costs and benefits resisted quantification. This approach is consistent with long-standing guidance, such as Clinton's Executive Order 12,866 and the George W. Bush-era Circular A-4, and also with basic cost-benefit principles: that an effect resists quantification does not mean that it does not have important welfare effects. But setbacks such as the *Business Roundtable* decision—which struck down the Securities and Exchange Commission's proxy access rule—and the Trump reversal of the Obama-era net neutrality rule illustrate the difficulties of successfully pursuing regulations where cost-benefit analysis methodologies remain underdeveloped.

In the final chapter of this book, we will return to ways in which cost-benefit analysis and regulatory review can be improved in the future, building on the advances of prior administrations. But before it is possible to push forward in a sustainable fashion, the bipartisan consensus supporting evidence, expertise, and analysis in regulatory decision making will need to be rebuilt. We now turn to the collapse of that consensus and the consequences for the American public.

4

Retreating from Reason

Given the Obama administration's embrace of cost-benefit analysis, Republican politicians and elites were placed in a difficult position: they had embraced a strategy of wholesale opposition to the new president, but the administration was using tools that had long been core Republican Party orthodoxy. They could have tempered their opposition when the administration adopted policies or approaches that were in line with their past priorities. But they did not.

The rise of the Tea Party and the 2010 midterm results exacerbated the oppositional tendency of many Republicans. With the financial crash-induced recession continuing to bite, a major talking point of Republican politicians was to accuse the administration of pursuing "job-killing regulations." Even a moderate figure like Mitt Romney embraced this new rhetoric and explicitly attacked cost-benefit analysis during his 2012 election. While the possibility of legislation offered an alternative policy pathway in 2009–2011, and the continuing jobs crisis and pending election hampered agency action in 2011–2012, after Obama's reelection, political conditions favored the use of agency action to pursue the administration's policy goals. One major example was the EPA's Clean Power Plan to address greenhouse gas emissions from power plants.

In light of the heightened agency action in Obama's second term, partisan conflict over regulation only increased. Many in the Republican coalition continued to level hyperbolic criticism of regulations adopted under Obama, despite the strong cost-benefit arguments in favor of many of the rules. This trend toward disregard for cost-benefit analysis became even more extreme in the run up to the 2016 election, with candidates in the Republican primary lambasting the Obama record on regulation.

In the aftermath of the 2016 election, the Trump administration accelerated the trend toward disregard for cost-benefit analysis. Agencies under Trump have engaged in absurd distortions, ignored evidence, and obviously twisted the methodology to achieve pre-desired outcomes. A new requirement for agencies to take two deregulatory actions for every new regulation is an example of the administration's approach: incoherent, counterproductive, and (ultimately) unsuccessful.

Appointment of incompetent personnel hostile to agency missions helped the Trump administration achieve one of its stated goals, which was a significant slowdown in agency action. However, proactive efforts by the administration to

Reviving Rationality. Michael A. Livermore and Richard L. Revesz, Oxford University Press (2020). © Oxford University Press. DOI: 10.1093/oso/9780197539446.001.0001.

delay or roll back rules have faced stiff opposition and fared poorly in court. Part of the reason for these failures is general incompetence and mismanagement. But the strong cost-benefit justifications that supported Obama-era rules also make them difficult to undo. The most successful deregulatory efforts were made possible by unified Republican control of the White House and Congress, which enabled the revival of a moribund statute from the 1990s called the Congressional Review Act. But even where official rollback efforts have failed, delay and a lack and of enforcement have achieved de facto rollbacks for many rules.

No Compromise

The 2008 election represented a major loss for the national Republican Party. Barack Obama won the presidency with nearly 10 million more votes than his opponent John McCain, a 7 percent margin in the national popular vote, and more than double the number of votes in the Electoral College. In the House of Representatives, the Democrats held over seventy five more seats than the Republicans, and in the Senate, the Democrats either verged on or held a fili-buster proof majority of sixty seats.[1] Outgoing President George W. Bush was extremely unpopular: polls taken in the lead up to the 2008 election found only 25 percent of voters with a positive view of his handling of the presidency, with 70 percent unhappy.[2] After experiencing long, grueling, expensive, and largely unsuccessful wars in Iraq and Afghanistan, and with the economy on the verge of collapse, the national electorate communicated a clear message of disapproval to the Republican Party.

Different political models make different predictions about how parties will react to these types of electoral setbacks. In a model of politics that was highly influential during the height of the twentieth century, political scientist Anthony Downs conceived of political parties as "teams" of politicians who sought out office for "the income, prestige, and power that go with running the governing apparatus."[3] Under Downs's model, parties "do not seek to gain office in order to carry out certain preconceived policies[,] . . . rather they formulate policies . . . to gain office."[4] This understanding of parties and their motivation led Downs to his view that parties will moderate their policies toward the median voter, with the goal of maximizing their share of the electoral vote.

Under the Downsian model of political behavior, after the Democratic tri-umph in 2008, the expected response of the Republican Party would have been moderation. The goals would be to alter policy positions on a few key issues where they were out of line with majority of Americans, work with the new president on a handful of signature issues where compromise was possible, and use the limited leverage afforded by the desire for bipartisanship and the sparing use of a filibuster threat to steer legislation and confirmations toward the center. Downs did not predict that politicians would always get along with each other, but his idea was that they would compete with each other to grab as much of the policy center as possible.

It turns out that, as far as predicting the Republican reaction to the Obama victory, the Downsian model could not have been more wrong. Rather than moving to the center and seeking conciliation with a popular new president, the Republican Party became intensely disciplined around a strategy of opposition and obstruction. This was especially true in the US Senate, where minority leader Mitch McConnell departed from prior norms of restraint and began engaging in filibusters of nearly every major piece of legislation.[5] The president's signature legislative policy on health care reform met with particularly strident opposition, perhaps surprisingly given that it drew one of its central features—an individual mandate to purchase health insurance—from a plan promoted by the conservative Heritage Foundation, and a similar program that was implemented successfully in Massachusetts under Republican governor Mitt Romney.[6] The Democrats ultimately had to rely on the process of budget reconciliation, which cannot be blocked by a filibuster, to overcome partisan opposition to the legislation.[7]

McConnell's use of the filibuster had more success in other areas. Immigration reform, for example, is an issue that has vexed both parties for a generation, with Presidents Clinton and George W. Bush both failing to adopt any significant updates to the law, despite widespread unhappiness with the current system. Obama, like his predecessors, also favored comprehensive reform, but the difficult politics of the issue made that impossible.[8] Instead, he focused his energies on a more limited measure, the DREAM Act, first introduced in 2001 by sponsors Dick Durbin (D-Illinois) and Orrin Hatch (R-Utah), which would have granted residency status to certain undocumented immigrants who entered the United States as children. After passing the House in late 2010, the bill died when the Republican minority again invoked the filibuster and the Democrats were unable to muster the sixty votes needed for passage.[9]

Aggressive use of the filibuster by the Republican minority also damned cap-and-trade legislation to control greenhouse gases. The dramatic shift in the posture of Republican politicians on environmental issues can be illustrated by comparing the 1990 Clean Air Act Amendments and the 2009 debate over climate change legislation.[10] For example, in 1990, Senator Mitch McConnell voted for the Clean Air Act Amendments, saying "I had to choose between cleaner air and the status quo. I chose cleaner air."[11] In 2010, as President Obama was encouraging Congress to pass a substantive climate change bill, Senator McConnell accused the Kerry-Lieberman bill of being "essentially written by BP,"[12] and ultimately proclaimed, "I think cap-and-trade, which is also known as the national energy tax, is dead in the United States Senate."[13]

There are many other prominent long-serving Republican senators who voted for the 1990 Clean Air Act Amendments but who did not support climate legislation after Obama's election.[14] After other leading senators refused to engage on the issue, Senator Lindsey Graham, was the sole Republican willing to attempt negotiating a Senate climate bill in 2010.[15] Even Graham eventually abandoned the legislative effort.[16] In 1990, Newt Gingrich and Jim Inhofe voted for the Clean Air Act Amendments;[17] by 2009, Gingrich—in his new role as a political pundit—was strident in his opposition[18] and Inhofe was the leading voice in the Senate questioning climate science.[19]

A particular irony of the near universal Republican opposition to climate legislation in 2009 was that the centerpiece of the bill was a market-based cap-and-trade program. For decades, a core Republican priority had been to shift environmental regulation in a more market-based direction.[20] Although there were many elements of the bill that were subjected to criticism,[21] in the course of attacking the Waxman-Markey bill, many Republicans focused on attacking what had been perhaps the defining characteristic of the party's approach to environmental issues.

The calling card of this transition was characterizing cap-and-trade as a tax.[22] In remarks before a group of conservative organizations in 2008, in preparation for the coming legislative battle, Myron Ebell, the director of Global Warming and International Environmental Policy at the Competitive Enterprise Institute, articulated the strategy: "If you want to fight this stuff . . . just remember: It's a tax. It's a tax. Just keep repeating that, it's a tax. . . . [W]e will win this debate if we just keep pointing out it's a tax . . . [C]ap and trade is another term for tax."[23]

Eventually, this framing morphed into the slogan "cap and tax," which was used as an epithet against Waxman-Markey and Kerry-Lieberman.[24] Even C. Boyden Gray, an early proponent of cap-and-trade in the H. W. Bush administration, himself called Waxman-Markey a "$3 trillion tax" in 2010.[25] The oppositional posture of the Republicans in Congress succeeded in stopping climate legislation but also salted the ground for future efforts to use market-based mechanisms to address environmental problems.

The Republican minority in the Senate not only blocked major portions of the new president's legislative agenda but also slowed down the confirmation process. Many senior political appointees require Senate approval, and the minority party can use similar powers to slow down or stop nominations as those used to block legislation—in particular the threat of a filibuster. Even when the Senate was controlled by Democrats, the minority frequently used these tools to oppose Obama nominees—delays associated with President Obama's nominees were more than twice those for President Reagan's nominees.[26]

Perhaps the strangest confirmation episode during the early Obama administration occurred when Cass Sunstein's nomination to head OIRA was before the Senate.[27] Despite the fact that Sunstein was a proponent of cost-benefit analysis whose nomination was popular with industry trade associations—and unpopular among left-leaning constituencies within the Democratic Party, including groups like the Center for Progressive Reform—Republican senators put holds on his nomination.[28] The ostensible justifications for these holds ranged from concerns that he would use his office to promote vegetarianism to fears that his embrace of behavioral economics would be a step along a slippery path to totalitarianism.[29] The holds and efforts to assuage these fears held up Sunstein's nomination for several months.

As a consequence of the Republicans' decisions to take the path of opposition rather than moderation and compromise, the Obama administration faced considerable difficulties and setbacks in pursuing its legislative agenda, even when the Democrats held majorities in both chambers. When the 2010 election strengthened McConnell's hand in the Senate and brought a new Republican majority in the House, the president's legislative agenda was effectively dead.[30] Instead, the administration would find itself fighting uphill battles on everything from moderate nominees for key government roles to basic funding measures. Given this hostility in Congress, the administration turned to its policy levers within the administration, and quickly began to draw from the cost-benefit progressive playbook discussed in chapter 3.

Countering the Playbook

In merging cost-benefit analysis with a regulatory agenda focused on achieving progressive priorities, the Obama administration placed its critics in a difficult position. Cost-benefit analysis has long been associated with an anti-regulatory agenda, and so when rules to protect the environment and public health and safety delivered massive net benefits, a standard point of criticism to those protections was eliminated. The administration's opponents in Congress, and more broadly the interest groups that were negatively affected by these socially beneficial rules had to turn to alternative arguments.

Rhetorical Tactic One: The Regulatory Tsunami

One tactic was to take the focus away from the wisdom of individual rules and instead redirect attention to the total regulatory burden, often characterized in rhetorically extreme language. An example of this hyperbolic rhetoric was the use of the phrase "regulatory tsunami" to characterize rulemaking under Obama. In remarks before the Des Moines Rotary Club, the president and CEO of the US Chamber of Commerce, Thomas J. Donohue, made the following claims:

> Today, American free enterprise indeed, the American Dream is being overwhelmed by a tsunami of government regulations. The more than 100,000 regulations issued over many decades are like plaque that slowly and silently accumulates in the arteries. They are depriving our economic system of the needed oxygen to grow and expand. Eventually they will silence the heartbeat of our economy. . . . America is sinking under the crushing weight of a vast and ever-expanding regulatory state. That burden threatens to short-circuit our recovery, hamper long-term growth, undermine our global competitiveness, and suffocate the entrepreneurial spirit so vital to America's success. . . .
>
> While many regulations provide valuable benefits to business and society, many are simply outdated, ineffective, overly complicated, and counterproductive. They are too numerous, too pervasive, and too costly.
>
> How costly? The Small Business Administration's Office of Advocacy puts the total price tag of complying with federal regulations at $1.75 trillion in 2008. That's trillion with a t.
>
> That's 12% of GDP. That's $500 billion more than the amount we pay in personal income taxes.
>
> Had every U.S. household paid an equal share of the federal regulatory burden, each would have owed $15,500 in 2008.[31]

This language was picked up by politicians as well: for example, in 2011, House Republicans released a report accusing the administration of a " 'regulatory tsunami' that stunts job creation."[32]

The reality was very different from these over-the-top characterizations. Careful analysis of the regulatory activity under President Obama found very little difference from prior administrations,[33] with an analysis by Bloomberg News finding that "Obama's White House has approved fewer regulations than his predecessor George W. Bush at this same point in their tenures, and the estimated costs of those rules haven't reached the annual peak set in fiscal 1992 under Bush's father." Bloomberg concluded that "Obama's 'tsunami' of new government regulations looks more like a summer swell." [34]

The quantitative estimates of regulatory costs quoted by Donahue were also baseless. These numbers were drawn from a study by Nicole V. Crain and W. Mark Crain, *The Impact of Regulatory Costs on Small Firms*, that had stunning methodological flaws. Perhaps the most damning was the method for estimating "economic" regulatory costs, which made up the lion's share of the total. The report describes the method as follows: "a cross-country regression analysis to examine the impact of a broad index of economic regulations on the national economic output."[35] The "broad index" was taken from the World Bank project on Worldwide Governance Indicators, which developed a Regulatory Quality Index. This variable was placed into a regression analysis alongside a set of controls (foreign trade, population, primary school enrollment, and broadband subscribers) to predict GDP.[36] The resulting coefficient was then used to create an estimate of regulatory costs.

This analysis is outlandishly misconceived. One set of problems arises from the use in the Crain and Crain report of this index as a measure of the aggregate level of regulation.[37] The index itself is a bit of hodgepodge and is based on surveys of businesses, information from risk management firms, and even the views of the Heritage Foundation.[38] It does not purport to measure the total *amount* of regulation, but instead the *quality* of regulation. This emphasis is reflected in some of the survey questions, which include soliciting the views of businesses about whether "anti-monopoly policy is lax and ineffective."[39] This means that the variable used by Crain and Crain to measure the extent of regulation in fact measures in part *the lack* of regulation and enforcement.

Just as important, the report entirely fails to examine whether the correlation between the Regulatory Quality index and GDP is causal. This question—separating causal effects from mere associations—is at the heart of social scientific research. A correlation between two variables in a regression like the one done by Crain and Crain does not imply that regulation *causes* a reduction in economic output. Even assuming the Regulatory Quality Index measures the amount of regulation, which it does not, the correlations they find need not be causal in the way they describe. Many possible confounding factors exist that could account for the correlations other than a causal effect from regulation to GDP. These include general economic or regulatory trends or reverse causation in which economic downturns trigger greater regulation. Given that the index is based on the perceptions of businesses, business advisors, and even political advocacy groups, it is quite possible that changes in the economy affect those perceptions—when the economy is good, the same regulatory requirements might seem less burdensome.

Nearly forty years ago, economist Edward E. Leamer urged the profession to "Take the Con out of Econometrics."[40] In the subsequent decades, economists spent considerable energy to improve the "credibility" of their work through research design.[41] The Crain and Crain report took none of these lessons and instead relied on outdated and discredited approaches that have been rejected by the professional community. But, notwithstanding the absolute flimsiness of these numbers, foes of the Obama administration's regulatory agenda were more than happy to draw on them to shore up their rhetoric.[42]

Rhetorical Tactic Two: Job-Killing Regulation

The second prong of the anti-regulatory counterattack on the Obama administration's playbook again attempted to shift focus away from costs and benefits, this time by claiming that regulations "killed" jobs. During a time of high unemployment, this claim carried considerable weight and was used as a blunt instrument to rhetorically hammer away at the president's policy agenda.

Blaming regulation for job losses was not a new rhetorical strategy for Republicans: Ronald Reagan used the phrase "job-killing regulation" during his 1980 presidential run.[43] However, Obama's election and subsequent use of the cost-benefit progressive playbook led his opponents to dig up and enthusiastically embrace this language: in 2007, the phrase (or close variants) showed up in just four newspaper articles; but by 2011 it appeared in nearly seven hundred.[44] John Engler, the CEO of the National Association of Manufacturers, models how the phrase was used by advocates in a quote in the *Washington Post* claiming that controls on the pollution that causes smog were "real job killers."[45] Republican politicians were also keen on the phrase; for example, House Speaker John Boehner criticized "the president's job-killing regulatory agenda" after the EPA clean air rules were announced and Representative Fred Upton declared "war on the regulatory state" and condemned "job-killing regulations the EPA is finalizing."[46]

It is worth noting that during a time of high unemployment, constituencies within the Democratic Party also focused on the employment effects of regulation. But progressives made the argument in the opposite direction, claiming the stronger environmental protections (for example) would lead to a surge in "green jobs."[47] One prominent advocate for this position was Van Jones, who called for a "green new deal" in his 2008 book *The Green Collar Economy: How One Solution Can Fix Our Two Biggest Problems*.[48] This vision resonated with core Democratic constituencies, in part because it offered a bridge between environmentalists, unions, and civil rights groups, which are core members of the Democratic Party coalition that have sometimes been at odds with each other. Jones served for a time as President Obama's special advisor for Green Jobs.

As with the "regulatory tsunami," claims about "job-killing regulation" (or, for that matter, the promise of "green jobs" as a response to unemployment) are overblown. Most regulations have only tangential effects on labor markets, and whatever employment effects they have are a small part of the overall picture. For example, one Obama-era rulemaking that received considerable pushback from industry was a rule on toxic air emissions from industrial boilers. The estimated net benefits from the rule were between $25.2 and $65.5 billion, which included up to 8,000 premature deaths avoided per year. The anticipated net employment effects were between 4,000 job losses and 8,300 jobs created, with a central estimate of a net of 2,100 jobs created.[49] Even taking the highest estimate for job losses and the low end estimate for net benefits, the rule generates over $6 million in social benefits for each job lost. In general, scholars who have studied this question have found that employment effects from regulation tend to cancel each other and be small compared to other regulatory effects.[50]

The only regulations that have direct effects on jobs are rules that directly govern labor or employment, such as the minimum wage or workplace safety regulation. But even in these cases, the current body of research indicates that effects are quite modest.[51] Reviewing research on workplace rules, the Office of Management and Budget has found that the "empirical literature does not offer unambiguous conclusions," and that some studies find that mandatory employment terms favorable to workers (such family leave, protection for disabilities, or minimum health insurance coverage) negatively affect wages or employment, while other studies find no such effects.[52] The minimum wage is a textbook example of a regulation that would be expected, under standard economic theory, to result in reduced employment.[53] However, the actual effects of modest minimum wage increases have been the subject of long-standing empirical scrutiny, starting with a landmark 1994 study by Alan Krueger and David Card, that questions the standard blackboard account.[54] A recent meta-analysis of research conducted on the subject finds that hiking the minimum wage has only very modest negative effects on employment, mostly confined to teenage workers.[55]

The negligible effects of regulation on employment—especially for non-labor regulation like environmental protections—did not stop advocates from trotting out studies that made extravagant jobs claims. Perhaps the most absurd example is a pair of studies that purported to forecast the employment effects of two Obama-era environmental rulemakings discussed in chapter 3: the Cross-State Air Pollution Rule (which was designed to cut down on interstate air pollution), and the Mercury and Air Toxics Rule (which was designed to reduce pollution for power plants).[56] One study, carried out by the consultant firm NERA for the trade group the American Coalition for Clean Coal Electricity anticipated 1.4 million *job losses* over seven years due to the rules. The other study, carried out by the Political Economy Research Institute at the University of Massachusetts Amherst and the environmental group CERES, predicted 1.4 million *jobs gained* from the regulation over five years. Both of these rules have now been fully implemented, yet no one appears to have noticed any substantial net employment effects from the two rules whatsoever. These results are in keeping with the EPA's own estimates, which anticipated only negligible net effects of the rules on jobs.[57]

It is important to recognize that regulations can have local or sectoral effects on employment that are important, even if, in the aggregate, there are countervailing effects and net impacts are small.[58] But the overheated rhetoric about jobs tends to obscure, rather than appropriately highlight, these fundamentally distributional consequences. Emphasis on regulation and jobs also tends to take focus away from more effective tools to address unemployment or under-employment, given the ineffectiveness of increasing or decreasing regulation as employment policy levers.

Rhetorical Tactic Three: The Deep State

The final rhetorical device used by opponents of the Obama administration to combat the cost-benefit progressive playbook was to raise fears about a tyrannical "deep state" filled with entrenched, power-hungry bureaucrats intent on undermining the public good. Concerns about the rising power of administrative agencies also have a long history,[59] as do concerns about the role of elites in American political life.[60] As a rhetorical strategy, "bureaucracy bashing" also has an unfortunately long pedigree and has been indulged in by politicians of both political parties.[61] But during the Obama administration, such longstanding critiques of active government and the structure of administrative agencies curdled into conspiratorial ruminations concerning the existence of an un-American deep state intent on undermining democracy itself.

The term "deep state" came to broad popularity as a term to describe Turkish politics, as in this usage by the *Washington Post* in 2003: "Turkish foreign policy is traditionally controlled by what is called the 'deep state,' generals and senior bureaucrats who remain in power as elected governments come and go."[62] The term has been applied to similar circumstances in countries such as Egypt.[63] An early application of the notion of the deep state to the United States is found in Peter Dale Scott's 2007 book, *The Road to 9/11: Wealth, Empire, and the Future of America*:

> Our supposed open society is in fact partly driven by deeper forces many of us do not clearly see, especially in matters of foreign policy. This weakness of civil society at the federal level allows policy to be dictated by special interests. . . .

I designate as the "deep state" (a term borrowed from Turkish analysts) that part of the state driven by top-down policy making, often by small cabals.[64]

Appearing on Alex Jones's radio show *Infowars,* after publication of this book, Scott—an emeritus professor of English at the University of California Berkeley—discussed his views.[65] Another early characterization of US policy-making as influenced by a nefarious deep state came in a 2011 interview with then-president of Afghanistan Hamid Karzai, who claimed that "behind the facade of Western assistance and the ambassadors lining up to offer support . . . the Deep State was working to undermine him."[66] In discussing the congressional run of Lynn Cheney, political reporter Mara Liasson characterized Cheney, then running in a Republican primary for a US Senate seat from Wyoming, as hailing from the "deep state wing of the Republican party on national security and foreign policy."[67]

Although the flowering of deep state rhetoric to describe career civil servants at most administrative agencies would await the election of Donald Trump, the latter period of the Obama presidency saw the term move beyond the conspiratorial fringes and national security context to apply as an all-purpose insult to US institutions. Writing in 2014, for example, Pat Buchanan explains what he sees as a leftward policy shift despite conservative electoral victories as arising from "the permanent powers and the deep state" characterized by a "mammoth bureaucracy—22 million municipal, county, state and federal employees— [with] a vital interest in the preservation and growth of government" alongside "the beneficiaries of [] social programs," a "higher education [system] dominated by tenured leftists and radicals" and a "popular culture, from movies to music to TV, [] dominated by the left."[68] Buchanan's views represent a distinctly partisan take on the deep state notion that has ultimately come to dominate the conversation.[69]

Applied to regulatory agencies such as the EPA, deep state rhetoric is silly. US administrative agencies are a far cry from the kinds of entrenched anti-democratic structures that gave rise to the term, which included military leaders in Turkey who maintained a central role in the country's government for half a century and engaged in multiple military coups to overthrow elected leaders. One need not endorse the current allocation of power among elected officials, their appointees, courts, and the civil service to recognize that the system in the United States falls well within the norm of other modern, democratic, economically developed countries. If anything, the US civil service is more tightly constrained and more deeply controlled by political appointees than in other economically advanced democracies.[70] Current institutions are also the consequence of many decades of compromise in which the value of impartiality, expertise, and professionalism was weighed against political responsiveness. Analogizing this compromise to a shadowy and conspiratorial influence on American politics is absurd.

Nevertheless, politicians have shown a willingness to adopt a tone in discussing administrative agencies that borders on deep state rhetoric. In recent years, two bills have been floated by Republicans in Congress that would radically change how agencies operate: the Regulatory Accountability Act (RAA) and the Regulations from the Executive in Need of Scrutiny Act (the REINS Act).[71] The RAA would impose a host of severe additional procedures on agencies—such as formal trial-type hearings—that would severely bog down all rulemakings, while the REINS Act would require congressional approval of all major rulemakings, which is a recipe to grind all agency action to an almost complete halt.[72] In supporting these extreme changes, politicians have leaned into the agency-as-boogeyman language, decrying "unelected, unaccountable bureaucrats"; criticizing "heavy-handed rule over the American people"; and describing "people [who] live in fear of what the EPA, Forest Service, BLM [Bureau of Land Management] or other agencies will do next."[73]

Neither the RAA nor REINS Act have become law. But by the end of the Obama administration, the paranoid style of deep state rhetoric had started to become normalized as it was used more frequently by mainstream Republican figures to describe the normal operations of a relatively moderate administration. Soon, the bounds around what counted for normal discourse over regulatory politics and administrative agencies would bend again, this time to the point of breaking.

The Deconstructionists

It is a bit unfair to fault Anthony Downs's model of political parties for its inability to predict how Republicans would respond to their 2008 electoral defeat—it was originally developed fifty years prior to Barack Obama's candidacy, a time of far more centrist parties, when policy overlap between politicians of different parties was common, and hard-core, polarized constituencies were rarer. In the decades since Downs, political scientists have refined his model and built new ones that better reflect contemporary realities, which include the importance of party "brands" and the role of "intense policy demanders" in shaping the behavior of politicians.[74] These models do a better job of predicting the kind of polarized, oppositional behavior that Obama faced when taking office.[75] But no political science model—no matter how well attuned to the contemporary political scene— predicted the rise of Donald Trump and the ways in which his candidacy and election transformed the Republican Party.

There are many facets of the phenomenon of Donald Trump the politician that are outside the scope of this book: his embrace of the birther conspiracy theory that claimed that President Obama was not a US citizen; his extreme violation of norms of decorum, up to and including bragging about his ability to sexually assault women with impunity; his temperament, demeanor, and work habits, all of which seem ill-suited to the presidency; and much else. Political scientists and historians will no doubt continue to puzzle for decades about how Trump captured the imagination of so many Republican primary voters, and what fueled the overwhelming negative partisanship that propelled him into the White House.[76] We will leave these questions to them.

For purposes of understanding contemporary US regulatory politics, what is most important about Donald Trump's posture toward these issues is the degree to which they are simply cruder renderings of the themes developed and deployed during the Republican campaign of opposition against the policies of Barack Obama. For example, in a post to Twitter on June 3, 2014, Trump states: "Obama's war on coal is killing American jobs, making us more energy dependent on our enemies & creating a great business disadvantage."[77]

By the time of Trump's tweet, the phrase "war on coal" had joined "job-killing regulation" and "regulatory tsunami" as a favorite talking point among industry lobbyists and Republican politicians.[78] In his tweet, Trump was simply using language that had been in heavy circulation among his co-partisans. Unlike on issues such as trade and immigration, where Trump departed from party elites, Trump's views and rhetoric concerning regulation fell in line with where the mainstream of the party had moved during the Obama presidency.

This is why upon taking office, a joint effort to roll back environmental, safety, and public health protections adopted in Obama's second term was among the most successful collaborations between the Trump White House and the Republican Congress. (The appointment of conservative judges was another.) Shortly after Trump's swearing in, his chief strategist at the time, Stephen K. Bannon, announced that the "deconstruction of the administrative state" was among the president's top priorities.[79] This was a grand, contradictory, and utterly unrealistic vision, given the administration's other purported priorities, such as cracking down on unauthorized immigration—a policy that requires a fairly substantial increase in administrative capacity. But it helped set the tone.

The first step of this campaign of deconstruction was built on the revival of the Congressional Review Act (CRA). For many years, regulatory statutes included provisions for legislative "vetoes" that empowered congressional actors (either a chamber or sometimes a committee) to vote to void certain types of regulation. In a 1983 decision *Immigration and Naturalization Service v. Chadha*, the US Supreme Court struck down these legislative vetoes as creating an unconstitutional route to legislating that impermissibly avoided the presidential veto.[80]

Adopted during the second term of the Clinton administration, the CRA was an attempt to create what amounted to a weaker version of the legislative veto through a fast-track process for Congress to "disapprove" a regulation within the sixty-legislative-day window (a somewhat difficult-to-calculate period extending for months) after it was finalized.[81] But the rub—and the reason the CRA largely fell into disuse—is that the president must sign the disapproval, just as with a normal piece of legislation, to avoid running afoul of *INS v. Chadha*. And typically, presidents approve of the actions of their administrative agencies, so the conditions for successful use of the CRA process are rare. Prior to Trump, it had been used only once, to repeal a rule on workplace ergonomics that had been adopted late in the Clinton administration. When the 2000 election placed George W. Bush in the White House with a unified Republican Congress, with the ergonomics rule still within the CRA window, the stars were properly aligned for its use. When a similar swing to unified Democratic control occurred in 2008, there were no Bush administration rules in the CRA window that Democrats determined were worth the effort.[82]

But Trump's surprise victory, alongside Republican majorities in the House and Senate with their strong anti-Obama sentiment, created the perfect conditions for the CRA to spring back to life. And the Trump White House and Republicans in Congress did use the CRA effectively, ultimately disapproving sixteen administrative actions.[83]

Many of the CRA disapprovals involve issues of some political salience, which helps explain why they were given priority by politicians in Congress. For example, one of the disapprovals targeted a rule by the Social Security Administration to identify individuals who receive disability benefits for reason of mental impairment and pass that information to the attorney general for inclusion in the system of national background checks for firearm purchases.[84] Other rules targeted by the CRA included a regulation that would have made it more difficult for states to engage in efforts to defund Planned Parenthood,[85] a rule limiting states' ability to require drug tests as a precondition for unemployment insurance payments,[86] and two rules related to primary and secondary education.[87] The political case for addressing these rules is fairly obvious, if only because they provided an opportunity for Republican politicians to engage in ideological signaling to their base.

There were two rule disapprovals with even more widespread substantive consequences. One targeted a rule by the Federal Communications Commission that would have restricted the ability of Internet Service Providers to collect and sell information about customers' online habits. Advocates of the rule argued that it was an important privacy protection at a time when companies are engaging in ever more intrusive data collection methods.[88] Opponents of the rule, which naturally included Internet Service Providers themselves, were pleased with the CRA disapproval, and argued that it would create a more robust market in online advertising, which is currently dominated by Google and Facebook.[89]

Another CRA disapproval targeted the Stream Protection Rule, a regulation by the Office of Surface Mining Reclamation and Enforcement (OSM) that addressed some of the damage associated with coal mining in the Eastern United States.[90] That rule was the culmination of many years of effort by groups such as Appalachian Voices to combat the devastating environmental consequences of surface-mining practices common in the region. Dubbed mountaintop removal, surface mining in the Appalachia Mountains often involves blasting away large portions of the natural landscape with industrial-scale explosives and then depositing the resulting waste, which often contains hazardous materials, into nearby streams and valleys.

The Stream Protection Rule did not go as far as groups such as Appalachian Voices would have liked: they favored a complete ban on mountaintop removal mining. Instead, the Obama administration adopted a more cautious approach, curtailing mining practices that generate "excess spoil," limiting the dumping of these wastes in streams, and restraining mining that occurs directly through existing streams. The costs of the rule were projected at $81 million per year, with a negligible impact on employment (a net gain of 150 jobs) and total coal production.[91] The agency did not provide a monetary estimate of most of the benefits, instead choosing to present benefits as natural units such as miles of stream water quality improvements and acres of forest preserved.[92] Even without monetary estimates, the value of these ecosystem improvements appear considerable, with water quality improvements in hundreds of downstream miles of stream and thousands of forest acres preserved.

Although the Stream Protection Rule was not a very expensive environmental measure compared to many others, it provoked an unhinged response from the coal industry, which warned of catastrophic job losses throughout the region.[93] Tarred as part of the "war on coal," the Stream Protection Rule became a priority item for incumbent coal operators with close ties to the Trump administration. On the other side of the issue were the rule's beneficiaries, largely less well-off Appalachian communities lacking the lobbying connections and media power of their opponents. It should come as little surprise that the coal industry walked away with the victory. The rollback of the Stream Protectio Rule saved coal operators tens of millions of dollars in compliance costs, but those saving came at a substantial cost for the environment and affected communities.

In addition to these more important rules, there were some odd choices of priorities for congressional attention. For example, one of the rules prohibited the use of bait in hunting brown bears, and the taking of black or brown bear cubs in Alaskan wildlife refuges.[94] When the Fish and Wildlife Service held hearings on the proposed rule, only 218 people showed up. The rule was no doubt important to a handful of bear hunters in Alaska, but not the stuff of Bannon's grand deconstruction. Other rules that fell to the CRA included a regulation by the Occupational Safety and Health Administration requiring employers to keep records of work-related injuries and illnesses,[95] rules making it easier for states and localities to facilitate retirement savings,[96] a rule by the Department of Defense to ensure that government contractors complied with federal labor laws,[97] a rule reforming the procedures for land-use planning on federal lands,[98] and an anti-corruption measure that required tracking of payments to foreign governments for natural resource extraction rights.[99] While various constituencies likely cared one way or another about these rules, it is perhaps surprising the Congress devoted its limited attention to targeting them with CRA disapprovals.

This spurt of deregulation was by far the most prolific use of the CRA in its history, and ultimately made up the most successful portion of the Trump administration's efforts at directly achieving Bannon's dreamed deconstruction.[100] But it would take far more to undo the policy achievements of the prior administration; we turn to the other attempts and assess their success in the next section.

Incompetence

Another element of the deconstructionist agenda has been the appointment of senior political officials who are a dangerous combination of hostile to their agencies' missions and unable to execute the duties of their office.

Norman Ornstein, a resident scholar at the American Enterprise Institute and a longtime Washington observer, offered this judgment of Trump's cabinet:

> We have a contingent of corrupt kleptocrats, some sadists, a racist, utter ideologues, at least one utter incompetent, another who has made as his mission devastating our diplomatic corps. Other administrations have had occasional embarrassments or individuals brought down by scandal. None in our lifetimes like this.[101]

Many Trump appointees for the most senior positions in government lacked significant government experience or knowledge about the departments they were charged with leading. To take just one example, Trump's secretary of education Betsy DeVos had no prior government experience, and instead was primarily involved in politics as a major donor and fundraiser for the Republican Party. Her knowledge of education policy mostly appears to involve the issue of school vouchers, of which she has been a long-standing advocate. In her confirmation hearing, she appeared to lack knowledge of basic education law and policy.[102]

Her appointment was the first in US history to require a vice president's tie-breaking vote in the Senate for a cabinet nomination.

In agencies with an environmental bent, the senior appointees have been particularly hostile to the agency's mission. During his 2012 presidential run, then Texas governor Rick Perry proposed that the Department of Energy be eliminated.[103] In 2017, he was confirmed as Trump's Secretary of Energy and shortly thereafter questioned the role of greenhouse gas emissions in climate change.[104] As attorney general for the state of Oklahoma, Scott Pruitt focused on aggressively challenging federal environmental protections.[105] He became Trump's EPA administrator, and, shortly thereafter, joined Perry in questioning the validity of climate science.[106] After a career in the Navy Seals, Ryan Zinke became a state politician and then made national headlines by referring to Hillary Clinton as the "Antichrist" during his (successful) 2014 run for Montana's US House representative seat.[107] He became Trump's secretary of the interior and, shortly thereafter, joined Perry and Pruitt in questioning the human contribution to climate change—going so far as to blame environmentalists, rather than greenhouse gas emissions, for the deadly 2018 California wildfire season.[108]

When it came to running their respective agencies, their policy inexperience and hostility toward their agencies showed. The debacles ran from the serious to the silly, and ultimately led to the resignations of all three under clouds of scandal.

On the serious side, Rick Perry pushed for a massive bailout of the coal and nuclear industry.[109] The Perry Coal Bailout Proposal was based on the entirely false premise that grid reliability was threatened by the retirement of old coal-generating power plants. The gist of the idea was to remove coal and nuclear power from competitive energy markets. Instead, the government would provide a guaranteed rate of return on their capital investments, coming out of the pockets of consumers. This new structure would create a massive subsidy that would hugely distort energy markets. It would also have resurrected a massive regulatory apparatus that had been gradually wound down over the course of several decades by leaders in both parties who favored free-market reforms in the energy sector—not exactly a dismantling of the administrative state.

Fortunately, the Perry coal bailout proposal was decidedly rejected by the Federal Energy Regulatory Commission, the oversight body with independent authority over regulating energy markets. The unanimous decision by the commission came in spite of the fact that the majority of its members were Republicans, and four of the five of them were appointed by Trump (although two were Democrats, in keeping with a statutory requirement of bipartisanship). In denying Perry's request, the commission found, in essence, that there was no reliability crisis to solve.[110] However, this failure did not stop Perry from pursuing similar efforts to bail out coal under different guises, some of which remain under consideration by the Energy Department and the Commission.[111]

The scandal that ultimately appears to have ended Perry's time at the Energy Department had nothing to do with his role there. Four years after referring to Donald Trump as a "cancer on conservatism" and two and a half years after taking a position on Trump's cabinet, Perry announced his plans to resign. Within days, he was implicated by Trump himself as the progenitor of the idea for Trump to call the president of Ukraine to pressure his government to investigate the family member of a Trump political rival—the crisis that ultimately led to Trump's impeachment.[112]

On the sillier side was Scott Pruitt's plan to facilitate a "red team blue team" debate on the science of climate change.[113] Borrowed from the military and business contexts, the idea is for a devil's advocate "red team" to assume an adversarial stance against a "blue team" tasked with defending a course of action or decision. The problem with this idea, as applied to climate science, is that it creates the impression that there are multiple equally valid alternative scientific views on the existence and causes of climate change. Actually, there is no legitimate disagreement; rather there is a massive consensus that human activities are the cause of global warming, ascribed to by 97 percent of climate scientists.[114] Only the strength of a decades-long industry-funded campaign continues to sow doubt on the subject.[115] The problem with Pruitt's absurd "red team blue team" proposal is that it creates the misleading impression of equivalence between the vast majority of the scientific community and those few who continue to question the reality of climate change. John Kelly, who was the White House chief of staff at the time that the proposal was circulated, reportedly killed the idea.[116]

There was also a consistent drumbeat of scandal and odd behavior, some of which may be attributable to simple inexperience and hubris. For example, Zinke issued the peculiar order that his official flag fly over the main Interior building whenever he was present—a ritual that has not been required for cabinet officials in living memory.[117] Zinke was also criticized for using government funds to charter flights and helicopters and for spending nearly $150,000 to upgrade the doors in his office.[118] Pruitt, for his part, compiled an extensive list of bizarre gaffes and ethical improprieties: spending over $100,000 on first-class flights for purported "security" reasons; renting a Washington, DC, apartment from a lobbyist at a subsidized rate; installing a $43,000 private phone booth in his office; using his position to secure his wife a job; and attempting to blacklist his twenty-six-year old former scheduler for perceived disloyalty.[119] Ultimately, after months of escalating scrutiny and bad press, both Zinke and Pruitt left the administration.

Benjamin Wittes, a senior fellow at the Brookings Institution and co-director of a joint Brookings and Harvard Law School project on law and national security, has summarized the Trump administration's early efforts to limit immigration through executive order as "malevolence tempered by incompetence."[120] For the environmental agencies, that characterization captures an important point   as will be discussed below, many of the Trump administration efforts to roll back environmental protections have foundered on the shoals of shoddy lawyering and economic ineptitude.

But it is also worth pausing to remember that incompetence alone causes substantial harm. The first-term EPA administrators in the two prior administrations were Lisa Jackson (under Obama) and Christine Todd Whitman (under George W. Bush). Of course, partisans on either side raised plenty of criticisms against the two administrators. But both Whitman and Jackson used their positions to forward the agency's mission within the confines of their political constraints. Whitman promoted efforts to expand the use of market-based tools to cut down on pollution,[121] including the rule that later served as the springboard for the Obama-era Cross-State Air Pollution Rule.[122] She also pushed back on pressure from the White House to ease pollution limits on existing power plants, albeit unsuccessfully.[123] Jackson spearheaded a number of major initiatives discussed in chapter 3, including the first federal limits on greenhouse gas emissions in the United States. Perhaps the single most important harm associated with Trump's reign of regulatory incompetence is the opportunity cost of what could have been accomplished by leaders who were loyal to their agencies' mission and capable of doing their jobs.

That said, incompetence also prevented Trump's political appointees from doing more active damage. As mentioned in chapter 1, agencies under Trump's supervision have had an absolutely abysmal record defending their decisions before the courts. Since taking office, the Trump administration has used agencies to deregulate as well as to implement many other administration priorities, spawning many lawsuits. According to one count, ninety- nine of those cases have come to some resolution.[124] In eighty-eight of those cases, the agency either lost in court, or withdrew its action after being sued: that is a loss rate of nearly 90 percent. This track record is absolutely terrible, especially in light of the considerable deference that federal courts typically offer agencies.

Many of the Trump administration's court losses came in response to unlawful delays. Upon taking office, many agencies were instructed to simply put on the brakes and stop the implementation of rules that had been duly adopted under the Administrative Procedure Act. However, once a rule is on the books, a separate action is needed to undo it, with the required opportunities for public comment and the demands that agencies justify their decisions.[125] In delay cases, the Trump administration's rollback efforts were denied in contexts as diverse as a Housing and Urban Development rule to increase access to housing for low-income tenants, a Bureau of Land Management rule to reduce the waste of natural gas from federal lands, and EPA controls on emissions of formaldehyde from composite wood products.[126]

In cases where agencies have attempted to go through the full process to actually undo (rather than delay) prior rules, courts have also found their reasoning lacking and have struck down those moves. One example is the case of the Valuation Reform Rule, which is discussed in more detail in chapter 10. During the Obama administration, the Department of the Interior issued a rule to improve the process used to determine the payments made by companies that had been granted access to federal lands to drill for oil and natural gas. These royalty payments are divided between the federal government and the states. By law, the Department of the Interior is charged with obtaining "fair market value" for use of public lands.[127] However, there were several loopholes that allowed companies to get away with paying deflated royalties, including a provision that allowed companies to set the value of coal, oil, and gas based on sales to captive entities, such as affiliates, rather than the true market value as reflected in arm's-length transactions.[128] This might sound like an obscure provision of an obscure procedure, but the upshot is that use of public lands was being given away to private companies for a sweetheart price, costing taxpayers millions of dollars. The Obama Valuation Reform Rule instilled some market discipline on the process.

Part of Zinke's agenda at Interior included getting rid of the Valuation Reform Rule. After first attempting to delay implementation, Interior issued a final action in August 2017 repealing the rule.[129] The agency's justification for its decision was seriously lacking and largely rested on a series of assertions that the rule would be "burdensome" and hamper energy development. Most damning was the fact that the agency failed to engage with the cost-benefit analysis that had been conducted by the Obama administration in support of the rule, which found that royalties would increase by roughly $80 million and reduce administrative costs. When the states of California and New Mexico sued Interior, these glaring flaws were readily apparent to the court, which struck down the repeal as arbitrary and capricious.[130]

Notwithstanding the general ineptitude, some deregulatory actions have been successfully finalized,[131] including a Federal Communication Commission action to repeal "net neutrality" rules governing internet service providers.[132] The fate of several other deregulatory actions, such as the repeal of emissions limits on greenhouse gases and weakening of standards for offshore oil drilling rigs, has not yet been decided by the courts. Although the litigation record of the Trump administration on regulation has been terrible, courts may not be willing to serve as the primary bulwark against the administration's regulatory irrationality forever. Finally, the slacked efforts to enforce existing rules under Trump have achieved some deregulatory effects similar to those of actual rollbacks.[133]

Delegitimization

From the perspective of immediate, concrete results, the Trump administration's efforts at deconstructing the administrative state have been only partially successful. Where victory has been achieved, it has often been through the incompetence of the senior political appointees put in charge: not exactly the most dignified pathway, but, in many cases, an effective one.

But in addition to deregulations achieved through specific actions or inactions, there has been broader damage done to the system of institutional and substantive guardrails that cabin agency decision making. This system has been constructed by presidential administrations of both parties and struck a delicate compromise between responsiveness to electoral politics and the need for impartial, expert decision making at agencies. That system includes the courts and various legal doctrines concerning judicial review, but it also includes OIRA and the substantive standard used in the process of executive review. During the Trump administration, the stabilizing role of OIRA and cost-benefit analysis have been under siege, and it is not clear that they will recover.

There have been two general prongs in this campaign. One has been a multifaceted effort to distort cost-benefit analysis so that it becomes less an honest account of the consequences of government decisions and more an advanced carnival game. In Part II of this book, we provide considerable detail about the various moves of the Trump administration to undermine the substantive meaning of cost-benefit analysis. An example of the larger point is the Trump administration's almost cartoonishly incompetent counting of the costs and benefits of its "SAFE" Vehicles Rule.

As discussed in prior chapters, one of the signature regulatory achievements of the Obama administration was rules to reduce greenhouse gas emissions from the transportation sector. In August 2018, the Trump administration issued proposed rule that would substantially roll back the Obama-era program. Dubbed the "Safer Affordable Fuel-Efficient (SAFE) Vehicles Rule," the Trump administration proposal called for freezing the increase in required fuel economy at thirty-seven miles per gallon. In its analysis of their proposal, the Trump agencies claimed that it would avoid over 12,000 traffic fatalities over several decades (hence the moniker "SAFE")[134] and lead to hundreds of billions of dollars in net benefits compared to Obama-era rules.[135] But these numbers were based on a transparently flawed set of economic models and assumptions. .

There are many analytic shortcomings in the legal and economic analysis of the proposed SAFE rule—too many to detail here.[136] But there is one modeling forecast that is particularly galling in how it flouts basic economic principles. The Trump administration predicted that by reducing the price of cars, it would decrease the number of cars on the road, and therefore reduce the number of automobile fatalities. This prediction—which contravenes basic principles of supply and demand—is the rough equivalent in economics of the Flat Earth hypothesis.

The main cost of the Obama vehicle greenhouse gas standards is an increase in the price of new cars. The EPA and Department of Transportation analysis at the time recognized and calculated that cost but found that it was more than offset by decreased spending on fuel and the environmental benefits of fewer air pollutants.[137] Under the principle of supply and demand, the increase in the price of new cars would also lead to fewer new cars sold—other things being equal, when the price of something goes up, the total amount demanded typically goes down. The consequence is that the size of the total "fleet" of cars on the road can be expected to decline: fewer new cars will be sold, which will be only partially offset by a decline in people scrapping their old cars.

Amazingly, the Trump administration predicted that rolling back the Obama-era standards and reducing the price of new cars would *decrease* the size of the fleet—to the tune of 6 million vehicles by 2029. This is an astonishing conclusion. Given the implausibility of this forecast, the underlying models that generated it should have been examined with a fine-tooth comb to look for errors. Instead, the leading experts within the agencies appear to have been shut out of the process until the last minute—at which point their objections were ignored.[138] This resulted in the use of models that the EPA's own peer review process characterized as having "weaknesses in their theoretical underpinnings [and] their econometric implementation," and that a group of leading economists argue "violate[] simple economic principles; lead[] to misleading conclusions related to the overall size of the fleet, fleet composition, and the amount of scrappage; and undermine[] [agency] modeling efforts."[139] Without the 6 million phantom cars, the purported benefits of the Trump rollback drop precipitously.[140]

Once it became clear that the analysis of the proposed rollback was so riddled with implausible assumptions that it would likely fail in court, the agencies changed tactics when they promulgated the final rule. In its main analysis, the Trump administration conceded that the rule would generate billions of dollars in net harms to society.[141] But to attempt to obscure this fact, the agencies engaged in other accounting gimmicks in their so-called "sensitivity analysis" to make it appear that the rule would not impose net costs on the American public. For example, the analysis of the final rule touts extra features such as more horsepower that would be facilitated by the rollback, while also assuming in its estimate of future car prices that no new features would be added. When these tricks are put to the side, the significant net costs of the rollback are clear.

A willingness to flagrantly distort the analysis of the costs and benefits is only one prong of the Trump administration's attack on expertise, evidence, and analysis. The other is perverting the role of regulatory review. This campaign started at the top: as elsewhere in the administration, Trump's choices for the senior leadership at OIRA departed from established norms. For several decades, there had been a tradition of appointing relatively moderate technocrats with expertise in cost-benefit analysis methodology for the role of OIRA administrator.[142] Prior administrators including Sally Katzen, John Graham, Cass Sunstein, and Howard Shelanski, who had all made major contributions in the areas of regulatory economics and practice, and cost-benefit analysis. Neomi Rao, Trump's initial appointee, had no background in these areas.[143]

Instead, Rao's most relevant prior work focused on constitutional questions in administrative law, especially those that could be used to undermine either the power or independence of administrative agencies. For example, in one article, Rao contributes to the effort by many conservative constitutional law scholars to resuscitate the "non-delegation doctrine," which was used by some judges in the 1930s in an attempt to thwart aspects of the New Deal, but has largely been abandoned by the courts.[144] Rao argues that when Congress empowers administrative agencies to act, it creates opportunities for individual members of Congress to influence policymaking outside the normal channels of lawmaking, because they can use their oversight tools to steer agency decision making. It is an interesting argument, because it turns on its head a traditional claim that legislative oversight of agencies helps cure whatever democratic deficit is created by delegation. But it has nothing to do with cost-benefit analysis. A second paper takes aim at limitations on the president's ability to fire senior officials within the executive branch, which have existed for many decades as a means of insulating certain agency decision makers from harsh political oversight.[145] Rao claims that the text of the constitution requires that the president be able to "control" agencies, and there is no ability to control without the ability to fire. This line of argument may have endeared her to the president with the famous "You're fired!" catchphrase from his reality television days, but is very far away from the bread and butter at OIRA and its focus on regulatory arcana.

Rao did, however, have deep political connections. She clerked for Justice Clarence Thomas, a highly valued credential in conservative circles, and served as counsel to the Senate Judiciary committee under Republican Orrin G. Hatch, as well as associate counsel to George W. Bush during his second term.[146] She also founded a center at George Mason University to provide a platform for some of her ideas on using constitutional or other legal arguments to limit the power of administrative agencies.[147]

A bit over a year after Rao was confirmed to her position at OIRA, Trump announced that he planned to nominate her to fill the seat on the US Court of Appeals for the District of Colubmia Circuit that had been occupied by now-Justice Brett Kavanaugh. Early the next year, she was confirmed in a party line vote in the Senate. The OIRA administrator role was filled by Paul Ray, who like

Rao lacked the standard background of prior administrators. After graduating from Harvard Law School in 2011 Ray clerked on the US Court of Appeals for the Second Circuit and then for Justice Samuel Alito on the US Supreme Court. He worked for several years as an associate at the law firm Sidley Austin LLP, and then served a short stint as a legal advisor in the Trump Labor Department before moving to OIRA under Rao. Although Ray is no doubt a rising talent within conservative political circles, his experience is not comparable to the group of prior OIRA administrators.[148]

In addition to Rao's and then Ray's appointments, another move of the Trump administration that broadcast the diminished status of cost-benefit analysis was the president's Executive Order 13,771, *Reducing Regulation and Controlling Regulatory Costs*.[149] That order had two main features: a directive for agencies to repeal at least two regulations for every new regulation issued; and a requirement that agencies impose no new net costs on businesses. Through this order, Trump changed the fundamental mission of OIRA, from ensuring that agencies accurately count costs and benefits with the goal of maximizing the well-being of the American people, to bean counting "regulatory" versus "deregulatory" actions and minimizing costs without accounting for the benefits of environmental, public health, or safety protections.

We discuss the regulatory budget component of Executive Order 13,771 in chapter 5, but the two-for-one requirement also clearly demonstrates the lowly status of OIRA review in the Trump administration. It may be the case that some regulations are ripe for repeal, either because they were ill-conceived from the beginning or because circumstances have changed and rendered them obsolete. But the order does not require that agencies target regulations that have net costs, instead simply counting "deregulatory" actions. In addition, agencies need not engage in any repeals, so long as they also engage in no new regulations. The requirement also fails to account for regulatory benefits, and so repealing a rule with very large net benefits and small costs would both count as a "deregulation" and be entirely permissible. Not only does the requirement not prioritize rules that should fall under a cost-benefit standard, but it also allows repeals that fail the cost-benefit test.

The basic irrationality of the two-for-one requirement is worth emphasizing. Often, a single rulemaking by an agency is actually a complex set of many related actions. Agencies decide what to bundle into a single rule based on considerations like administrative feasibility and clarity for the regulated industry. But an agency could, if it wanted to, bundle together more actions into a single rulemaking, or disaggregate a single rulemaking into several: such game-playing is invited by the two-for-one requirement.

The lack of consistent leadership familiar with the ins and outs of cost-benefit analysis, along with the new substantively meaningless bean-counting role given to OIRA in Executive Order 13,771, has led to a serious erosion of the office's capacity to fulfill its traditional role. The failure to screen the SAFE Vehicles Rule proposal for minimal analytic rigor provides one illustration of how far OIRA has fallen. But there are plenty of others.

Another clear example of OIRA's inability to enforce basic methodological standards occurred during review of a repeal by the Department of Labor of a rule by the Obama administration that specified the circumstances under which employers could require employees to pool tips with other staff and barred employers from participating in such pools. The Trump administration issued a proposed rulemaking to undo the Obama rule, freeing employers to, in effect, pocket money that was intended by consumers as an additional payment to staff.[150]

The Department of Labor purported to conduct a cost-benefit analysis of the tip pooling rule but engaged in only qualitative analysis, arguing that it "lack[ed] data to quantify possible reallocations of tips."[151] In reality, however, the agency had conducted a quantitative analysis that found that employees would lose billions of dollars in tips transferred to and pocketed by employers.[152] It turned out that Rao had learned of this study and initially blocked Labor from moving forward with the regulation without including it in the rulemaking record. Then, Labor Secretary Alexander Acosta worked with Office of Management and Budget Director (and Rao's boss) Mick Mulvaney to undermine OIRA's authority by publishing the proposal despite OIRA's objections.[153] Given that policing cost-benefit analysis has been the core of OIRA's mission and competency for decades, that Mulvaney and Acosta saw fit to overrule Rao on such a basic question is a striking illustration of the severely diminished stature of analytic rigor in the Trump administration.

One additional example helps drive home the point. In the summer of 2019, the Food and Nutrition Service in the Department of Agriculture issued a rule that changed who would be eligible for food stamps—eliminating assistance for 3 million people. In chapter 10, we will discuss some of the dishonest ways that the Trump administration has analyzed rules that have substantial distributional consequences by transferring (or not) resources to different groups. But the problem with the economic analysis of the food stamp rule does not require much time to explain: the agency estimated that 500,000 children would lose their automatic eligibility for free school lunch due to their parents being removed from the food stamp rolls but did not include this finding in its cost-benefit analysis.[154] This failure again shows how little respect has been given to cost-benefit analysis within the Trump administration.

***

The Republican Party did not respond to its losses in the 2008 election through a moderate opposition to the Obama administration, which might have been characterized by a willingness to work across the aisle on issues where the parties appeared to be moving toward agreement—such as on the value of cost-benefit analysis and the use of market-based mechanisms to control pollution. Instead, the Obama administration found no support, even when embracing traditional Republican approaches. Rather, it found itself attacked by a wave of harsh rhetoric: condemned for initiating a "tsunami" of regulation and being intent on "killing" American jobs. This rhetoric, and the declining prestige of cost-benefit analysis within the Republican Party during the Obama years, set the stage forefforts during the Trump administration to attack agencies, delegitimize the regulatory process, appoint incompet senior agency officials, and undermine OIRA's traditional role in enforcing cost-benefit norms.

In Part II of this book, we turn to the many specific ways that the Trump administration has treated cost-benefit analysis as a charade: one that attempts to ignore the benefits of regulations; that questions those benefits at every opportunity; and that, when convenient, invents sham benefits out of thin air to support a favored deregulatory action. In this process, the administration has attempted to convert the practice of cost-benefit analysis from a guardrail that cabins agency discretion into a shell game that does nothing more than obscure the harmful consequences of the administration's actions.

PART II
CHARADE

5

The Illusion of Costs without Benefits

The core of the Trump administration's regulatory agenda is to focus exclusively on the costs of regulations while ignoring, trivializing, and mischaracterizing their benefits. This agenda is most visibly embodied in Executive Order 13,771, titled *Reducing Regulation and Controlling Regulatory Costs*, which the president issued during his second week in office.[1] The order explicitly leaves in place Clinton's Executive Order 12,866, which requires that regulatory actions—regardless of whether they impose new requirements or repeal existing requirements—be justified by cost-benefit analysis.[2] Nonetheless, the Trump order directs agencies to control costs and eliminate two regulations for every new one, but it makes no reference at all to regulatory benefits.

This one-sided approach is also reflected in significant regulatory efforts to delay or repeal important initiatives of the Obama administration designed to protect public health and the environment. In some of these proceedings, the Trump administration has altogether ignored the benefits of the rules it seeks to eliminate or suspend, instead focusing solely on cost savings to regulated industry. In others, it has considered a rule's *quantified* benefits but essentially disregarded the benefits that were not quantified.

The Trump administration's approach makes a mockery of the notion of cost-benefit analysis. In our daily lives, we might decide that it is not worth spending $50 to prevent a stubbed toe. But we are likely to feel quite differently if, instead, the effect is the loss of a limb. To set a goal of saving $50, no matter the consequences, is obviously foolish.

The central tenet of cost-benefit analysis involves comparing the costs and benefits of an action and choosing the alternative that maximizes net benefits. Evaluating the cost savings of deregulatory action without reference to forgone benefits bears no resemblance to cost-benefit analysis. Saving regulatory costs is attractive only if the benefits forgone as a result of these savings are lower than those costs. A rule that reduces compliance costs by giving up an even larger set of social benefit is hardly an attractive proposition.

Moreover, the Trump administration's approach does more than mock rationality and cost-benefit analysis. If this approach succeeds, the effects would be significant and pernicious for public health and the environment. Fortunately, so far the courts have systematically struck down most of the administration's efforts to roll back regulations when those rollbacks were justified through

Reviving Rationality. Michael A. Livermore and Richard L. Revesz, Oxford University Press (2020). © Oxford University Press. DOI: 10.1093/oso/9780197539446.001.0001.

one-sided consideration of cost savings and the erasure of the associated regulatory benefits.

A One-Sided Executive Order

As discussed in chapter 4, Trump's Executive Order 13,771 has two components. First, agencies must repeal two existing rules for each new rule they promulgate.[3] We have already shown why the requirement makes little sense. The second component is a regulatory budget, which caps new regulatory costs at zero for fiscal year 2017 and at a level set by the director of the Office of Management and Budget (OMB) for each agency in the following years.[4] To meet the 2017 zero cost budget, agencies needed to offset any costs associated with a new rule by delaying, suspending, or repealing other rules with equivalent costs.[5]

The cost cap for fiscal year 2017, which ran through September 30, 2017 (roughly eight months into the new administration) could be seen as a moratorium on regulations during that period, since one way to meet it would be by not promulgating any new rules. There are antecedents for moratoria of various kinds at the beginning of a new administration, though they were for shorter periods of time. For example, on taking office, President Reagan asked federal agencies to postpone the effective date of pending final rules for sixty days and to refrain from proposing any new regulations for the same two-month period.[6] Presidents Clinton,[7] George W. Bush,[8] and Obama[9] placed more flexible moratoria by prohibiting agencies from submitting final or proposed rules to the *Federal Register*, and withdrawing any rules that had not yet been published, until those rules could be approved by an agency head appointed by the new president.[10]

The Trump administration's approach differs primarily from prior moratoria in that a cap on regulatory costs continues indefinitely.[11] And while the executive order leaves open the possibility that agencies could impose net costs on the regulated entities following fiscal year 2017,[12] they in fact have shown no inclination to do so. For fiscal year 2018, no major agency sought an increase in net regulatory costs.[13] Similarly, for fiscal year 2019, no major agencies proposed imposing net costs through their regulatory initiatives.[14]

As with the text of the executive order itself, statements by senior administration officials praised these cost caps and paid almost no attention to what societal benefits might thereby be forgone.[15] Most significant are the statements by Office of Information and Regulatory Affairs (OIRA) Administrator Neomi Rao. Rao celebrated the "cost-savings" associated with the administration's deregulatory actions, gleefully tallying a \$23 billion dollar reduction in "burdensome regulations" by the end of fiscal year 2018.[16] She claimed that these reductions were "unleashing the freedom of American workers, innovators and businesses,"[17] and justified the regulatory budgets as "an important backstop to make sure deregulatory actions are not just paper revisions and repeals, but actions that generate real regulatory cost savings for the American public."[18] And Rao insisted that "the benefits of deregulation are felt far and wide" and gave the Trump administration's deregulatory agenda credit for the nation's low unemployment rate and GDP growth.[19]

Each of the empirical claims about the virtues of the Trump administration's approach—the cost savings, and the effects on economic growth and unemployment—has been the subject of significant criticism.[20] But, more important for the purposes of this discussion, what is missing from this self-congratulatory narrative is an accounting for the forgone benefits and new risks the public faces as a result of the deregulatory actions. Even if cost savings were high, how do we know that corresponding increases in the public's risk of premature death, heart disease, asthma, and other serious negative consequences are not even higher?[21]

Rao does not even attempt to answer that question. Not doing so is expedient for her purposes, though a serious abdication of the responsibilities of her office. One does not need to search far for the reason. As explained in part in the following subsections and throughout this book, the regulatory initiatives that the Trump administration is trying to dismantle had benefits that far exceeded their costs. Repealing or rolling them back will therefore make the American people substantially worse off. Instead of celebrating the cost savings, we should be mourning the far larger consequences for well-being of additional deaths and serious illnesses.[22]

To the extent that the Trump administration is treating Executive Order 13,771 as imposing a budget constraint under which no new net costs can be imposed on regulated industry, not only for fiscal year 2017 but subsequently as well, the negative consequences fall into two discrete categories. First, this constraint might stand in the way of promulgating regulations that produce net benefits to society.[23] And second, it might lead to the repeal of other net beneficial regulations. On both scores, the impacts are pernicious.[24]

Properly designed, regulatory budgets could be socially beneficial, increasing net benefits to society.[25] For this to be the case, however, agencies would necessarily need to consider benefits in setting those budgets. In fact, early proponents of regulatory budgets, including Chris DeMuth, OIRA's head during the Reagan administration and subsequently president of the American Enterprise Institute, acknowledged explicitly that benefits should be taken into account in allocating regulatory budgets to particular agencies.[26] Similarly, John Graham, the OIRA head during the George W. Bush administration explained that "programs with a strong benefit justification should receive more generous treatment under a regulatory budget [than other programs]."[27]

This type of nuanced approach is technically possible under the Executive Order for fiscal years beyond 2017, during which the director of OMB is required to designate a regulatory budget for each agency after considering the agency's regulatory plan.[28] But, in fact, the Trump administration has done nothing of the sort, focusing only on costs and entirely ignoring the associated benefits.

Any respected economist would cringe at this one-sidedness. It is simply absurd for the economic analysis of policy to ignore the deaths averted, the reduced number of hospitalizations, the morbidity reductions, and other significant impacts on the well-being of Americans.[29]

Ignoring Benefits Leads to Losses in the Courts

The Trump administration has justified a number of its efforts to delay, stay, or suspend Obama administration regulations by reference only to the cost savings to regulated industries, without looking at the forgone benefits to the regulatory beneficiaries. Not surprisingly, the courts have set aside a significant number of these misguided initiatives.

For example, in June 2017 the Bureau of Land Management attempted to suspend the Methane Waste Prevention Rule,[30] originally promulgated by the Obama administration in 2016, which reduces the loss of natural gas from leaks during the extraction of oil and natural gas.[31] The rule was expected to generate up to $204 million in net benefits per year as well as cost savings from the sale of captured natural gas, along with ancillary benefits like improvements in quality of life for nearby residents.[32] The agency justified its decision to suspend the rule based on the "substantial cost" that industry would incur to comply with the rule, but it did not consider the $204 million dollars in forgone benefits resulting from the suspension.[33] When this deregulatory action was challenged, the United States District Court for the Northern District of California struck down the suspension, finding that the administration had "entirely failed to consider the benefits of the Rule, such as decreased resource waste, air pollution, and enhanced public revenues."[34] The government initially appealed to the United States Court of Appeals for the Ninth Circuit, but subsequently agreed to have its appeal dismissed, thus letting the lower court decision stand and signaling the death knell of the Waste Prevention Rule's suspension.[35]

Similarly, in its December 2017 delay of the publication of training materials for farmers exposed to pesticides,[36] the Environmental Protection Agency (EPA) did not consider the resulting harms to farmworkers and their families.[37] Instead, the agency focused exclusively on the savings to the regulated community, explaining that its objective was to "prevent extra work and costs to developers of the training materials and EPA reviewers."[38] When challenged in court, the agency responded by publishing the training documents instead of defending the delay.[39]

In June 2017, the EPA also attempted to postpone compliance deadlines for the Chemical Disaster Rule,[40] a rule that was promulgated by the Obama administration and was meant to reduce the frequency and magnitude of chemical accidents, resulting in savings in damages and other, unquantified benefits.[41] Commenters complained that the Trump administration action would cause harm by failing to prevent or mitigate chemical accidents during the period of the delay and that the agency had not explained why it was appropriate to forgo such benefits during this period.[42] The EPA's response was that because the rule had not yet gone into effect, a delay of the compliance dates would simply maintain the status quo and therefore not cause any harms.[43] The United States Court of Appeals for the District of Columbia Circuit roundly rejected this argument, determining that the agency had not provided any good explanation "for delaying provisions that [the] EPA previously determined would help keep first responders safe and informed about emergency-response planning."[44]

The DC Circuit explicitly rejected the agency's argument that the delay would impose no costs because it simply maintained the status quo. The court reasoned that "the baseline for measuring the impact of a change or rescission of a final rule is the requirements of the rule itself, not the world as it would have been had the rule never been promulgated."[45] And the court noted the inconsistency in the agency position: that the rule would not lead to forgone benefits because it had not yet gone into effect but that, nonetheless, it would produce cost savings to regulated industry. It concluded that "[the] EPA cannot have it both ways."[46]

The Trump administration relied on the same flawed logic when, in May 2017, the Food and Drug Administration postponed compliance deadlines of a 2014 Obama administration nutritional labeling rule.[47] Here, too, the agency justified the delay based on "the reduction in costs to covered establishments."[48] It acknowledged, however, that delay would produce forgone benefits to consumers.[49] Combining these two effects, the FDA determined "average annualized net benefits [would] decrease by $5 million"[50] as a result of the delay. Apparently, the FDA did not find this outcome troubling. Following a court challenge,[51] the agency agreed to enforce the rule.[52].

Equating Unquantified Benefits with Nonexistent Benefits

In addition to illegally ignoring benefits altogether, the Trump administration has also attempted to justify some of its deregulatory actions by removing *unquantified* benefits from consideration in its cost-benefit analyses. To justify this approach, it has improperly equated unquantified benefits with speculative, insignificant, and uncertain benefits.

As discussed earlier, the executive orders and guidance governing regulatory analysis instruct agencies to give due consideration to all important unquantified costs and benefits. Clinton's Executive Order 12,866 requires agencies to assess "qualitative measures of costs and benefits that are difficult to quantify, but nevertheless essential to consider."[53] The Office of Management and Budget's Circular A-4 guidance on regulatory analysis cautions agencies against ignoring the potential magnitude of unquantified benefits, because the most efficient rule may not have the "largest quantified and monetized . . . estimate."[54] The economic literature has widely recognized that cost-benefit analysis requires proper consideration of effects that "defy quantification but are thought to be important."[55]

Uncertainty about an effect does not mean the effect is worthless. Quite to the contrary, unquantified benefits can explicitly be brought to bear in a cost-benefit calculation. For example, break-even analysis, which is contemplated in Circular A-4,[56] seeks to determine the minimum value of an unquantifiable benefit that would give a regulation net positive benefits.[57]

There is a long-standing practice by agencies under administrations of both political parties of recognizing that unquantified benefits can sometimes be substantial. For example, in April 1982—just months after President Reagan signed Executive Order 12,291,[58] which, like its successor Executive Order 12,866, required agencies to conduct regulatory impact analyses—the Bureau of Land Management (BLM) prepared an analysis of oil and gas leasing in Alaska's National Petroleum Reserve.[59] BLM explained that "[b]ecause of information gaps and scientific uncertainty," the "social costs" of allowing oil and gas drilling in sensitive Alaskan land "cannot be quantitatively predicted."[60] BLM noted, however, that drilling operations could entail the "risk of significant environmental harm,"[61] and particularly insisted that sociocultural, nutritional, and economic effects to the subsistence activities of Native communities, while unquantifiable, were "real and very important."[62] Ultimately, in BLM's 1982 regulatory impact analysis, the agency concluded that "these costs must, therefore, be analyzed in terms of the potential risks (or cost) posed to environmental values in relation to the perceived benefits to accrue through oil and gas development."[63]

Similarly, under the Clinton administration BLM developed new regulations for hardrock mining and determined that while the benefits are "difficult to quantify" due to information gaps, the net economic benefits could be "substantial" and the "environmental benefits of protecting even a small number of unique resources over time could easily offset the costs."[64] Even when BLM later repealed portions of those hardrock mining regulations during the George

W. Bush administration, the agency noted that certain effects could be "substantial" even though uncertainty prevented quantification.[65]

Along the same lines, for the last twenty-five years, under administrations of both political parties, the EPA has consistently recognized the importance of considering unquantified benefits. In response to criticism of its benzene regulations under Section 112, the EPA under President George H. W. Bush "reject[ed] the position that only quantified information can be considered in the decisions."[66] And the EPA under President Clinton considered the "real, but unquantifiable benefits" of emissions standards for hazardous waste combustors.[67] Likewise, the EPA under President George W. Bush evaluated a rule restricting emissions from non-road diesel engines based on "consideration of all benefits and costs expected to result from the new standards, not just those benefits and costs which could be expressed here in dollar terms."[68] Departing from the well-accepted approaches to considering unquantified benefits and the consistent regulatory practices of prior administrations, the Trump administration has just pretended that unquantified benefits do not exist. A few examples illustrate how the administration has engaged in this conduct that flouts both the law and the economic consensus.

The EPA disregarded unquantified benefits in delaying the Chemical Disaster Rule, discussed earlier in this chapter. When the EPA, during the Obama administration, initially promulgated this rule, it engaged in a far more thorough analysis of the costs and benefits.[69] The agency found that the rule would result in extensive, but unquantified, benefits.[70] The EPA said that though it was "unable to quantify what specific reductions may occur as a result of the[] revisions, [it was] able to present data on the total damages that currently occur at . . . facilities each year," damages that would be reduced by some amount.[71] The EPA also pointed to other unquantified benefits, such as avoiding catastrophes, lost productivity, significant emergency response costs, transaction costs caused by accidents, property value impacts in nearby neighborhoods, and environmental damages.[72] The agency determined that annualized costs would be just over $130 million.[73] It estimated that monetized accident damages for facilities covered by the rule were $274.7 million per year and "some portion of [these] future damages would be prevented through implementation of [the] final rule" due to a "reduction of the frequency and magnitude of damages from releases."[74] The agency, however, could not estimate the exact amount of this decrease.[75] The EPA concluded that "when considering the rule's likely benefits that are due to avoiding some portion of the monetized accident impacts, as well as the additional non-monetized benefits . . . [the] EPA believes the costs of the rule are reasonable in comparison to its benefits."[76]

In delaying the effective date of the Chemical Disaster Rule, the Trump EPA ignored the agency's own prior findings about the benefits of the rule. The EPA dismissed the forgone benefits caused by the delay of the rule as "speculative at best,"[77] because of the "lack of a quantification of benefits in the final rule regulatory impact analysis."[78]

This conclusion is unsupportable. While insufficient data may render a particular benefit unquantifiable, that does not mean the benefit is "speculative." The term "speculative" (defined as "based on a guess and not on information"[79]), suggests that there may be no benefit at all, whereas an unquantified benefit is an expected benefit that cannot currently be quantified because of the lack of analytical techniques for doing so. Agencies cannot rationally ignore benefits just because they are unquantified. As the DC Circuit has held, "The mere fact that the magnitude of [an effect] is *uncertain* is no justification for *disregarding* the effect entirely."[80] In vacating the delay of the Chemical Disaster Rule, the DC Circuit took issue with the fact that the EPA did not "explain why the detailed factual findings regarding the harm that would be prevented upon implementation of the . . . Rule are now only 'speculative.'"[81]

In another example, in October 2018, the Trump administration attempted to extend various compliance deadlines for the Landfill Rule,[82] promulgated by the Obama administration in 2016, which was designed to reduce the emissions of greenhouse gases and other pollutants from landfills.[83] The rule was estimated to deliver significant monetized benefits—$440 million in the year 2025 alone—reducing methane and carbon dioxide emissions, which contribute to climate change, and by capturing otherwise wasted landfill gas and redirecting it to productive uses.[84] The EPA estimated that the corresponding annualized costs would be just $54 million, in the form of equipment installation, testing, and monitoring.[85] The rule could therefore be justified on the basis of the monetized costs and benefits alone.[86] The Landfill Rule also reduced emissions of volatile organic compounds, which are precursors to particulate matter and ozone, and reduced some organic hazardous air pollutants.[87] The agency found that reducing all of these pollutants would improve air quality and related health effects associated with exposure.[88] However, these benefits, unlike those resulting from methane and carbon dioxide reductions, could not be readily quantified.[89] The Obama administration made clear that the fact that it was difficult to model the direct and indirect impacts of the reductions in emissions with the data available at that time did not mean that benefits from such reductions did not exist.[90] In contrast, when justifying the delay, the Trump administration largely ignored the impact of forgone emissions reduction benefits, quantified or not.[91] It merely said that "although the costs and benefits of harmonizing the timing requirements of state plans cannot be quantified due to inherent uncertainties, the EPA believes that they will be minimal . . . ."[92]

But the mere fact that a benefit cannot currently be quantified does not mean that the benefit is "minimal." That an agency presently lacks the necessary data to quantify a given benefit has no relationship with the magnitude of the benefit, or the certainty that the benefit exists. In fact, some of the most substantial categories of monetized benefits of environmental regulation were at one time considered to be unquantifiable. Mortality risks, for example, were once ignored by agencies due to unsatisfactory methods for assigning a value to a regulation's expected lifesaving effects.[93] The development of the willingness-to-pay methodology allowed economists to determine how much people, on average, were willing to spend on reductions in risk.[94] This information could then be aggregated to determine the value of statistical life. The integration of the value of life in agency cost-benefit analysis has become standard practice and has been instrumental in supporting regulations with life-saving benefits that justify their cost.[95]

Not surprisingly, the Trump administration's effort to delay the Landfill Rule met with fierce resistance and was blocked in court. A judge on the United States District Court for the Northern District of California ordered the EPA to implement and enforce the requirements within a specific timeframe.[96] The states bringing the action and the EPA agreed that the agency had a mandatory duty to so. While the court noted the harmful impact of the types of pollution produced in landfill gas,[97] due to the parties' stipulation it did not analyze whether the EPA adequately considered the forgone benefits caused by delaying the rule but rather proceeded to determine a feasible timeline under which the EPA must implement the rule.[98]

Another example of the Trump administration's failure to take unquantified benefits into account involves BLM's repeal in December 2017 of the Fracking Rule,[99] promulgated by the Obama administration in 2015 in order to address the adverse consequences of extracting natural gas and oil through hydraulic fracturing.[100] The rule sought to "ensure wellbore integrity, protect water quality, and enhance public disclosure of chemicals and other details of hydraulic fracturing operations."[101] At the time of its promulgation, BLM had stated that "the primary challenge in monetizing benefits lies in the quantification of a baseline risk associated with specific operating practices and in the measurement of the change in that risk that the BLM can attribute to the rule's requirements."[102] For example, the agency indicated that while data are not clear about the exact difference between risk of spills using storage tanks or pits, there is widespread agreement that tanks—which the rule generally required—are the less risky option.[103] Quantifying the rule's benefits would require understanding this incremental risk reduction.[104] However, BLM underscored that this lack of quantification did not mean that the rule is without benefits[105] and expressed confidence that the overall risk reductions would be significant.[106] Ultimately, the agency concluded that the standards were "prudent," "necessary," and "common-sense,"[107] and that "potential benefits of the rule are significant."[108]

In repealing the Fracking Rule, the Trump administration repeatedly assumed that forgone benefits must be small or non-existent because they were unquantified, improperly equating quantification with significance. The repeal, for example, concluded that "any *marginal benefits* provided by the 2015 rule *do not outweigh* the rule's costs, even if those costs are a small percentage of the cost of a well. *In fact, benefits were largely unquantified* in the 2015 rule."[109]

The clear implication was that *because* the Fracking Rule's benefits were unquantified, they must have been very small and would therefore be outweighed by its costs. Along similar lines, the agency also indicated in the repeal that "there were *no monetary estimates of any incremental benefit* that the 2015 rule provides" and concluded that "such incremental benefits, however, are *likely to be too small . . .* to justify compliance *costs that are both monetized and certain to exist.*"[110] BLM thus implied that forgone benefits were not "certain to exist" because they were not monetized, and so assumed that in no case could non-monetized benefits possibly be large enough to justify a rule's monetized costs. A corollary to this analysis is that unquantified benefits, no matter how significant, could never justify the expenditure of any monetized costs, no matter how small. This position defies logic and is inconsistent with long-accepted and judicially approved approaches for dealing with unquantified benefits. The United States District Court for the Northern District of California rejected a legal challenge to the rule,[111] but the case is now on appeal to the Ninth Circuit.[112]

***

In a variety of ways discussed in this chapter, the Trump administration has shown how it privileges regulatory costs over benefits, leading to one-sided analyses of regulatory policies that contravene the most basic tenet of cost-benefit analysis: that costs and benefits should be compared on an equal footing. Right out of the gate, the president issued Executive Order 13,771, a one-sided policy that pays lip service to cost-benefit analysis while totally disregarding its central goal, which is to maximize net benefits to society, not to reduce regulatory costs for a favored few. A reduction of regulatory costs that is accompanied by a larger reduction of benefits is an affront to cost-benefit analysis. But the Trump administration celebrates such cost-reducing measures regardless of the magnitude of the forgone benefits. And it is particularly galling that OIRA —the institution charged with protecting the integrity of cost-benefit analysis—conducted this celebration and that Neomi Rao, the office's head before her appointment to the DC Circuit, vocally celebrated this affront.

Sometimes Executive Orders are written to please political constituencies and have little substantive significance.[113] That has not been the case here. The order was followed with significant regulatory actions seeking to delay or repeal signature initiatives of the Obama administration, focusing exclusively on the cost savings to industry and ignoring forgone benefits. And, in other cases in which the Trump administration actually acknowledged a rule's benefits, it did so only in a partial way, crediting the quantified benefits but ignoring the benefits that could not be quantified.

The Trump administration's one-sided approach to considering regulatory costs and ignoring the associated benefits has so far suffered a near-total rout in the courts, which, not surprisingly, have found this approach to be arbitrary and capricious. Similarly, the administration's treatment of unquantified benefits as speculative, insignificant, and uncertain, and therefore not worthy of attention, has also been met with successful court challenges because the law requires that agencies give due consideration to all benefits, regardless of whether they can be quantified.

These losses, however, do not make the affront on cost-benefit analysis any less pernicious, in part because the Trump administration is getting its way until a court can set aside its illegal actions—a process that is often lengthy. More significantly, these practices might be taken up by future administrations, particularly if over time the judiciary becomes less vigilant after repeated exposure to bad practices.

6

Erasing Public Health Science

In addition to acting as if deregulatory measures can be justified without regard to forgone benefits, the Trump administration is also engaged in more targeted but similarly unsupportable strategies. Chapter 5 analyzed the effort to assume away benefits entirely, justifying deregulatory actions solely on the basis of cost savings. In addition, the administration has called into question the scientific studies supporting the most significant health benefits of many rules. These included benefits that result from reducing particulate matter in the air. These air quality improvements are widely acknowledged to produce the largest monetized net benefits of all federal regulations. By ignoring validly conducted and well-respected peer-reviewed studies, the Trump administration is not just placing a light thumb on the scale against regulation—it is pressing down hard.

In this connection, in April 2018, the EPA, then headed by Administrator Scott Pruitt, proposed the Strengthening Transparency in Regulatory Science rule.[1] The EPA claimed that the proposal was "intended to strengthen the transparency of EPA regulatory science"[2] and would "help ensure that [the] EPA is pursuing its mission of protecting public health and the environment in a manner that the public can trust and understand."[3] Pruitt himself stated that the proposed rule signified that "the era of secret science at [the] EPA is coming to an end," adding that "the ability to test, authenticate, and reproduce scientific findings is vital for the integrity of [the] rulemaking process" and "Americans deserve to assess the legitimacy of the science underpinning EPA decisions that may impact their lives."[4] But, quite to the contrary, the main effect of the proposed rule would be to undermine the EPA's ability to use peer-reviewed epidemiological studies when setting standards to protect public health and the environment. These studies present the most direct and persuasive evidence of the adverse health effects of pollutants. Ignoring them will lead to uninformed and inadequately stringent standards that will cause unnecessary and avoidable disease and death.

There are two predominant sources of evidence on the adverse health effects of environmental contaminants: epidemiological studies on humans; and toxicological studies on laboratory animals.[5] The EPA-proposed "science transparency" rule will make it more difficult to use the first. Without these studies, the EPA will find it difficult to justify the regulation of harmful substances that cause tens of thousands of premature deaths each year. The Trump administration has now indicated that it wants to undermine the second source as well. The EPA has

Reviving Rationality. Michael A. Livermore and Richard L. Revesz, Oxford University Press (2020). © Oxford University Press. DOI: 10.1093/oso/9780197539446.001.0001.

proposed to reduce its requests for, and funding of, mammal studies by 30 percent by 2025 and to eliminate them altogether by 2035, though some may still be approved on a case-by-case basis.[6] Administrator Wheeler has alleged concerns for animal welfare in arguing for limits on animal testing. But, more likely, this action is undertaken at the behest of the chemical industry, which favors these moves because they will make it more difficult for the agency to regulate the harmful effects of their products.[7]

The efforts to impede these two sources of scientific support for environmental regulation are part of an overarching strategy by the Trump administration to obscure the significant benefits of regulation in general and of environmental regulation in particular. Some of the most serious risks posed by pollution could go unregulated if the administration has its way.

While the focus of this chapter is on epidemiological studies, which as discussed below, are the proposed "science transparency" rule's main target, its impact would extend far more broadly. For example, to monetize the benefits of reductions in premature deaths, the simple largest quantified component of the benefits of environmental regulation, economists have developed estimates for the value of statistical life. These widely used estimates are based on the Census of Fatal Occupational Injuries fatality data.[8] The CFOI data, which are confidential and never reported in journals that require data posting, could be just as vulnerable under the proposed rule as epidemiological studies.[9]

A Wolf in Sheep's Clothing

On first impression, the proposed "science transparency" rule might look like a beneficial attempt to improve the quality of scientific evidence used by the EPA. The rule states that "for the science pivotal to its significant regulatory actions, [the] EPA will ensure that the data and models underlying the science [are] publicly available in a manner sufficient for validation and analysis."[10] The proposed rule is also intended to ensure that decision making is marked by "reproducibility."[11] The EPA explained that "information is considered 'publicly available in a manner sufficient for validation and analysis' when it includes the information necessary for the public to understand, assess, and replicate findings."[12] According to the EPA, the proposed rule is "informed by the policies recently adopted by some major scientific journals,"[13] including *Science, Nature,* and the *Public Library of Science (PLoS),*[14] and "is consistent with . . . the focus on transparency in OMB's *Guidelines for Ensuring and Maximizing the Quality, Objectivity, Utility and Integrity of Information Disseminated by Federal Agencies.*"[15] And although the proposed rule "includes a provision allowing the Administrator to exempt significant regulatory decisions on a case-by-case basis if he or she determines that compliance is impracticable,"[16] the document gives virtually no guidance on when that might happen.

One does not need to scratch much below the surface to understand that the "science transparency" proposed rule would exclude a myriad of valid scientific studies from EPA consideration. Instead of a beneficial, good government measure, it is an effort to disregard the leading peer-reviewed epidemiological studies of the past and to make it virtually impossible for such studies to be considered in the future.

The EPA's proposed "science transparency" rule is the newest incarnation of past failed attempts to undermine the role of science in regulatory decision making. Prior to Pruitt's proposed rule, congressional Republicans had attempted to pass the Secret Science Reform Act of 2014,[17] the Secret Science Reform Act of 2015,[18] and the Honest and Open New EPA Science Treatment (HONEST) Act of 2017.[19] These past bills were similar to the proposed rule and all of them would have prohibited the agency from acting on valid scientific research. The proposed rule is a direct outgrowth of these efforts. Indeed, after the HONEST Act failed in the Senate, Representative Lamar Smith, its House sponsor, met with Pruitt to urge him to administratively adopt the legislation's policies.[20] In March 2018, during a closed-door meeting at the Heritage Foundation, Pruitt agreed to do so.[21] Pruitt's resignation in July 2018 seemed to call the future of the rule into question, but his successor, Andrew Wheeler, has repeatedly affirmed his commitment to seeing the rule through[22] and has issued a supplemental proposal doubling down on the Pruitt approach.[23]

The "science transparency" proposed rule would make it very difficult, in many cases downright impossible, for the EPA to rely on epidemiological studies—studies of the impact of pollutants on human populations—because of the confidentiality agreements necessary to obtain personal health data. These studies, which enjoy the support of the scientific community, provide the main justification—in some cases the only possible justification—for some of our most important environmental protections, which have significantly improved the lives of the American people.

The EPA makes several arguments in support of its "science transparency" proposal. It wrongly asserts that its proposal is consistent with the data-sharing policies of the leading scientific journals and with the replication standards of the Office of Management and Budget. The agency also maintains that the confidentiality of health data can be protected through data anonymization. The leading researchers in the area compellingly show that not to be the case. And the EPA's proposal is inconsistent with standard precepts of decision theory and cost-benefit principles. The proposed rule would cripple the ability to conduct future epidemiological studies and, if applied retroactively, would threaten to remove from consideration the leading research demonstrating the link between airborne pollutants and devastating public health consequences. In sum, as shown in the subsequent sections, the agency's claims that the proposed rule would make the science it relies on more credible and reliable do not withstand scrutiny. Instead, the agency—and the American people, whom it is charged with protecting—would be deprived of the benefit of studies meeting the high standards of the scientific community.

Ignoring Epidemiological Studies

The "science transparency" proposed rule could bar the agency from relying on epidemiological studies in the rulemaking process. Such studies typically collect years' worth of extensive, sensitive data on medical history, personal habits, and socioeconomic status from thousands of individuals. Data of this sort is generally protected by confidentiality agreements that bar researchers from sharing it in a manner that would allow an individual to be identified. Without such confidentiality protections, individuals typically would not agree to participate in studies requiring personal information.[24]

Many experts have expressed their concern about the impact that the proposed rule would have on the use of scientific data to inform EPA regulations, especially epidemiological studies. Nearly seventy public health, medical, academic, and scientific organizations wrote a joint letter to Pruitt explaining that while they support transparency in the scientific process, they strongly opposed the approach taken by the proposed rule.[25] The signatories explained that excluding studies simply because the raw data cannot be made publicly available would result in inadequately informed regulatory decisions that could subject people to real harm: "The result would be decisions affecting millions based on inadequate information that fails to include well-supported studies by expert scientists. These efforts are misguided and will not improve the quality of science used by [the] EPA nor allow the agency to fulfill its mandate of protecting human health and the environment."[26]

For example, there are many studies for which the underlying data cannot be made publicly available because doing so would be infeasible, counterproductive, or dangerous.[27] In particular, epidemiological studies would be especially vulnerable to exclusion.[28] Environmental epidemiologist Douglas Dockery, director of Harvard's Center for Environmental Health and a co-author of the Harvard Six Cities study, discussed later in this chapter, stated that the "science transparency" proposed rule would undermine how scientists track the effects of pollution and chemical exposure on public health, concluding that the proposed rule is "a direct assault on epidemiology."[29]

Indeed, under the "science transparency" proposed rule, many epidemiolog-   .
ical studies that are pertinent to the EPA's work could not be considered during
the rulemaking process due to data confidentiality obligations. For example,
in a study published in the *American Journal of Respiratory and Critical Care
Medicine* in June 2018, researchers found, for the first time, that fine particulate
matter exposure was more strongly associated with respiratory emergency hospital visits for children than for adults, while ozone exposure was more strongly
associated with respiratory emergency hospital visits for adults than for children.
The researchers concluded that in light of this finding, relying on Medicare data
and other studies that restrict their analysis to populations over age sixty-five
"could underestimate population respiratory health impacts of $PM_{2.5}$ or ozone."[30]
However, because the study was based on confidential emergency room visit
records aggregated by state agencies to protect the patients' privacy, the proposed
rule would bar the EPA from considering it.[31]

In addition to excluding studies that have already been conducted, the rule
will have a devastating effect on future research. Most obviously, absent confidentiality agreements, it would be very difficult to recruit subjects for epidemiological studies. Few people want their most private habits—that they
engage in risky activities, for example—or detailed information about their
health disclosed publicly for everyone to see. Peter Thorne, a toxicologist at the
University of Iowa and former chair of the EPA's science advisory board, said that
with the "science transparency" proposed rule in place, researchers might have
more trouble recruiting participants for epidemiological studies in the future because of a fear that their personal information would ultimately be shared with
the government.[32]

Some scientists have considered alternative study designs that would allow for
the public disclosure of some data while maintaining confidentiality obligations,
but these efforts are unlikely to satisfy the proposed rule's requirements. For example, Joel Kaufman, an epidemiologist at the University of Washington, is currently conducting a study for which he is attempting to create a "limited" dataset
that could be shared with other researchers consistent with confidentiality
restrictions under which he obtained the data, but believes that any reasonable
efforts to protect confidentiality will not satisfy the rule.[33]

The "science transparency" proposed rule is likely to have particularly pernicious effects for studies using data from low-probability but high-impact
events, including natural disasters, environmental catastrophes, wars, or terrorist attacks. If replication becomes a requirement for the use of scientific data,
then a great deal of data collected in the real world might be barred. Obvious
examples of non-replicable events include data of human exposure to pollution
or toxins resulting from natural disasters, including oil spills, such as the 2009

BP Deepwater Horizon catastrophe in the Gulf of Mexico; events like the nuclear plant failures in Chernobyl and Fukushima; fallout from deployment of nuclear weapons in Hiroshima and Nagasaki; or the long-term health effects for first responders to the September 11, 2001, terrorist attacks. In its own data guidelines developed during the George W. Bush administration, the Office of Management and Budget explicitly identified this problem, noting that "it may not be feasible to replicate the radiation exposures studied after the Chernobyl accident."[34]

Focusing on studies of this sort, a group of nearly 1,000 scientists from across the United States sent a letter to Pruitt explaining that the proposed rule would exclude critically important public health studies because their underlying data cannot be replicated.[35] And, at the proposed rule's public hearing, the American Pediatric Association, the American Lung Association, and former government employees with regulatory experience in the multiple agencies all raised these concerns as well.[36]

Meta-Analysis and Decision Theory

The "science transparency" proposed rule could also cast a pall over meta-analyses, another significant category of studies linking exposure to contaminants and adverse health effects. Meta-analyses, which aggregate the results of large numbers of studies, including epidemiological studies, have become increasingly prevalent and are an important, standard tool in the field of public health.[37] There would be negative consequences if, in order to meet the requirements of the proposed rule, researchers begin to exclude from their meta-analyses studies for which the underlying data are not publicly available. Excluding these studies risks introducing systemic bias into the meta-analyses, undercutting their ultimate quality. For an optimal meta-analysis, researchers first select studies based on how relevant they are to answering the question of interest. In aggregating the relevant pool of studies, researchers would weigh each study based on that study's evidentiary value. As long as a study has any evidentiary value whatsoever, researchers would include it. Failing to do so would result in a less precise aggregate estimate. Thus, the proposed rule would allow the EPA to consider meta-analyses only if researchers violate the best practices, endorsed in the scientific community, for how meta-analysis should be conducted.[38] Of even more immediate concern, existing meta-analyses may need to be disregarded if they are based on at least some studies that rely on confidential data.

Designating a study as having no evidentiary value simply because the underlying data cannot be made publicly available is arbitrary and would result in a less accurate average estimate.[39] Moreover, it would reduce the sample size of a meta-analysis so that drawing legitimate statistical conclusions from the data would be more difficult.[40] Additionally, excluding studies based on whether the data are publicly disclosed may result in biased estimates if the estimates in studies for which the data are not publicly disclosed differ from the estimates in other studies.[41] And doing so is inconsistent with the EPA's own guidance for conducting meta-analyses.[42]

Even if epidemiological studies in the future are conducted in a manner that complies with the "science transparency" proposed rule, past studies still could not be included in meta-analyses. The entire purpose of a meta-analysis is to aggregate large numbers of scientific studies that incorporate different datasets and research methods. The proposed rule would make it impossible for scientists to conduct scientifically appropriate meta-analyses.

The proposed rule's all-or-nothing approach, in which scientific evidence is credited if it meets its data transparency requirements and must be ignored if it does not, is also inconsistent with key precepts of decision theory. In particular, outright exclusion of scientific studies based on arbitrary criteria, such as whether a study's underlying data are publicly available, will result in the exclusion of relevant, valid, peer-reviewed science from EPA consideration. Given accepted approaches to decision theory, the agency should take account of all available evidence and update its assessments in light of new evidence.[43] Under this approach, the agency would use all studies that include potentially valuable information to inform its belief about the costs and benefits of regulation. And it would place weight on each study in proportion to that study's evidentiary value.

If the agency had a defensible reason to believe that studies have higher evidentiary value if their data are publicly available, then, other things being equal, it should place a higher weight on those studies. But there is no justification for treating the availability of information as more important than any other consideration by altogether ignoring studies that do not have publicly available data. Indeed, data availability is not the only factor that could plausibly affect the weight accorded to a particular study. Other factors include the size of the sample, the age of the study, the publication in a peer-reviewed journal, and the transparency of the estimation technique.

Taken to its logical conclusion, the EPA's approach could lead to a nihilistic situation in which all scientific data are excluded. As anyone who submits articles to peer-reviewed journals can attest, referees almost always subject articles to criticism. If every departure from perfection, which is necessary given data or methodological limitations, were a reason to ignore a study's conclusions, we might end up in a world in which no scientific studies could be used for regulatory purposes. In such a world, of course, deadly harms would go unregulated. For this reason, the scientific community uses peer review and widely accepted disciplinary norms, as opposed to perfection, as the standard for crediting scientific work. And, as indicated above, the peer-review practices of the leading journals do not require the data-disclosure straitjacket of the EPA's proposed rule.

False Claims about the Scientific Consensus

The EPA's justifications for its radical proposal, which would allow dangerous pollutants to be inadequately regulated or unregulated altogether, are based on false claims that do not withstand serious scrutiny. For example, in its proposal, the EPA wrote that the "science transparency" proposed rule is "informed by the policies recently adopted by some major scientific journals,"[44] including *Science, Nature,* and *Public Library of Science (PLoS).*[45] The head editors of those journals published a joint statement in response to the proposed rule, emphasizing that while they require that all data be made available to other researchers for the purposes of reproducing or extending the analysis of a study, the data need not be made publicly available.[46] Moreover, the editors stress that "exceptional circumstances, where data cannot be shared openly with all, include data sets featuring personal identifiers," thus recognizing that full transparency is not appropriate for epidemiological studies. And they explain that "the merits of studies relying on data that cannot be made publicly available can still be judged" because "reviewers can have confidential access to key data and as a core skill, scientists are trained in assessing research publications by judging the articulation and logic of the research design, the clarity of the description of the methods used for data collection and analysis, and appropriate citation of previous results." The editors conclude by stressing the importance that public policies rely on "the full suite of relevant science vetted through peer review" and that "excluding relevant studies simply because they do not meet rigid transparency standards will adversely affect decision-making processes."

More generally, these leading journals, along with over 1,000 other journals, have adopted the 2015 Transparency and Openness Promotion guidelines, which are graduated transparency standards that provide flexibility to reflect disciplinary needs while observing a set of principles that are shared throughout the scientific community.[47] Unlike the proposed rule, these guidelines recognize that the ability of researchers to share data differs across scientific disciplines. Accordingly, the guidelines facilite the production of reliable science while allowing for flexibility in situations where data cannot be made publicly available.

Science, Nature, and *PLoS* have all incorporated these guidelines in their research data-sharing policies, allowing them to encourage data transparency while acknowledging that public data disclosure is not feasible in studies where researchers must protect the confidentiality of personal information. Unlike the proposed rule, the policies of these journals encourage data transparency but do not strictly require that the data underlying scientific studies be made publicly available in order to evaluate the credibility of a study.

Prominent scientists similarly took issue with the EPA's approach. For example, John Ioannidis, chair in Disease Prevention at the Stanford University School of Medicine, published an article criticizing the "science transparency" proposed rule.[48] Although Ioannidis believes that direct access to data is an indicator of transparency[49] and making data widely available is an "exciting, worthy aspiration,"[50] he explained that the proposed rule would be harmful to EPA decision making because "most of the raw data from past studies are not publicly available."[51] Ioannidis pointed out that in a random sample of 268 biomedical papers published from 2000 to 2014, none of them provided access to all of their raw data, and "the proportion of studies that have had their raw data independently re-analyzed is probably less than one in a thousand."[52] Thus, he concluded that the proposed rule would lead the EPA to exclude so much relevant research that it would practically eliminate science from the decision-making process, leaving regulations to be designed "on opinion and whim."[53]

Inconsistency with Established Government Practices

In another false assertion seeking to claim support for its misguided policy proposal, the EPA suggested that the "science transparency" proposed rule is consistent with the focus on transparency in OMB's *Guidelines for Ensuring and Maximizing the Quality, Objectivity, Utility and Integrity of Information Disseminated by Federal Agencies.*[54] Unlike the proposed rule, the OMB Guidelines do not try to strictly link data transparency to scientific credibility. Instead of the one-size-fits-all approach of the EPA proposal, the OMB Guidelines contemplate a broader scope for the requirement of reproducibility. In particular, they urge caution, particularly in the case of epidemiological studies, "because it may often be impractical or even impermissible or unethical to apply the reproducibility standard to such data."[55] And the guidelines ask "that agencies consider, in developing their own guidelines, which categories of original and supporting data should be subject to the reproducibility standard and which should not."[56] The guidelines recognize that "even in a situation where the original and supporting data are protected by confidentiality concerns, or the analytic computer models or other research methods may be kept confidential to protect intellectual property, it may still be feasible to have the analytic results subject to the reproducibility standard."[57] For example, they note that the results could be replicated by "a qualified party, operating under the same confidentiality protections as the original analysts."[58] The proposed rule misleadingly cites the OMB Guidelines without acknowledging any of these essential distinctions.

Neither the scientific practices of the leading journals nor the OMB Guidelines do anything remotely similar to what the EPA proposal attributes to them. Instead of adopting the EPA's wooden, inflexible approach, which is at odds with the way science is conducted, the scientific journals and the OMB Guidelines explicitly tailor the data disclosure requirements to the needs of particular types of research and recognize that for epidemiological studies there are serious limits on what data can be disclosed.

Data Anonymization

In its proposal, the EPA acknowledges that a significant amount of raw data cannot be made entirely publicly available for legal and ethical reasons. However, the EPA suggested that these concerns can be addressed with "simple" techniques such as data masking, coding, and de-identification measures.[59] Along these lines, some of the most prominent trade associations representing regulated entities closely aligned with the deregulatory policies of the Trump administration, including the National Association of Manufacturers, American Chemistry Council, and American Petroleum Institute, encouraged the EPA to implement or develop de-identification strategies and protected data-sharing mechanisms, arguing that this would be sufficient for maintaining anonymity and protecting individuals' privacy.[60] Going further, the Fertilizer Institute claimed that arguments that confidentially protected data is a barrier to implementing the "science transparency" proposed rule are "red herrings."[61]

The EPA and the trade associations supporting its position have vastly oversimplified the nature of the confidentiality problem. Indeed, measures like data de-identification and masking are widely known to be ineffectual because anonymized datasets can be combined with additional publicly available information to uniquely identify individuals. As an illustration of this problem, Latanya Sweeney, a professor of government and technology at Harvard University and one of the leading scholars in the field of data privacy, used data from the 1990 census to determine that 87 percent of Americans are uniquely identified by the combination of their ZIP code, birthdate, and gender.[62] And it is especially easy to re-identify individuals living in small rural communities.[63]

Sweeney powerfully identified this phenomenon while she was still in graduate school, using an ostensibly anonymous dataset containing every Massachusetts employee's hospital visits. William Weld, the governor at the time, had assured the public that patient privacy had been protected because the dataset excluded obvious individual identifiers, such as name, address, and social security number. However, the dataset still contained the ZIP code, birthdate, and gender of every individual. To prove how easy it was to re-identify the individuals using this information, Sweeney used publicly available voter roll information—which included the name, address, ZIP code, birth date, and gender of every voter—and cross-referenced it with the health data. By combining these datasets, Sweeney was able to uniquely identify Governor Weld's health data, which she sent to his office.[64] As a result, Paul Ohm, a professor at Georgetown University Law Center and a prominent expert in information privacy and computer crime law, argues that "data can be either useful or perfectly anonymous but never both."[65]

Similarly, a group of Belgian scientists recently published an article in *Nature Communications* setting forth a method that can accurately estimate the likelihood of a specific person being re-identified from a de-identified dataset.[66] Using their model, the scientists found that 99.98 percent of Americans would be re-identified in any dataset using fifteen demographic attributes. The scientists concluded by explaining that "even heavily sampled anonymized datasets are unlikely to satisfy the modern standards for anonymization set forth by [the European General Data Protection Regulation] and seriously challenge the technical and legal adequacy of the de-identification release-and-forget model."

At the same time, when datasets are stripped of so much useful identifying information, like age, gender, and occupation, they become less useful for epidemiological research. For example, in a dataset that contains individuals' names, gender, birthdate, ZIP code, and health conditions, a researcher may want to redact the names, gender, and birthdate of the individuals to protect anonymity before sharing the dataset with other researchers. However, with this new dataset, future researchers would be able to correlate health issues only with ZIP code, without taking into account potentially confounding variables like age and gender. A new, redacted dataset of this sort would certainly not be as valuable as the original in reproducing results or conducting further analysis.

Instead of redaction, researchers' standard protocol is to protect anonymity by aggregating the data. Speaking to this point, Peter Thorne, director of the Environmental Health Sciences Research Center at the University of Iowa College of Public Health and former chairman of the EPA's Science Advisory Board, said that if he had to redact a dataset, "it would have far less value than it has when [he] aggregate[s] it," because he would have to "redact so much of it, there would be nothing left."[67] Thorne explained that "when researchers disclose their datasets, they don't black out personal health information; instead, they group the results."[68] Thorne offered an example, explaining that "if [he] enrolled 100 people in a specific ZIP code, and 70 developed asthma and 30 didn't [he would] disclose data on those groups rather than individuals [to] protect people's privacy."[69] But this aggregation procedure, though more scientifically appropriate, would run afoul of the "science transparency" commands in the proposed rule.

The Likely Target

A particularly problematic consequence would follow if the EPA applied the proposed rule retroactively to prior studies. The proposal did not take a position on this enormously important issue, instead soliciting comments on whether the "science transparency" proposed rule should apply to scientific studies that were completed before the rule's effective date.[70]

If the proposed rule only applies to future regulations—that is, if it applies solely prospectively—researchers and scientists may be able to start adapting the design of some studies to meet the requirements of the proposed rule.[71] However, if the proposed rule applies retroactively to studies that have already been completed, then the EPA could not rely on these studies, even if they were published in the leading peer-reviewed journals, in setting regulations to protect public health and the environment. Some of the most important environmental regulations, which save tens of thousands of lives each year, would be deprived of their scientific support. Even if the existing rules relying on these studies were not called into question, they could be weakened when they are next amended.

Not surprisingly, the EPA received numerous comments on this issue. The major scientific organizations vigorously opposed the retroactive application of the proposed rule. For example, the American Association for the Advancement of Science urged that all prior studies be exempt from the proposed rule.[72] And the EPA's own Science Advisory Board, even after Pruitt purged it of many of the academic scientists and filled the positions with employees of regulated entities,[73] called the wisdom of retroactive application into question. The Science Advisory Board indicated instead that "it might be easier to accomplish the rule's objectives if the focus were on future studies rather than on studies that are already designed and published with terms that make complete transparency difficult or impossible to accomplish."[74]

The regulated community was divided on the question. The American Chemistry Council, a prominent trade association representing chemical companies that generally opposes regulation, took issue with the retroactive application of the "science transparency" proposed rule. It indicated that "retrospective application of any regulation (and its underlying scientific evaluations) is rife with complication, confusion, and significant ambiguity for the EPA and stakeholders alike."[75] Using the National Ambient Air Quality Standards

(NAAQS) under the Clean Air Act as an example, it explained that "each NAAQS review under the [act] is based on a substantial amount of scientific and policy information" and "the retroactive application of this proposal to those administrative records would only serve to confuse, distress, and impede a NAAQS review process that is already severely overburdened."[76]

In contrast, the American Petroleum Institute, a prominent trade association representing oil companies, which normally is aligned with the American Chemistry Council, parted ways with its usual ally on this matter. It argued that the proposed rule should apply retroactively to studies that the EPA has previously relied on in promulgating regulations.[77]

Among the most significant consequences of the proposed rule is the potential exclusion of two landmark studies that reveal the health consequences of particulate matter. The Harvard Six Cities study, a large-scale epidemiological study published in 1993,[78] and a subsequent epidemiological study from the American Cancer Society, published in 1995,[79] are widely regarded as the leading studies of the adverse health consequences of particulate matter in the ambient air. These two studies were foundational to the EPA's subsequent strengthening of the NAAQS for particulate matter.[80]

The reason that so much is at stake is that reductions in particulate matter prevent a large number of premature deaths. According to a 2016 OMB report, EPA rules accounted for 61 percent to 80 percent of the monetized benefits from all major federal regulations over the past ten years, with 98 percent to 99 percent of those monetized benefits coming from air quality rules.[81] Moreover, the estimated benefits of air quality rules "are mostly attributable to the reduction in public exposure to fine particulate matter."[82] Reductions in exposure to fine particulate matter under the Clean Air Act have yielded myriad health benefits, including preventing, annually, nearly 230,000 premature deaths, 180,000 cases of acute bronchitis, 200,000 heart attacks, and 2.4 million cases of asthma exacerbation.[83] As a result, the consequences of not considering the Harvard Six Cities study and American Cancer Society study in future revisions of the particulate matter standards could be extremely serious, needlessly placing at risk the lives of large numbers of Americans.

This is not the first time that anti-regulatory figures have attempted to cast doubt on the Harvard Six Cities and American Cancer Society studies in an effort to undermine EPA regulations. In 2013, Republican representative Lamar Smith, then the chairman of the Committee on Science, Space, and Technology, who years later pressed Pruitt to propose the "science transparency" rule, subpoenaed the raw data of the two studies, arguing that "regulations based on secret data have no place in a democracy."[84] He was ultimately unsuccessful in his legislative quest, as the studies' research teams refused to turn over the data, explaining that they had to protect the participants' confidentiality.

These complaints are being leveled even though both the Harvard Six Cities study and the American Cancer Society study have been the subject of independent verification. When the findings of the Harvard Six Cities study were first published, industry groups attacked the research, primarily by claiming that it contained "secret science."[85] In the original publication of the study, the researchers provided the participant data only in an aggregated format. The data for each individual could not be made publicly available due to the patient confidentiality agreements under which the information was obtained.[86] For each city, the researchers provided summary statistics for twenty-one metrics such as the percentage of males and females, the percentage of smokers, and the average age.[87]

In July 2000, in response to the industry complaints, the researchers asked the Health Effects Institute, an organization co-funded by the EPA and the automobile industry, to determine whether the study's conclusions were correct.[88] To do so, the institute was given access to the individual-level data. Like the original researchers, it had to sign strict confidentiality agreements.[89]

The Reanalysis Team of the Health Effects Institute (HEI) performed a quality assurance audit of a sample of the original data of both the Harvard Six Cities study and the American Cancer Society study, which "revealed the data to be of generally high quality with a few exceptions" due to a small number of coding errors.[90] Correcting these errors did not materially change the original results.

In addition to verifying data quality, the Reanalysis Team tested the robustness of the original results with alternative models. For example, it controlled for more variables and added interactions between variables that the original studies had not included. The work of the Reanalysis Team was then "intensively and independently peer reviewed by a Special Panel of the HEI Health Review Committee."[91] The Health Effects Institute concluded that "the Reanalysis Team identified relatively robust associations of mortality with fine particles, sulfate, and sulfur dioxide, and they tested these associations in nearly every possible manner within the limitations of the datasets."[92]

Opposing the "science transparency" proposed rule, George Thurston, a scientist at the New York University School of Medicine who worked on the Reanalysis Team, explained that the EPA already has the ability to independently verify scientific studies through organizations like the Health Effects Institute. Thurston wrote that instead of requiring that data be made publicly available through the proposed rule, the EPA should fund "such independent assessments, without risking private research data." [93]

And, ironically, the OMB Guidelines—on which, as discussed above, the EPA relies for support of its proposed rule—use the Health Effects Institute's reanalysis of the Harvard Six Cities study and American Cancer Society study as an example of how to comply with a reproducibility standard for scientific studies without violating the confidentiality agreements necessary to obtain the data on which the studies are based.[94]

If the EPA truly cared about increasing transparency, credibility, and reliability, it would at least consider expanding the role of unbiased third-party organizations to perform independent analyses of the scientific studies the EPA relies on. Instead, the EPA has chosen to propose a rule that would make it impossible for the agency to rely on a vast literature of important epidemiological studies and would completely throw out some of the most important public health science available. The EPA has tried to mask the proposed rule as a policy that would increase scientific credibility and reliability. In reality, the proposed rule is a thinly veiled attempt at excluding science from the EPA's rulemaking process, particularly the Harvard Six Cities study and the American Cancer Society study.

***

The "science transparency" proposed rule attempts to undermine the EPA's ability to set effective public health and environmental protections. Epidemiological studies, which are especially vulnerable to exclusion, have been instrumental in determining the benefits of EPA regulations that protect public health and the environment. Promoting transparency is clearly desirable, but the EPA's blunt, one-size-fits-all approach, as opposed to the contextually sensitive approaches of the scientific community, threatens to erase the conclusions of well-conducted, peer-reviewed, and appropriately replicated studies, cutting the legs from under regulations that have brought enormous benefits to the American people in the form of large numbers of avoided deaths, heart attacks, strokes, and serious respiratory problems. And there is good reason to suspect, given the long-standing efforts of congressional Republicans and of the Trump administration's interest group allies, that behind this seemingly general proposal is the very specific objective of, once again, casting doubt on the Harvard Six Cities study and American Cancer Society study.

These two studies are largely responsible for providing the scientific support for the air quality rules that constitute a majority of all the monetized benefits of federal regulations. Ignoring studies such as these will significantly worsen the quality of regulatory outcomes. If the EPA's genuine aim is to improve the scientific integrity of its rulemaking processes, there are good-faith alternatives that, unlike the proposed rule, enjoy the support of the scientific community. That it has chosen not to do so is an indication that the rule's purported goal of transparency is merely a means to the true end of erasing the scientific basis for major environmental protections.

7
Resurrecting Discredited Models

Chapters 5 and 6 analyzed alternative strategies used by the Trump administration to provide a veneer of rationality to its deregulatory agenda. First, it has tried to justify deregulation by looking exclusively at cost savings to regulated industry and ignoring forgone public health and environmental benefits. Second, disregarding the consensus of the scientific community and consistent regulatory practices by administrations of both parties over decades, the Trump administration has called into question the validity of epidemiological studies, which are one of the two main categories of studies of the adverse health effects of contaminants.

This chapter focuses on an additional strategy undertaken by the Trump administration in its effort to undermine cost-benefit analysis. In case both tactics criticized in the prior two chapters fail, the Trump administration is pushing another argument, also flatly inconsistent with the scientific consensus: that the most prevalent air pollutants in general, and that particulate matter in particular, have thresholds below which they produce no adverse health effects. In doing so, it can hide an important proportion of the health benefits of regulation.[1]

When confronted with the potential for pollutants to cause serious health effects, scientists need to identify the relationship between exposure to these substances and damage to the body. One refrain common among medical experts for generations was that "the dose makes the poison."[2] This phrase evoked the idea that exposures are harmless until some threshold is reached; only after being subjected to a high enough amount would people experience any negative health consequences.

But, as scientists began studying pollutants like radiation and particulate matter in greater detail, they concluded that while there are certain substances that do cause harm only above an exposure threshold, many dangerous chemicals do not have a threshold below which no harm occurs. Instead, any amount of exposure can cause damage to the human body, though the effects are more severe at higher concentrations.[3] As a result of these more modern scientific understandings, for more than four decades, under administrations of both parties, federal agencies have treated two important classes of pollutants as non-threshold contaminants: carcinogens, and the six so-called criteria pollutants regulated by the Clean Air Act (ground level ozone, particulate matter, carbon monoxide, lead, sulfur dioxide, and nitrogen dioxide).

Reviving Rationality. Michael A. Livermore and Richard L. Revesz, Oxford University Press (2020). © Oxford University Press. DOI: 10.1093/oso/9780197539446.001.0001.

The Trump administration is now trying to act against the scientific consensus and, without any plausible justification, depart from settled administrative practices. A major focus of this effort is particulate matter, which poses extraordinarily serious threats to public health. If the Trump administration can lower the estimated benefits associated with particulate matter reductions, it will have an easier task in providing a cost-benefit justification for its deregulatory actions.[4]

The Trump administration is engaged in this effort with the support of industry advocates, who have discredited themselves repeatedly over more than half a century by attacking the scientific consensus behind government regulation of tobacco, acid rain, and other threats to health and the environment.[5] In contrast, the administration's efforts are opposed, as was the case with the Science Transparency Rule discussed in chapter 6, by the leadership of the scientific community and by the EPA's own science advisors.

Emergence of a Non-Threshold Consensus

The earliest studies demonstrating that pollution could cause harm even at very low doses concerned carcinogenic pollutants. Research into how carcinogens damage the body expanded dramatically following the development of nuclear technology and increasing concerns about the release of radioactive isotopes through atomic testing.[6] This work led to the realization that there was no threshold below which cells showed no damage once exposed to radiation.[7]

Over many decades, the EPA built off this insight to model the relationship between many different types of carcinogens and human health impacts. For example, the EPA has taken the position stated in its Guidelines for Carcinogen Risk Assessment that a carcinogen does not have a threshold below which it poses no adverse health effects unless there is sufficient pollutant-specific data suggesting that a threshold exists for that pollutant. Other federal regulatory agencies like the Occupational Safety and Health Administration and Food and Drug Administration have similarly taken the position that, presumptively, carcinogens have no thresholds.

The basic approach taken by the EPA and other federal agencies involves first identifying the "mode of action" for carcinogens, which describes the sequence of events and processes resulting in cancer formation. The mode of action can help scientists discern whether there is a threshold for the substance as well as whether the association between exposure and harm is linear in nature. A linear relationship means that negative effects increase proportionally as the amount of exposure rises. Non-linear associations can show different patterns. For example, an additional unit of concentration might produce more negative health impacts at higher concentrations than at lower ones. Once the EPA determines the mode of action, it models how exposure relates to risk of harm based on that mode of action. As one would expect, if the mode suggests a linear, non-threshold relationship, the EPA will model the relationship in that way. If, in contrast, the mode suggests a non-linear relationship or a threshold, the EPA will use those models instead. In situations where the EPA does not have enough data to model the mode of action for carcinogens, it adopts a linear, non-threshold model as a default.[8]

Research into noncarcinogenic chemicals eventually revealed that many of them, such as carbon monoxide and ozone, also did not appear to have a threshold below which no injuries occurred. Nevertheless, in its earliest analyses in the 1970s, the EPA, in formulating regulations for the criteria pollutants— ground level ozone, particulate matter, carbon monoxide, lead, sulfur dioxide, and nitrogen dioxide—used language suggesting threshold models for these pollutants.[9]

By 1977, only a few years after the federal government began formulating these regulatory standards, studies of air pollutants had provided strong evidence of a non-threshold relationship between exposure and harm. The evidence was so strong that a congressional committee referred to the notion of a " 'no-effect' concentration" as a "chimera."[10] As a result, in the 1977 amendments of the Clean Air Act, it adopted a regulatory program called Prevention of Significant Deterioration, which constrains the degradation of ambient air quality in areas that have air quality that is better than the required ambient standards, contained in the National Ambient Air Quality Standards (NAAQS).[11] If criteria pollutants had thresholds and if the standards were set at these thresholds, then there would be no reason for Congress to provide additional protection. Thus, in the 1977 amendments to the Clean Air Act, Congress rejected the threshold argument now being made by the Trump administration.

Also in the late 1970s, the emerging scientific consensus led the EPA to adopt linear, non-threshold modeling for criteria pollutants. Since then, the agency has consistently treated criteria pollutants as non-threshold pollutants under administrations of both parties, in line with the scientific consensus, an enormous body of literature, and the practice of other federal agencies.

There is also growing evidence that the EPA should stop using the threshold concept for other noncarcinogenic substances, not just those classified as criteria pollutants under the Clean Air Act. Unlike its approach to modeling risk for carcinogens and criteria pollutants, for other compounds the EPA does assume that there is a threshold below which exposure will not lead to adverse health impacts. However, epidemiological studies have documented human health impacts at lower and lower levels of exposure to a variety of chemicals. These findings led the National Research Council of the National Academy of

Sciences to conclude in an influential 2009 report, *Science and Decisions*, that the threshold assumption model for most noncarcinogens currently used by the EPA is based on an outdated scientific understanding developed between the 1950s and the 1980s and "does not make the best possible use of available scientific evidence."[12] For these substances, instead of assuming a threshold model as the default and a non-threshold model as the exception, the better approach would be the opposite: a non-threshold model as the default and a threshold model as the exception where specific evidence for a given pollutant suggests it would be appropriate.[13] Though the EPA has consistently applied, for decades, the non-threshold assumption for carcinogens and criteria pollutants, the agency has not yet attempted to follow the 2009 recommendation to do away with using thresholds for evaluating the health impacts of other chemicals.[14] The European Commission, however, has signaled that, in at least some contexts, it may be moving more broadly toward using non-threshold models.[15]

Moreover, non-threshold models are generally more appropriate for analyzing population-level risk, which is what environmental standards are designed to reduce, because of the differential sensitivity that individuals exhibit toward contaminants. Each individual person has a unique sensitivity to pollution exposures, and there is considerable evidence that certain segments of the population are particularly susceptible to harm.[16] For example, very young children, pregnant women, or the elderly frequently will be more sensitive to toxins when exposed at the same level as the average population.[17] As a result, even if there were a threshold for a person of average sensitivity, the threshold for an exceptionally sensitive person would necessarily be lower. And the threshold would be lower still, or even non-existent, for the most sensitive individuals in the population. In other words, even if individual toxicity thresholds existed, population-level toxicity would still be best modeled with non-threshold models. If an agency instead modeled the health risks of pollutants according to a toxicity threshold for the average person, it would be leaving more sensitive people unprotected.[18]

Particulate Matter and Public Health

As mentioned earlier, the EPA has long relied on a linear, non-threshold model for particulate matter, a criteria pollutant that is especially dangerous to human health. Particulate matter is a mixture of very small particles and liquid droplets that are found in the air. Some particles, such as dust, dirt, soot, and smoke, are large enough to be visible, while others are too small to be seen with the naked eye. The EPA regulates particulate matter differently depending on the size of the particles because of variations in risk; smaller particles pose more of a danger because they penetrate farther into the lungs. Exposure to particulate matter can have negative effects on lung and heart health, causing coughing or difficulty breathing, aggravating asthma, decreasing lung function, and contributing to heart attacks and irregular heartbeat. Exposure can be deadly, particularly for people with heart or lung disease.[19]

As indicated in chapter 6, two studies have provided the most important evidence on the adverse health effects of particulate matter: the Harvard Six Cities study[20] and an American Cancer Society study.[21] Published in the 1990s based on data collected over decades, they present robust evidence on the negative effects of particulate matter from exposures at very low concentrations.[22] More recent follow-up research has confirmed the original findings of the two studies,[23] and the EPA has continued to rely on their assessments in formulating air quality standards for particulate matter,[24] as well as other emission controls that affect particulate levels.[25]

Experts outside of the EPA widely agree that the findings of the Harvard Six Cities study and the American Cancer Society study demonstrate that particulate matter is a non-threshold pollutant. In 2002, relying on the American Cancer Society study, the National Research Council's Committee on Estimating the Health-Risk-Reduction Benefits of Proposed Air Pollution Regulations[26] concluded that "there is no evidence for any . . . indication of a threshold" for particulate matter.[27] Additionally, the Health Effects Subcommittee of the Advisory Council on Clean Air Compliance Analysis relied on both the Six Cities Study and the American Cancer Society study to conclude that it "fully supports [the] EPA's use of a no-threshold model to estimate the mortality reductions associated with reduced particulate matter exposure."[28] It reasoned that the EPA's "decision is supported by the data, which are quite consistent in showing effects down to the lowest measured levels."[29]

The findings have also been corroborated by additional research conducted separately from the follow-up work to the two studies. For instance, the American Thoracic Society has found adverse health effects even in areas meeting current air quality standards for particulate matter set through the NAAQS.[30] A separate investigation by the Harvard School of Public Health produced similar results, and concluded that there is no evidence to suggest a threshold exists for particulate matter risks.[31] Global data compiled by the World Health Organization, a specialized agency of the United Nations, also supports the absence of a threshold for particulate matter; research throughout the world has found damage even at very low concentrations below current US standards.[32]

The body of scientific evidence overwhelmingly supports the conclusion that particulate matter causes negative health effects at even the lowest levels of exposure, meaning there is no safe threshold below which risks would be eliminated for all individuals in a population. In 2006, the EPA solicited a report from experts in epidemiology, toxicology, and medicine to offer their expert opinions on the scientific evidence regarding the concentration-response relationship between small particulate matter particles and mortality.[33] All the contributors agreed that there was no epidemiological evidence to support the existence of a threshold.[34] The consensus of the group was that using a threshold model would also be inappropriate for determining potential harm from particulate matter, given that variations in genetic, environmental, and socioeconomic factors can make certain people experience negative effects at even small exposure levels.[35] A 2010 scientific report by the American Heart Association reached similar conclusions.[36] The report comprehensively reviewed studies on the relationship between particulate matter and heart health that had been published in the preceding five years.[37] It concluded that there was no safe threshold of exposure for particulate matter.[38]

A Consistent Regulatory Approach

As a result of the plethora of evidence on the absence of a threshold for particulate matter, the EPA has, under administrations of both parties, set air quality standards for particulate matter using non-threshold models for decades. The EPA has incorporated the models in its regulatory impact analyses, which calculate the costs and benefits of pollution restrictions. In these evaluations, the EPA estimates benefits for reducing particulate matter all the way to zero in order to account for the harm caused by even the lowest levels of the pollutant.

Beginning with the Reagan administration, the EPA stated that no evidence supported the use of a threshold for particulate matter and adopted a linear non-threshold model for the pollutant.[39] Likewise, the Clinton EPA issued NAAQS for particulate matter using linear, non-threshold modeling, noting that "the level or even existence of population thresholds below which no effects occur cannot be reliably determined."[40] It initiated the practice of calculating benefits for reducing particulate matter at levels below the standards it ultimately chose to implement. This analysis revealed that further reductions beyond the standards the agency promulgated would actually be cost-benefit justified.[41] The George W. Bush EPA, after analyzing new studies on particulate matter, found that no threshold could be found for the pollutant and maintained the Clinton administration's practice of calculating benefits below the standards it set through the NAAQS.[42] Again, the agency found that even stricter restrictions on particulate matter emissions would have additional net benefits because of the enormous health improvements from lower levels of the pollutant.[43] For example, twice as many deaths would be avoided by just a small reduction in emissions.[44]

The Obama EPA continued the use of linear, non-threshold modeling for particulate matter. For example, in the EPA's most recent revision of particulate matter standards, the agency stated that because "there was no discernible population-level threshold below which effects would not occur[,] ... it is reasonable to consider that health effects may occur over the full range of concentrations observed in the epidemiological studies, including the lower concentrations."[45] Again, as it had done in earlier administrations, the EPA analyzed the costs and benefits of controls assuming negative health effects at the lowest levels of exposure and found net benefits would actually be greater below the standards it chose to implement.[46] While acknowledging that all extrapolations of effects contain some degree of uncertainty, the agency noted that recent research had continued to find damage from very low levels of exposure.[47]

Questioning Threshold Models

During the Obama administration, the use of non-threshold modeling for particulate matter and other pollutants began to prompt a backlash from industry, as the EPA tightened regulatory controls.[48] Organizations like the American Chemistry Council and American Petroleum Industry, two trade groups representing regulated entities, advocated using thresholds in modeling health effects despite the significant scientific research challenging the existence of a threshold for a vast array of pollutants.[49] Industry representatives seized on the uncertainties associated with modeling effects at these lower levels of pollution to try to argue that the agency should not attempt to calculate possible benefits from reductions below the current air quality standards.[50]

The Trump administration's EPA, prompted by industry lobbying for less regulation, is considering reinstating the use of thresholds for carcinogens, criteria pollutants, and other chemicals.[51] Yet the agency has not done the work required under the law to justify departing from prior EPA modeling. And such work could not be done because it would fly in the face of established, well-developed science.

In particular, the Trump EPA has called the non-threshold treatment of particulate matter into question in at least three important policies: the Strengthening Transparency in Regulatory Science proposed rule discussed in chapter 6; the repeal of the Clean Power Plan, an important Obama administration initiative to control the greenhouse gas emissions of existing power plants; and the Affordable Clean Energy rule, which replaced the Clean Power Plan with a far weaker approach. If the EPA were to follow its current course of action, the absence of any reasonable explanation for its adoption of thresholds will leave the agency vulnerable to multiple legal challenges.

In the "science transparency" proposed rule, the EPA suggested it intended to reconsider non-threshold modeling for pollutants by challenging the studies on which these models are based. Most of the rule is focused on justifying the disregard of studies based on confidential data, but buried in the proposed regulation is a short paragraph stating that the agency is seeking to "increase transparency of the assumptions underlying dose response models" by considering approaches other than linear, non-threshold models.[52] According to the EPA, "there is growing empirical evidence of non-linearity in the concentration-response function for specific pollutants and health effects," requiring a reevaluation of whether thresholds are a better approach. The EPA does not cite a single scientific study to support these statements, or any other research that would explain its departure from long-standing agency practice on evaluating the health effects of pollution. Without details about the research the agency is relying on to support incorporating threshold models, outside experts and the public are unable to adequately assess and comment on the proposed rule.[53]

The Trump administration's EPA has also proposed threshold modeling for the harmful effects from particulate matter to justify its proposal to repeal the Clean Power Plan. As part of its cost-benefit analysis of the rule, the EPA examined a number of indirect effects, including deaths that would be prevented from reductions in particulate matter that occur as the energy sector becomes cleaner. Consistent with its established practice spanning decades, the agency first applied a linear, non-threshold model to calculate the potential for harm at all levels of exposure. The proposed repeal, however, also included modeling estimates that assumed that no individual would suffer a health impact from reducing particulate matter pollution below a certain population threshold level.[54] The agency chose to examine two different potential thresholds: first, the level set by the NAAQS, and second, the lowest measurable level detected in epidemiological studies, which is below the limit set by the NAAQS.[55] The regulatory impact analysis accompanying the proposed repeal acknowledged that prior scientific studies have supported a finding that particulate matter does harm to human health below these two thresholds.[56] But the agency then emphasized the supposed uncertainties surrounding extrapolations below pollutant concentrations that can be measured in epidemiological studies. The EPA was particularly critical of the fact that models of non-observable effects assume that the relationship between exposure and harm occurs in a linear fashion, suggesting that it was unwise to place much confidence in the "shape and magnitude" of the curve. The agency relied on these supposed uncertainties to argue that the two threshold models were relevant to the regulatory analysis.

The EPA eventually abandoned an outright repeal of the Clean Power Plan. Instead, Administrator Andrew Wheeler announced that the agency would promulgate the Affordable Clean Energy rule, which would regulate the greenhouse gas emissions of existing power plants but significantly less stringently than had been the case under the Clean Power Plan.[57] But, in switching course on the proposed repeal, the EPA did not abandon its effort to change the modeling of particulate matter's health effects.

As it did with the proposed Clean Power Plan repeal, the EPA introduced thresholds into its calculations of health effects from reducing particulate matter emissions.[58] In the proposal for the Affordable Clean Energy rule, the agency asserted that it was "less confident" in risk estimates from exposures that are extrapolated to lower doses through modeling rather than directly observed in observational studies.[59] This uncertainty, it claimed, underscored the need to calculate benefits from particulate matter reductions using a threshold, or what the agency surreptitiously called "concentration benchmark analyses."[60] While acknowledging that its own scientists endorsed a non-threshold, linear approach, the EPA nevertheless contended that inserting these alternative calculations would give the government and the public a better appreciation for the rule's costs and benefits.[61]

The EPA's attempted shift from non-threshold to threshold modeling appears to be responsive to the pressure of industry groups, which had cast doubt on non-threshold models as part of their deregulatory toolkit.[62] For example, shortly before the Trump administration took office, an industry-funded think tank called the Heartland Institute began attacking the Clean Power Plan's use of non-threshold modeling, claiming that it was biased and based on fearmongering about risks to children.[63] Their strategy was soon adopted by other groups like the Competitive Enterprise Institute, a think tank with extensive ties to the tobacco, chemical, and fossil fuel industries that has asserted that "the Obama EPA's linear-no-threshold (LNT) assumption that PM2.5 [particulate matter] kills at any concentration above zero is non-validated, contrary to considerable evidence, and a license for regulatory excess."[64]

The vast majority of scientific experts have been extremely critical of the suggestion that the use of threshold modeling is better supported by the scientific evidence than non-threshold modeling.[65] At an EPA hearing on the Clean Power Plan repeal, outside scientific experts on lung diseases agreed that the Trump EPA's use of particulate matter thresholds is contrary to the latest research on effects from low levels of exposure and underestimates the health benefits from reductions below current air quality standards.[66] As groups like the Union of Concerned Scientists have noted, these changes are likely to particularly harm children and others who are sensitive to low levels of pollution.[67]

Even the EPA's own scientific advisory board opposed the use of thresholds in evaluating the risk of harm from the repeal of the Clean Power Plan.[68] And it did so even after the Trump administration purged it of many of its academic scientists and replaced them with scientists employed by regulated industry.

The industry assault on non-threshold models for particulate matter continued after the proposal of the Affordable Clean Energy rule, which, as the EPA's own analysis revealed, would lead to an additional 1,400 deaths per year under linear, non-threshold modeling.[69] In response, groups like the Institute for Energy Research, an industry funded non-profit with ties to the Koch brothers, claimed the media was wrongly focusing on only "one estimate" from the EPA's analysis and that linear, non-threshold modeling should be done away with because it inaccurately represents health impacts from particulate matter.[70] The argument was picked up by conservative outlets like *The Daily Caller*, which asserted that "[the] EPA is just estimating premature deaths based on current epidemiological studies that are still the subject of debate."[71] Industry creation of a manufactured scientific debate, despite a clear consensus to the contrary, is a well-trod path to attempt to avoid regulation.[72] And it is a path that the Trump administration is skipping along with enthusiasm.

***

The effort to reinvigorate threshold modeling for environmental regulation is a thinly disguised attempt to undermine cost-benefit justified regulation and aid industry at the expense of public health. Where epidemiological studies have not demonstrated a threshold toxicity level for a pollutant, the best current scientific evidence suggests that a linear, non-threshold model is the best assumption for predicting the toxicity for the pollutant at a population level. Most important, with respect to particulate matter, the pollutant that produces the largest number of quantifiable premature deaths and hospitalizations for serious injuries, the dominant scientific consensus is that a linear, non-threshold model is most appropriate for modeling the pollutant's toxicity. In contrast, arguments for threshold modeling for particulate matter, which the Trump administration is embracing in important regulatory proceedings, have virtually no support in the modern scientific literature and would undo over thirty years of scientific progress.

8

Ignoring Indirect Benefits

Another component of the cost-benefit charade carried out by the Trump administration concerns its treatment of the indirect consequences of regulation. Established and well-accepted practices for conducting cost-benefit analysis require the consideration not only of the direct consequences of rules but also of their indirect consequences. Such indirect effects must be considered whether they are negative (indirect costs) or positive (indirect benefits, also referred to as ancillary benefits or co-benefits). These standards have been embodied in the guidance documents under which federal agencies operate, in the regulations promulgated by these agencies, and in decisions of the federal courts reviewing these regulations.

In its zeal to repeal or severely weaken enormously beneficial environmental regulations, the Trump administration has assumed away tens of billions of dollars in yearly benefits from a large number of averted premature deaths, strokes, heart attacks, and severe respiratory problems. The pseudo-logic to support this assumption has been that these effects are "indirect" and result from reductions in "non-target" pollutants. But, even as the administration has willfully ignored massive co-benefits for some rules, it has embraced them for others, when doing so helps justify deregulation. The frank inconsistency cleanly demonstrates that there is no principle at play in the treatment of indirect effects other than the expediency of creating an illusion of rationality for actions that will severely harm the American people.

Development of the Administrative Practice

The question of how to account for the indirect consequences of regulation first received sustained attention in the 1990s with the publication of *Risk Versus Risk* by John Graham, who later became the head of the OIRA in the George W. Bush administration, and Jonathan Wiener.[1] That book took issue with prior administrative practices of looking only at the direct consequences of regulation and argued that the direct benefits of regulation were sometimes coupled with indirect negative consequences.[2] In particular, Graham and Wiener focused on the fact that regulations seeking to reduce certain risks can increase other risks, which they referred to as "countervailing risks."[3] Graham and Wiener maintained

Reviving Rationality. Michael A. Livermore and Richard L. Revesz, Oxford University Press (2020). © Oxford University Press. DOI: 10.1093/oso/9780197539446.001.0001.

that an accurate accounting of regulatory effects would consider these countervailing risks through what they termed risk-trade-off analysis,[4] or risk-risk analysis.[5] Risk-risk analysis quickly picked up traction among academics specializing in administrative law.[6]

Judges embraced risk-risk analysis as well. Justice Breyer concurred in *Whitman v. American Trucking Ass'ns*, agreeing with the Court's unanimous ruling that the Clean Air Act prohibits the consideration of costs in setting the NAAQS. But he wrote separately to argue that the "statute . . . permits the [EPA] Administrator to take account of comparative health risks."[7] Under Breyer's approach, if the steps taken to reduce ambient pollution reduced the risk of one type of health harm but increased the risk of another (for example, if cutting ozone pollution reduced respiratory risk but increased melanoma risk), the EPA could take that countervailing risk into account.[8]

Judge Stephen Williams of the United States Court of Appeals for the District of Columbia Circuit, was also a notable early proponent of risk-risk analysis. For example, in a concurrence in *International Union, United Automobile, Aerospace & Agricultural Implement Workers v. Occupational Safety and Health Administration*, Judge Williams used risk-risk analysis to challenge what he viewed as the "casual assumption that more stringent regulation will always save lives."[9] He argued that the health-wealth connection required consideration of negative economic effects of regulation and their purported effect on health: "More regulation means some combination of reduced value of firms, higher product prices, fewer jobs in the regulated industry, and lower cash wages. All the latter three stretch workers' budgets tighter. . . . And larger incomes enable people to lead safer lives."[10] And while the health-wealth trade-off has been criticized as an empirical matter, Judge Williams's embrace of risk-risk analysis is independent of the theoretical or empirical support for the health-wealth relationship.[11]

The George W. Bush era Circular A-4 explicitly requires the consideration of both countervailing risks and ancillary benefits.[12] The circular instructs agencies to "look beyond the direct benefits and direct costs" to "consider any important ancillary benefits and countervailing risks."[13] Further, it states that "the same standards of information and analysis quality that apply to direct benefits and costs should be applied to ancillary benefits and countervailing risks."[14]

Consistent Application

The EPA, the agency most in the crosshairs of the Trump administration's unwarranted attack on co-benefits, has long taken co-benefits into account in its economic analyses of environmental rules. The EPA's current guidelines for cost-benefit analyses, which were adopted in 2010 after extensive peer review, instruct the agency to assess "all identifiable costs and benefits" and state that an economic analysis of regulations should include both "directly intended effects . . . as well as ancillary (or co-) benefits and costs."[15]

The EPA's guidelines build on principles applied during previous administrations. For example, the George W. Bush EPA used similar language in its 2008 draft "Guidelines for Preparing Economic Analyses," declaring that "an economic analysis of regulatory or policy options should present all identifiable costs and benefits that are incremental to the regulation or policy under consideration. These should include directly intended effects and associated costs, as well as ancillary (or co-) benefits and costs."[16] The proposed George W. Bush era guidelines also stated that "for a regulation that is expected to have substantial indirect effects beyond the regulated sector, it is important to choose a model that can capture those effects."[17]

Likewise, the Clinton EPA's guidelines for conducting cost-benefit analyses endorsed the importance of considering indirect costs and benefits.[18] Issued in 2000, the Clinton guidelines included indirect costs as a component of its calculations for health and social costs.[19] Emphasizing the importance of a "complete benefits analysis"[20] the guidelines explained that indirect benefits should be counted.[21] Moreover, the guidelines noted that "immediately following a net benefit calculation, there should be a presentation and evaluation of all benefits and costs that can only be quantified but not valued, as well as all benefits and costs that can be only qualitatively described."[22] The implication is that, even for effects that cannot be monetized, informed decision making requires consideration of all benefits and costs, not just direct ones. In short, EPA's guidelines adopted during administrations of both parties called for the use of co-benefits in cost-benefit analyses.

In addition to being discussed in multiple iterations of the EPA's guidelines, co-benefits have been included in decades of actual regulatory cost-benefit analyses performed by the agency—stretching back at least as far as the 1980s.[23] The agency began acknowledging these benefits in Clear Air Act rules at least as far back as the 1980s. In 1985, the EPA under President Ronald Reagan conducted an extensive analysis of co-benefits from reductions of non-target pollutants in its landmark 1985 regulation reducing lead in gasoline, including an analysis of benefits from reductions in ozone, nitrogen oxides, and hydrocarbons.[24] As part of this analysis, the EPA found monetized annual co-benefits from reducing hydrocarbons, nitrogen oxides, and carbon monoxide, benzene, and other non-targeted pollutants to be worth an estimated $222 million.[25] Also, in its proposal for developing New Source Performance Standards for municipal waste combustors, the Reagan-era EPA discussed the importance of considering "indirect benefits" from its regulation of toxic emissions from municipal waste combustors and explained that its analysis would include "indirect benefits accruing from concomitant reductions in other regulated pollutants."[26]

Under President George H. W. Bush, the EPA in 1991 justified performance standards in a proposed rule for landfill gases in part on "the ancillary benefit of reducing global loadings of methane."[27] Further, the EPA examined countervailing climate change risks. The agency noted that carbon dioxide emissions under the proposed standard would increase, but justified regulation in part because of the climate change benefits from methane emission reductions.[28] The EPA took into consideration both the ancillary benefits of methane reductions in reducing greenhouse gas pollution and the countervailing risk of increasing carbon dioxide emissions.[29] The EPA's judgment on how to regulate was thus guided by the full scope of the regulatory effects.

The EPA under President Bill Clinton, in a 1998 rule establishing standards for hazardous air pollutant emissions from pulp and paper producers, analyzed indirect effects, both co-benefits from reductions in emissions and indirect costs from increases in emissions, for criteria pollutants regulated by the NAAQS.[30] With respect to the standards for existing sources, the agency estimated small increases in emissions of carbon monoxide, nitrogen oxides, and sulfur dioxides from the rule, but a significant decrease in particulate matter emissions.[31] And, with respect to the standards for new sources, the EPA concluded that in addition to decreasing hazardous air pollutants, the rule would also decrease the emissions of several other criteria pollutants, including particulate matter.[32] Thus, the agency relied on co-benefits in justifying the rules for both new and existing standards.

In 2005, the EPA under George W. Bush noted that its Clean Air Interstate Rule, which targeted particulate matter and ozone emissions, would also reduce mercury emissions,[33] and included the co-benefits from mercury reductions in its cost-benefit analysis for the rule.[34] The Bush EPA also discussed co-benefits as part of a regulation governing hazardous air pollutants from mobile sources, primarily cars.[35] The agency noted that though the rule was designed to control air toxics, it also reduced particulate matter and ozone, a "co-benefit" the agency considered "significant."[36] The EPA calculated that the standards would reduce exhaust emissions of direct particulate matter nationwide by over 19,000 tons in 2030.[37] The agency also analyzed the effects of the rule on ozone emissions, concluding that some areas would have "non-negligible improvements in projected 8-hour ozone."[38]

Similarly, high-profile Obama-era EPA regulations like the Mercury and Air Toxics Standards and the Clean Power Plan, discussed below, reflect the requirement of Circular A-4 that the agency consider co-benefits, and the requirement of the EPA's own guidelines to consider "all identifiable costs and benefits." The inclusion of co-benefits in these regulations is well in line with the long-standing practice of the EPA to include co-benefits and countervailing risks in its assessment of clean air regulations.

In sum, the EPA has consistently examined a full range of effects from regulations. Rather than arbitrarily ignoring certain effects because they are ancillary or indirect, the EPA discusses and analyzes indirect costs and co-benefits. The agency has done so through multiple presidential administrations of different parties and in a wide range of clean air regulations. These practices have been standard from the Reagan administration through the Obama-era EPA regulations discussed below.

Judicial Treatment of Indirect Costs

Courts are sometimes asked to review the adequacy of an agency's cost-benefit analysis, and in this context they have addressed the issue of indirect benefits and costs.[39] Reviewing courts have frequently required agencies to include ancillary impacts in their economic analyses of regulatory actions.

In 1991, the United States Court of Appeals for the Fifth Circuit rejected the EPA's attempt to ban asbestos-based brakes under the Toxic Substances Control Act.[40] A central part of the court's holding was its finding that the EPA needed to consider the indirect safety effects of other potential, non-asbestos options for car brakes.[41] The court determined that under the Toxic Substances Control Act, the EPA "was required to consider both alternatives to a ban and the costs of any proposed actions."[42] The court noted with disapproval that the agency had not evaluated the harm from increased use of substitute products, including "the dangers posed by the substitutes, including cancer deaths from the other fibers used and highway deaths occasioned by less effective, non-asbestos brakes." According to the court, the agency's "failure to examine the likely consequence of the EPA's regulation render[ed] the ban of asbestos friction products unreasonable."[43] In short, the EPA's cost-benefit analysis did not, in the court's view, adequately address indirect costs and was therefore unsupported by "substantial evidence" as required under the statute.[44]

A year later, the DC Circuit struck down a rule promulgated by the National Highway Traffic Safety Administration, for failing to consider potential indirect costs.[45] The agency had attempted to increase fuel-efficiency standards for cars but had not considered the potential safety risks that might arise if more fuel-efficient cars were less protective in a crash.[46] The court found that the agency had not met the requirement of reasoned explanation and required that it "reconsider the matter and provide a genuine explanation for whatever choice it ultimately makes."[47]

Other circuit court decisions have likewise addressed the issue of indirect costs and have rejected cost-benefit analyses that lacked an estimate of these effects. In 1993, the United States Court of Appeals for the Seventh Circuit partially vacated a regulation by the Occupational Safety and Health Administration putting standards in place to limit the transmission of communicable diseases.[48] The agency failed to consider the indirect health effects that might result if the rule increased health care costs and thus limited access to care.[49] The court found that the agency's analysis "[was] thus incomplete."[50]

The DC Circuit has explicitly addressed the "mirror image" of indirect costs: co-benefits.[51] In 2016, the court's decision in *United States Sugar Corp. v. EPA* upheld the EPA's consideration of co-benefits in regulating the effects of reducing hazardous air pollutants from boilers, process heaters, and incinerators.[52] Specifically, the EPA decided not to adopt more lenient hydrogen chloride emission standards, reasoning that it could weigh additional factors such as the "cumulative adverse health effects due to concurrent exposure to other [hazardous air pollutants] or emissions from other nearby sources" and the "potential impacts of increased emissions on ecosystems."[53] Industry groups argued that the EPA's consideration of these co-benefits invalidated the agency's decision.[54] In response, the EPA asserted that "its consideration of these co-benefits was not a regulation of other pollutants; rather, it was simply choosing not to ignore the purpose of the [Clean Air Act]—to reduce the negative health and environmental effects of [hazardous air pollutant] emissions—when exercising its discretionary authority under the Act."[55] The DC Circuit held that the EPA acted within its legal authority when it considered not only the direct benefits of reducing hydrogen chloride but also the co-benefits from that reduction—namely, indirect reductions of other hazardous air pollutants.[56] The court agreed that the use of co-benefits conforms with the Clean Air Act's purpose, finding that "the EPA was . . . free to consider potential co-benefits that might be achieved" from enforcing the more stringent standard.[57]

Courts that have examined cost-benefit analyses have acknowledged the logic of evaluating the indirect effects of regulations and using this information to guide the rule-making process. While there have been more cases concerning indirect costs, modern cases have addressed indirect benefits as well and no court has said there is any reason to treat them differently. This approach is the only plausible one since the terms *costs* and *benefits* are merely convenient descriptors that helpfully depict whether effects are positive or negative. Such characterizations provide no justification for focusing on some effects while ignoring others.[58]

Underscoring this important point, Christopher DeMuth and Judge Douglas Ginsburg, both of whom led OIRA during the Reagan administration, noted that "OIRA . . . recommends that agencies account for ancillary benefits as well as countervailing risks,"[59] and that "there appear to be no legal, political, or intellectual . . . impediments to treating ancillary benefits and countervailing risks equally in cost-benefit analysis and regulatory design."[60] DeMuth and Ginsburg are absolutely correct: it would be incoherent to consider indirect consequences of regulation if they are negative but ignore them if they are positive.

Ignoring Reality

The effort to veer away from this long-standing consensus, supported by economic theory, logic, and a consistent administrative practice by administrations of both parties over decades, first appeared in June 2018, when the EPA published an Advance Notice of Proposed Rulemaking inviting comments on "perceived inconsistency and lack of transparency in how the Agency considers costs and benefits in rulemaking."[61] The document, issued by Administrator Scott Pruitt one month before his resignation, asked the following question with respect to co-benefits: "To what extent should [the] EPA develop a general rule on how the Agency will weigh the benefits from reductions in pollutants that were not directly regulated (often called 'co-benefits' or 'ancillary benefits')?"[62] Tellingly, the EPA did not raise similar questions about the consideration of indirect costs.[63]

In the advance notice, the EPA did not explicitly answer the question on how co-benefits should be treated, but its intent was clear enough. Industry and conservative groups allied with the Trump administration had been railing against the use of co-benefits for some time. For example, the US Chamber of Commerce termed the consideration of co-benefits "a controversial and legally dubious accounting method"[64] and the Cato Institute called them a "sleight of hand."[65] Even more obvious, in April 2018, two months before the advance notice's publication, Pruitt said in a speech to the Heritage Foundation that "[the] EPA will soon stop relying on 'co-benefits' in crafting new regulations"[66]—a stark indication that the administrator's mind had already been made up. After Pruitt's departure, his successor Andrew Wheeler abandoned the attempt to fashion an across-the-board policy on co-benefits. [67] Rather, Wheeler announced that the agency would proceed in a piecemeal fashion, examining the issue separately depending on the regulatory context.[68] But there is no mystery over whether the agency will proceed with the goal announced by Pruitt at the Heritage Foundation event. In February 2019, the agency, under Wheeler's leadership, proposed to reverse the foundation of the Obama administration's Mercury and Air Toxics Standards (MATS) rule, arguing that the agency improperly relied on co-benefits.

In order to regulate hazardous air pollutant emissions from power plants, the Clean Air Act, in section 122(n), requires the EPA to first determine whether it is "appropriate and necessary" to do so.[69] The agency made this determination in 2012, and, at the same time, it promulgated the MATS rule, setting forth the emissions limitations that would apply to power plants.[70] Subsequently, in *Michigan v. EPA*, the Supreme Court remanded the "appropriate and necessary" finding on the grounds that the EPA had failed to consider costs before making it.[71] The EPA had, in fact, conducted a formal cost-benefit analysis for MATS, but the agency had not relied on this analysis as a basis for the threshold appropriate-and-necessary finding; this analysis, therefore, did not satisfy the Court's requirement.[72]

The Supreme Court left it "up to the Agency to decide [on remand] (as always, within the limits of *reasonable* interpretation) how to account for cost."[73] In 2016, the EPA, under the Obama administration, reaffirmed its 2012 appropriate-and-necessary finding. As one basis for this decision,[74] the agency relied on the conclusions of the formal cost-benefit analysis contained in the regulatory impact analysis justifying the emission limitations in the MATS rule.[75] That analysis projected that the rule would impose $9.6 billion per year in compliance costs but yield between $37 and $90 billion per year in quantifiable benefits, in addition to many other positive health and environmental effects that were not quantified.[76]

The "great majority" of these quantified benefits were "attributable to co-benefits from reductions in [particulate matter]-related mortality."[77] These particulate matter reductions would occur as a direct consequence of the steps that the EPA expected power plants to take to reduce their emissions of hazardous air pollutants. Consistently with prior practices, the agency referred to particulate matter reductions as "co-benefits" because they were "not the primary objective" of MATS and took them into account in its analysis.[78] Because the EPA's formal cost-benefit analysis showed that MATS's benefits would "exceed the costs by 3 to 9 times," the agency found that it "provide[d] an independent basis to support the finding that a consideration of cost does not cause the agency to alter its [2012 appropriate-and-necessary] determination."[79]

Now, under the Trump administration, the EPA proposes to reverse the agency's prior "appropriate and necessary" determination because the quantified *direct* benefits did not justify the costs.[80] In addition to ignoring the unquantified benefits of the rule, the agency argues that its refusal to consider *indirect* benefits is a "reasonable approach . . . to considering costs in response to *Michigan*."[81] In other words, according to the EPA, even if section 112(n) does not unambiguously preclude the full consideration of co-benefits, the agency has discretion to fully or partially disregard such benefits. In alleged accordance with this new interpretation of section 112(n), the EPA ignored the vast co-benefits at stake and then "propose[d] to conclude that it is not appropriate and necessary to regulate HAP from EGUs [Electric Generating Units] . . . because the costs of such regulation grossly outweigh the [direct] HAP benefits."[82]

There is no support for the EPA's claim that section 122(n) precludes it from considering co-benefits, because that section does not contain the words "costs" or "benefits" and the operative words, which are "appropriate and necessary," undoubtedly permit the consideration of co-benefits. But the resolution of this question of statutory interpretation is not necessary to an understanding of the EPA's approach to co-benefits. That is because the agency made the alternative argument that even if the statute did not preclude the consideration of co-benefits, it would nonetheless exercise its discretion to ignore co-benefits.

While ignoring co-benefits is by itself illogical enough, in proposing to reverse the "appropriate and necessary" finding, the agency went even further. Even though the EPA ignored the co-benefits of the rule, it considered the indirect costs of the MATS rule: the $9.6 billion annual cost estimate included costs "beyond [those] borne by owners of coal- and oil-fired units regulated by MATS."[83] The EPA relied on a cost estimate that includes indirect costs but declined to give equal consideration to indirect benefits, thereby engaging in a lopsided, opportunistically framed economic analysis to justify the reversal of its prior finding, which supported a rule that generates tens of billions of dollars of net benefits for society each year.

Selective Embrace of Co-benefits

The Trump administration's treatment of co-benefits is an affront to reasoned decision making. Even worse is its lack of a consistent position on the issue. When co-benefits stand in the way of its deregulatory zeal, it cavalierly calls them into question, as discussed above. But, in other cases, where co-benefits would further its deregulatory agenda, the administration embraces them with great enthusiasm. Two recent examples illustrate the point.

Under the Trump administration, the EPA relied heavily on co-benefits to support its Affordable Clean Energy rule, which is a toothless replacement for the Clean Power Plan, the signature climate initiative of the Obama administration.[84] The Trump rule abandons the Obama administration's goals of boosting clean energy in favor of requiring only modest efficiency gains at coal plants. Perversely, the Trump strategy runs the risk of *raising* emissions because older plans will become more cost-competitive.

The Trump EPA's economic justification proceeded in two steps. First, the agency evaluated an outright repeal of the Clean Power Plan. For reasons unrelated to the treatment of co-benefits, it concluded, bizarrely, that this repeal would have no costs and no benefits.

In the second step, the EPA compared the Affordable Clean Energy rule to a baseline with no Clean Power Plan. The agency's cost-benefit analysis considered three elements: direct benefits, which resulted from greenhouse gas reductions; co-benefits, which resulted from reductions in particulate emissions; and costs. Under every scenario that the agency analyzed, the costs were higher, by a considerable amount, than the direct benefits. It was only by relying on co-benefits that the agency was able to justify its new, much weakened rule. For example, the impact of the rule in 2030, at a 3 percent discount rate, was as follows: direct benefits of $52 million, co-benefits of $320 to $780 million, and costs of $180 million. Thus, the Trump rule would have net costs of $128 million if co-benefits were not taken into account. But rather than ignore the co-benefits this time, the agency included them and concluded that the ACE rule had positive net benefits of $192 to $652 million.[85]

The Trump EPA played the same trick in its proposed rollback of greenhouse emission standards for cars and light trucks, the so-called SAFE rule discussed in Chapter 4. In arguing in favor of this rule, the Trump administration relies heavily on co-benefits in both its rhetoric and its economic analysis.[86]

The proposal, authored jointly by the EPA and the National Highway Traffic Safety Administration, claims that the increases in pollution and fuel costs resulting from the rollback are justified by supposed safety benefits. As discussed earlier, the agencies assume that the stricter efficiency standards adopted under Obama would raise the purchase price of vehicles. This may well be true. But the agency goes on to assume that somehow (contrary to basic economic principles), higher prices will lead people to buy more cars. More cars means more miles driven and more accidents. From this line of reasoning, the Trump EPA concludes that the rollback will save lives.

These purported safety benefits are co-benefits, which—unlike in the case of the MATS rule—the agency is happy to advertise. For example, EPA administrator Andrew Wheeler conceded that, as a result of the rollback, "more oil will be consumed,"[87] which necessarily leads to the emission of more greenhouse gases. But Wheeler was quick to justify these bad effects because the rule will "save 12,000 lives."[88] Along the same lines, Heidi King, the National Highway Traffic Safety Administration's deputy administrator, stated: "Most importantly, this rule promises to save lives."[89] The name of the rule was even chosen so that its acronym could telegraph this message: The Safer Affordable Fuel-Efficient (SAFE) Vehicles Rule for Model Years 2021–2026 Passenger Cars and Light Trucks.[90] The economic analysis of the rule reveals that more than half of its benefits were attributable to the asserted safety benefits.[91]

From the EPA's perspective, the direct benefits of greenhouse gas standards for motor vehicles are the reduction of greenhouse gases: that is the objective of the section of the Clean Air Act under which it has the authority to promulgate the rule.[92] And the National Highway Traffic Safety Administration's authority for setting fuel-economy standards stems from the Corporate Average

Fuel Economy program, which dates back to the energy crisis of the 1970s and is designed to conserve fuel.[93] As a result, from the perspective of both agencies, any safety benefits are co-benefits, not direct benefits.[94]

The EPA is trying to have it both ways. On the one hand, it appears to be engaged in a broad effort to discredit reliance on co-benefits to justify regulatory actions. But, on the other hand, it is happy to tout such benefits when doing so furthers its deregulatory objectives.

***

The Trump administration's actions on co-benefits ignore settled economic theory and the precepts of rationality; fly in the face of clear, long-standing guidance from the executive branch on how cost-benefit analysis should be conducted; and are inconsistent with the regulatory practices of administrations of both parties over several decades.

The Trump administration manages to compound this intellectual dishonesty through its brazen inconsistency. While decrying the use of co-benefits, it acknowledges indirect costs with enthusiasm. Thus, it takes the wholly implausible position that the indirect consequences of regulation should be taken into account if they are negative but should be ignored if they are positive. And it disregards co-benefits only when doing so furthers the administration's deregulatory agenda. In contrast, when invoking co-benefits can support deregulation, the administration celebrates them with zeal.

9

Trivializing Climate Change

The prior chapters focused primarily on the Trump administration's efforts to hide entirely the benefits of environmental regulation to human health. The administration is also engaged in a related illusion: to make very large benefits looks small. Climate change is one of the most pressing issues of our time. In late 2018, the Intergovernmental Panel on Climate Change released a stark report—at the current warming rate, the planet is on track to reach a 1.5° Celsius increase from pre-industrial temperatures by 2040.[1] Increasing global temperatures are expected to have far-reaching impacts on global food security, national security, and human health. Already, scientists have identified the impacts of climate change on food production, rainfall, regional drought, and ocean chemistry.[2] The report also showed that while a 1.5° C increase will have far reaching impacts, the consequences of 2° C or larger increase—also on the horizon unless policy steps are taken—are markedly more severe.[3]

Despite these concerning findings and a 2018 National Climate Assessment prepared by thirteen federal agencies that outlined the serious climate impacts in the United States,[4] the Trump administration has, at every turn, taken actions to reverse the climate progress achieved during the Obama administration. The Trump EPA has moved to repeal or significantly roll back three significant rules to reduce the emissions of greenhouse gases from existing power plants, passenger cars and light trucks, and oil and gas installations. President Trump has also used the presidential bully pulpit to mock climate change science. For example, on January 20, 2019, he tweeted: "Be careful and try staying in your house. Large parts of the Country are suffering from tremendous amounts of snow and near record setting cold. Amazing how big this system is. Wouldn't be bad to have a little of that good old-fashioned Global Warming right now."[5]

To mask the true effects of its policies, the Trump administration has targeted the social cost of carbon, which is a way to express the global climate damage inflicted by carbon dioxide emissions in monetary terms. It represents the harm caused by a ton of carbon dioxide emissions. The Trump administration has used two principal techniques, unsupported by economic theory, to reduce the estimate of the damages of greenhouse emissions by around a factor of 10. As a consequence, the cost-benefit analysis of its rollbacks hide their enormous adverse consequences.

Reviving Rationality. Michael A. Livermore and Richard L. Revesz, Oxford University Press (2020). © Oxford University Press. DOI: 10.1093/oso/9780197539446.001.0001.

Genesis of the Social Cost of Carbon

The Obama administration developed the social cost of carbon following a 2008 decision by the United States Court of Appeals for the Ninth Circuit that required the government to estimate the adverse consequences of greenhouse gas emissions. In *Center for Biological Diversity v. National Highway Traffic Safety Administration*, a large group of petitioners, including eleven states and four public interest groups, challenged the National Highway Traffic Safety Administration's corporate average fuel-economy (CAFE) standards on several grounds, one of which was the agency's failure to account for the adverse consequences of greenhouse gas emissions.[6] The agency had employed a cost-benefit analysis to justify the standards, but it did not include the reduction of greenhouse gas emissions that would accompany more stringent CAFE standards as a benefit in this calculation, citing the uncertainty in the valuation of greenhouse gas impacts.[7] The Ninth Circuit rejected this argument, stating that while "the record shows that there is a range of values, the value of carbon emissions reduction is certainly not zero."[8]

Following this decision, in 2009 President Obama convened an Interagency Working Group (IWG) on the social cost of carbon. The working group consisted of members from a broad set of federal agencies: the Council of Economic Advisers, Council on Environmental Quality, Department of Agriculture, Department of Commerce, Department of Energy, Department of Transportation, EPA, National Economic Council, Office of Energy and Climate Change, Office of Management and Budget, Office of Science and Technology Policy, and Department of the Treasury.[9]

In developing the social cost of carbon, the IWG relied on the three most widely cited, peer-reviewed models that link the physical impacts of carbon dioxide emissions to economic damages, including the Dynamic Integrated Climate Economy (DICE) model developed by William Nordhaus.[10] Each model translates emissions into changes in atmospheric carbon concentrations, atmospheric concentrations into temperature changes, and temperature changes into economic damages. The IWG weighted each model equally when calculating the social cost of carbon values.[11]

To produce the social cost of carbon estimates, the IWG used three different discount rates (2.5 percent, 3 percent, and 5 percent) to translate future impacts into present-day dollars. It also modeled five scenarios based on peer-reviewed estimates of relevant parameters such as socioeconomic and emissions trajectories.[12] The combination of three models, three discount rates, and five scenarios produced forty-five different social cost of carbon distributions per year. For each discount rate, the IWG computed the average social cost of carbon values across all models and scenarios.[13] Consistent with the economics literature and the Circular A-4 guidance, the IWG selected a central social cost of carbon value based on a 3 percent discount rate. Additionally, the IWG produced a fourth value representing "lower probability, higher impact" climate damages using the 95th percentile social cost of carbon values from each of the three models at the 3 percent discount rate,[14] and emphasized the importance of considering the full range of social cost of carbon values.[15]

The IWG issued its first social cost of carbon value in 2010 and updated it several times, most recently in 2016, to reflect the latest scientific and economic data.[16] Under the 2016 update, the central social cost of carbon value for emissions in the year 2020 was $52/ton CO_2, expressed in 2019 dollars.[17] For emissions in later years, the social cost of carbon value is higher because future emissions are expected to produce more damage as the effects of climate change become more serious.[18] In addition, under the IWG's approach, many climate damage categories are modeled proportionally to gross GDP, which means that the social cost of carbon increases as the GDP grows over time.[19] Under the 2016 estimates, the social cost of carbon is valued at $62/ton in 2030, $74/ton in 2040, and $85/ton in 2050, all in 2019 dollars.[20]

In 2016, the social cost of carbon was the subject of litigation in the United States Court of Appeals for the Seventh Circuit.[21] In *Zero Zone, Inc. v. U.S. Department of Energy*, a group of businesses and trade associations challenged two Department of Energy rules regulating the energy efficiency of commercial refrigeration equipment.[22] One of the issues raised in an industry challenge to the rule was the agency's use of the social cost of carbon to estimate the value of greenhouse gas emissions reductions. The court soundly rejected that challenge, finding that the social cost of carbon was an appropriate value to include in cost-benefit analysis of agency rulemakings.[23] This decision was an important step in cementing the legitimacy of the social cost of carbon as a rulemaking tool. Today, the IWG's 2016 estimate of the social cost of carbon remains the best metric for monetizing climate change damages.[24]

A Lower Bound

According to the IWG, the social cost of carbon is primarily intended to reflect "changes in net agricultural productivity, human health, property damages from increased flood risk, and the value of ecosystem services due to climate change."[25] But, because of empirical limitations, the current social cost of carbon does not include several other significant categories of damages. These include catastrophic climate events, climate-induced migration and conflict, certain human health costs, natural disturbances (which include erosion, air pollution, fire, pests, and other pathogens), damages to ecosystem services and biodiversity, inter-regional damages, and the impacts from the interaction among climate damages.[26]

In 2018, California endured the state's deadliest wildfire on record, and a recent study found its annual burned area has increased by more than five times since 1972, attributing this increase to climate change.[27] Yet wildfire damages are currently not included in the social cost of carbon.

As a result of these limitations, an article in *Nature* that we co-authored with Nobel Prize winner Kenneth Arrow and a group of prominent scientists and economists concluded that "the bulk of the literature and arguments indicates that social-cost models are underestimating climate-change harms."[28] For this reason, the social cost of carbon should be regarded as a "lower bound" of the true damage of carbon dioxide emission.[29] Echoing this conclusion, a 2015 survey of individuals publishing on climate change in peer-reviewed economics and environmental economics journals found that 69 percent of respondents believed the social cost of carbon "should be greater than or equal to the figure currently used [as of 2015] by the U.S. government."[30]

This expert consensus is not reflected in current United States environmental policy. In March 2017, through an executive order, President Trump disbanded the IWG and ordered that all its technical support documents be withdrawn as "no longer representative of governmental policy."[31] However, the executive order clearly contemplated that agencies would continue to monetize climate change costs because it directed them to use the guidelines in Circular A-4 when estimating such values.[32]

The EPA, under then-administrator Scott Pruitt, released a revised interim social cost of carbon estimate of between $1 and $6 per metric ton of CO_2 (in 2011 dollars) for the year 2020, down from the IWG's estimate of $42 (in 2007 dollars).[33] The Trump administration accomplished this drastic decrease by making two unjustified changes to the IWG's social cost of carbon calculations. First, it raised the discount rates from the IWG's 2.5 percent, 3 percent, and 5 percent range to using only a 3 percent and a 7 percent rate. Second, it switched from a global to a domestic-only value of the social cost of carbon. Neither change can withstand scrutiny.

Ignoring Future Generations

One of the most significant changes reflected in the EPA's interim social cost of carbon numbers was the inclusion of a 7 percent discount rate in the calculation of the social cost of carbon and the dropping of the 2.5 percent and 5 percent rates from the analysis.[34] Doing so gives the Trump administration the opportunity to justify policies by reference to a social cost of carbon derived using a 7 percent discount rate, as opposed to the 3 percent discount rate used by the IWG.

Prominent economists are in near-unanimous agreement that the choice of a 7 percent discount rate is indefensible, particularly because the time frame over which climate change damages occur is so long. For example, Maureen Cropper, a professor at the University of Maryland, explained that "if you use a rate above 5 percent, you're essentially saying that we shouldn't worry today about anything that happens 100 years from now."[35] Damages of $100 that occur 100 years from now would be worth $5.20 today at the 3 percent discount rate used by the IWG but only 12 cents, 43 times less, at a 7 percent rate.[36] With this new discount rate, the Trump administration is effectively saying that Americans today are willing to pay virtually nothing to avoid drastic climate impacts that will affect their grandchildren.

In fact, the IWG's social cost of carbon was criticized for not using *lower* discount rates. Chris Hope, author of one of the three models on which the social cost of carbon is based, argued that the IWG had selected estimates on the higher end of the acceptable range and had failed to adequately justify this choice.[37] The EPA's own 2008 proposed guidance, dating back to the George W. Bush administration, suggested a 0.5–3 percent discount rate when discounting costs and benefits that will affect multiple generations.[38] And a 2015 survey of economists found that a majority favored a long-term social discount rate of between 1 and 3 percent.[39]

At first glance, the Trump administration's use of the 7 percent discount rate might appear to be a defensible position. The most recent OMB guidance on conducting cost-benefit analyses, Circular A-4, which is discussed at length in earlier chapters, instructs agencies to use a 3 percent and a 7 percent discount rate when calculating costs and benefits of regulatory actions.[40] Not surprisingly, in deploying the 7 percent discount rate in 2017, the EPA cited Circular A-4.[41]

However, the same document states that the 3 percent and 7 percent may be problematic when intergenerational impacts are at stake.[42] It notes that "although most people demonstrate time preference in their own consumption behavior, it may not be appropriate for society to demonstrate a similar preference when deciding between the well-being of current and future generations."[43] Further, the circular indicates that individuals who will be affected by our present decisions cannot participate in the decision-making process, "and today's society must act with some consideration of their interest."[44] It also notes that there is "increased uncertainty about the appropriate value of the discount rate, the longer the horizon for the analysis," which counsels in favor of lower discount rates.[45]

Apart from existing guidance and common sense, there are three analytical arguments that provide strong support for the proposition that the 7 percent discount rate is inappropriate for the analysis of climate change, where the damages accrue over a very long term.

First, using a 7 percent discount rate in this context stems from a category mistake. As Circular A-4 notes, the 7 percent discount rate is linked to the average rate of return to private capital in the US economy and is appropriate when the effects of regulation fall exclusively or primarily on the allocation of capital.[46] In contrast, a "lower discount rate is appropriate" when a regulation "primarily and directly affects private consumption (e.g., through higher consumer prices for goods and services)."[47] For such cases, the social rate of time preference—the rate at which society discounts future consumption flows—is appropriate.[48] The circular linked this rate to the real rate of return on long-term government debt, which at the time had averaged 3 percent.[49]

After thoroughly examining the academic literature, the IWG concluded that "the consumption rate of interest is the correct concept to use in evaluating the benefits and costs of a marginal change in carbon emissions"[50] because of the impacts of climate change on private consumption. And it chose this estimate, in accordance with Circular A-4, in computing the central value (3 percent) of its social cost of carbon estimate.

Second, economists have stressed that the rates set forth in Circular A-4, which was issued in 2003, may be inappropriate today because of the fall of long-term interest rates. In basing the 3 percent discount rate on the real rate of return on long-term government debt, the Circular stated that "the yield on 10-year Treasury notes has averaged 8.1 percent since 1973 while the average annual rate of change in the CPI [Consumer Price Index] over this period has been 5.0 percent, implying a real 10-year rate of 3.1 percent,"[51] which rounded to 3 percent. In early 2017, the Council of Economic Advisers noted in an issue brief that the real rate of return on ten-year government bonds had fallen to 1.4 percent and that the 3 percent discount rate should therefore be revisited.[52] It also suggested that downward adjustment might be appropriate for the 7 percent discount rate.[53]

Third, low, declining discount rates should be used when discounting over very long horizons when there is uncertainty about the appropriate rate.[54] This concept is generally attributed to Martin Weitzman, the prominent late Harvard economist.[55] The insight is that if there is uncertainty about the discount rate, as there is bound to be when the time frame for analysis is very long, the discount rate at the lower end of the range dominates over the very long term and becomes the only relevant one to consider.[56] As Weitzman explains, events in the "distant future" should be discounted at their "lowest possible limiting value."[57] So, even if there were genuine uncertainty about whether the correct discount rate is 3 percent or 7 percent, which there is not, only the 3 percent discount rate would be relevant over the long term. Other governments, like the United Kingdom and France, have already embraced the approach of using declining discount rates for official public projects.[58]

A mathematical example helps to illustrate this concept.[59] Let us assume that the yearly discount rate over the next ten years is equally likely to be either 10 percent or 2 percent. Weitzman argues that we should not simply average the discount rates and discount at 6 percent. Instead, we should average the expected values at each of those discount rates. One dollar in 10 years is worth either $.39 (10 percent rate) or $.82 (2 percent rate) now. This gives us an expected (average) present value of $.60, which would result from using a discount rate of 5.2 percent, rather than 6 percent. The corresponding discount rate declines to 2.7 percent in 100 years and to 2.1 percent in 1,000 years, eventually approaching 2 percent.[60]

Blinkered Climate Nationalism

In additional to trivializing the climate damages that will be experienced by future generations, the Trump administration has also adopted a form of climate nationalism that ignores the fundamentally global nature of climate change.[61]

Since its inception in 2010, the social cost of carbon has priced the global impacts associated with increases in carbon emissions. This meant that United States agencies would account for the worldwide impact of any carbon dioxide emissions. The IWG had considered the domestic versus global distinction in its 2010 Technical Support Documentation and concluded that a global focus for the social cost of carbon was appropriate for two primary reasons. First, climate change involves a global externality, in that greenhouse gases will affect all countries regardless of where these gases originate.[62] Second, the United States cannot solve climate change alone; international cooperation is an essential aspect of any climate change plan.[63]

Under Trump, the EPA has instead adopted a "domestic only" social cost of carbon. This approach overlooks enormously significant aspects of the climate change problem.[64] Most obviously, greenhouse gases emitted in the United States have effects all over the world; therefore, to accurately account for their consequences, one needs to use a global value. To do otherwise would treat foreign lives as if they had no value. But even if one accepted the (morally troubling) premise that only people in the United States matter, the domestic-only approach fails to account for significant concepts like spillovers and reciprocity, and, as a result, ultimately harms the US residents that it seeks to protect.

Because of the world's interconnected financial, political, health, security, and environmental systems, climate impacts occurring initially beyond the geographic borders of the United States cause significant costs that accrue to US citizens and residents. The IWG analyzed climate damages worldwide precisely to account for important aspects of public welfare like international spillover effects,[65] and the *Zero Zone* court upheld the reasonableness of this approach.[66] In contrast, the "domestic only" approach ignores how international spillovers, reciprocal foreign actions, and extraterritorial interests will affect the interests of the United States and public welfare, thereby overlooking enormously important parts of the problem.

With respect to international spillovers, as the IWG explained, attempts to cordon climate effects into strict geographic boundaries will inevitably underestimate damages by ignoring "how damages in other regions could affect the United States" through factors such as "economic and political destabilization" and "global migration."[67] For example, as one of us explained in a court filing "climate-induced flooding in Thailand interrupts US supply chains for electronic components; climate-related financial shocks in China will reverberate through Chinese holdings of US debt; water and food scarcity in Latin American can trigger mass emigration to the United States; infectious diseases exacerbated by climate will spread from abroad through air travel and vectors like mosquitos; a drought in Syria erupts into civil war and pulls the United States into conflict; and global climate effects become, according to the Department of Defense, 'threat multipliers' that 'increase the frequency, scale, and complexity of future [military] missions.'"[68]

The "domestic only" approach also ignores the effects of foreign reciprocity.[69] Greenhouse gases are global pollutants that mix through the planet's atmosphere and affect climate worldwide. Each ton of greenhouse gases abated in other countries thus directly benefits the United States. Direct US benefits from existing international climate policies could reach over $2 trillion in the next decade.[70] But if foreign countries instead set their climate policies by considering only certain domestic climate effects and ignoring the impact of climate change in other countries, the United States would suffer. Richard G. Newell, president of Resources for the Future, put it very aptly when he explained that the "United States is only 14 percent of global emissions, which means that 86 percent of the damages we will face will be caused by emissions from other countries."[71]

The United States is engaged in a repeated strategic dynamic with other countries that have already adopted values for the social cost of their greenhouse gas emissions based on worldwide damages, including the United Kingdom, Germany, Sweden, Canada, and others. Departing from this collaborative dynamic, by reverting to an estimate that ignores the externalities of US emissions, could trigger a similar response from other countries.[72] If other countries likewise ignore the effects of their emissions on the United States, they will weaken their climate efforts in ways that cause climate damage to the United States. As the IWG noted, accounting for the global benefits of US actions "can encourage reciprocal action by other nations, leading ultimately to international cooperation that increases both global and U.S. net benefits relative to what could be achieved if each nation considered only its own domestic costs and benefits."[73]

The negative impacts of climate change to citizens and residents of the United States also extend far beyond our geographic borders. US citizens have investments in climate-vulnerable foreign businesses, foreign properties, and other assets; US citizens have interests in consuming climate-vulnerable foreign goods and services, including tourism; eight million US citizens live abroad and therefore suffer from climate change impacts in other countries; the United States has legal obligations and a willingness to pay to protect global commons like the oceans and Antarctica, which are adversely affected by climate change; and US citizens value and are willing to pay to protect foreign natural resources like rainforests, foreign charismatic megafauna like pandas, and the health and welfare of foreign citizens.

Thus, the Trump administration's "domestic only" approach ignores international spillovers, foreign reciprocity, and extraterritorial interests. As a result, even if the goal was to measure the negative impacts of climate change in the United States, the measure that the administration uses is arbitrary and inadequate. Indeed, the administration excludes important impacts that accrue in the United States. It explains its approach by reference to the admonition in Circular A-4 to "focus on benefits and costs that accrue to citizens and residents of the United States."[74] But instead of actually carrying out this command, the administration arbitrarily excludes important negative impacts that do affect the United States.

**

The Trump administration's new interim social cost of carbon values is indefensible. The 7 percent discount rate is empirically incorrect and ethically dubious. Similarly, the domestic-only focus treats people in other countries as if their lives did not matter, and, even from a purely nationalistic perspective, will likely impose *more* climate costs on Americans in the future as a result of ignoring the international spillovers of climate change and the international tragedy of the commons characteristic of the climate change problem. Cost-benefit analyses based on the Trump social cost of carbon treat the most important environmental issue of our time as though it were an easily ignorable distraction.

10

Manipulating Transfers

In addition to obscuring the *costs* of its deregulatory agenda—by ignoring or minimizing the health harms associated with repealing or weakening environmental and public health standards—the Trump administration has used methodological tricks to exaggerate the *benefits* of its actions. One way it has done this is by characterizing certain transfers between two parties as a benefit to one, contravening established techniques of cost-benefit analysis going back decades.

Imagine a regulation that sets a per-ton fee on emitters of a particular pollutant, with the fee deposited into a fund for environmental remediation. Is this fee a cost or a benefit? For the regulated industry, clearly it imposes a cost, but from the perspective of the recipient of the funds (like a local government), the fee definitely looks like a benefit. Because economic analysis takes the perspective of society as a whole, this type of payment, called a transfer payment, is not included when agencies analyze the net impacts of regulation. Instead cost-benefit analysis is concerned with the incentives these transfer payments can create. In the case of the per-ton pollution fee, for example, existing emitters might invest in technology that reduces their emissions and, in turn, the amount they must pay into the remediation fund. The benefits of the policy then stem from the resulting public health and environmental improvements from less pollution. The costs are the additional expenditures for the new technology. The policy is desirable if the benefits outweigh the costs. But the tax itself does not enter in this calculation.

Why are transfer payments not included in cost-benefit analyses? It is because the amount of money leaving the hands of one party is equal to the amount reaching the hands of the other party. To the extent that a payment involves transaction costs—writing and mailing a check, for example—those costs should be counted in a cost-benefit analysis. But the payment itself is not. In the case of the tax, the amount paid by polluters is equal to the amount received by the government. Any transfer will have this feature of symmetry, so it does not make sense to treat one side of a transfer payment as a cost or a benefit, because the transaction ends in a wash. Unfortunately, another way in which the Trump administration is mangling cost-benefit analysis is by treating one side of a transfer payment as an impact of regulation while ignoring the other side. What is more, it does so inconsistently: sometimes negative impacts to the federal Treasury are

Reviving Rationality. Michael A. Livermore and Richard L. Revesz, Oxford University Press (2020). © Oxford University Press. DOI: 10.1093/oso/9780197539446.001.0001.

treated as costs and at other times as benefits. This approach is the antithesis of appropriate analysis and, as this chapter shows, leads to truly perverse results.

A Clearly Established Consensus

The George W. Bush era Circular A-4 instructs agencies to first develop a baseline against which to evaluate the proposed regulation ("the way the world would look absent the proposed action") and to "describe the alternatives available . . . and the reasons for choosing one over another."[1] The agencies then "should discuss the expected benefits and costs of the selected regulatory option."[2] This discussion is the heart of cost-benefit analysis, covering how the proposed action is expected to produce those benefits and costs, what incentives the regulation may generate, the methodology used to monetize these benefits and costs, and any unquantifiable benefits and costs.[3] In so doing, agencies analyze the impacts of the regulation from the perspective of society as a whole, comparing well-being if the regulation went into effect to well-being in the baseline.

As defined in Circular A-4, "transfer payments are monetary payments from one group to another that do not affect total resources available to society."[4] The circular explicitly tells agencies they "should not include transfers in the estimates of the benefits and costs of a regulation."[5] It explains that "benefit and cost estimates should reflect real resource use" and transfer payments "do not affect total resources available to society."[6] Instead, transfer payments should be "address[ed] . . . in a separate discussion of the regulation's distributional effects."[7]

This approach does not imply that transfer payments do not affect economic behavior. In fact, the opposite is often true. As indicated above, a pollution tax is a transfer payment because the money that leaves the coffers of private parties is equal to the money that enters the coffers of the government. But such a tax provides an incentive to make investments in pollution reduction, which are costs, that lead to improved health and environmental outcomes, which are benefits. And those costs and benefits, of course, would be counted in the cost-benefit analysis used to evelute the policy.

As traditionally carried out, cost-benefit analysis seeks to maximize the net benefits of government policies to society and is indifferent to how those costs and benefits are distributed among the various affected actors.[8] But that does not imply that government policies should be indifferent to distributional effects. The government might prefer, for example, to shift money from richer people to poorer people. In the United States, this kind of progressive transfer is accomplished in part through an income tax on the relatively wealthy coupled with an earned income credit on those who are less well off. Cost-benefit analysis does not shed light on whether this transfer is desirable.[9] Instead, the transfer would need to be justified on independent normative grounds.[10]

Over four decades, presidential administrations with very different views on regulatory policy and on the optimal level of redistribution have come and gone, but transfer payments have always been treated separately from economic impacts. For example, a 1996 best practices document issued during the Clinton administration formalized the conceptual distinction between transfers and impacts, directing agencies that "transfers should not be included in the [economic analysis] estimates of the benefits and costs of a regulation."[11] A later guidance counseled agencies to "address [transfers] in a separate discussion of the regulation's distributional effects."[12] Early in George W. Bush's first term, the administration reissued guidelines that instructed agencies to "report transfers separately and avoid the misclassification of transfer payments as costs or benefits."[13] It explained that transfers do not reflect "net welfare gains to society."[14] And Circular A-4, discussed above, followed two years later. Under President Obama, the OMB reaffirmed that transfer payments must be described and accounted for, distinct from net economic impacts, as part of an agency's analysis of "distributive impacts and equity."[15]

For decades, administrations of both parties, despite their different political perspectives, have treated transfer payments as analytically distinct from the assessment of costs and benefits. On paper, the Trump administration has followed the long-standing consensus. In addition to instructing agencies to follow Circular A-4,[16] the administration issued a guidance document stating that federal spending actions that cause income transfers between taxpayers and program beneficiaries are "transfer rules" and specifically directs agencies to the circular "for a discussion of the distinction between transfers and costs generally."[17]

In practice, however, the Trump administration has blatantly departed from the prior consensus and from established economic theory. As the following examples demonstrate, Trump-era economic analysis features transfer payments split into their two halves, with one held up as a cost or benefit and the other not taken into account in the cost-benefit analysis. When it is convenient to promote the wishes of a favored interest group, an avoided tax payment to the federal government is treated as an economic benefit to the entities not having to pay the tax, while the loss to the public fisc is ignored. But when the beneficiaries of a federal transfer program are a group disfavored by the current administration, the savings to taxpayers from curtailing the program are treated as a benefit and the loss to the beneficiaries is ignored.

Neither of the rules discussed below is currently in effect. They were both struck down by the courts, though on grounds unrelated to the distinction between cost-benefit analysis and transfer payments. But they are revealing of an approach to rulemaking by the Trump administration that does violence to economic theory and to the long-standing and well-accepted practices on how cost-benefit analysis should be conducted.

Preferring Fossil Fuel Companies to the Federal Treasury

After years of study and outreach, the Department of Interior under President Obama issued a rule reforming the way royalty payments for mining on federal lands are calculated. This rule, creating a much simpler valuation system, was projected to save millions in administrative costs and to ensure a return to the public that more accurately represents the value of public resources. When it came into office, the Trump administration promptly delayed implementation of the rule, citing the increased royalty payments made by coal companies as an economic cost. It ignored the other side of these averted payments, the shortfall to the federal government and to state governments, which are the recipients of these royalties. As discussed above, these royalties are transfer payments, and therefore should not be included as either costs or benefits for the purposes of cost-benefit analysis.

The reserves of fossil fuels on federal land are enormous, and more than one-third of all American coal production comes from federal coal leases.[18] In exchange for use of the public resources, the Department of Interior manages a royalty payment program on federal energy leases,[19] charging a fee (between 8.5 and 12.5 percent, depending on the type of mining) based on the "amount or value of the production removed or sold from the lease."[20] Except in Alaska, which receives a larger share of the fees, these royalties are then split in half between the federal government and the state governments where the mining takes place.[21] Due to the size of the coal reserves, these royalty payments from energy leases on public lands are important funding sources: they represent the largest source of income for the federal government outside of taxes,[22] and go to roads, schools, and municipal governments in the states where mining takes place.[23]

Historically, managing these leases has been plagued by problems of transparency, high administrative costs, and low returns to US taxpayers.[24] The management of the leases was widely criticized for decades by both economists and environmental groups: the former, for the systematic undervaluation of reserves, and the latter, for the lack of attention to the environmental impact of coal extraction.[25]

In 2007, during the George W. Bush administration, the Interior Department created a committee to review and improve the procedures for conducting auctions for leasing lands for mineral extraction and assessing royalty payments.

This review identified a number of problems with the current system.[26] First, over 90 percent of auctions had only one bidder. As a result, competition did not drive prices up to ensure adequate compensation for the use of public resources.[27] Second, royalty payments were calculated based on the first sale of the coal after mining.[28] If this sale was from a company to a third party, the market price was used to calculate royalties; if it was from a company to one of its own affiliates (as is common), the Interior Department would review it using a complicated series of benchmarks to determine if the price was fair.[29] These benchmarks were prone to abuse, and companies would pay a royalty based on the low price they charged their own subsidiaries, as opposed to the far higher actual market price they later received for the coal.[30]

Pressure for reform grew during the Obama presidency, as the share of domestic crude oil production that was extracted from federal lands reached a historic high of 36 percent,[31] and a Reuters investigation conducted in 2012 detailed the ways coal producers were avoiding paying full royalties for mining on federal land.[32] The report detailed how companies would sell to one of their subsidiaries at a low price, and how this would slip through the cracks during the review process.[33] The companies would then turn around and sell coal on the international market, taking in a much higher profit.[34]

In response, the Government Accountability Office called on the Interior Department to reform its valuation system, stressing the system's unnecessary complexity and low royalty payments that did not reflect the real market price.[35] As the push for reform grew, it even attracted some limited bipartisan support, with western Republicans such as Alaska senator Lisa Murkowski and Wyoming governor Matt Mead offering support.[36]

After years of studying the problem, a series of public workshops, and review of thousands of comments, in July 2016 the Department of the Interior issued the Valuation Rule.[37] The rule closed the loopholes in calculating royalties, setting the value of the resource for the purposes of the royalty payment at the first arm's-length sale between non-related parties. Thus, companies would no longer be able to reduce their royalty payments by selling the resource at depressed prices to their own subsidiaries.

In the economic analysis accompanying the Valuation Rule, the Interior Department treated as benefits the reduced administrative costs of valuing mineral resources by reference to the first arms-length transaction, which it estimated to be $3.6 million per year.[38] Distinct from these avoided administrative costs—a net benefit to society—the rule was also expected to increase royalty revenues to the federal government and the states by $80 million per year.[39] Consistent with economic theory and long-standing cost-benefit practices, the agency did not treat the larger royalty payments as either a net benefit or a cost. Because the increased government revenues would be offset by higher costs to fossil fuel companies, the higher royalties were instead a transfer payment.[40]

Following the promulgation of President Trump's Executive Order on Energy Independence and Growth,[41] which sought to ease regulatory burdens on energy production,[42] the Interior Department proposed to rescind the Valuation Rule.[43] The economic analysis accompanying the proposal calculated the changes in royalty payments, describing the "costs and benefits . . . this rule will have on all potentially affected groups," including industry and various governments.[44] The rule noted "cost impacts" leading to a "net impact" of "decreased royalty collections" of up to $74.8 million, and noting the "roughly corresponding" effect on the Treasury and states.[45] The analysis also indicated that "industry [would] incur additional administrative costs," due to the more complex valuation formula used before the policy change, and that there would be one-time costs of switching reporting systems for those companies that had prepared for the new requirements, but these costs are not quantified.[46] In justifying the repeal, the Interior Department focused on the fact that the repeal would result "in an overall savings to the industry,"[47] because it concluded that the quantified reduction in royalty payments exceeded the unquantified increase in administrative costs.

Thus, the Trump administration treated the reduction in royalty payments as the benefit of the rescission, the additional administrative costs as its costs, and the amount by which the first amount exceeded the second as the net benefit. But in a proper conducted analysis, royalty savings for fossil fuel companies would be considered one side of a transfer payment, with the other side being the lost royalty revenue for federal and state treasuries. Both sides, taken together, would cancel each other out, leaving the forgone administrative cost savings as the net impact of the repeal. A proper analysis would thus have clearly shown that the repeal was net costly.

After the Interior Department finalized the rescission,[48] the states of California and New Mexico sued, arguing that the department's action violated the Administrative Procedure Act.[49] The United States District Court for the Northern District of California agreed, vacating the government's action.[50] Though the court did not specifically address the economic justification beyond noting Interior's "obligation to conduct a cost-benefit analysis," it found that the department had undertaken its action without providing an adequate explanation, considering alternatives, or allowing a sufficient opportunity to comment on its proposal.[51] The government did not appeal the decision.[52] Nonetheless, this rescission will remain an example of how the Trump administration has mangled cost-benefit analysis in ways that any respected economist would find unrecognizable simply to serve the agenda of favored interest groups.

Preferring the Federal Treasury to Student Borrowers

In its repeal of the Borrower Defense Rule, the Trump administration attempted to undo more than two decades of efforts to protect defrauded student borrowers.[53] In 1994, Congress directed the Department of Education to establish regulations allowing students who had been defrauded by their educational institutions to present that fact as a defense against repayment of their loans.[54] The resulting regulation, promulgated later that year, was only one page long[55] and was largely unused for decades.[56]

In May 2015, Corinthian Colleges, a chain of for-profit colleges, filed for bankruptcy following a number of lawsuits and fraud investigations.[57] Seeking to avoid the obligation to repay the outstanding balance on their student loans, many Corinthian graduates, who had attended the chain of colleges based on fraudulent employment statistics, asserted the borrower defense claims authorized by the regulation. Under the applicable legal standard at the time, they needed to show that "a cause of action would have arisen under applicable State law" against the educational institution.[58] This requirement led to inconsistent results for similarly situated debtors and a serious administrative burden for the Department of Education, which had to evaluate more than fifty different standards.[59] Compounding these administrative difficulties was the sheer volume of the claims: tens of thousands of borrowers sought to assert the defense.[60]

On November 1, 2016, the Education Department promulgated the Borrower Defense Rule, which changed the applicable standard for when a borrower could assert the defense and created clear procedures for filing and granting claims.[61] The new uniform federal standard allows for a borrower defense to be raised if one of three conditions is present: "a substantial misrepresentation, a breach of contract, or a favorable, nondefault contested judgment against the school."[62]

In the accompanying cost-benefit analysis, the department determined that the rule's benefits justified its costs.[63] The discharges themselves are transfer payments, because they shift money from creditor to debtor (here from the government to the student borrower) and therefore should be treated separately for purposes of economic analysis. Consistent with standard practices and relying on Circular A-4, the rule explicitly treated these transfers as categorically distinct from the rule's cost and benefits.[64] Thus, the sizable disbursements to students (up to $5.8 billion annually) were not included among the rule's benefits in the cost-benefit analysis, and the corresponding payments by the government were not included among its costs.[65]

The rule was expected to significantly increase the number of borrowers who succeeded in discharging loans. The benefit of the rule was not the discharge itself, but that such borrowers would "become bigger participants in the economy," including by "buying a home, saving for retirement, or paying for other expenses."[66] In reaching this conclusion, the analysis described how high student debt can hinder marriage, home ownership, access to credit, and finding steady employment.[67] The rule, therefore, was forecast to lead to "significant positive consequences for affected borrowers" and as a consequence, "associated spillover economic benefits."[68]

In June 2017, the Education Department, now under the leadership of Betsy DeVos, who had characterized the Obama-era rule as "free money" for anyone who "raise[d] his or her hands,"[69] delayed implementation of the rule, which had been set to go into effect July 1.[70] The department indicated that postponing the rule "will help to avoid the[] significant costs to the Federal government" of discharging additional loans.[71] Left unmentioned in the analysis was the cost to student loan borrowers, who would no longer be eligible for relief from their debt.[72]

The Education Department eventually proposed a replacement policy in July 2018 that would sharply limit the circumstances under which a borrower could assert a defense to repayment.[73] However, while the department was formulating this replacement policy, students who would have been eligible for loan discharges and various states sued.[74] The court agreed with their claims that delaying the implementation of the Borrower Defense Rule was unlawful,[75] finding that the department had "failed to consider how the public interest or the interest of student borrowers would be affected by its decision."[76]

As a result of the court's ruling, the Obama-era rule finally took effect in October 2018.[77] But less than a year later, DeVos promulgated a replacement rule that would make it much more difficult for borrowers to take advantage of debt relief.[78] The final replacement closely resembles the July 2018 proposal, albeit with some of the most criticized provisions omitted.[79] The economic analysis accompanying the rule noted that borrowers would receive $11.1 billion less in discharges over ten years, and these reduced discharges were nominally treated as transfer payments.[80] However, the rule repeatedly refers to the savings to the federal government. In contrast, the positive effects of loan forgiveness for borrowers are not discussed at all.[81] As a result of this Trump administration rollback, only loans disbursed from July 2017 to July 2020 will be covered by the Obama-era rule.[82]

Who Counts

As with the rescission of the Valuation Rule, the delay of the Borrower Defense Rule was improperly justified on the basis of one side of a transfer payment, touting a gain for one party to a transaction without acknowledging a corresponding loss to the other party. In both proceedings, the Trump administration's approach is clearly inconsistent with economic theory and long-standing administrative practices, which would consider both sides of the transfer as part of the distributional consequence of the rule and include neither in the cost-benefit analysis.

For the rescission of the Valuation Rule, the Trump administration treated reduced payments by fossil fuel companies as benefits, while ignoring the symmetric deficit to the federal Treasury and to the states. In turn, for the delay of the Borrower Defense Rule, the administration treated reduced outlays by the federal Treasury and private lenders as benefits, while ignoring the symmetric cost imposed on student borrowers. In one proceeding, the Trump administration said that society is better off with less money in the federal Treasury. In the other proceeding, it said exactly the opposite.

In both proceedings, the transfer was between the federal government and private parties. In its rescission of the Valuation Rule, the Trump administration revealed that it prefers money to be in the hands of coal companies rather than in the coffers of the federal Treasury. Delaying the Borrower Defense Rule showed that it prefers money in the coffers of the Treasury rather than in the hands of students. The implication, by transitivity, is that the government prefers coal companies to students. In order to achieve this perverse result, the Trump administration twisted cost-benefit analysis beyond recognition

***

In summary, the Trump administration counts as a benefit a shortfall to the federal Treasury that helps a group it favors: companies extracting fossil fuels from federal lands. In contrast, it counts as a cost a use of Treasury funds to help a group it disfavors: student borrowers in disputes with for-profit colleges and universities. Under any properly conducted cost-benefit analysis neither would count as either a cost or a benefit. Instead, each is one half of a transfer payment. To properly evaluate the distributional consequences of a regulation, both sides need to be considered. And neither side is relevant to determine whether the rule is economically efficient, which is the basis for the cost-benefit inquiry that federal agencies are required to undertake.

PART III
REBUILDING

11

Future Directions

The Trump administration has crashed hard against the guardrails. These norms developed over the past several decades to balance the competing demands of competent administration of the nation's laws and accountability to the political process. Although the system of guardrails was far from perfect, the Trump administration's many failures demonstrate the value of this system for the American public. With a diminished Office of Information and Regulatory Affairs (OIRA) and cost-benefit analysis treated by the administration like a charade, the question facing both political parties is whether they want to, and can, commit themselves to rebuilding—and even improving—the system that Trump inherited.

For Democrats, the fundamental question they face is, "If the Republicans refuse to play by the rules, why should we?" As discussed in chapter 2, there have long been constituencies within the Democratic Party that oppose the use of cost-benefit analysis and the institution of regulatory review. They view OIRA as beholden to big business and cost-benefit analysis as embodying a flawed set of moral views that irredeemably bias review against regulatory protections. When the use of cost-benefit analysis was an area of bipartisan consensus, these groups had good reason to reconcile themselves to that reality and learn to work within its parameters. But the Trump administration has upended that status quo, and progressives who oppose cost-benefit analysis have a new opening to push for it to be abandoned.

Republicans, in contrast, must decide whether to repudiate the approach of the Trump administration or double down. Doing away with constraints is liberating, and Donald Trump has signaled his affiliation with core Republican constituencies in ways that prior Republicans have been hesitant to do—and he has been repaid with extreme loyalty in return. For a substantial portion of Republican voters, Trump is a heroic figure, relentlessly defending ordinary Americans against the deception and hypocrisy of despised elites.[1] Departing from this pose in favor of the type of managerial competence once embraced by figures like Mitt Romney is not a clearly winning proposition for politicians who must compete in Republican primaries.

Despite the incentives of some actors in each of the parties to abandon cost-benefit analysis, all hope of retaining a robust role for OIRA and cost-benefit analysis is not lost. The synthesis achieved by the Obama administration between

Reviving Rationality. Michael A. Livermore and Richard L. Revesz, Oxford University Press (2020). © Oxford University Press. DOI: 10.1093/oso/9780197539446.001.0001.

cost-benefit analysis and a progressive policy agenda remains an attractive approach for Democratic politicians, who must balance a variety of competing pressures within their party. Cost-benefit analysis also helped make it more difficult for the Trump administration to roll back Obama-era rules. Doing away with cost-benefit analysis would also reinforce the narrative that regulatory policies are blatant power grabs by agencies seeking to maximizing their budgets, or political appointees promoting an ideological agenda, rather than good faith efforts to deliver value for the public. Among Republicans, there is some recognition that limiting their coalition to Trump's core base is a recipe for demographic disaster as the country becomes more diverse and tolerant. Embracing cost-benefit analysis may be part of a larger strategy for Republican politicians to draw from formerly discarded components of their intellectual tradition to reposition themselves for this future.

How these politics shake out will have substantial normative consequences. If future administrations seek to reestablish cost-benefit analysis and genuine regulatory review, there will be an important opportunity to keep what has worked in the prior system while making much needed improvements going forward. There are many good reasons to believe that some set of guardrails to constrain political influence at agencies is desirable, and good reasons to specifically endorse cost-benefit analysis and centralized review—when they are done well. But the past success of a practice or institution does not guarantee its future existence. If the party system has shifted in ways that generate incentives for both parties to defect from their prior consensus, it is possible that the Obama administration will represent the high-water mark for cost-benefit analysis and OIRA.

The Democrats' Choice

The Obama synthesis of cost-benefit analysis and a progressive policy agenda did not sit well with all Democratic constituencies, and some advocates have called for future Democratic administrations to take a different path. Writing for *The Prospect*, Jeff Hauser of the progressive Center for Economic and Policy Research calls for a series of reforms with an ultimate goal of turning "OIRA to a shell of its former self."[2] In Hauser's view, OIRA and cost-benefit analysis were largely an impediment to the progressive agenda he favors. He is particularly critical of Obama's choice of Sunstein to run OIRA,[3] arguing that "when Obama gave Sunstein the keys to the regulatory castle at OIRA, he ensured that his first term would fail to seize the opportunity to rapidly bring about the 'change' he had promised to the country." In response to what he believes were the failures of the Obama administration, he calls for a series of reforms, including "modify[ing] the Reagan-era executive order that mandates a cost-benefit analysis for all rules," or even "strip[ping] OIRA of much of its authority."

Hauser's critique resonates with the views of other figures who are influential among progressive on these issues. In particular, after leaving the administration, Lisa Heinzerling has been quite critical of the relationship between OIRA and agencies, based on her experiences at the Environmental Protection Agency (EPA).[4] Heinzerling offers the following summary of her views:

> The process [of regulatory review] is utterly opaque. It rests on assertions of decision-making authority that are inconsistent with the statutes the agencies administer. The process diffuses power to such an extent—acceding, depending on the situation, to the views of other Cabinet officers, career staff in other agencies, White House economic offices, members of Congress, the White House Chief of Staff, OIRA career staff, and many more—that at the end of the day, no one is accountable for the results it demands (or blocks, in the case of the many rules stalled during the OIRA process). And, through it all, environmental rules take a particular beating, from the number of such rules reviewed to the scrutiny they receive to the changes they suffer in the course of the process.[5]

In addition to these process concerns, Heinzerling reiterates long-standing substantive objections, arguing that

> the cost-benefit lens through which OIRA viewed agency rules proved to skew against some kinds of rules, in particular environmental rules, since so many of the benefits of environmental rules are difficult or impossible to quantify and monetize, and since so many of these benefits occur in the future while the settled practice of cost-benefit analysis is to steeply discount future consequences.[6]

In Heinzerling's view, these substantive issues are more difficult to address than the process concerns, many of which (she argues) could be dealt with by more faithfully following the procedures laid out in the Clinton executive order on regulatory review.[7] By contrast, she argues, "so long as the culture at OIRA does not change and so long as cost-benefit is the decision tool of choice, environmental protection will suffer."[8]

It is not surprising that not everyone was ultimately happy with the Obama administration's version of cost-benefit progressivism. The Democratic Party is made up of a diverse array of groups and interests, and while their goals sometimes overlap, other times they do not. The Obama administration successfully pursued many progressive policy goals, but others stalled or never made it onto the agenda.[9]

But at the same time, the administration faced criticisms from within the party that it was going too far. For example, in 2010, Mark Warner, a Democratic senator from the swing state of Virginia, laid blame for the slow pace of the economic recovery on "executives' belief that Washington regulators are stifling fresh investment and discouraging innovation through new rules and requirements."[10] In response, he proposed a "pay-go" system for regulation that called for agencies to "eliminate one existing regulation for each new regulation they wanted to add" and to "offset [the costs of new rules] by cost burden reductions on existing regulations."[11] Versions of these two proposals—pushed by a senior voice in the Democratic Party during the Obama administration—were incorporated into Donald Trump's executive order on regulation.[12]

The Trump administration has also led some traditional opponents of cost-benefit analysis to see at least some value in the technique. Rena Steinzor, who was a founder and former president of the Center for Progressive Reform, has leveled a number of critiques against cost-benefit analysis and OIRA over the years.[13] Nevertheless, she recognizes that it provides a standard that can be used to hold agencies to account, and she criticizes the EPA under Trump for some of the same violations of established cost-benefit methods discussed in this book, including for the agencies' refusal to properly account for co-benefits in seeking to undermine the Mercury and Air Toxics Standards rule.[14] Amy Sinden, another longtime critic of cost-benefit analysis, similarly condemns the Trump administration for failing to hew to its purported cost-benefit principles and instead moving toward "a brave new politics of populism in which expertise in all forms is suspect and intellectual integrity (or even just its pretense) is vilified and dispensable."[15]

Looking forward, then, there are several factors that are likely to influence the path taken by future Democratic administrations. With respect to the institution of regulatory review, there are a number of reasons to believe that it will be resilient to many of the critiques that have been leveled against it. As noted by Justice Kagan nearly two decades ago, presidents are held accountable for the actions of administrative agencies and they face considerable pressure to deliver policy results that are achievable only through administrative action—especially during periods of political gridlock.[16] OIRA review has proven useful for presidents of both political parties as a means to assert control over regulatory policymaking at the many agencies spread out across the federal government. If OIRA review were to be dismantled entirely, some centralized mechanism for reasserted centralized control over agencies would almost certainly move into the void in a Democratic administration.

The experience of the Carter administration is instructive. As recounted by Thomas Weko, Carter's campaign came in "the wake of the Watergate affair [when] journalists, scholars, and politicians concluded that a large and powerful White House staff was a dangerous excrescence on the national political system."[17] Accordingly, Carter, who campaigned as the anti-Nixon, promised to severely curtail the power of White House staff and reinstitute a "cabinet government" that "permit[ted] cabinet departments to enjoy their customary prerogatives in formulating policy and advising the president."[18] This experiment with decentralized power was widely perceived to be a disaster for the administration, with appointees who "didn't feel that they work[ed] for Jimmy Carter," who were unable or unwilling to forge strong relationships between the president and party constituencies, and who had a "multiplicity of voices" on policy issues—rather than a coherent administration-wide position— that "embarrassed the administration" and "contributed to doubts about the president's leadership ability."[19] After two years, Carter attempted to reverse course, but it was too late and he lost after his first term in a landslide defeat to Ronald Reagan, who immediately abandoned the failed experiment with decentralization through a muscular assertion of presidential authority.

Carter's experience amply demonstrated the costs of decentralization. If Democratic constituencies simply could not be forged together into a coherent government platform, then even with all of the downsides of decentralization, it might be the only way to accommodate diverse interests within the party: in essence allowing the environmentalist to control the EPA, the labor unions to control the Labor Department, and the teachers' unions to control the Department of Education. But the vast political costs of such an approach—made clear during the Carter administration—makes such a solution the best course of action only under extreme conditions of party discord. Despite important intraparty disagreement, the Democrats do not appear to be forced into such an arrangement. (The situation may be different for the Republican Party, a point to which we return below.)

The questions of whether OIRA will be the primary office for centralized regulatory review, and whether cost-benefit analysis will continue to be the substantive standard, however, remain open. Given the substantive expertise and reputation of OIRA staff, the logic for OIRA review is diminished if a cost-benefit standard is no longer used. At the very least, such a shift would require a substantial retooling of the office.

With respect to cost-benefit analysis, the Democrats will face the same choice that they have for administrations dating back to Bill Clinton, but with a twist. The perennial issue is how best to balance the progressive demands for more aggressive regulatory protections against the concerns among moderates about regulatory costs, and a more general electoral fear of being cast as zealots who are bent on imposing rules on industry at the expense of the American economy. The twist is that when prior Democrats have made this decision at the start of their administration, it has been during periods when the Republican establishment embraced cost-benefit analysis. Now, after years of attacking the methodology during the Obama presidency, and degrading it during the Trump administrations, that mantle has largely been abandoned.

This twist creates several countervailing pressures. In the past, it would have been costly for Democrats to depart from the bipartisan consensus; that cost is lower now that the consensus has evaporated.[20] On the other hand, the Republican Party's move away from cost-benefit analysis gives Democrats an opportunity to pitch themselves as the better protectors of rationality in regulatory decision making.

The experience under Trump of using cost-benefit analysis to critique the administration also shows the value of the technique as a means of providing public accountability for bad policies. Groups have found that the administration's blatant departures from established methods and disclosure of severe negative net consequences for the American public have proven useful in criticizing its regulatory policies, both in court and in the public debate. If Democrats were to abandon cost-benefit analysis or engage in similar Trump-style manipulation, they will find themselves on the receiving end of similar critiques. The threat of losses in court may loom especially large. In addition, once a Republican president again occupies the White House, the Democrats may find that their regulations are more easily overturned.

Nevertheless, once in power, Democrats may decide that cost-benefit analysis is an unnecessary constraint, even if that means being criticized for regulatory zealotry or losing in court. Indeed, Democrats may decide that they will face those criticisms no matter what approach they use, pointing to the experience under President Obama. And court losses may come notwithstanding quality cost-benefit analysis, especially if the current trend among conservative jurists and legal scholars of extreme skepticism of government agencies continues to gain momentum.[21]

That a Republican president was the first to attempt to cast off this constraint undermines whatever norm of reciprocity helped support the system of guardrails inherited by Trump. Cost-benefit analysis, like the other guardrails that exist within the executive, has survived as long as it has in part because administrations of both political parties were willing to play by the rules. In an interview with Cass Sunstein 2018, writer Dylan Matthews posed the following argument in favor of future Democratic administrations moving away from the Obama synthesis that Sunstein contributed to:

> Liberals and leftists are being hampered by the generosity of their principles. . . . [T]hey need to learn to play dirtier and can't afford to hamstring themselves by, say, subjecting their policies to cost-benefit analysis when faced with a figure like Trump who's not hamstrung by anything.

An analogy might be drawn to the prisoners' dilemma, where two strategic actors are collectively better off cooperating than defecting, but each individual actor has incentives to drop out of the agreement. Under these conditions, it can be difficult to maintain a cooperative posture, with each party knowing that the other has an incentive to defect. There is a famous experiment by political scientist Robert Axelrod where he showed that, especially under uncertainty, the best strategy to play in a prisoners' dilemma was the "tit-for-tat" approach that starts with cooperation, but then immediately strikes back with defection at the first sign of bad faith.[22] By defecting from the long-term agreement to carry out cost-benefit analysis within the range of accepted norms, the current administration has destabilized what was a very beneficial cooperative equilibrium. It is possible that the Democrats will respond to this violation of the settled arrangement by defecting themselves, initiating a feedback that ultimately does away with cost-benefit analysis in any rigorous form altogether.

The choices of the next Democratic administration may turn, in part, on predictions about the relationship of future Republicans to cost-benefit analysis. If the approach of the Trump administration, which built on the heated anti-regulatory rhetoric used by Republicans during the Obama administration, is anticipated to continue, then Democrats may ultimately decide that they need not continue to antagonize activists within their base who have always strongly opposed cost-benefit analysis. If, on the other hand, they can anticipate that forces within the Republican Party who would like to rebuild the guardrails will be ascendant in the future, Democrats may be more inclined to invest their own political capital in upholding them.

Cost-Benefit Analysis and the GOP

The challenges posed by Donald Trump to the future of the Republican Party extend far beyond the question of whether cost-benefit analysis is used to evaluate regulatory decisions or whether OIRA will continue to play its traditional role in the White House. Nevertheless, leaders within that party will have to make decisions about these questions, and so we now attempt to sketch out some of the alternative paths that are available and the pitfalls that leaders are likely to face along the way.

As with a future Democratic administration, one question for a future Republican administration is institutional, concerning the role of OIRA and centralized regulatory review more generally. Republicans can likewise learn lessons from Jimmy Carter about the value of centralization, but they face the additional, perhaps confounding, example of Donald Trump. Few Democrats would argue that the Trump administration has been a success, and many would be happy to attribute at least some of these failures to the president's management style. For Republicans, the conclusion is less clear: some may view the administration as a policy failure for its inability to deliver many concrete substantive results to core party constituencies; but others may view the administration as a resounding political success based on its bond with the Republican base and ability to survive a string of scandals while incessantly attacking political rivals. The particular management style of the Trump administration, with its many inconsistencies and diminished role for centralizing institutions like OIRA, may be seen as generating important political benefits, if not policy success.

An additional complicating factor is the degree of tumult within the Republican Party. Trump's election brought to the front a substantial split between party elites and the voting base on issues such as immigration and trade. In placing those issues at the center of his primary campaign, he forced a confrontation with party leaders who sought to expand the party's appeal beyond its core base of white voters.[23] His success in rallying the voting base and rising from a political non-entity to the White House has demonstrated at least the short-term power of his approach. There is now an energized Trump wing of the Republican Party—hardline anti-immigration; skeptical of trade, international institutions, and military intervention; harshly critical of the media and academia—that competes with more traditional actors within the party. Managing this conflict is likely to be a dominant challenge for the party in the coming years.

In light of this difficulty, the advantage of a more decentralized approach is that it avoids the need to arrive at a single coherent administration-wide policy and message. The multiplicity of voices that led to the impression of failed leadership during the Carter administration may be an advantage in the current state of affairs within the Republican Party, as a range of different constituencies can feel as though they have some representation in the government: Treasury Secretary Steven Mnuchin for the banks; Stephen Miller drafting executive orders to please anti-immigration constituencies; and Scott Pruitt and Andrew Wheeler at the EPA for coal voters. Officials publicly disagreeing with each other, and the president, both during and after their time in government, could be understood as a pressure valve for a loose coalition facing deep rifts. This president has also been much more aggressive in turning over staff. That churn as led to instability and a degree of chaos. But the lack of coherent and consistent policy positions also gives various constituencies the impression that they can continue to influence future decisions, as any given policy direction might turn on a whim.

However future Republicans manage the problem of centralization, there is the additional question of cost-benefit analysis. Like its predecessors, the Trump administration has embraced the language of cost-benefit analysis. But it has done so while flagrantly violating established methods and, frankly, the entire spirit of the enterprise. One possible road forward for the party would be to continue the approach of the Trump administration of engaging in this charade. It may be that future Republican administrations will simply assert that they are carrying out cost-benefit analysis, while doing nothing of the kind. One of the major downsides of this approach has been trouble in court, but if the party is able to install a critical mass of judges willing to ignore these failures, then that cost may decline over time.

A second, perhaps less likely alternative, would be a principled rejection of cost-benefit analysis in favor of a more explicitly libertarian approach to governing. In discussing the Trump administration's approach to regulation, former OIRA administrator John Graham along with co-author Keith Belton observed that Trump appeared to "offer[] a . . . philosophical and quasi-Constitutional rationale for deregulation that is rooted in a defense of individual liberty and democracy."[24] This rationale "suggests that the administration might be inclined to remove or scale back some regulations, even if it cannot be shown that those acts of deregulation have tangible cost savings that justify the forgone benefits of regulation." In this way, liberty—in the sense of the absence of "intrusion on the freedoms of private citizens and enterprises"[25]—is not valued because it contributes to people's well-being but for other reasons.[26] Among their recommendations for the Trump administration is developing some means of estimating the effects of deregulation on this value of freedom.

This approach presents hazards for a Republican administration for several reasons. Most obviously, the party is not uniformly libertarian. Anti-immigration constituencies favor extremely intrusive application of government force to achieve their goals, which require a substantial administrative and enforcement apparatus that subjects private individuals and businesses (large and small) to considerable regulatory demands. Social conservatives within the party favor increased regulation of the reproductive choices of women. Libertarianism may appeal to some conservative think tanks, but it is not clear that—other than as a mere rhetorical devise—it has much purchase with the average Republican voter.

An additional problem that might arise for Republicans who are enthusiastic about a more explicitly libertarian approach is that it might not always produce the results they anticipate. Were an intellectually coherent formal method of measuring freedom to be developed, it would need to account for both sides of the equation. A pollution control regulation might limit the freedom of regulated companies, which have less latitude to spend their money as they might choose. On the other side are the freedom benefits associated with fewer lifetimes spent under the restrictions imposed by asthma. The liberty constraints on automakers that wish to produce less safe cars would have to be balanced against the restrictions on liberty associated with being confined to a wheelchair after an avoidable car accident. Large banks might chafe under the restrictive constraints of financial regulation, but that freedom cost must be balanced against the curtailment of life prospects that many people suffered as a consequence of the Great Recession. If a future Republican administration attempts to engage in an inquiry with liberty at its foundation, it may find itself back in the same position it currently faces: with a methodology that it developed clearly demonstrating the value of government protections.[27]

A final approach for a future Republican administration would be to reembrace serious use of cost-benefit analysis and recommit itself to honestly evaluating the positive and negative effects of its decisions. It may be that a political climate may arise in which such a move would be possible, and even rewarded—perhaps as part of a strategy to distance the party from its Trump period. The Republican Party can justifiably take credit for pushing cost-benefit analysis when faced with Democratic opposition, just as it once pushed for cap-and-trade and—a long time ago—the use of expansive federal authority to protect the rights of formerly enslaved people in the American South.[28] American parties are flexible entities with a large stock of historical and intellectual resources. As the political situation changes, incentives to draw from some of these prior traditions within the party may arise.

The Judicial Refuge

If future Democratic or Republican administrations choose to move away from cost-benefit analysis—either by formally abandoning the practice or continuing some version of the cost-benefit analysis charade initiated under Trump—the reality of judicial review will be an important limiting constraint. As we have emphasized several times in this book, the Trump administration has accumulated an abysmal record in challenges to its agency actions, in part because it has refused to stay within the traditional guardrails around agency action, including cost-benefit analysis. Future administrations will have to defend their actions before courts, which creates another forum where cost-benefit norms can be enforced. The prospect of judicial review may also provide a reason for administrations to avoid at least explicitly rejecting cost-benefit analysis.

Increasingly over the past several decades, courts have demonstrated a willingness to impose cost-benefit analysis requirements on agencies. A trio of Clean Air Act cases in the US Supreme Court helps demonstrate the trend.[29] In the first, the Court was extremely skeptical about the use of cost-benefit analysis to evaluate clean air regulations. In a 2001 decision, *Whitman v. American Trucking*, the Court heard a challenge to a decision by the Clinton-era EPA to increase the stringent National Ambient Air Quality Standards (NAAQS) for particulate matter and ozone.[30] In keeping with its prior practice, the EPA had not considered costs when setting the standards. The language of the statute it-self was silent on cost considerations, requiring the agency to adopt standards "requisite to protect the public health" with "an adequate margin of safety" but without explicitly requiring or prohibiting that costs be considered.[31] Industry argued that given the substantial costs imposed by the EPA's new standard, not weighing the costs and benefits was irrational and violated the statute. Writing for a unanimous court, Justice Scalia upheld the EPA's approach, finding that the relevant provision of the Act "unambiguously bars cost considerations from the NAAQS-setting process."[32]

A decade later, the Court's position shifted. In *EPA v. EME Homer City Generation*,[33] the Court heard a challenge to the Cross-State Air Pollution Rule discussed in chapter 2. The portion of the Clean Air Act at issue in that case re-quired states to prohibit sources "from emitting any air pollutant in amounts which will . . . contribute significantly" to air quality violation in downwind states.[34] As in *Whitman*, the statute was silent on whether the agency could con-sider costs, but unlike in *Whitman* that agency had used cost to set the relevant standards. And, unlike in *Whitman*, the Court found that there was sufficient discretion for the agency to take costs into account, even when not explicitly au-thorized to do so by the statute.

On the heels of *EME Homer*, the Court decided the third in this Clean Air Act trifecta, this time hearing a challenge to the Mercury and Air Toxics Standards discussed in chapter 8. In this case, the portion of the act at issue required the EPA to regulate if, after carrying out a study of the public health effects of hazardous pollutants emitted from power plants, it determined that "such regulation is ap-propriate and necessary."[35] As in the two earlier cases, the statute did not specify whether costs should be considered. Unlike for the Cross-State Air Pollution Rule, the Obama administration had decided not to consider costs when making that appropriate and necessary determination, based on its reading of what was permissible under the statute. Only later in the rulemaking process did the EPA engage in a cost-benefit analysis. In *Michigan v. EPA*, the Court decided that, un-like in *Whitman* (where statutory silence implied that cost-considerations were prohibited) and unlike in *EME Homer* (where statutory silence allowed, but did not necessarily require cost-considerations), in this case, the vague language in the statute *required* that costs be considered.[36]

This trio of cases shows a fairly clear trend line in the Court's attitude toward cost-benefit analysis: from skepticism to embrace. This trend has been mirrored elsewhere in the federal judiciary, and legal scholars have argued that something akin to a common law doctrine has emerged in federal courts in favor of cost-benefit analysis of major agency decisions.[37] If this is true, then perhaps courts can drag along agencies and the White House, even if both political parties de-cide that they would prefer to do away with cost-benefit analysis.

The prospect that the judiciary might provide at least a limited refuge for cost-benefit analysis is not entirely misplaced.[38] But it will be a temporary refuge at best. Courts have some degree of separation from the political process: judges are appointed for life, and various norms and practices in American legal and political culture help preserve judicial independence. Even if both political parties decide to abandon cost-benefit analysis, sitting judges who have become convinced of its merits have no direct incentive to change their positions. US judges are not apparatchiks accustomed to immediately conforming their views to the current official doctrines of their parties, and there are few mechanisms for political actors to discipline judges once they are safely ensconced on the bench. So courts can successfully continue to enforce cost-benefit norms even if both parties decide that they would prefer to leave the practice behind.

However, the US judiciary is not fully divorced from politics: indeed, the appointment of judges (and especially Supreme Court justices) has become among the most contested and polarizing decisions in American political life. Over time, judges selected through this political process are bound to reflect the governing views in their respective parties. And if both parties decide that they would prefer not to be bound by cost-benefit analysis, then they will eventually find jurists who share that opinion. And so, although the judiciary may serve as a final bastion of support for cost-benefit analysis, once the parties have moved on, it may be only a matter of time before the courts follow.

***

For the first time since at least 1992, and perhaps 1981, the immediate future of cost-benefit analysis and OIRA are uncertain. In one sense, the failures of the Trump administration have amply demonstrated the value of cost-benefit analysis and meaningful OIRA review. But, by breaking with decades of consensus, the Trump administration has also opened the door for one or the other political parties to permanently abandon these guardrails. For Democrats, the progressive wing of the party has a long history of opposition to both cost-benefit analysis and OIRA, and post-Trump Democratic administrations are likely to face at least some pressure to give in to these long-standing demands. For Republicans, rebuilding centralized review and engaging in rigorous cost-benefit analysis will require rejecting much of how the Trump administration has done business—a difficult proposition in a party that has become in part defined by loyalty to the Trump brand.

12

Improving the Guardrails

Apart from the political calculations discussed in the last chapter, from a normative perspective, there is very little to recommend the Trump approach to regulation. For conservatives who believe that government should be particularly cautious when interfering with private markets, the Trump administration's rejection of expertise and evidence has tarnished what might otherwise have been an attractive opportunity to pursue deregulatory actions. For progressives, the Trump approach is wrongheaded in its devotion to undoing regulatory protections and demonstrates the pitfalls of pursuing a policy agenda that is unleavened by careful analysis.

Future Democratic and Republican administrations could do much to improve on the status quo simply by abandoning this failed experiment in bad government. There is great value in simply reestablishing the guardrails that were in place prior to January 20, 2017. Decades of bipartisan consensus is not something to cast away lightly, and it is worth investing in rebuilding that foundation.

But, while the past can provide an important starting place, future administrations can be more ambitious. Reinstating prior norms concerning cost-benefit analysis and meaningful regulatory review is a good first step, but there are several reforms that can improve on the system as it was inherited by Donald Trump. We focus on three areas where improvements to cost-benefit analysis are needed and where some measure of bipartisan consensus may be possible.

One reform involves rethinking the role of ex-post analysis of regulation. There have long been calls among experts and administrations of both parties for agencies to engage in "retrospective review" of their decisions.[1] The idea is that after a regulation has been adopted, agencies can look back to investigate whether the rule achieved its goals, and, more generally, what the costs and benefits of the decision were. Although attractive on its face, there are a number of important practical and political challenges that have long interfered with more widespread adoption of the practice. We propose ways to refocus retrospective review that can help overcome these challenges.

A second area where improvements can be made is unquantified costs and benefits. Clinton's Executive Order 12,866 acknowledges the importance of regulatory effects that may be difficult to measure or monetize, but the reality is that unquantified benefits and costs are often downplayed or ignored altogether. One

Reviving Rationality. Michael A. Livermore and Richard L. Revesz, Oxford University Press (2020). © Oxford University Press. DOI: 10.1093/oso/9780197539446.001.0001.

way to address this problem is to deploy tools such as break-even analysis when there are important categories of costs and benefits that defy quantification. These can be useful half-measures, but agencies should continue to push forward in developing techniques that can bring a larger class of regulatory effects into the cost-benefit fold through quantification.

The final area for improvement involves the distributional effects of regulatory decisions. This issue has received considerable attention over the years, both from academics and—to a lesser extent—agency officials. The questions of whether, and how, distributional effects ought to be considered is controversial, and they intersect with contested areas of morality and political philosophy. Nevertheless, there is a growing consensus that distributional analysis of some form is needed. Future administrations should develop a set of consistent guidelines to provide some clarity concerning when and how distributional analysis should be carried out, including in the evaluation of existing regulations.

Please Rewind

There are several steps that a future administration can take to break with the Trump administration and reinstate prior norms concerning regulatory decision making. The choice of an OIRA administrator will be an early first signal of change in direction. The tradition of selecting OIRA administrators who have a strong background in cost-benefit analysis, who lack close ties to any particular interest group, and who have solid reputations for fairness and pragmatism should be reaffirmed. A second important step will be rescinding the Trump executive order *Reducing Regulations and Controlling Regulatory Costs* that included the incoherent and biased two-for-one requirement, put exclusive emphasis on regulatory costs, and instituted a zeroed out regulatory budget. The administration can also quickly reaffirm its commitment to the principles and processes described in Clinton's Executive Order 12,866 and Obama's Executive Order 13,563.

One question that any new administration will face is whether to issue its own executive order on regulatory review, and if so, what the content of that order should be. Two weeks into the Obama administration, the president issued a memorandum asking the Office of Management and Budget (OMB) "to produce within 100 days a set of recommendations for a new Executive Order on Federal regulatory review." The presidential memorandum specifically solicited feedback on "the relationship between OIRA and the agencies," "disclosure and transparency," "public participation," "the role of cost-benefit analysis, . . . distributional considerations, fairness, and concern for the interests of future generations," "the role of the behavioral sciences," and "best tools for achieving public goals through the regulatory process."[2] In responding to this directive, OMB solicited feedback from agencies and the public.

This process was, in retrospect, likely a mistake. It created expectations, especially among constituencies that had long disfavored regulatory review and cost-benefit analysis, that a major change was on the horizon.[3] In reality, the Obama administration did not upend the process. Instead, as discussed in chapter 2, regulatory review continued under the Clinton order, which was eventually affirmed in Obama's Executive Order 13,563, two years after the beginning of the administration.[4] In part, the Obama administration may have come to realize the value of leaving long-existing policies and procedures in place as a way to maintain consistency with prior administrations.

Despite the lack of an executive order that made basic changes to the goals or procedures of regulatory review, the Obama administration nonetheless made a number of valuable incremental improvements to the existing system. These included demonstrating, through its regulatory actions, that there can be considerable overlap between cost-benefit analysis and a progressive regulatory agenda. The estimate for the social cost of carbon generated by its interagency working group was also an extremely important contribution to federal regulatory practice. In addition, during his time at OIRA, Cass Sunstein issued guidance for agencies on how best to incorporate insights from behavioral economics into certain types of regulatory design.[5]

The value of the incremental approach taken by the Obama administration to gradually improving the system of regulatory review has been amply demonstrated by the Trump administration, which has recklessly abandoned the work of prior administrations. The instinct under the Obama administration was ultimately to keep processes, procedures, and methods used during earlier administrations in place so long as they worked well enough, focusing efforts on the most important reforms while accepting that the system that it inherited might not be perfect.[6] This freed the administration to undertake initiatives on new issues—such as the social cost of carbon—without the need to revisit every prior decision made by previous administrations. It also made it more difficult to roll back Obama-era rules, as they were supported by long-standing practices that courts are more likely to respect.

Maintaining continuity with the past also helps reinforce the normative importance of the guardrails. The basic structure of regulatory review by OIRA using cost-benefit analysis has been in place for nearly four decades, and even the Trump administration purports to operate within this tradition. After the completion of the Obama administration, Bill Clinton's Executive Order 12,866 had been endorsed and used in three administrations, of both political parties, over a twenty-four-year period. This continuity has made the choices of the Trump administration to abandon these practices in all but name more stark. Had the

Obama administration issued an executive order that substantially reformed the process, then the decisions of the Trump administration to break with the past may have appeared less radical.

Assuming that one of the priorities of a future administration will be to restore, to a large degree, the pre-Trump status quo, the question arises whether any of the changes adopted during the Trump administration ought to be maintained. The two candidates that seem the most plausible involve exerting formal review of the decisions of independent agencies and extending review to tax regulations—both of which cut against the broader trend of the Trump administration to reduce OIRA's role.

With respect to independent agencies, there has been a long debate about whether OIRA review is appropriate.[7] Both advocates of a more unified executive and proponents of greater use of cost-benefit analysis have argued against excluding independent agencies (such as the Federal Communications Commission and the Securities and Exchange Commission) from OIRA review. Most of the arguments on the other side invoke the value of insulating some agencies from political influence and raise questions about the legality of requiring review.[8] The Obama administration took a step toward extending OIRA review to independent agencies in the President's Executive Order 13,579 that suggested (but did not require) that independent agencies should carry out cost-benefit analysis.[9] The Trump administration took a step further by effectively extending regulatory review to independent agencies.[10] The lack of a legal challenge to this move strengthens the case that OIRA review of independent agencies is, at the very least, lawful. Given general presidential incentives to influence agency decision making, this innovation of the Trump administration may prove resilient.

With respect to review of tax regulations, there is a fundamental difference between tax and other policy areas where regulatory review has traditionally been carried out: unlike other regulatory contexts, tax rules are not primarily justified as a means to address market failures.[11] Rather, the tax system raises revenue to fund the government, while also attempting to avoid distortive incentives and balancing distributional goals.[12] That said, the tax code is also full of various "expenditures" that amount to special carve-outs intended to subsidize groups or activities.[13] It is possible that OIRA review can be helpful for tax regulations, but only if it is given the capacity and mandate to tailor its review to the specific circumstances involved in the tax context. OIRA staff must also include experts in tax who are well positioned to understand the often complex incentive effects of tax rules—otherwise, its feedback is likely to be ill-informed. And any requirement that cost-benefit analysis of tax rules be carried out should require an appropriate means of formally accounting for distributional effects, given the centrality of distribution to tax regulation.

Reorienting Retrospective Review

At its most fundamental, cost-benefit analysis involves two separable inquiries. The first is an effort to anticipate the consequences of different regulatory alternatives in terms of "natural units."[14] For a public health regulation, the natural unit of regulatory benefits might be the number of lives saved; for an environmental rule, a natural unit might include the number of acres of land that are protected. Costs in natural units might include investments in pollution control technology or compliance-related hiring. Only after forecasts in natural units are generated does cost-benefit analysis move to the second inquiry, which is translating these effects to a single metric that can be used to make comparisons. In current US practice, the common metric is monetary, and natural units are given monetary value through the concept of willingness to pay.

Anticipating the consequences of regulations is often a difficult and fraught task. The task is difficult because regulations interact with physical, biological, behavioral, and social systems that are complex, adaptive, and not well understood. One cannot simply take the status quo as a given, change a single part of the system, and expect the rest to remain static. Rather, one can expect regulatory effects to extend into the broader system, generating feedbacks that can dull or intensify the initial effect while also generating second-order effects elsewhere. The task is fraught because forecasts about regulatory effects have political consequences. Understanding the effect of exposure to secondhand smoke on cancer rates, the consequences of greenhouse gas emissions for climate change, or the risks of pesticide residue on foods are not neutral scientific questions of interest based only on human curiosity about the world. Rather, they inform regulatory, legal, and moral judgments with the potential to fundamentally shape social relationships.

Despite these challenges, cost-benefit analysis requires that regulatory effects be anticipated to the degree possible. Over the past several decades, agencies have devoted considerable resources to developing general methods for estimating regulatory effects and then applying those methods to individual rulemakings. Often this task involves the construction of models: simplified representations of some relevant portion of the world as networks of relationships that can be described in mathematical terms. These models help aggregate the existing knowledge base within a relevant domain but often have important areas of uncertainty where data gaps exist. Professional judgment based on existing empirical research is used to fill in these gaps using assumptions about how relationships work in the real world. These models are then used to forecast the effects of regulatory choices under different policy scenarios. These forecasts serve as the first step in cost-benefit analysis, as a set of predictions about the consequences of a regulatory choice in natural units.

It is widely acknowledged, including by agencies engaged in cost-benefit analysis, that forecasts of regulatory consequences have many sources of uncertainty. Well-conducted analyses are clear about the sources of uncertainty and will use various ways to communicate that uncertainty, for example, by presenting estimates of costs and benefits in terms of ranges rather than point values. But, although communicating uncertainty is useful, cost-benefit analysis has greater value when predictions can be made with at least a reasonable degree of confidence. If the net benefits of a potential rule are estimated to be equally likely to be large and negative, large and positive, or zero, then the analysis does not really offer much useful information to decision makers.

In light of these well-known limitations, there have long been calls for agencies to improve the evidence base that is used as inputs into cost-benefit analysis, especially through the use of retrospective analysis. While cost-benefit analysis is prospective in nature, retrospective analysis looks in the other direction and attempts to understand what the consequences of a regulation have been after it has been implemented. The information generated from retrospective review can, at least in theory, be used both to make decisions about the rule in question—such as whether it should be expanded or curtailed—and can also be used to improve the quality of ex-ante cost-benefit analysis going forward.

Advocates of retrospective review cross the political spectrum. Every president since Jimmy Carter has, in one way or another, called on agencies to assess the existing stock of regulations.[15] A group of former OIRA administrators from the Reagan, George H. W. Bush, Clinton, George W. Bush, and Obama administrations has endorsed the idea,[16] as have groups as diverse as the conservative Mercatus Center and the more liberal Progressive Policy Institute.[17] A number of scholars have called for retrospective review and made specific recommendations on how it can be improved,[18] as has the Administrative Conference of the United States, a federal agency charged with making recommendations to improve administrative processes and procedures.[19]

Notwithstanding this impressive bipartisan consensus, actual attempts to implement retrospective review have been fairly minor.[20] The most extensive push came under President Obama. Three different Obama executive orders mention and emphasize the need for comprehensive retrospective review.[21] Perhaps most important, the president made clear that this issue was a genuine priority, and OIRA became deeply involved in the effort to push "regulatory lookback," circulating memoranda on the subject,[22] and facilitating a government-wide effort in which agencies submitted review plans and reported any resulting regulatory changes.[23] The Government Accountability Office assessed the Obama regulatory review initiative and found that substantial steps were taken: 22 agencies had completed nearly 250 regulatory actions by August 2013 that were intended to improve regulatory effectiveness, reduce burdens, or increase the clarity of existing rules.[24]

Despite the general success of the Obama regulatory lookback effort, it had several limitations. One major problem was an emphasis on reducing regulatory burdens rather than improving regulatory performance overall or collecting information that would usefully inform future decision making. A particular focus of the lookback process was "the problem of cumulative burdens."[25] Sunstein has described such cumulative burdens as arising from "requirements [that] may be sensible taken individually, but taken as a whole . . . might be redundant, inconsistent, overlapping, and immensely frustrating, even crazy-making (to use the technical term)."[26] As discussed in chapter 4, Republicans often focused their criticisms during the Obama administration on the overall scope of the regulatory system, rather than the costs and benefits of individual rules. Perhaps the administration's emphasis in its regulatory lookback was partially meant as a response to this criticism, but it also skewed and limited the ultimate value of the exercise.

Even the most successful effort in retrospective review to date, then, was ultimately one-off and ad hoc, with priorities that may have been distorted by the political needs of the day, and which produced some policy changes but little in the way of long-term insight. If retrospective review is going to become a consistent and valuable institution, the Obama administration experience is unlikely to serve as the template.

Advocates of retrospective review have long recognized that there are two sets of challenges to its implementation. One difficulty is that agencies are reluctant to review their own rules. It is not extremely surprising that agencies, under constant scrutiny by politicians who are often happy to engage in bureaucrat bashing at the slightest provocation, might be hesitant to engage in probing criticism of their past decisions. The political costs of finding that programs are underperforming are obvious. Outside experts can sing the praises of impartial review and policy evaluation, but until the basic incentive structure facing agencies changes, their participation is likely to be tentative at best.

The second challenge is that it is often quite difficult to estimate the effects of regulation.[27] The basic issue is generic to a range of scientific inquiries and involves the conditions necessary to draw causal conclusions from data. There is a natural human tendency to infer causation from temporal priority, based on our daily experiences: we watch a glass fall to the floor and immediately shatter, and then we infer that the impact caused the shattering. That intuitive notion of causal inference works well enough in common situations, but in the context of regulation, things are much more complicated. If a clean air regulation is adopted, and then air quality improves, we might naturally infer causation, but that inference may not be warranted. It could be that some other factor led to the air quality improvements, and the regulation was incidental. Or there might be a third cause, such as technological change or political, economic, or social pressures, that independently led to the regulation and the air quality improvement.

In many scientific settings, researchers use experiments, with randomly assigned control groups and treatment groups and a small number of differing variables, to generate the kinds of data that can support causal claims. Observational data from the real world lack the tight controls of experimental settings, but social science researchers have developed a number of ingenious methods to engage in causal inference from data generated outside the lab.[28] One example is to look for discontinuities, especially those that are quasi-random. For example, Michael Greenstone and Justin Gallagher used the arbitrary cutoff at the end of the Superfund National Priorities List to examine the effects of the toxic site cleanup program.[29] Research using these techniques has led to many important insights, but it depends on peculiar data structures that may not exist for the types of questions that have the most policy relevance. In the context of regulations that are rolled out in widespread fashion, with no control groups and a vast number of other temporally correlated changes, estimating causal effects can be particularly difficult.

Various remedies have been proposed to address the problems of political incentives and causal inference that have previously limited retrospective review. These proposals include allocating review responsibilities to an independent agency that was not involved in the initial regulation and asking agencies to design their regulations in ways that involve elements of random assignment to facilitate future efforts to tease out causal effects.[30] At least to date, none of the more ambitious programs of reform have been given serious consideration by political actors, even during the Obama administration's major regulatory lookback push.[31]

In the event of a future administration that is genuinely interested in implementing and improving cost-benefit analysis, moving beyond the current impasse over retrospective review should be a major priority. An important first step will be to frankly acknowledge the past failure to successfully implement consistent retrospective review and to recognize the stable sources of that failure. In particular, framing retrospective review efforts in terms of evaluating individual rules and addressing "the problem of cumulative burdens" has not worked. This framing has led to understandable and predictable resistance by agencies. It also draws attention toward past policy choices rather than improving decision making going forward. Finally, it does not focus analytic resources on contexts where learning is possible and will have the most value.

Instead of the largely negative emphasis of past efforts, a renewed push for retrospective review should separate two different priorities. One priority of review should focus on questions rather than rules.[32] The idea would be to identify areas of uncertainty in regulatory decision making and then undertake a consistent and sustained program of research to reduce that uncertainty. This research program could involve partnerships among government, academic institutions, and perhaps regulated industry and the advocacy community. One such partnership that has been a considerable success is the Health Effects Institute, which is an independent non-profit corporation that receives funding from the automobile industry and the EPA, and that then supports high-quality and well-respected public health research on the effects of air pollution. The Health Effects Institute has played an important role as a "credible neutral arbiter" on issues such as the public health science of particulate matter.[33]

Emphasizing a questions-focused research program has several advantages for overcoming the traditional roadblocks that have hampered retrospective review. Politically, it places much less pressure on agencies. In its current form, retrospective review is a gauntlet that agencies are forced to periodically run, absorbing blows from politicians on both sides along the way. This may be good sport for the politicians, but it is surely no fun for the civil servants at agencies. Substantively, a questions-focused research program targets analytic resources where they are most needed for future decisions, creates at least the potential for sustained progress, and identifies key areas where agencies can facilitate the development of high-quality data.

The second priority would be a regulatory "checkup," which should be framed as a neutral and non-threatening periodic assessment that is a normal part of the regulatory process—not an opportunity for political point scoring. There are many regulations on the books, and changing circumstances or updated information could mean that rules that were once justified no longer make sense, existing requirements could be consolidated or streamlined, or current rules are insufficient to attain their policy goals. Some mechanism to periodically examine existing rules would identify those opportunities. These periodic regulatory checkups should be focused on maximizing net benefits rather than simply reducing burdens. This means that eliminating, modifying, or expanding existing regulations should all be equally favored. The best rules to select for checkup are those that have been on the books for some time, to reduce the risk that checkups will serve as an opportunity for interest groups to re-litigate recent decisions. In addition, rules should be targeted where there is a relatively high likelihood that changed circumstances or new information on costs and benefits would lead to some kind of reform. Checkups can also be an opportunity to identify areas of inaction where new rules could help address lacunas in existing regulatory regimes.

The political rhetoric around these checkups can also help set the tone. In his 2012 State of the Union Address, in the lead up to his reelection campaign,

President Obama touted the regulatory lookback overseen by Sunstein in the following way:

> There's no question that some regulations are outdated, unnecessary, or too costly. In fact, I've approved fewer regulations in the first 3 years of my Presidency than my Republican predecessor did in his. I've ordered every Federal agency to eliminate rules that don't make sense. We've already announced over 500 reforms, and just a fraction of them will save business and citizens more than $10 billion over the next 5 years. We got rid of one rule from 40 years ago that could have forced some dairy farmers to spend $10,000 a year proving that they could contain a spill, because milk was somehow classified as an oil. With a rule like that, I guess it was worth crying over spilled milk.[34]

Sunstein acknowledged his role in the groaner of a joke,[35] but the larger point is the emphasis on reducing regulatory costs (rather than maximizing net benefits) and the use of retrospective review as an opportunity for the president to cast agencies in a negative light. Obama's spilled milk joke was fairly harmless, but it perpetuated the association between retrospective review and public embarrassment for agencies. A more positive framing in both the executive orders and related public statements that emphasizes rules that work well, the benefits of regulation, and changes based on new circumstances or learning could help reduce the perception within agencies that retrospective review is largely a losing proposition.

Improving Quantification

After the consequences of a regulatory decision have been estimated in natural units, cost-benefit analysis requires that they be converted to a common metric so that comparisons can be made. Without this step, it would be impossible to assess whether various regulatory alternatives were superior to each other because some might be an improvement along one unit (such as lives saved) while others are better on another metric (such as number of asthma cases avoided). Placing all effects on a common scale avoids these problems. The US practice has been to convert natural units to a monetary scale, based on the value placed on those effects by the population that experience them. For example, a reduction in air pollution is valued in terms of the preferences of the people who enjoy that benefit, and the costs are valued in terms of the preferences of those who pay them.

There is a long-standing discussion about alternative metrics that could be used in cost-benefit analysis, which might convert natural units to some other scale, such as utility or happiness.[36] One of the advantages of a monetary scale is that it fits fairly comfortably with the standard justification of cost-benefit analysis. The goal of cost-benefit analysis is to identify market failures where government intervention can improve on the results generated by private transactions alone. At least for the most fundamental market failures, which arise from externalities, any regulation that is cost-benefit justified is also a "potentially Pareto" improvement. What this means is that, at least in theory, every person could be made better off with the regulation than without. Because money is fungible and can (in theory) be transferred, it makes sense to use in the context of the potential Pareto test.

Even if everyone agrees that a monetary scale is appropriate, a major challenge in cost-benefit analysis is that many benefits do not have obvious monetary values because they are not directly traded on markets. There is no direct price for reducing general mortality risk, avoiding asthma, or receiving ecosystem services such as clean water or crop pollination. Without a way to make these conversions, estimates of regulatory effects will be left unquantified in the final analysis. Although, in theory, agencies can take these unquantified benefits into account, in reality, these benefits are often de-emphasized, either by agencies themselves, in the public debate, or in the process of judicial review.

One improvement on the current system of simply reporting unquantified benefits is the use of what is sometimes called "break-even analysis."[37] The idea with break-even analysis is that when there are important categories of benefits that have not been quantified, cost-benefit analysis can report what the value would need to be in order to justify the regulation compared to the status quo. For example, if a rule would cost $10 million and save 100 acres of sensitive habitat, then the value of that habitat would have to be over $100,000 per acre to justify the rule. This type of break-even analysis is useful, because it makes explicit what would otherwise be an implicit judgement on the part of the decision maker. Courts may also favor this type of analysis as a way to avoid unquantified benefits being used as "trumps" to justify rules in ways that avoid judicial scrutiny.[38]

Although break-even analysis can be useful in some situations, actually developing valuation methods that can be used to monetize benefits is far superior. In essence, break-even analysis amounts to the declaration of a specific assumption concerning some value in a cost-benefit analysis. This can be useful, from the perspective of transparency and to help clarify the regulatory decision at hand. But it does not itself provide guidance concerning whether a policy choice is justified. A second limitation of break-even analysis is that it can be applied only in contexts where there a relatively small number of types of regulatory effects. To extend the case of the habitat rule above, if the decision saves 100 acres of habitat, results in the lost opportunity to construct a housing tract, shopping center, and medical facility, and slightly increases risks of mosquito-borne disease, there is no single variable that can be subjected to a break-even analysis—the decision has effects on too many dimensions. Only once the dimensions have been reduced down to nearly those needed to conduct a full cost-benefit analysis, with only one missing value, can break-even analysis be done.

For these reasons, investing in efforts to improve valuation methods for regulatory benefits such as healthier ecosystems or more stable financial markets is an important step that a future administration can take to increase the usefulness of cost-benefit analysis. These efforts can build on successful prior examples where important non-market benefits have been given reliable and well-justified values. In chapter 9, we discussed the process used by the Obama administration to create a credible estimate of the social cost of carbon, drawing together voices throughout the federal government and grounding the final estimate on the best peer-reviewed models currently available. This systematic effort to create a harmonized value across the federal government provides an excellent example of how future administrations can improve valuation methods going forward.

Perhaps the best other example of a sustained effort to value an important class of regulatory benefits that is not traded on markets has been the development of the value of statistical life. For many environmental, public health, and safety regulations, the largest and most important category of benefits is the reduction of morality risks. But valuing this benefit presents a range of tricky issues. Most basically, like other non-market values, there is no simple, observable price that can be used. There are also concerns about the ethics associated with placing an arbitrary "price" on human life.[39]

During the early days of the use of cost-benefit analysis to evaluate regulation, the most common method for valuing mortality risks was the "human-capital approach," which used earning potential (sometimes minus consumption) to reflect economic productivity.[40] Some agency officials preferred versions of this approach because they felt it was more consistent with the view that "life was too sacred to value."[41] But this approach leads to an extremely low value compared to alternatives that are more theoretically well grounded, specifically those that use people's willingness to pay for risk reduction.[42] For example, the human capital approach attaches no value to saving the lives of retired people, which is an absurd result. W. Kip Viscusi recounts a story during the Reagan administration in which Occupational Safety and Health Administration's insistence on using the human capital approach almost resulted in OIRA rejecting a workplace safety regulation that was cost-benefit justified when the (more appropriate) willingness to pay method was used.[43] Over the years, the human-capital approach was eventually rejected, both by agencies and by OIRA guidance, in favor of metrics based on willingness to pay.[44]

Beyond making decisions about the most basic theoretical basis for valuing mortality risk reduction, the EPA especially has devoted considerable attention to addressing additional conceptual issues as well as many methodological challenges in its effort to generate a justifiable estimate of the value of statistical life. One important conceptual issue concerns the unit of measure, in natural units, that should be the focus of valuation. The traditional approach takes mortality risk itself as the measure and examines willingness to pay to reduce that category of risks. An alternative approach takes changes in life expectancy as the appropriate natural unit. This "life-years" approach, which was floated during the George W. Bush administration, results in lower valuation when an intervention will reduce risks for people with lower life expectancy.[45] After considerable study, both the EPA and OIRA ultimately rejected the life-years approach as inconsistent with the more general willingness to pay methodology, because, throughout large portions of their lives, people do not appear to adjust their preferences for risk reduction significantly based on life expectancy.[46]

On the methodological side, the most contentious issue has to do with how best to elicit people's preferences about mortality risk reduction. There are two general methods. One, the "revealed preference" method, uses actual market behavior to understand how people trade money against mortality risk. The main market decision used relates to employment in risky jobs, which typically carry a wage premium. The alternative method is based on "stated preferences," which are elicited using surveys. Over the years, a number of studies have been carried out using these methods: in 2000, the EPA did a general survey of the existing research and generated an overall central estimate of $5.8 million dollars per statistical life (1997 dollars).[47] For the past decade, the agency has used values between $9 million and $11 million in its rulemakings (2017 dollars),[48] which is roughly consistent with the views of leading experts.[49] Other agencies that generate life savings benefits generally draw from a similar list of studies and come to similar numbers, albeit with some variation.[50]

The lesson from the history of developing the value of statistical life is that, even for a regulatory benefit as complex and morally fraught as mortality risk reduction, it is possible to develop a value that is well grounded in economic theory and has a sound empirical basis. Of course, developing such values can be controversial, and important decisions must be made along the way. Nevertheless, it is possible to successfully negotiate these difficulties to generate meaningful estimates: the value of statistical life has been used in scores of rulemakings to help illustrate the value of federal regulatory protections and has become a fixture of cost-benefit analysis as practiced in the United States.

There are a number of common regulatory benefits that are either currently not given explicit value or where valuation could be improved. In the environmental context, there is a long tradition of using stated preference studies to elicit information about how people value protections for endangered species or unspoiled wilderness. This "existence value" is not even indirectly traded on markets, so there is no mechanism to observe revealed preferences. Despite decades of work by academics to develop the methodology, many agencies do not explicitly value these types of effects, even when there are relatively reliable techniques to do so.[51] For example, in an Obama-era rulemaking to reduce the ecological effects of coal-fired power plants that draw water from rivers and lakes for cooling purposes, the EPA conducted a stated preference study to estimate the value people place on reducing those effects but then ignored that study in the final rulemaking.[52] Developing methods that agencies have sufficient confidence in to actually use should be a priority in this area.

Another category of benefits where improvements to valuation can be made are ecosystem services, which include providing goods such as water, food, and wood; regulating and supporting natural processes (as happens in the case of flood control and soil formation); and the creation of cultural and recreational value.[53] Valuing ecosystem services is difficult because it requires understanding complex functions that ecosystems serve and monetizing those often non-market benefits.[54] Despite these difficulties, economists have made important headway toward monetizing ecosystem services, which agencies can use as the basis for further progress.[55]

Real options are another area where existing research can be used to improve cost-benefit analysis of government decisions, especially in the context of non-renewable resources.[56] Real options are the value of delaying decisions in the hopes of acquiring better information over time. For example, in making decisions about leasing offshore oil drilling rights, the government typically conducts a cost-benefit analysis in which it compares the social welfare consequences of drilling now with those of leaving the resource in the ground forever. If the net benefits of the former option are higher, the way is cleared for auctioning the leases.[57] But by failing to take option values into account, agencies do not consider the possibility that the net benefits of delaying a decision might be even higher—for example, as the risk of environmental catastrophes are better understood, or new technologies are developed to reduce the harms when failures happen. There are existing tools within the finance literature that can be applied to the context of natural resource planning, and the Obama administration took some steps in the direction of applying these tools,[58] but more can be done.

Other regulatory benefits that are ripe for additional research into valuation fall into the category of emotional and psychological effects. For example, the EPA has begun investigating whether special value should be given to rules that reduce cancer effects because of the psychological distress that accompanies a cancer diagnosis.[59] Rules to reduce terrorism risk might have similar types of psychological benefits beyond their direct effect on more tangible risks. As discussed in the previous chapter, John Graham and Keith Belton have suggested that effects on individual liberty be given more specific accounting in cost-benefit analysis. Cass Sunstein and Eric Posner have argued that people's willingness to pay to discharge moral obligation can be given a monetary value.[60]

Despite decades of work to improve valuation methodologies, there remains much work to do. In its current incarnation, cost-benefit analysis does a reasonably good job of providing estimates of many important categories of value. The value of statistical life, especially, plays an important role in many regulatory contexts. With the development of the social cost of carbon, the Obama administration took an important step in valuing an crucial category of benefits. These examples demonstrate that, with effort, it is possible to derive monetary estimates for regulatory effects that are largely outside of markets and therefore difficult to value. Future administrations should contribute to better cost-benefit analyses that are accurate for a wider range of regulatory contexts by developing similarly robust methods for values that currently fall outside of quantitative cost-benefit analysis.

Accounting for Distribution

A final area where a future administration can improve cost-benefit analysis is by tackling the question of how best to assess and respond to the distribution of regulatory costs and benefits. Although it has long been recognized that regulations can have important distributional consequences (in addition to their aggregate effects), and both the Clinton and Obama executive orders on regulatory review explicitly call on agencies to consider distribution, there has never been a consistent cross-government effort to examine how the costs and benefits of regulation are distributed across society.[61] As with expanding the evidence base for cost-benefit analysis and improving valuation techniques, this is an area where substantial steps can be taken to improve on existing practice.

There are many reasons that the distribution of the costs and benefits of regulation matter. If the goal of cost-benefit analysis is to identify regulations that improve people's well-being,[62] then a rule that imposes substantial costs on those worse off in society in order to generate benefits for the very wealthy raises a problem, even if the rule appears to have net benefits overall. The reason is that the reduction in consumption for people who struggle to make ends meet may have a very serious negative impact on their well-being, while the boost in consumption for the well-off might not matter very much. Stated plainly, the negative effects on well being from a $1,000 cost imposed on a family at the federal poverty line (with an income of roughly $25,000 a year) are far greater than the positive effects on well-being from a $2,000 benefit delivered to a family at the top 1 percent of the income scale (earning over $400,000 a year).[63]

There is nothing new about the claim that distribution matters: scholars and government officials have long recognized its importance and considered how best to incorporate distributional effects into policymaking. Among academic commentators, there are broadly two views on the subject. One view is that the best way to account for distribution is through the tax-and-transfer system rather than by revising regulations that are otherwise efficient.[64] The shorthand for this view is that regulation should increase the size of the pie, while the tax-and-transfer system can decide how to distribute the pieces. In the example above, the best way to respond to a regulation that imposes a cost on a less-well-off family to generate a benefit for those in the 1 percent is *not* to drop the regulation. Rather, adherents of this view would argue that it is best to adopt the regulation, increase the size of the pie, and then tax the wealthy family and transfer funds to the less-well-off family. If the initial cost is $1,000, and the benefit is $2,000, then the tax could transfer $1,500 from the beneficiaries (who are well off) to the burdened group (who are not), making everyone better off by $500.

The institutional corollary to the standard view is that agencies, which are responsible for regulation, should focus on efficiency (i.e., maximizing the size of the pie), while Congress, which is responsible for writing the tax rules, can handle distributional issues. This view is largely reflected in the practice of cost-benefit analysis, which focuses nearly exclusively on aggregate costs and benefits and only rarely considers distributional impacts.

One alternative to the increase-the-pie view does not reject the basic premise that efficient regulations coupled with transfers may indeed be optimal.[65] Rather, the issue is whether such transfers can and do actually occur in practice. The current state of policy in the United States has facilitated large and growing inequality, with a small fraction of the population capturing a massive amount of the total production of the economy.[66] The huge disparities in consumption within the US population are clear evidence that the distributional policies necessary to maximize well-being are not happening. General gridlock in Congress also prevents more targeted measures to compensate groups that might be disadvantaged by particular policies. As more policymaking power is shifted to agencies, and Congress is less able to fulfill its traditional role in managing transfers, the necessity to engage in some form of distributional analysis increases. If compensation does not occur in practice, then a focus on maximizing efficiency through rulemaking, while ignoring distribution, might simply result in a large pile of pie for those who already have enough, while leaving crumbs for the rest of society.[67]

The problem of the practical inadequacy of transfers is especially acute in cases where costs or benefits (i.e., the costs of inaction) are highly concentrated on the least well off. Rules that protect wilderness areas for recreational enjoyment but that have substantial localized costs for rural communities may be net beneficial overall, but the concentrated costs on those who are ill suited to bear them raise concerns. Likewise, the environmental justice movement has long worked to raise awareness about the special pollution burdens placed on certain communities. Even assuming that the costs of reducing that pollution (borne by consumers and shareholders) might sometimes be larger than the benefits, there are clear fairness issues raised when politically and economically disadvantaged communities are asked to absorb more than their fair share of exposure to public health risks.

An additional argument in favor of distributional considerations informing regulatory decision making is that sometimes, distributional issues are central to a statutory scheme. In that case, a failure to account for the distribution of costs and benefits would interfere with Congress's attempts at distributing wealth in a way that improves well-being, which would then undercut the more general argument that agencies ought to focus primarily on efficiency rather than distribution. Statutory regimes where distribution is central include various assistance programs (such as food stamps), health care regulations and the administration of Obamacare, and regulations that affect the immigration system. During the Trump administration, OIRA also extended its review of tax regulations,[68] where distributional impacts are absolutely central. Engaging in cost-benefit analysis of regulatory decision making in these contexts without accounting for distributional effects is highly distorting.

Accepting that consideration of distribution of costs and benefits should at least sometimes inform regulatory decision making, there are many questions that must be addressed to carry out distributional analysis in practice. One important issue concerns the dimensions of difference that ought to be considered. Generally speaking, within welfare economics, the relevant dimension is income or wealth, with the idea being that costs and benefits have greater consequence when they are imposed on or enjoyed by those with lower levels of income/wealth. More generally, well-being might be the relevant dimension, so that income/wealth is augmented by other factors, such as health status.[69] Other dimensions that might be relevant in the context of the United States include race, gender, geography, and economic sector.

There is a second set of issues that are empirical and involve the question of how to estimate the distribution of costs and benefits. For standard cost-benefit analysis, the incidence of a cost or benefit (i.e., who pays the cost or who receives the benefit) is immaterial, and so analysts can simply calculate the total amounts without considering how they might be passed along. Distributional analysis adds complexity to the problem. For example, the initial incidence of the costs of an air quality regulation might fall on polluting companies—which have to pay for new technologies—but those costs might be passed along to ratepayers through higher prices or to workers through lower wages. Likewise, the benefits of cleaner air might appear to go to local residents who have fewer health problems, but if rents increase to reflect the improved environmental amenities, then property owners would be able to extract at least some of the value. Predicting how costs and benefits will ultimately flow within the economy can be a difficult empirical undertaking.

A third set of issues concerns how to respond to information that is contained in distributional analysis. There are two general options: one is to alter a rule to reduce undesirable (or increase desirable) distributional effects. For example, a rule that imposes costs on less-well-off communities might be made less stringent to reduce those costs. A second option is to engage in some kind of transfer program to supplement a regulation that would otherwise have harmful distributional consequences. Such transfers might be done by Congress through the tax-and-transfer systems, as is envisaged by the increase-the-pie model. But a range of tools is available within the executive branch that could be leveraged to achieve similar results: the president plays a central role in the budgeting process, he is charged with spending already appropriated funds in general, and agencies have considerable power over the distribution of discretionary grants (which total well over $100 billion per year).[70]

Experience has amply demonstrated that agencies are unlikely to start spontaneously conducting rigorous distributional analysis on their own. Some push from the White House will be necessary. A future administration that is serious about promoting distributional analysis should, at the very least, issue a set of guidelines, on par with Circular A-4, that explains the contexts where distributional analysis is most important and provides a set of techniques and best practices for agencies to draw on. Especially for controversial questions—such as the dimensions of difference that ought to be studied—agency officials are likely to feel much more comfortable proceeding if a clear path is set before them.

When moving forward with guidance on distributional analysis, the White House should consider an open process of peer review, as was undertaken during the creation of Circular A-4. These types of documents can have considerable staying power, and it is important that they reflect the best available thinking. Given the complex and value-laden nature of many of the relevant questions, the views of a diverse range of voices should be considered, including those outside the constituency of whichever party happens to be in power.

Once guidelines are in place, OIRA could require that distributional analysis be carried out when appropriate. The mere imposition of a purported requirement is rarely enough to push agencies to devote resources to additional analysis. One clear example of an analytic mandate that is routinely ignored by agencies is the requirement in Executive Order 13,132 that agencies assess the "federalism" impacts of their rules.[71] Because OIRA does not enforce this mandate, agencies simply include boilerplate in the regulatory record stating that there are no important consequences for the balance of state and federal power for a rule (even when there clearly are). To avoid the continuation of a similar fate for distributional analysis, OIRA must play a more aggressive role.

A second step to promote distributional analysis would be to incorporate it into the system of regulatory checkups that we described in the prior section. When many existing regulations were adopted, their costs and benefits were forecast, so there is at least some basis for the belief that many represent improvements in efficiency from the status quo. But since distributional analysis has rarely been carried out, there is no basis for an analogous belief with respect to the desirability of their distributional consequences. As agencies evaluate existing regulations to consider whether they should be expanded, retracted, or revised, their role in contributing to, or helping alleviate inequality is a relevant factor.

***

There is no guarantee that future administrations will enthusiastically embrace cost-benefit analysis and regulatory review. But for an administration that is committed to rebuilding and improving the guardrails, there is considerable work that can be done. The first and most important step is to reverse the course set by the Trump administration by abandoning its attempt to treat cost-benefit analysis as a charade, restoring OIRA review to its former place, and recommitting to carrying out rigorous analysis of costs and benefits. From that foundation, steps to reorient retrospective review in a more productive direction, improve valuation techniques for regulatory consequences that currently fall outside of quantitative cost-benefit analysis, and facilitate distributional analysis can help give new life to rationality in US regulatory decision making.

Notes

Acknowledgments

1. These earlier works include: RICHARD L. REVESZ & MICHAEL A. LIVERMORE, RETAKING RATIONALITY: HOW COST-BENEFIT ANALYSIS CAN BETTER PROTECT THE ENVIRONMENT AND OUR HEALTH (2008); Nicholas Bagley & Richard L. Revesz, *Centralized Oversight of the Regulatory State*, 106 COLUM. L. REV. 1260 (2006); Kimberly M. Castle & Richard L. Revesz, *Environmental Standards, Thresholds, and the Next Battleground of Climate Change Regulations*, 103 MINN. L. REV. 1349 (2019); Caroline Cecot & Michael A. Livermore, *The One-In, Two-Out Executive Order Is a Zero*, 166 U. PENN. L. REV. ONLINE 1 (2017); Madison E. Condon, Michael A. Livermore & Jeffrey G. Shrader, *Assessing the Rationale for the U.S. EPA's Proposed "Strengthening Transparency in Regulatory Science" Rule*, 14 REV. ENVTL. ECON. & POL'Y 131 (2019); Bethany A. Davis Noll & Richard L. Revesz, *Regulation in Transition*, 104 MINN. L. REV. 1 (2019); Michael A. Livermore & Daniel Richardson, *Administrative Law in an Era of Partisan Volatility*, 69 EMORY L. J. 1 (2019); Michael A. Livermore & Jason A. Schwartz, *Analysis to Inform Public Discourse on Jobs and Regulation, in* DOES REGULATION KILL JOBS? 239 (Cary Coglianese, Adam M. Finkel & Christopher Carrigan eds., 2013); Michael A. Livermore, *Cost-Benefit Analysis and Agency Independence*, 81 U. CHI. L. REV. 609 (2014); Michael A. Livermore & Richard L. Revesz, *Interest Groups and Environmental Policy: Inconsistent Positions and Missed Opportunities*, 45 ENVTL. L. 1 (2015); Michael A. Livermore, *Political Parties and Presidential Oversight*, 67 ALA. L. REV. 45 (2015); Michael A. Livermore & Richard L. Revesz, *Regulatory Review, Capture, and Agency Inaction*, 101 GEO. L. J. 1337 (2013); Michael A. Livermore & Richard L. Revesz, *Retaking Rationality: Two Years Later*, 48 HOUS. L. REV. 1 (2011); Michael A. Livermore & Richard L. Revesz, *Rethinking Health-Based Environmental Standards*, 89 N.Y.U. L. REV. 1184 (2014); Laura J. Lowenstein & Richard L. Revesz, *Anti-Regulation Under the Guise of Rational Regulation: The Bush Administration's Approaches to Valuing Human Lives in Environmental Cost-Benefit Analyses*, 34 ENVTL. L. REP. 10,954 (2004); Samuel J. Rascoff & Richard L. Revesz, *The Biases of Risk Tradeoff Analysis: Towards Parity in Environmental and Health-and-Safety Regulation*, 69 U. CHI. L. REV. 1763 (2002); Richard L. Revesz & Matthew R. Shahabian, *Climate Change and Future Generations*, 84 S. CAL. L. REV. 1097 (2011); Richard L. Revesz, *Congress and the Executive: Challenging the Anti-Regulatory Narrative*, 2018 MICH. ST. L. REV. 795; Richard L. Revesz, *Cost–Benefit Analysis and the Structure of the Administrative State: The Case of Financial Services Regulation*, 34 YALE J. REG. 545 (2017); Richard L. Revesz, *Environmental Regulation, Cost-Benefit Analysis, and the Discounting of Human Lives*, 99 COLUM. L. REV. 941 (1999); Richard

L. Revesz, *Institutional Pathologies in the Regulatory State: What Scott Pruitt Taught Us About Regulatory Policy*, 34 J. LAND USE & ENVTL. L. 211 (2019); Richard L. Revesz, *Quantifying Regulatory Benefits*, 102 CALIF. L. REV. 1423 (2014); Richard L. Revesz, *Regulation and Distribution*, 93 N.Y.U. L. REV. 1489 (2018).

Introduction

1. Romney for President, Inc., Believe in America: Mitt Romney's Plan for Jobs and Economic Growth 55 (2011).
2. *See generally* Albert L. Nichols, *Lead in Gasoline*, *in* ECONOMIC ANALYSES AT EPA: ASSESSING REGULATORY IMPACT 49 (Richard D. Morgenstern ed., 1997).
3. *See* EPA, The Benefits and Costs of the Clean Air Act from 1990 to 2020 (2011).
4. *See, e.g.*, EPA, Federal Implementation Plans: Interstate Transport of Fine Particulate Matter and Ozone and Correction of SIP Approval, 76 Fed. Reg. 48,208 (Aug. 8, 2011); EPA, Finding of Significant Contribution and Rulemaking for Certain States in the Ozone Transport Assessment Group Region for Purposes of Reducing Regional Transport of Ozone, 63 Fed. Reg. 57,356 (Oct. 27, 1998).
5. *See* John D. Graham, *Saving Lives Through Administrative Law and Economics*, 157 U. PA. L. REV. 395 (2008).
6. *See, e.g.*, California v. U.S. Dep't of the Interior, 381 F. Supp. 3d 1153, 1168 (N.D. Cal. 2019) (vacating the Department of Interior's repeal of an Obama era rule that reformed the process for determining royalties for the use of federal lands for the extraction of coal, oil, and gas, finding that the agency "fail[ed] to satisfy its obligation to explain the inconsistencies between its prior findings in enacting the Valuation Rule and its decision to repeal such Rule").
7. James Goodwin, Ctr. for Progressive Reform, Regulation as Social Justice: A Crowdsourced Blueprint for Building a Progressive Regulatory System 4 (2019).
8. *See, e.g.*, N. Gregory Mankiw, *"Republican Economist" Sheds a Party Label*, N.Y. TIMES, Nov. 17, 2019, at BU5.

Chapter 1

1. *See generally* Jack M. Beermann, *Congressional Administration*, 43 SAN DIEGO L. REV. 61 (2006); Elena Kagan, *Presidential Administration*, 114 HARV. L. REV. 2245 (2001).
2. Agency personnel have varying degrees of direct accountability to the president. Some are appointed directly, others with Senate confirmation, and others are hired through the civil service process. Some serve at will, others are protected by "for cause" statutory clauses at independent agencies, and still others are shielded by civil service protection. The senior leadership at agencies are generally understood to be quite responsive to the president and the party in the White House.
3. *See* DANIEL CARPENTER, REPUTATION AND POWER: ORGANIZATIONAL IMAGE AND PHARMACEUTICAL REGULATION AT THE FDA (2010).

4. Dan Farber, *How Trump Officials Abuse Cost-Benefit Analysis to Attack Regulations*, WASH. MONTHLY (Jan. 9, 2019), https://washingtonmonthly.com/2019/01/09/how-the-trump-administration-abuses-cost-benefit-analysis-to-attack-regulations/; Amit Narang, *The Stunning Triumph of Cost-Cost Analysis*, REG. REV. (Feb. 19, 2017), https://www.theregreview.org/2017/02/19/narang-stunning-triumph-cost-cost-analysis/; Jonathan S. Masur, *The Deep Incoherence of Trump's Executive Order on Regulation*, YALE J. REG.: NOTICE & COMMENT (Feb. 7, 2017), http://yalejreg.com/nc/the-deep-incoherenceof-trumps-executive-order-on-regulation-by-jonathan-s-masur/.

5. In this book, we focus on cost-benefit analysis and regulatory review as two important guardrails, but there are many others, such as those protecting scientific integrity or ensuring competence in government staff. A recent report prepared by a group of bipartisan experts with senior government experience during administrations of both parties focused on the breakdown of these two guardrails. *See* National Task Force on Rule of Law & Democracy, Brennan Ctr., Proposals for Reform Volume II (2019).

6. Richard B. Stewart, *The Reformation of American Administrative Law*, 88 HARV. L. REV. 1667, 1684 (1975).

7. Russell E. Train, *The Environmental Record of the Nixon Administration*, 26 PRESIDENTIAL STUD. Q. 185, 188–89 (1996).

8. *Presidential Veto Message: Nixon Vetoes Water Pollution Act*, *in* CQ ALMANAC 1972 11-78-A (28th ed. 1973).

9. N. William Hines, *History of the 1972 Clean Water Act: The Story Behind How the 1972 Act Became the Capstone on a Decade of Extraordinary Environmental Reform*, 4 GEO. WASH. J. ENERGY & ENVTL. L. 80, 98 (2013).

10. *See generally* ANGIE MAXWELL & TODD SHIELDS, THE LONG SOUTHERN STRATEGY: HOW CHASING WHITE VOTERS IN THE SOUTH CHANGED AMERICAN POLITICS (2019). There are some dissenting views concerning the centrality of backlash to progress on civil rights to the realignment of the South. *See, e.g.*, BYRON E. SHAFER & RICHARD JOHNSTON, THE END OF SOUTHERN EXCEPTIONALISM: CLASS, RACE, AND PARTISAN CHANGE IN THE POSTWAR SOUTH (2006). For a long view of developments in the two parties, see JOHN H. ALDRICH, WHY PARTIES? A SECOND LOOK (2011).

11. Thomas O. McGarity, *Regulatory Reform in the Reagan Era*, 45 MD. L. REV. 253 (1986). For a discussion of the factors that influenced changing attitudes toward environmental policy within the Republican Party, see JAMES MORTON TURNER & ANDREW C. ISENBERG, THE REPUBLICAN REVERSAL: CONSERVATIVES AND THE ENVIRONMENT FROM NIXON TO TRUMP (2018).

12. WILLIAM A. NISKANEN, JR., BUREAUCRACY AND REPRESENTATIVE GOVERNMENT (1971).

13. *See* Toni Makkai & John Braithwaite, *In and Out of the Revolving Door: Making Sense of Regulatory Capture*, 12 J. PUB. POL'Y 61, 62 (1992) (discussing Nader's views).

14. *See* James G. Benze, Jr., *Presidential Reorganization as a Tactical Weapon: Putting Politics Back into Administration*, 15 PRESIDENTIAL STUD. Q. 145, 146 (1985); RICHARD P. NATHAN, THE ADMINISTRATIVE PRESIDENCY (1983).

15. OIRA itself was created in the Paperwork Reduction Act during the waning days of the Carter administration, although without its regulatory review function. Paperwork Reduction Act of 1980, Pub. L. 96–511, § 3503, 94 Stat. 2812, 2814–15 (Dec. 11, 1980). There were other precursors to the system created by Reagan during the Nixon and Carter administrations. *See* Jim Tozzi, *OIRA's Formative Years: The Historical Record of Centralized Regulatory Review Preceding OIRA's Founding*, 63 ADMIN. L. REV. 37, 40–62 (2011)(providing an overview of pre-Reagan efforts at regulatory review). Cost-benefit analysis itself also long precedes the institution of regulatory review. *See* Jonathan B. Wiener, *The Diffusion of Regulatory Oversight*, *in* THE GLOBALIZATION OF COST-BENEFIT ANALYSIS IN ENVIRONMENTAL POLICY 123 (Michael A. Livermore & Richard L. Revesz eds, 2013).

16. Executive Order 12,291, 46 Fed. Reg. 13,193 (Feb. 19, 1981).

17. *See* Stewart, *supra* note 6.

18. Calvert Cliffs' Coordinating Committee, Inc. v. U.S. Atomic Energy Commission, 449 F.2d 1109, 1111 (1971). Judge Wright was appointed to the United States District Court for the Eastern District of Louisiana by Harry S. Truman and then elevated to the DC Circuit Court by John F. Kennedy.

19. Patricia M. Wald, *The D.C. Circuit: Here and Now*, 55 GEO. WASH. L. REV. 718, 718 (1986).

20. *See* Vermont Yankee Nuclear Power Corp. v. Natural Resources Defense Council, 435 U.S. 519, 558 (1978).

21. *Id.*

22. Chevron v. Natural Resources Defense Council, 467 U.S. 837 (1984). As is discussed below, courts continue to engage in review of agency reason-giving. *See* Motor Vehicle Manufacturers Association v. State Farm Mutual Auto. Ins. Co., 463 U.S. 29 (1983).

23. Scholars disagree about whether Justice Scalia's enthusiasm for the doctrine gradually diminished, especially during the Obama administration. *See* Robin Bravender, *Scalia and* Chevron: *It's Complicated*, E&E NEWS (Feb. 19, 2016), https://www.eenews.net/stories/1060032640.

24. Antonin Scalia, *Regulatory Reform—The Game Has Changed*, REGULATION, Jan./Feb. 1981, at 13, 13–14.

25. Samuel Issacharoff, *Outsourcing Politics: The Hostile Takeover of Our Hollowed-Out Political Parties*, 54 HOUS. L. REV. 845 (2017); Joseph Fishkin & Heather K. Gerken, *The Party's Over:* McCutcheon, *Shadow Parties, and the Future of the Party System*, 2014 SUP. CT. REV. 175.

26. BYRON E. SHAFER, THE AMERICAN POLITICAL PATTERN: STABILITY AND CHANGE, 1932–2016, 121–78 (2016).

27. Executive Order 12,866, 58 Fed. Reg. 51,735 (Oct. 4, 1993).

28. One important set of transparency requirements in the Order mandates that OIRA maintain "a publicly available log" with the status of regulations under review, and records of written and oral communications received by the office. *Id.* § 6(b)(4).

29. *Id.* § 1(b)(6) (emphasis added).

30. Kagan, *supra* note 1, at 2249.

31. The goal of shifting the Overton window is sometimes used by advocates of extremist ideologies to justify violence and other confrontational tactics. *See* David C. Atkinson, *Charlottesville and the Alt-Right: A Turning Point?*, 6 POL., GROUPS, & IDENTITIES 309, 313 (2018).

32. Office of Mgmt. & Budget, Circular A-4, at 2 (Sept. 17, 2003).

33. OIRA has its critics, who argue, *inter alia*, that the office is beholden to regulated industry and unlawfully interferes with agency discretion. *See, e.g.*, Rena Steinzor, *The Case for Abolishing Centralized White House Regulatory Review*, 1 MICH. J. ENVTL. & ADMIN. L. 209 (2012); Lisa Heinzerling, *Statutory Interpretation in the Era of OIRA*, 33 FORDHAM URB. L.J. 1097 (2006).

34. *See* STUART SHAPIRO, ANALYSIS AND PUBLIC POLICY: SUCCESSES, FAILURES AND DIRECTIONS FOR REFORM (2016).

35. *Cf.* Joseph Stiglitz, *Looking Out for the National Interest: The Principles of the Council of Economic Advisers*, 87 AM. ECON. REV. 109 (1997) (discussing role of the Council of Economic Advisers in resisting special interests pressure in governmental decision making).

36. John D. Graham, *Saving Lives Through Administrative Law and Economics*, 157 U. PENN. L. REV. 395, 404 (2008). *But see* Simon F. Haeder & Susan Webb Yackee, *Presidentially Directed Policy Change: The Office of Information and Regulatory Affairs as Partisan or Moderator?*, 28 J. PUB. ADMIN. RES. & THEORY 475 (2018) (arguing, *contra* Graham, that OIRA's primary role is deregulatory during both Democratic and Republican administrations).

37. *See* Ben Geman & Kevin Bogardus, *Obama Regulations Chief Pressed Attacks on Ozone Standards*, THE HILL (Aug. 8, 2012), https://thehill.com/policy/energy-environment/242667-obama-regs-chief-pressed-attacks-on-ozone-standards.

38. John M. Broder, *Re-election Strategy Is Tied to a Shift on Smog*, N.Y. TIMES, Nov. 17, 2011, at A1.

39. Art Fraas & Richard Morgenstern, *Identifying the Analytical Implications of Alternative Regulatory Philosophies*, 5 J. BENEFIT COST ANALYSIS 137 (2014).

40. There are many reasons that an agency's reason giving may be defective, outside of flaws in a cost-benefit analysis. However, there is an important line of cases in which courts specifically police how agencies examine and weigh costs and benefits. *See* Caroline Cecot & W. Kip Viscusi, *Judicial Review of Agency Benefit-Cost Analysis*, 22 GEO. MASON L. REV. 575 (2015).

41. Food and Drug Admin. v. Brown & Williamson Tobacco Corp., 529 U.S. 120 (2000).

42. Massachusetts v. EPA, 549 U.S. 497 (2007).

43. Michigan v. EPA, 135 S. Ct. 2699 (2015). The issue in this case was whether EPA was required to consider costs before making a determination that it was "appropriate and necessary" to regulate hazardous air pollutants from power plants under the Clean Air Act. Justice Scalia, for the majority, found that the agency must examine costs prior to making that determination. Justice Kagan, in dissent, argued that the agency had adequately factored costs into its decision making during the rulemaking process, after the initial "appropriate and necessary" determination was made.

44. 538 F.3d 1172, 1198 (2008).

45. Graham, *supra* note 36, at 479. The Department of Transportation did not include a social cost of carbon in the original rulemaking, despite the (apparent) views of OIRA under Graham. As this example illustrates, although OIRA has traditionally been an influential institution, that does not mean that its views are always heeded.

46. Securities and Exchange Comm'n, Facilitating Shareholder Director Nominations, 75 Fed. Reg. 56,668 (Sept. 16, 2010). Agencies that have been designated as "independent" have not traditionally been required to conduct cost-benefit analysis or submit their rules to OIRA. *See* Kirti Datla & Richard L. Revesz, *Deconstructing Independent Agencies (and Executive Agencies)*, 98 CORNELL L. REV. 769 (2013). Partially as a consequence of this structure, the quality of cost-benefit analysis varies across agencies. Some, such as the EPA, have responded to consistent OIRA oversight by devoting considerable resources to economic analysis. Others, such as the Securities and Exchange Commission, which is not subject to OIRA review, have not built out their cost-benefit capacity to the same degree. *See* Richard L. Revesz, *Cost-Benefit Analysis and the Structure of the Administrative States: The Case of Financial Services Regulation*, 34 YALE J. REG. 545 (2017).

47. Business Roundtable v. Securities & Exchange Comm'n, 647 F.3d 1144, 1148–49 (2011).

48. For examples of OIRA's reduced influence in the Trump administration, see chapter 4. Part II discusses in details the way in which the administration has attempted to manipulate cost-benefit analysis. It is possible that OIRA review has improved agency analyses compared to some even worse baseline. But given the poor quality of analysis in the proposed and final rules that have been published, OIRA has not ensured a minimum quality standard.

49. There is a now decades-long trend toward partisan polarization in the nomination and confirmation of federal judges—the process did not start with Donald Trump. *See* Keith E. Whittington, *Partisanship, Norms, and Federal Judicial Appointments*, 16 GEO. J. L. & PUB. POL'Y 521 (2018).

50. MARTY COHEN ET AL., THE PARTY DECIDES: PRESIDENTIAL NOMINATIONS BEFORE AND AFTER REFORM 7 (2008).

51. *See generally* DAVID FARBER, CHICAGO '68 (1988).

52. *See* ALDRICH, *supra* note 10.

53. COHEN ET AL., *supra* note 50. This work defines political parties in a broad way, arguing that the highly involved activists function as a single political party, even without formal affiliations with the national organization.

54. *See id.* at 5, 187–88.

55. *Id.* at 5–6.

56. Indeed, the authors used returns from some of the early primaries to argue that these endorsements still mattered and were helping Clinton to pull together the party's core voters. *See id.* at 302–3 (noting "the apparent ability of black leaders to swing black voters away from Obama").

57. Indeed, the 2016 election put *The Party Decides* in the public spotlight in a way that is rare for an academic text. *See* Steve Kolowich, *The Life of "The Party Decides,"*

CHRONICLE HIGHER EDUC. (May 16, 2016), https://www.chronicle.com/article/The-Life-of-The-Party/236483.

58. *See* Harry Enten, *The Four Things I Learned from the Donald Trump Primary*, FIVETHIRTYEIGHT (May 6, 2016), https://fivethirtyeight.com/features/the-four-things-i-learned-from-the-donald-trump-primary/.

59. Ali Dukakis, *Rick Perry Calls Donald Trump a "Cancer on Conservativism,"* ABC NEWS (Jul. 22, 2015), https://abcnews.go.com/Politics/rick-perry-calls-donald-trump-cancer-conservatism/story?id=32622991. As we discuss in chapter 4, Perry later recanted his views and went on to head the Department of Energy in the Trump administration.

60. *See generally* ALAN I. ABRAMOWITZ, THE GREAT ALIGNMENT: RACE, PARTY TRANSFORMATION, AND THE RISE OF DONALD TRUMP (2018); RACHEL BITECOFER, THE UNPRECEDENTED 2016 PRESIDENTIAL ELECTION (2017).

61. On legal changes that have weakened political parties, see Issacharoff, *supra* note 25.

62. Cynthia R. Farina, *False Comfort and Impossible Promises: Uncertainty, Information Overload, and the Unitary Executive*, 12 U. PA. J. CONST. L. 357 (2010); Eric A. Posner, *Controlling Agencies with Cost-Benefit Analysis: A Positive Political Theory Perspective*, 68 U. CHI. L. REV. 1137, 1142–43 (2001).

63. Terry M. Moe, *The Politicized Presidency, in* THE MANAGERIAL PRESIDENCY 144 (James P. Pfiffner ed., 2d ed. 1999).

64. David E. Lewis, *The Contemporary Presidency: The Personnel Process in the Modern Presidency*, 42 PRESIDENTIAL STUD. Q. 577, 580 (2012).

65. Institute for Policy Integrity, Roundup: Trump-Era Agency Policy in the Courts, https://policyintegrity.org/deregulation-roundup (last updated July 15, 2020) (counting 88 unsuccessful outcomes and 11 succesful outcomes for Trump agencies in administrative law cases).

66. David Zaring, *Reasonable Agencies*, 96 VA. L. REV. 135, 170 (2010); Connor Raso, *Trump's Deregulatory Efforts Keep Losing in Court—And The Losses Could Make It Harder for Future Administrations to Deregulate*, BROOKINGS (Oct. 25, 2018), https://www.brookings.edu/research/trumps-deregulatory-efforts-keep-losing-in-court-and-the-losses-could-make-it-harder-for-future-administrations-to-deregulate/.

67. Li Zhou, *Study: Trump's Judicial Appointees Are More Conservative Than Those of Past Republican Presidents*, Vox (Jan. 25, 2019), https://www.vox.com/2019/1/25/18188541/trump-judges-mconnell-senate.

68. The Trump administration has put forward an unusually large number of nominees who were rated as "not qualified" by the American Bar Association. *See ABA Ratings During the Trump Administration*, Ballotpedia, https://ballotpedia.org/ABA_ratings_during_the_Trump_administration.

69. Charles M. Cameron & John M. de Figueiredo, *Quitting in Protest: Presidential Policymaking and Civil Service Response* (Duke Law Sch. Pub. Law and Legal Theory Series No. 2020-17, 2020).

70. Tom Fox, *Morale Is Down, but Federal Employees Remain Dedicated to Their Agency Missions*, WASH. POST (May 12, 2017), https://www.washingtonpost.com/news/on-leadership/wp/2017/05/12/morale-is-down-but-federal-employees-remain-dedicated-to-their-agency-missions/.

71. Andrew Restuccia, *Federal Workers Spill on Life in Trump's Washington*, POLITICO (Mar. 30, 2018), https://www.politico.com/story/2018/03/30/trump-washington-civil-servants-492347.

72. *Id.*

73. *See* Rachel M. Cohen, *"I Fully Intend to Outlast These People": 18 Federal Workers on What It's Really Like to Work for the Trump Administration*, WASHINGTONIAN (Apr. 7, 2019), https://www.washingtonian.com/2019/04/07/18-federal-workers-what-its-really-like-to-work-for-the-trump-administration/.

74. *Id.* In one particularly aggressive move, the Trump administration has relocated two major research agencies within the Department of Agriculture from Washington DC to the Kansas City area, prompting a round of departures of agency personnel. *See* Frank Morris, *Critics of Relocating USDA Research Agencies Point to Brain Drain*, NPR (Sept. 10, 2019), https://www.npr.org/2019/09/10/759053717/critics-of-relocating-usda-research-agencies-point-to-brain-drain.

75. *See, e.g.*, Coral Davenport & Hiroko Tabuchi, *4 Car Companies Defy Trump E.P.A.*, N.Y. TIMES, July 26, 2019, at A1.

76. *See* Cary Coglianese, *The Semi-Autonomous Administrative State* (Univ. of Pa. Pub. Law and Legal Theory Research Paper Series No. 19-35, 2019)(arguing that legal structures should both facilitate political accountability and protect expert decision making at administrative agencies).

Chapter 2

1. There also may be a trade-off between centralization and competence, if issue-specific agencies build greater expertise. Rachel E. Barkow, *Insulating Agencies: Avoiding Capture Through Institutional Design*, 89 TEX. L. REV. 15, 34 (2010) (explaining that "the relationship between expertise and OIRA is [] a complicated one").

2. James P. Pfiffner, *Presidential Transitions, in* THE OXFORD HANDBOOK OF THE AMERICAN PRESIDENCY 85, 94 (George C. Edwards III & William G. Howell eds., 2009).

3. *See* Michael Nelson, *Barack Obama: Domestic Affairs*, U. VA. MILLER CTR., https://millercenter.org/president/obama/domestic-affairs.

4. RICHARD L. REVESZ & MICHAEL A. LIVERMORE, RETAKING RATIONALITY: HOW COST-BENEFIT ANALYSIS CAN BETTER PROTECT THE ENVIRONMENT AND OUR HEALTH 23–26 (2008) [hereinafter RETAKING RATIONALITY].

5. MURRAY L. WEIDENBAUM & ROBERT DEFINA, THE COST OF FEDERAL REGULATION OF ECONOMIC ACTIVITY (1978).

6. Murray L. Weidenbaum, *The High Cost of Government Regulation*, CHALLENGE, Nov.–Dec. 1979, at 32, 39.

7. WILLIAM A. NISKANEN, JR., BUREAUCRACY AND REPRESENTATIVE GOVERNMENT (1971).

8. James C. Miller & Robert L. Greene, *Environmental Protection: The Need to Consider Costs and Benefits*, HIGHWAY USERS Q., Summer 1976, at 10.

9. Christopher DeMuth, *Defending Consumers Against Regulation*, AM. SPECTATOR, Jan. 1978, at 1.

10. *See, e.g.,* Christopher C. DeMuth, *Constraining Regulatory Costs—Part Two: The Regulatory Budget*, REGULATION, Mar./Apr 1980, at 29.

11. *See infra* chapter 5 on the resurgence of the concept of a regulatory budget—in a less rational form—in the Trump administration.

12. *Compare 1980 Democratic Party Platform*, AM. PRESIDENCY PROJECT, https://www.presidency.ucsb.edu/node/273253 (section on "Regulatory Reform"), *with Republican Party Platform of 1980*, AM. PRESIDENCY PROJECT, https://www.presidency.ucsb.edu/node/273420(section on "Fairness to the Employer").

13. *See Republican Party Platform of 1980, supra* note 12.

14. *See, e.g.,* David J. Lanoue, *One that Made a Difference: Cognitive Consistency, Political Knowledge, and the 1980 Presidential Debate*, 56 PUB. OPINION QUART. 168 (1992).

15. *See Oct. 28, 1980 Debate Transcript*, COMMISSION ON PRESIDENTIAL DEBATES, http://www.debates.org/index.php?page=october-28-1980-debate-transcript.

16. Richard H. Pildes & Cass R. Sunstein, *Reinventing the Regulatory State*, 62 U. CHI. L. REV. 1, 3 (1995).

17. Alan Morrison, then of Public Citizen, provided a nice summation of some of the central concerns of the time. Alan B. Morrison, *OMB Interference with Agency Rulemaking: The Wrong Way to Write a Regulation*, 99 HARV. L. REV. 1059 (1986).

18. Clyde H. Farnsworth, *Move to Cut Regulatory Costs Near*, N.Y. TIMES, Feb. 14, 1981, § 2, at 29 (quoting Saul Miller, a spokesman for the AFL-CIO).

19. Philip Shabecof, *Reagan Order on Cost-Benefit Analysis Stirs Economic and Political Debate*, N.Y. TIMES, Nov. 7, 1981, § 2, at 28.

20. *Id.*

21. *Id.*

22. *See, e.g.,* IAN AYRES & JOHN BRAITHWAITE, RESPONSIVE REGULATION: TRANSCENDING THE DEREGULATION DEBATE (1992); JERRY L. MASHAW, GREED, CHAOS, AND GOVERNANCE: USING PUBLIC CHOICE TO IMPROVE PUBLIC LAW (1997); Susan Rose-Ackerman, *Progressive Law and Economics—And the New Administrative Law*, 98 YALE L. J. 341 (1988); Cass R. Sunstein, *The Cost-Benefit State* (Coase-Sandor Inst. for Law & Econ. Working Paper No. 39, 1996).

23. The intellectuals and political figures involved might reject this comparison. Nevertheless, in our view, there are sufficient parallels to draw a rough analogy between the two.

24. *See* RETAKING RATIONALITY, *supra* note 4, at 32.

25. THOMAS O. MCGARITY, REINVENTING RATIONALITY: THE ROLE OF REGULATORY ANALYSIS IN THE FEDERAL BUREAUCRACY 256 (1991).

26. Sunstein and Heinzerling here stand in for a substantial intellectual debate with many participants. *See* Don Bradford Hardin, Jr., *Why Cost-Benefit Analysis? A Question (and Some Answers) About the Legal Academy*, 59 ALA. L. REV. 1135, 1136–37 (2008) (documenting the rise in cost-benefit-related legal scholarship from 27 articles in 1981 to 628 by 2005).

27. Cass R. Sunstein, *Incompletely Theorized Agreements*, 108 HARV. L. REV. 1733 (1995).

28. *Id.* at 1736.
29. Regulatory Review, Memorandum for the Heads of Executive Departments and Agencies from President Barack Obama, 74 Fed. Reg. 5977 (Jan. 30, 2009).
30. *See* Gabriel Nelson, *Obama Overhaul of Regulatory Reviews Now Seen as Unlikely*, GREENWIRE (July 14, 2010), https://archive.nytimes.com/www.nytimes.com/gwire/2010/07/14/14greenwire-obama-overhaul-of-regulatory-reviews-now-seen-45978.html?.
31. Executive Order 13,563, 76 Fed. Reg. 3821 (Jan. 21, 2011).
32. *See* ERIC POOLEY, THE CLIMATE WAR: TRUE BELIEVERS, POWER BROKERS, AND THE FIGHT TO SAVE THE EARTH (2010); Ryan Lizza, *As the World Burns*, NEW YORKER (Oct. 3, 2010), https://www.newyorker.com/magazine/2010/10/11/as-the-world-burns.
33. Democrats voted in favor of the bill by a margin of 211 to 44 (with one not voting); Republicans voted against by a margin of 168 to 8 (with two not voting). *See H.R. 2454 (111th): American Clean Energy and Security Act of 2009*, GOVTRACK, https://www.govtrack.us/congress/votes/111-2009/h477.
34. We return to Republican opposition to cap-and-trade during this period *infra* chapter 4.
35. For an overview, see Jody Freeman, *The Obama Administration's National Auto Policy: Lessons from the "Car Deal,"* 35 HARV. ENVTL. L. REV. 343 (2011).
36. Other methods include transition to zero emissions vehicles, reducing vehicle miles traveled, and improving vehicles' air conditioning system.
37. A supplemental approach to improve fuel economy is to require alternative fuels (such as ethanol) that—at least theoretically—have less net carbon content (because biofuels extract carbon content from that air). In practice, the renewable fuel standard in the United States has faced stiff criticism for its environmental effects and questionable net impacts on greenhouse gases. *See* Dina Cappiello, *The Secret Environmental Cost of U.S. Ethanol Policy*, ASSOCIATED PRESS (Nov. 12, 2013), https://www.apnews.com/7250a40e0b1e49a5988ef31259728ef0; C. Ford Runge, *The Case Against More Ethanol: It's Simply Bad for Environment*, YALE ENV'T 360 (May 25, 2016), https://e360.yale.edu/features/the_case_against_ethanol_bad_for_environment.
38. California is the only state with independent regulatory authority under the Clean Air Act to regulate automobile pollution. *See* Clean Air Act § 209, 42 U.S.C. § 7543 (2012); Engine Mfrs. Ass'n v. EPA, 88 F.3d 1075, 1079 n. 9 (D.C. Cir. 1996) (discussing California's special role). During his campaign, then candidate Obama had pledged to respect California's role, and so cutting the state out of the loop to simplify matters was not an option. *See* Freeman, *supra* note 35, at 351.
39. *See, e.g.*, Robert C. Crandall & John D. Graham, *The Effect of Fuel Economy Standards on Automobile Safety*, 32 J. L. & ECON. 97 (1989).
40. Because the rulemaking was jointly undertaken by the EPA and the Department of Transportation, the two agencies conducted separate cost-benefit analyses, which treated the main categories of effects somewhat differently. In particular, the Department of Transportation treated fuel savings as a direct benefit and pollution

reductions as an ancillary benefit, while the EPA treated pollution reductions as direct benefits and fuel savings as "negative costs."

41. EPA, Final Rulemaking to Establish Light-Duty Vehicle Greenhouse Gas Emission Standards and Corporate Average Fuel Economy Standards, Regulatory Impact Analysis, at 8-13 to 8-25 (2010). This is the sum of the greenhouse gas reduction benefits at the preferred social cost of carbon at the time (3 percent discount rate) plus the benefits from reductions in local pollutants. Additional benefits were derived from energy security impacts, reduced refueling time, and the value of increased driving. Additional costs of accidents, noise, and congestion were associated with the increased driving (but overall net benefits). The annual net benefits of the rule by 2030 with the preferred social cost of carbon were estimated to be over $87 billion.

42. A challenge to these standards was included in broader litigation by a conservative think tank against several greenhouse gas related actions during the Obama administration. *See* Coalition for Responsible Regulation. v. EPA, 684 F.3d 102 (D.C. Cir. 2012), *aff'd in part, rev'd in part sub nom.* Utility Air Regulatory Group v. EPA, 134 S. Ct. 2427 (2014). The DC Circuit upheld the rule against an "arbitrary and capricious" challenge. The Supreme Court took the case to decide other issues and did not review the car standards.

43. *See generally* EPA, *supra* note 41.

44. *See* supra notes 5–10 and accompanying text.

45. John F. Morrall III, *A Review of the Record*, REGULATION, Nov./Dec. 1986, at. 25, 30 tbl. 4. The Morrall study has faced criticism on several grounds. *See, e.g.*, Richard W. Parker, *Grading the Government*, 70 U. CHI. L. REV. 1345 (2003).

46. *See* Tammy O. Tengs & John D. Graham, *The Opportunity Costs of Haphazard Social Investments in Life-Saving, in* RISKS, COSTS, AND LIVES SAVED: GETTING BETTER RESULTS FROM REGULATION (Robert W. Hahn ed., 1996).

47. *See, e.g.*, ROBERT W. HAHN, REVIVING REGULATORY REFORM: A GLOBAL PERSPECTIVE (2000).

48. Whitman v. Am. Trucking Ass'ns, 531 U.S. 457 (2001).

49. Michael A. Livermore & Richard L. Revesz, *Rethinking Health-Based Environmental Standards*, 89 N.Y.U. L. REV. 1184, 1261 (2014).

50. *Id.* at 1261–62.

51. We have argued that the best interpretation of *American Trucking* is that it precludes the consideration of costs "only in cases in which [considering costs] would lead to compromising the stringency of the health-based standards." *See id.* at 1263. For the reasoning behind the conclusion, see *id.*

52. *See, e.g.*, EPA, National Ambient Air Quality Standards for Lead, 73 Fed. Reg. 66,964, 67,046 (Nov. 12, 2008) (stating "although an RIA has been prepared, the results of the RIA have not been considered in issuing this final rule").

53. The selected standards have net benefits compared to the status quo, although when compared to more stringent standards they are less than optimal.

54. *See* Michael A. Livermore & Richard L. Revesz, *Rethinking Health-Based Environmental Standards and Cost-Benefit Analysis*, 46 ENVTL. L. REP. 10674 (2016).

55. Alexander Volokh, *Rationality or Rationalism? The Positive and Normative Flaws of Cost-Benefit Analysis*, 48 Hous. L. Rev. 79, 80–81 (2011).

Chapter 3

1. *See generally* Richard L. Revesz, *Environmental Regulation, Cost-Benefit Analysis, and the Discounting of Human Lives*, 99 Colum. L. Rev. 941 (1999).
2. *See generally* Cass R. Sunstein, Valuing Life: Humanizing the Regulatory State (2014).
3. *See, e.g.*, Robert W. Hahn et al., *Assessing Regulatory Impact Analysis: The Failure of Agencies to Comply with Executive Order 12,866*, 23 Harv. J. L. & Pub. Pol'y 859 (2000).
4. *See, e.g.*, Nathaniel O. Keohane, *The Technocratic and Democratic Functions of the CAIR Regulatory Analysis*, *in* Reforming Regulatory Impact Analysis 33 (Winston Harrington, Lisa Heinzerling & Richard D. Morgenstern eds., 2009).
5. One example was in a rulemaking by the Obama EPA to regulate the cooling structures used by power plants. The rule reduced harms to fish and other marine life that occur when cooling water is drawn from freshwater bodies. The agency commissioned a study of the value placed by the public on those benefits and decided not to use those estimates to inform the final rulemaking. EPA, National Pollutant Discharge Elimination System—Final Regulations to Establish Requirements for Cooling Water Intake Structures at Existing Facilities and Amend Requirements at Phase I Facilities, 79 Fed. Reg. 48,300, 48,304 (Aug. 15, 2014) ("In estimating the benefits of today's rule, EPA did not rely on the results of the stated preference survey conducted by the Agency . . . .").
6. The Federalist No. 51 (James Madison).
7. Here we are channeling a cost-benefit analysis version of "Hercules," the judge of "superhuman skill, learning, patience, and acumen" proposed by Ronald Dworkin. *See* Ronald Dworkin, Taking Rights Seriously 105 (1978).
8. Break-even analysis can be used when some values in a cost-benefit analysis are highly uncertain. The inquiry in a break-even analysis is to identify the "break-even" point of those uncertain values, such that a rule would or would not be cost-benefit justified. For example, if a rule has cost of $100 million and reduces one million tons of pollution, the break-even value of pollution avoided is $100 per ton. If the value of pollution reduction is greater than $100 per ton, the rule is cost-benefit justified (at least compared to the status quo). *See generally* Cass R. Sunstein, *The Limits of Quantification*, 102 Calif. L. Rev. 1369 (2014). Another technique that is sometimes used by agencies in the face of uncertainty is cost-effectiveness analysis, which seeks to identify the cheapest path to achieving regulatory goals. Cost-effectiveness analysis is appropriate when regulatory goals are set exogenously.
9. Executive Order 12,866, 58 Fed. Reg. 51,735 (Oct. 4, 1993).
10. Externalities can be both negative and positive. A negative externality, such as pollution, justifies a government intervention to control it—say, through a pollution tax.

A positive externality is a useful effect enjoyed by a third party. For example, a person who maintains private property in a way that facilitates habitat for beneficial species creates a positive externality enjoyed by others. Positive externalities imply that private parties will have too little incentive to engage in such conduct, and government intervention to promote the underlying activity, such as subsidies, may be justified. *See infra* note 98 concerning the distinction between real and pecuniary externalities. It is only the first that provides a prima facie case for regulation, and so in keeping with common convention, we restrict our definition of externalities to only the category of real externalities that indicate market failure.

11. One mechanism to "internalize" the costs of pollution is through the tort system, if aggrieved parties can sue for damages. However, in many environmental contexts the tort system is not sufficient because of the nature of the harms involved.

12. Bargaining between the relevant parties is another mechanism that can, in theory, internalize the costs of pollution to the polluter, as long as the allocation of property rights is clear. *See* R.H. Coase, *The Problem of Social Cost*, 3 J. L. & ECON. 1 (1960). As a practical matter, however, private bargaining will not address many environmental threats because property rights are imperfect and there are too many affected parties involved to efficiently transact. It is possible that public pressure without direct government intervention may also be able to change conduct that generates externalities; but the circumstances where such efforts will achieve efficient results are likely to be rare.

13. *See* Richard L. Revesz, *Federalism and Interstate Environmental Externalities*, 144 U. PA. L. REV. 2341, 2350–54 (1996).

14. North Carolina v. EPA, 531 F.3d 896 (D.C. Cir. 2008). The court objected to the trading provision in the rule because it could not guarantee that an upwind state that was significantly contributing to non-attainment with air quality standards in downwind states would reduce its pollution, because it was possible that the upwind sate would purchase allowances rather than control emissions. That there would be relatively inexpensive aggregate reductions from all upwind states was insufficient for the court.

15. The limitations on trading in the Cross-State Air Pollution Rule were put in place so that all relevant states would reduce their emissions to the point that they would no longer be significantly contributing to non-attainment with air quality standards in any downwind state.

16. EPA, Regulatory Impact Analysis for the Federal Implementation Plans to Reduce Interstate Transport of Fine Particulate Matter and Ozone in 27 States: Correction of SIP Approvals for 22 States 1–21 (2011).

17. EPA v. EME Homer Generation L.P., 134 S. Ct. 1584, 1593 (2014) (citing Revesz, *supra* note 13, at 2343.) (abbreviations and citations ommitted).

18. Amanda Giang & Noelle E. Selin, *Benefits of Mercury Controls for the United States*, 113 PROC. NAT. ACAD. SCI. 286 (2016). During the rulemaking process, the EPA did not quantify these direct benefits.

19. We return to the issue of co-benefits and the MATS Rule in chapter 8.

20. EPA, Regulatory Impact Analysis for the Final Mercury and Air Toxics Standards, at ES-1 (2011).

21. Michigan v. EPA, 135 S. Ct. 2699 (2015).

22. EPA, Supplemental Finding That It Is Appropriate and Necessary to Regulate Hazardous Air Pollutants from Coal- and Oil-Fired Electric Utility Steam Generating Units, 82 Fed. Reg. 24,420 (Apr. 25, 2016).

23. EPA, National Ambient Air Quality Standards for Ozone, Final Rule, 80 Fed. Reg. 65,292 (Oct. 26, 2015); EPA, National Ambient Air Quality Standards for Particulate Matter, Final Rule, 78 Fed. Reg. 3086 (Jan. 15, 2013); EPA, Primary National Ambient Air Quality Standard for Sulfur Dioxide, Final Rule, 75 Fed. Reg. 35,520 (June 22, 2010); EPA, Primary National Ambient Air Quality Standards for Nitrogen Dioxide, Final Rule, 75 Fed. Reg. 6473 (Feb. 9, 2010). *See* Michael A. Livermore & Richard L. Revesz, *Rethinking Health-Based Environmental Standards and Cost-Benefit Analysis*, 46 ENVTL. L. REP. 10674 (2016).

24. EPA, National Ambient Air Quality Standards for Ozone, 73 Fed. Reg. 16,436 (Mar. 27, 2008).

25. *See* Paul Kiel, *States, Enviro Orgs Sue EPA over Ozone Rule*, PROPUBLICA (May 29, 2008), https://www.propublica.org/article/states-enviro-orgs-sue-epa-over-ozone-rule.

26. EPA, National Ambient Air Quality Standards for Ozone, 75 Fed. Reg. 2938 (Jan. 19, 2010).

27. *See* Denise Robbins, *Experts: Pro-Smog Pollution Report Is "Unmoored from Reality,"* MEDIAMATTERS (Aug. 20, 2014), https://www.mediamatters.org/wall-street-journal/experts-pro-smog-pollution-report-unmoored-reality.

28. *See id.*

29. Compared to the George W. Bush–era standard, the central estimate from the EPA's regulatory impact assessment shows that more stringent standards have smaller expected net benefits, although with considerable uncertainty. *See* EPA, Summary of the Updated Regulatory Impact Analysis (RIA) for the Reconsideration of the 2008 Ozone National Ambient Air Quality Standard (NAAQS) (2009), at S1-6 to S1-8.

30. Letter from Cass Sunstein, OIRA Administrator, to Lisa Jackson, EPA Administrator (Sept. 2, 2011).

31. *Id.*

32. *See* EPA, Regulatory Impact Analysis of the Final Revisions to the National Ambient Air Quality Standards for Ground-Level Ozone (Sept. 2015).

33. EPA, *supra* note 5.

34. EPA, Hazardous and Solid Waste Management System; Disposal of Coal Combustion Residuals from Electric Utilities, 80 Fed. Reg. 21,302 (Apr. 17, 2015).

35. Office of Surface Mining Reclamation and Enforcement, Stream Protection Rule, 81 Fed. Reg. 93,066 (Dec. 20, 2016).

36. Critics of cost-benefit analysis have often focused on the fact that agencies often ignore benefits that are difficult to quantify. *See* Amy Sinden, *The Problem of Unquantified Benefits*, 49 ENVTL. L. 73 (2019).

37. EPA, *supra* note 5 at 48,303.

38. *Id.* at 48,304.

39. *Id.*

40. *See generally* Robert J. Johnston et al., *Contemporary Guidance for Stated Preference Studies*, 4 J. Ass'n Envtl. & Res. Econ. 319 (2017).

41. *See, e.g.,* Contingent Valuation of Environmental Goods: A Comprehensive Critique (Daniel McFadden & Kenneth Train eds., 2017).

42. Kenneth Arrow et al., Report of the NOAA Panel on Contingent Valuation, 58 Fed. Reg. 4602 (Jan. 15, 1993).

43. Office of Mgmt. & Budget, Circular A-4 at 22–24 (Sept. 17, 2003). In the words of the Circular:

> Since [stated preference methods] generate data from respondents in a hypothetical setting, often on complex and unfamiliar goods, special care is demanded in the design and execution of surveys, analysis of the results, and characterization of the uncertainties. A stated-preference study may be the only way to obtain quantitative information about non-use values, though a number based on a poor quality study is not necessarily superior to no number at all. Non-use values that are not quantified should be presented as an "intangible" benefit or cost.

44. *See* Michael A. Livermore, *Cost-Benefit Analysis and Agency Independence*, 81 U. Chi. L. Rev. 609, 647–48 (2014) (discussing alternative approaches to valuing life savings).

45. EPA, Guidelines for Preparing Economic Analyses (2010).

46. *See generally* Daniel Bodansky, Jutta Brunnée & Lavanya Rajamani, International Climate Change Law (2017).

47. Adam Vaughan & David Adam, *Copenhagen Climate Deal: Spectacular Failure—Or a Few Important Steps?*, Guardian (Dec. 22, 2009), https://www.theguardian.com/environment/2009/dec/22/copenhagen-climate-deal-expert-view (collecting views of various experts on the merits of the Accord).

48. EPA, Technical Support Document for Endangerment and Cause or Contribute Findings for Greenhouse Gases under Section 202(a) of the Clean Air Act (2009).

49. Clean Air Act § 202(a), 42 U.S.C. § 7521(a) (2012) (punctuation omitted).

50. Ctr. for Biological Diversity v. Nat'l Highway Traffic Safety Admin., 538 F.3d 1172, 1227 (9th Cir. 2008).

51. The range of estimates also included two estimates exploring the sensitivity of the calculations to assumptions about the appropriate discount rate. The central estimate is based on a 3 percent discount rate; two other estimates explore the sensitivity to using instead a 2.5 percent or a 5 percent discount rate. *See generally* Interagency Working Group on Social Cost of Greenhouse Gases, Technical Support Document: Technical Update of the Social Cost of Carbon for Regulatory Impact Analysis under Executive Order 12866 (Aug. 2016).

52. The original estimates were given in 2007$. Using the Consumer Price Index inflation tables, the central estimate of $42 in 2007$ for year 2020 emissions equals $51.79 in 2019$, and a high-impact estimate of $123 in 2007$ for year 2020 emissions equals $151.66 in 2019$.

53. Iliana Paul, Peter Howard & Jason A. Schwartz, Inst. for Policy Integrity, The Social Cost of Greenhouse Gases and State Policy (2017).

54. EPA & Nat'l Highway Traffic Safety Admin., 2017 and Later Model Year Light-Duty Vehicle Greenhouse Gas Emissions and Corporate Average Fuel Economy Standards, 77 Fed. Reg. 62,624 (Oct. 15, 2012).

55. EPA & Nat'l Highway Traffic Safety Admin., Greenhouse Gas Emissions and Fuel Efficiency Standards for Medium- and Heavy-Duty Engines and Vehicles—Phase 2, 81 Fed. Reg. 73,478 (Oct. 25, 2016); EPA & Nat'l Highway Traffic Safety Admin., Greenhouse Gas Emissions Standards and Fuel Efficiency Standards for Medium- and Heavy-Duty Engines and Vehicles, 76 Fed. Reg. 57,106 (Sept. 15, 2011).

56. EPA, Carbon Pollution Emission Guidelines for Existing Stationary Sources: Electric Utility Generating Units, 80 Fed. Reg. 64,662 (Oct. 23, 2015).

57. *Id.* at 64,680 tbl. 1.

58. Editorial Board, *The Supreme Court Puts the Brakes on Clean Power*, WASH. POST (Feb. 10, 2016), http://wapo.st/1QsAI4A? .

59. *See generally* Richard L. Revesz et al., *Global Warming: Improve Economic Models of Climate Change*, 508 NATURE 173 (2014).

60. Press Release, Royal Swedish Acad. of Sci., The Prize in Economic Sciences 2018 (Oct. 8, 2018).

61. Peter Howard, Omitted Damages: What's Missing from the Social Cost of Carbon (2014).

62. *See* Thomas Sterner & U. Marin Persson, *An Even Sterner Review: Introducing Relative Prices into the Discounting Debate*, 2 REV. ENVTL. ECON. & POL'Y 61 (2008).

63. *See* Kenneth J. Arrow et al., *Should Governments Use a Declining Discount Rate in Project Analysis?*, 8 REV. ENVTL. ECON. & POL'Y 145 (2014); Richard G. Newell & William A. Pizer, *Discounting the Distant Future: How Much Do Uncertain Rates Increase Valuations?*, 46 J. ENVTL. ECON. & MGMT. 52 (2003); Martin L. Weitzman, *Why the Far-Distant Future Should Be Discounted at Its Lowest Possible Rate*, 36 J. ENVTL. ECON. & MGMT. 201 (1998).

64. Richard L. Revesz et al., *Best Cost Estimate of Greenhouse Gas Emissions*, 357 SCIENCE 655 (2017).

65. *See generally* DANIEL KAHNEMAN, THINKING, FAST AND SLOW (2011); RICHARD H. THALER & CASS R. SUNSTEIN, NUDGE: IMPROVING DECISIONS ABOUT HEALTH, WEALTH, AND HAPPINESS (2008).

66. *See generally* SANJIT DHAMI, THE FOUNDATIONS OF BEHAVIORAL ECONOMIC ANALYSIS (2016) (providing an extensive introduction to the field).

67. *See* Colin Camerer et al., *Regulation for Conservatives: Behavioral Economics and the Case for "Asymmetric Paternalism,"* 151 U. PA. L. REV. 1211 (2003) (early example of the application of insights from behavioral economics to law and public policy).

68. Beyond the well-being of users or potential users, a ban on heroin could be justified on the basis of secondary effects, such as addiction-induced theft, harm done to family members, or costs imposed on public institutions such as the health care or criminal justice systems. However, to some degree, these secondary effects—especially crime—may be exacerbated, rather than reduced, through a ban.

69. Lindsay F. Wiley, Micah L. Berman & Doug Blanke, *Who's Your Nanny? Choice, Paternalism and Public Health in the Age of Personal Responsibility*, 41 J. L. MED. & ETHICS 88 (2013).

70. Some of this opposition was funded by the affected industry. *See* Michael M. Grynbaum, *Fighting Soda Rule, Industry Focuses on Personal Choice*, N.Y. TIMES, July 2, 2012, at A10.

71. *See* Wiley, Berman & Blanke, *supra* note 69. *See generally* Gregory Mitchell, *Libertarian Paternalism Is an Oxymoron*, 99 Nw. U. L. REV. 1245 (2005).

72. *See* EPA, Final Rulemaking to Establish Light-Duty Vehicle Greenhouse Gas Emission Standards and Corporate Average Fuel Economy Standards, Regulatory Impact Analysis (2010). These fuel savings can be understood as negative costs, since they decrease the costs that consumers ultimately pay for vehicles that produce less pollution.

73. EPA & Nat'l Highway Traffic Safety Admin., Light-Duty Vehicle Greenhouse Gas Emission Standards and Corporate Average Fuel Economy Standards, Final Rule, 75 Fed. Reg. 25,324, 25,328–29 (May 7, 2010).

74. *Id.* at 25,510–15.

75. David L. Greene, EPA, How Consumers Value Fuel Economy: A Literature Review (2010).

76. EPA & Nat'l Highway Traffic Safety Admin., *supra* note 73 at 25,510–15.

77. Not every expert agrees with the conclusions reached by the Obama EPA on this question. For example, Ted Gayer and W. Kip Viscusi have argued that "the evidence in the economics literature on the existence and magnitude of [] an energy efficiency gap is mixed and does not provide a compelling justification for overriding consumer decisions in the absence of supporting evidence." Ted Gayer & W. Kip Viscusi, *Overriding Consumer Preferences with Energy Regulations*, 43 J. REG. ECON. 248, 249 (2013). The question may turn on the best conclusion to draw from "mixed" evidence. In a related paper, Gayer and Viscusi argue that "the burden of proof for any [cost-benefit analysis] conducted as part of a review of regulatory proposals should be placed heavily on justifying any presumption of a deviation from consumer sovereignty." Ted Gayer & W. Kip Viscusi, *Overriding Consumer Preferences with Energy Regulations* 8–9 (Mercatus Center at George Mason University Working Paper 12-21, 2012). This high burden of proof may not be justified, at least in the context of fuel-economy decisions. For example, EPA cites research showing that consumers misperceive the relationship between miles per gallon and fuel consumption—a fact that calls into question how well positioned consumers are to make informed decisions in this context. *See* Richard P. Larrick & Jack B. Soll, *The MPG Illusion*, 320 SCIENCE 1593 (2008).

Under standard rational choice theory, a social decision maker facing uncertainty ought to maximize expected utility based on the probability that it assigns to various outcomes. Here, the existing state of the empirical literature was not entirely conclusive and required the agency to exercise its judgment concerning whether more fuel-efficient cars (which have a higher purchase price but save fuel) would generate a genuine improvement in consumer well-being. The agency's reasoning, relayed in the rulemaking record, took account of the existing literature in behavioral economics more broadly, as well as research that had been done on consumer decision making in the context of automobile purchases specifically. This review of the available evidence was consistent with long-standing norms concerning how agencies should make decisions under conditions of uncertainty—a common situation. Of course, that does not imply that every expert need accept the agency's conclusions; healthy debate and continued research can certainly help improve future decisions in this area.

78. *See* Inst. for Policy Integrity, Supplemental Comments to NHTSA and EPA on Vehicle Emissions Standards 6–8 (Dec. 21, 2018) (documenting consistent approach to valuing fuel savings during the Carter, Reagan, George H. W. Bush, Clinton, George W. Bush and Obama administrations).

79. Pub. L. No. 109-280, 120 Stat. 780 (codified as amended in scattered sections of 26 and 29 U.S.C.).

80. *See* Eric J. Johnson & Daniel Goldstein, *Do Defaults Save Lives?*, 302 SCIENCE 1338 (2003). For a discussion of some of the mechanisms that might drive this effect, see Shai Davidai, Thomas Gilovich & Lee D. Ross, *The Meaning of Default Options for Potential Organ Donors*, 109 PROC. NAT'L ACAD. SCI. 15201 (2012).

81. The efficacy of the law's automatic enrollment provisions has been questioned by some, in part because the default savings rate may have been set too low. *See* Ryan Bubb & Richard H. Pildes, *How Behavioral Economics Trims Its Sails and Why*, 127 HARV. L. REV. 1593, 1616–25 (2014).

82. Federal Reserve System, Electronic Fund Transfers, 74 Fed. Reg. 59,033 (Nov. 17, 2009).

83. Novantas, Understanding Consumer Choice: A Review of Consumer Overdraft Behaviors 4 (2015) (study funded by Consumer Bankers Association).

84. Comments of Consumer Bankers Association to Consumer Financial Protection Bureau (July 1, 2019) (on file with authors).

85. A rational overdraft might result when a bank customer intentionally uses a checking account as a source of short-term credit. One study by a consulting firm working with the Fed used an extended interview technique in an attempt to gauge consumers' responses to the new disclosure. *See* ICF Macro, Design and Testing of Overdraft Disclosures: Phase Two (2009).

86. *See, e.g.*, RICHARD A. POSNER, A FAILURE OF CAPITALISM: THE CRISIS OF '08 AND THE DESCENT INTO DEPRESSION (2009); John Cassidy, *After the Blowup*, NEW YORKER, Jan. 11, 2010 at 28.

87. *See generally* Herbert Hovenkamp, *Post-Chicago Antitrust: A Review and Critique*, 2001 COLUM. BUS. L. REV. 257, 257–75 ; Laura Phillips Sawyer, *U.S. Antitrust Law and Policy in Historical Perspective* (Harvard Business School Working Paper 19-110, 2019).

88. *See generally* ALAN DEVLIN, FUNDAMENTAL PRINCIPLES OF LAW AND ECONOMICS 303–94 (2015).

89. *See* JOEL B. EISEN ET AL., ENERGY, ECONOMICS, AND THE ENVIRONMENT (4th ed. 2015).

90. *See* Ohio v. Am. Express Co., 138 S. Ct. 2274 (2018) (holding that credit card companies' "anti-steering" policies are not anti-competitive); Herbert J. Hovenkamp, *Platforms and the Rule of Reason: The* American Express *Case*, 2019 COLUM. BUS. L. REV. 35, 46 (criticizing the Supreme Court's "regressive, antieconomic conclusion" and flawed reasoning in the *American Express* case).

91. One example of this deregulatory effort was the decommissioning of the Civil Aeronautics Board, which regulated airlines from 1939 to 1985. *See* Airline Deregulation Act, Pub. L. 95–504, 92 Stat. 1705 (1978).

92. Promoting Wholesale Competition Through Open Access Non-Discriminatory Transmission Services by Public Utilities, Order 888, 75 FERC ¶ 61,080 (Apr. 24, 1996); Regional Transmission Organizations, Order 2000, 89 FERC ¶ 61,285 (Dec. 20, 1999).

93. Fed. Reserve Sys., Regulatory Capital Rules: Implementation of Risk-Based Capital Surcharges for Global Systemically Important Bank Holding Companies, 80 Fed. Reg. 49,081 (Aug. 14, 2015); Fed. Reserve Sys., Regulatory Capital Rules: Regulatory Capital, Implementation of Basel III, Capital Adequacy, Transition Provisions, Prompt Corrective Action, Standardized Approach for Risk-Weighted Assets, Market Discipline and Disclosure Requirements, Advanced Approaches Risk-Based Capital Rule, and Market Risk Capital Rule, 78 Fed. Reg. 62,018, 62,023 (Oct. 11, 2013).

94. Dep't of the Treasury, Office of the Comptroller of the Currency, Fed. Reserve Sys., Federal Deposit Insurance Corporation and Securities and Exchange Commission, Prohibitions and Restrictions on Proprietary Trading and Certain Interests in, and Relationships With, Hedge Funds and Private Equity Funds, 79 Fed. Reg. 5,536 (Jan. 31, 2014).

95. The underlying causes of the housing bubble and subsequent financial crisis are deeply contested. *See generally* ALAN S. BLINDER, AFTER THE MUSIC STOPPED: THE FINANCIAL CRISIS, THE RESPONSE, AND THE WORK AHEAD (2013); BETHANY MCLEAN & JOE NOCERA, ALL THE DEVILS ARE HERE: THE HIDDEN HISTORY OF THE FINANCIAL CRISIS (2010).

96. Bureau of Consumer Fin. Prot., Ability-to-Repay and Qualified Mortgage Standards Under the Truth in Lending Act (Regulation Z), 78 Fed. Reg. 6408 (Jan. 30, 2013).

97. *Compare* John C. Coates IV, *Cost-Benefit Analysis of Financial Regulation: Case Studies and Implications*, 124 YALE L.J. 882 (2015) [hereinafter Coates, *Case Studies*] (raising concern of "camouflage") *with* Cass R. Sunstein, *Financial Regulation and Cost-Benefit Analysis*, 124 YALE L.J.F. 263, 263 (2015). For other works in the back and forth, see Sumit Agarwal, *A Simple Framework for Estimating Consumer Benefits from Regulating Hidden Fees*, 43 J. LEGAL STUD. S239 (2014); Robert P. Bartlett III, *The Institutional Framework for Cost-Benefit Analysis in Financial Regulation: A Tale of Four Paradigms*, 43 J. LEGAL STUD. S379 (2014); Omri Ben-Shahar & Carl E. Schneider, *The Futility of Cost-Benefit Analysis in Financial Disclosure Regulation*, 43 J. LEGAL STUD. S253 (2014); Ryan Bubb, *Comment: The OIRA Model for Institutionalizing CBA of Financial Regulation*, 78 L. & CONTEMP. PROBS. 47 (2015); John C. Coates IV, *Towards Better Cost-Benefit Analysis: An Essay on Regulatory Management*, 78 LAW. & CONTEMP. PROBS. 1 (2015); John H. Cochrane, *Challenges*

for Cost-Benefit Analysis of Financial Regulation, 43 J. LEGAL STUD. S63 (2014); James D. Cox, *Iterative Regulation of Securities Markets after* Business Roundtable: *A Principles-Based Approach*, 78 LAW. & CONTEMP. PROBS. 25 (2015); Robert J. Jackson. Jr., *Comment: Cost-Benefit Analysis and the Courts*, 78 L. & CONTEMP. PROBS. 1 (2015); Bruce Kraus & Connor Raso, *Rational Boundaries for SEC Cost-Benefit Analysis*, 30 YALE J. REG. 289 (2013); Gillian E. Metzger, *Through the Looking Glass to a Shared Reflection: The Evolving Relationship Between Administrative Law and Financial Regulation*, 78 LAW & CONTEMP. PROBS. 129 (2015); Eric A. Posner & E. Glen Weyl, *Benefit-Cost Paradigms in Financial Regulation*, 43 J. LEGAL STUD. S1 (2014); Matthew Spitzer & Eric Talley, *On Experimentation and Real Options in Financial Regulation*, 43 J. LEGAL STUD. S121 (2014).

98. The National Research Council provides the following definition:

> An externality, which can be positive or negative, is an activity of one agent (for example, an individual or an organization, such as a company) that affects the well-being of another agent and occurs *outside the market mechanism.*

NAT'L RESEARCH COUNCIL OF THE NAT'L ACADEMIES, HIDDEN COSTS OF ENERGY: UNPRICED CONSEQUENCES OF ENERGY PRODUCTION AND USE 29 (2010).

This extra-market dimension of pollution is what distinguishes it from effects on third parties that occur within the market, which are sometimes referred to as "pecuniary externalities." Imagine a new market entrant begins to purchase a good, driving up prices. The diminished welfare of other consumers, who can purchase less of the good at the higher price, are pecuniary externalities. In complete and functioning markets, pecuniary markets do not interfere with efficiency—negative welfare effects (e.g., loss consumer surplus) are offset by symmetrical welfare increases (e.g., producer surplus). *See* Tibor Scitovsky, *Two Concepts of External Economies*, 62 J. POL. ECON. 143 (1954). This means that pecuniary externalities alone are insufficient to indicate a market failure. When markets are incomplete, pecuniary externalities can lead to inefficiencies. *See, e.g.,* Lee Hsien Loong & Richard Zeckhauser, *Pecuniary Externalities Do Matter when Contingent Claims Markets are Incomplete*, 97 Q. J. ECON. 171 (1982). Pecuniary externalities are contrasted with "real" externalities. *See* Richard P. Adelstein & Noel M. Edelson, *Subdivision Exactions and Congestion Externalities*, 5. J. LEGAL STUD. 147 (1976). It is the latter category of real externalities that fits the National Research Council definition.

99. Government intervention generates various administrative costs and is only justified to correct for a market failure when the net benefits of the (often imperfect) improvement in efficiency are greater than those costs.

100. The issue of how best to describe market failures in the context of systemic risk and financial crises is quite complex. Systemic risk does not fit in the definition of a real externality (defined above, *supra* note 98) because its effects occur through rather than outside the market system. The notion of pecuniary externalities (defined above, *supra* note 98) has been used in the context of macroeconomic policy analysis. *See, e.g.,* Olivier Jeanne & Anton Korinek, *Managing Credit Booms and Busts: A Pigouvian Taxation Approach*, 107 J. MONETARY ECON. 2 (2019). Systemic

risk in financial markets has been characterized as an externality that arises from relationships between financial firms, as bank failures propagate through a system. *See, e.g.*, Viral V. Acharya, *A Theory of Systemic Risk and Design of Prudential Bank Regulation*, 5 J. FIN. STABILITY 224 (2009).

Even the notion of real externalities has long-standing critics, at least as far back as Coase. *See* Coase, *supra* note 12. Under the Coasian view, no effect is (at least in theory) outside the market because actors can always bargain over them—the victims of pollution could pay the polluter to reduce emissions. Government action is justified not because effects are in principle outside the market, but because transaction costs prevent private actors from efficiently bargaining over terms.

The Coasian transaction cost view also has critics. Harold Demsetz, for example, argues that transaction costs themselves arise from private ordering and, accordingly, "there is no difference between transaction cost and other costs" in relevant respects. Harold Demsetz, *The Problem of Social Cost: What Problem?*, 7 REV. L. & ECON. 1, 10 (2011). Transactions occur when the expected value of the bargain for the parties is greater than the cost of transacting, full stop. For Demsetz, government intervention is justified (according to a neoclassical framework) only when a good (such as clean air or a stable climate) is indivisible/non-excludable and cannot, even in principle, be brought into the system of private property (in part because people will not be honest about their willingness to pay for the good).

Working backward, it may be possible to provide a neoclassical justification for regulatory interventions to reduce systemic risk either because a stable financial system is an indivisible/non-excludable good (on the Demsetzian view) or based on transaction cost reasoning if those costs prevent private parties from efficiently allocating and controlling such risks (under the Coasian view). The definition of a (real) externality adopted by the National Research Council, *supra* note 98, can be understood as a short-hand for a family of inefficient outcomes that occur either due to the indivisibility/non-excludability of a good or due to transaction costs, such that effects from private decisions are transmitted entirely outside the market. Systemic risks do not fit this definition (because such risks propagate through markets) and so the short-hand is not applicable, even though a justification for regulation could be made on Demsetzian or Coasian grounds (or, for that matter, on the basis of pecuniary externalities that combine with other market characteristics to lead to non-optimal outcomes).

101. *But see* GARY B. GORTON, SLAPPED BY THE INVISIBLE HAND: THE PANIC OF 2007 (2010); ROBERT J. SHILLER, IRRATIONAL EXUBERANCE (3d. ed. 2015); Robert J. Shiller, *Human Behavior and the Efficiency of the Financial System*, *in* HANDBOOK OF MACROECONOMICS (John B. Taylor & Michael Woodford eds., 1999).

102. Of course, it may take an extensive line of credit and a steel will to exploit such failures if they are particularly widespread. *See* MICHAEL LEWIS, THE BIG SHORT: INSIDE THE DOOMSDAY MACHINE (2010).

103. Government officials can also misdiagnose the causes of prior financial crises. For an argument that this has often been the case, see PAUL G. MAHONEY, WASTING A CRISIS: WHY SECURITIES REGULATION FAILS (2015).

104. Although the US regulators did not publish formal cost-benefit analyses, the Basel Committee, in consultation with the International Monetary Fund did. *See* Basel Comm. on Banking Supervision, An Assessment of the Long-Term Economic Impact of Stronger Capital and Liquidity Requirements (2010); Macroeconomic Assessment Grp., Final Report: Assessing the Macroeconomic Impact of the Transition to Stronger Capital and Liquidity Requirements (2010). Commentators have been critical of the quality of these analyses. *See, e.g.,* Coates, *Case Studies, supra* note 97, at 960 ("A review of these publications does not leave a reader with much confidence . . . .").

105. See Coates, *Case Studies, supra* note 97, at 959 n. 276 and accompanying text, 974–77.

106. The CFBM articulated the systemic risk concern as follows: "Throughout the housing boom, most lenders and borrowers entering into such agreements failed to consider the costs that default would inflict on other properties (and the consumers who inhabited them) and on the financial system and economy writ large." Bureau of Consumer Fin. Prot., *supra* note 96, at 6561.

107. Richard L. Revesz, *Cost-Benefit Analysis and the Structure of the Administrative State: The Case of Financial Services Regulation,* 34 YALE J. REG. 545 (2017).

108. *See* Sawyer, *supra* note 87.

109. For a discussion of how shareholder activism by union pension funds can be used to achieve labor-oriented policy goals, see DAVID WEBBER, THE RISE OF THE WORKING-CLASS SHAREHOLDER: LABOR'S LAST BEST WEAPON (2018).

110. Rulemaking efforts were initiated, but never completed, in 1942, 1977, 1992, and 2003. Sec. and Exch. Comm'n, Facilitating Shareholder Director Nominations, Proposed Rule, 74 Fed. Reg. 29,024, 29,029 & n.73 (June 18, 2009).

111. Business Roundtable v. Sec. and Exch. Comm'n, 647 F. 3d 1144, 1151 (D.C. Cir. 2011).

112. Under the Trump administration, the Securities and Exchange Commission has moved in the opposite direction by proposing to make it more difficult for shareholders to submit proposals to corporate boards of directors for considera-tion. *See* Securities and Exchange Commission, Procedural Requirements and Resubmission Thresholds Under Exchange Act Rule 14a–8, 84 Fed. Reg. 66,458 (Dec. 4, 2019). The move was hailed by the Business Roundtable, "an association of chief executive officers," and strongly opposed by progressive groups engaged in shareholder advocacy. *Compare* Public Comments of Business Roundtable on Procedural Requirements and Resubmission Thresholds under Exchange Act Rule 14a-8 (Feb. 3, 2020), *with Proposed SEC Rules to Restrict Proxy Access Break Faith with Investors,* INTERFAITH CTR. ON CORP. RESP. (Nov. 5, 2019), https://www.iccr.org/proposed-sec-rules-restrict-proxy-access-break-faith-investors.

113. Fed. Commc'ns Comm'n, Protecting and Promoting the Open Internet, 80 Fed. Reg. 19,738, 19,747 (Apr. 13, 2015).

114. *Id.* at 19,740.

115. *Id.* at 19,747

116. *Id.* at 19,739

117. So-called "independent" agencies were excluded from both the Reagan and Clinton executive orders on regulatory review. *See* Kirti Datla & Richard L. Revesz, *Deconstructing Independent Agencies (and Executive Agencies)*, 98 CORNELL L. REV. 769 (2013).

118. Mozilla Corp. v. Fed. Commc'ns Comm'n, 940 F. 3d 1 (D.C. Cir. 2019). The court's decision in that case upholds the agency's use of a qualitative cost-benefit analysis and rejects challengers' assertion that the discussion failed to appropriately examine the possible costs of the rollback.

119. Revesz, *supra* note 107.

120. Executive Order 13,563 § 1(c), 76 Fed. Reg. 3821, 3821 (Jan. 21, 2011).

121. A major challenge involved is in coming to agreement on the underlying values. One sophisticated normative defense of cost-benefit analysis as it is practiced in the United States (with its emphasis on Kaldor-Hicks efficiency, willingness to pay, and preference satisfaction) is that it provides a rough guide of the effects of a policy on human well-being. *See* MATTHEW D. ADLER & ERIC A. POSNER, NEW FOUNDATIONS OF COST-BENEFIT ANALYSIS (2006). Under one interpretation of this account, policy choices matter because of their consequences for well-being, and other values (such as dignity) enter the calculus inasmuch as they bear on well-being. *Cf.* Louis Kaplow & Steven Shavell, *Fairness Versus Welfare: Notes on the Pareto Principle, Preferences, and Distributive Justice*, 32 J. LEGAL STUD. 331 (2003). This view has critics. Libertarians, for example, argue that certain rights are inviolable, even with the goal of maximizing welfare. *See generally* ROBERT NOZICK, ANARCHY, STATE, AND UTOPIA (1974). In the language of Obama's order 13,563, some may argue that "dignity" requires that certain property interests be respected, whatever the net social costs of doing so.

122. *See generally* Ted Gayer & W. Kip Viscusi, *Determining the Proper Scope of Climate Change Policy Benefits in U.S. Regulatory Analyses: Domestic Versus Global Approaches*, 10 REV. ENVTL. ECON. & POL'Y 245 (2016) ("The standard practice for benefit-cost analysis would be to ignore the preferences of citizens outside of the state since they are not bearing any of the costs of providing the good."). We do not agree with this view.

123. There are classes of benefits of DACA that would be counted under the Gayer-Viscusi approach, including altruistic benefits enjoyed by US citizens (based on their desire to help others) and general economic benefits.

124. Ctrs. for Medicare & Medicaid Servs., Regulatory Impact Analysis, Patient Protection and Affordable Care Act; Establishment of Exchanges and Qualified Health Plans, Exchange Standards for Employers (CMS-9989-FWP) and Standards Related to Reinsurance, Risk Corridors and Risk Adjustment (CMS-9975-F) (2012).

125. AJIT K. DASGUPTA & D.W. PEARCE, COST-BENEFIT ANALYSIS: THEORY AND PRACTICE (1972).

126. Some question the empirical foundations for the claim that marginal utility actually declines in consumption. *See* Sarah B. Lawsky, *On the Edge: Declining Marginal Utility and Tax Policy*, 95 MINN. L. REV. 904 (2011).

127. Matthew Adler, Well-Being and Fair Distribution: Beyond Cost-Benefit Analysis (2012); Derek Parfit, *Equality and Priority*, 10 Ratio 202 (1997).

128. HM Treasury, The Green Book: Appraisal and Evaluation in Central Government 77–81 (2018).

129. Executive Order 12,866, *supra* note 9, § 1(a).

130. *See* Louis Kaplow & Steven Shavell, *Why the Legal System Is Less Efficient than the Income Tax in Redistributing Income*, 23 J. Legal Stud. 667 (1994).

131. Richard L. Revesz, *Regulation and Distribution*, 93 N.Y.U. L. Rev. 1489 (2018).

132. Prison Rape Elimination Act of 2003, 42 U.S.C. §§ 15601–09, § 15602(1), (2) (2012).

133. The agency did not do a full cost-benefit analysis due to uncertainty about the rule's effects. Rather, it opted for a "break-even approach" that estimated the efficacy that the rule would need to achieve to have net benefits, vis-à-vis the status quo. U.S. Dep't of Justice, Regulatory Impact Assessment, Final Rule National Standards to Prevent, Detect, and Respond to Prison Rape Under the Prison Rape Elimination Act (PREA) 9 (2012).

134. *Id.* at 39–66.

135. Lisa Heinzerling, *Cost-Benefit Jumps the Shark*, Geo. L. Fac. Blog (June 13, 2012), https://gulcfac.typepad.com/georgetown_university_law/2012/06/cost-benefit-jumps-the-shark.html.

Chapter 4

1. Whether or not the Democrats held a filibuster-proof majority depends on how Joe Lieberman and Bernie Sanders, independents who caucused with the Democrats, are treated. There was also some variation over time due to special elections.

2. *Presidential Approval Ratings—George W. Bush*, https://news.gallup.com/poll/116500/presidential-approval-ratings-george-bush.aspx (see table, "Do you approve or disapprove of the way George W. Bush is handling his job as president?," entry for week of 2008 Oct. 31-Nov. 2).

3. Anthony Downs, *An Economic Theory of Political Action in a Democracy*, 65 J. Pol. Econ. 135, 137 (1957).

4. *Id.*

5. *McConnell: Democrats' Big Senate Majority Forces Obstructionism*, PBS News Hour (Aug. 5, 2010), https://www.pbs.org/newshour/politics/mcconnell-says-big-dem-majority-in-senate-forces-obstruction. Use of the filibuster under McConnell increased when the Democrats took control of the Senate, following the 2006 midterm elections. *See Cloture Motions*, U.S. Senate, https://www.senate.gov/legislative/cloture/clotureCounts.htm. Norms concerning the use of the filibuster in the Senate began eroding in the mid-twentieth century:

> In the 1950s, the filibuster, despite requiring fewer senators to maintain, was employed only rarely. The norms for its use were far more restrictive. Specifically, when we speak of norms, we mean the perception by the senators themselves that the use of the filibuster was a legitimate tactic to prevent bills they disliked from being passed. In the early 1970s, a general rise in the

legitimacy of obstructionist tactics and individualism among senators legitimized the filibuster. By 1975, when the cloture rule was changed, the filibuster had become a more regular (if still infrequent) part of the Senate's processes. Over time, under the 60-vote rule, the permissiveness of obstruction and filibustering as legislative strategy has only risen. Today, the filibuster is employed to block almost anything that the minority party in the Senate does not want to see passed. Its legitimacy as a tactic is absolute.

Thomas R. Gray & Jeffery A. Jenkins, *Unpacking Pivotal Politics: Exploring the Differential Effects of the Filibuster and Veto Pivots*, 172 Pub. Choice 359, 364 (2017).

6. After the mandate was incorporated into Obamacare, the Heritage researcher who had previously supported the idea recanted his earlier views. *See* Stuart Butler, *Don't Blame Heritage for ObamaCare Mandate*, Heritage (Feb. 3, 2012), https://www.heritage.org/health-care-reform/commentary/dont-blame-heritage-obamacare-mandate. This public disavowal was part of a broader trend and provides an additional illustration of the role of partisanship in influencing policy views. Michael Cooper, *Conservatives Sowed Idea of Health Care Mandate, Only to Spurn It Later*, N.Y. Times, Feb. 14, 2012, at A15. There were also conservatives who opposed individual mandates before this idea was taken up by Obama and whose opposition has remained consistent over time. *See* Avik Roy, *The Tortuous History of Conservatives and the Individual Mandate*, Forbes (Feb. 7, 2012), https://www.forbes.com/sites/theapothecary/2012/02/07/the-tortuous-conservative-history-of-the-individual-mandate/.

7. The first version of the Affordable Care Act passed the Senate using the regular procedure, garnering the sixty votes needed to close debate. However, adoption of the final complete version that was negotiated with the House and included important adjustments (such as higher health care subsides) was accomplished through reconciliation as a set of amendments. Kevin Drum, *Obamacare Was Not Passed via Reconciliation*, Mother Jones (Jan. 3, 2017), https://www.motherjones.com/kevin-drum/2017/01/obamacare-was-not-passed-reconciliation/.

8. Shan Carter et al., *On the Issues: Immigration, Election Guide*, N.Y. Times (May 23, 2012), https://www.nytimes.com/elections/2008/president/issues/immigration.html .

9. David M. Herszenhorn, *Senate Blocks Bill for Young Illegal Immigrants*, N.Y. Times (Dec. 18, 2010), https://www.nytimes.com/2010/12/19/us/politics/19immig.html.

10. There are a number of substantive differences between the 1990 Clean Air Amendments and the 2009 cap-and-trade bill. Most obviously, they address different pollutants. Nevertheless, the contrast is instructive. In 1990, it was still possible to muster some degree of bipartisan consensus to engage in serious environmental lawmaking, and Republican politicians made an important contribution to that law by pushing for a cap-and-trade approach to air pollution reduction. In 2009, leading Republican politicians denied the reality of one of the most important environmental issues of the day, and criticized in harsh terms the very market-based approach that they had favored.

11. Jean Chemnick & Manuel Quiñones, *Clean Air Act Debates Show How Much Politics Have Changed*, E&E News (Feb. 13, 2014), https://www.eenews.net/stories/1059994544.

12. Louis Jacobson, *McConnell Says that Kerry-Lieberman Climate Bill "Essentially Written" by BP*, POLITIFACT, https://www.politifact.com/truth-o-meter/statements/2010/jun/14/mitch-mcconnell/mcconnell-says-kerry-lieberman-climate-bill-essent/.

13. Jordan Fabian, *McConnell: Cap-and-Trade "Dead,"* THE HILL (Aug. 24, 2010), http://thehill.com/blogs/blog-briefing-room/news/115501-mcconnell-pronounces-cap-and-trade-dead; Ezra Klein, *Cap-and-Trade Is Dead*, WASH. POST (July 19, 2010), http://voices.washingtonpost.com/ezra-klein/2010/07/were_not_getting_a_price_on_ca.html.

14. These include Dan Coats, Chuck Grassley, Lisa Murkowski, John McCain, and Thad Cochran. *See* Roll Call Vote 101st Congress–2nd Session, Measure Number S. 1630 (Clean Air Act Amendments of 1990 Clean Air Employment Transition Act).

15. *See* Ryan Lizza, *As the World Burns*, NEW YORKER (Oct. 3, 2010), https://www.newyorker.com/magazine/2010/10/11/as-the-world-burns.

16. *Id.*

17. *H.R. 3030 (101st): Clean Air Act Amendments of 1990*, GOVTRACK, https://www.govtrack.us/congress/votes/101-1990/h137.

18. Alex Kaplun, *Gingrich Group's Campaign Takes Aim at House Bill*, E&E NEWS (June 23, 2009), https://www.eenews.net/stories/79559.

19. *See, e.g.,* Juliet Eilperin & Brady Dennis, *How James Inhofe Is Upending the Nation's Energy and Environmental Policies*, WASH. POST (March 14, 2017), http://wapo.st/2mprPlv? (quoting Inhofe as claiming that climate change is a "hoax").

20. Richard Schmalensee & Robert N. Stavins, *The SO2 Allowance Trading System: The Ironic History of a Grand Policy Experiment*, 27 J. ECON. PERSP. 103 (2013).

21. *See, e.g.,* Editorial, *Buried Code*, WASH. POST (June 7, 2009), https://www.washingtonpost.com/wp-dyn/content/article/2009/06/06/AR2009060601797.html (criticizing supplemental measures in the bill, such as building codes).

22. *See* Jonathan S. Masur & Eric A. Posner, *Toward a Pigouvian State*, 164 U. PA. L. REV. 93, 142 (2015) ("When Obama eventually proposed a cap-and-trade system, opponents attacked it as 'cap and tax.' . . . The word 'tax' is toxic, particularly for political conservatives.")

23. *See* ERIC POOLEY, THE CLIMATE WAR: TRUE BELIEVERS, POWER BROKERS, AND THE FIGHT TO SAVE THE EARTH 51 (2010).

24. *See* Press Release, U.S. Senate Comm. on Env't and Pub. Works, Inhofe Exposes Cap and Tax Scheme in Obama Budget (Mar. 18, 2009).

25. John M. Broder, *"Cap and Trade" Loses Its Standing as Energy Policy of Choice*, N.Y. TIMES, Mar. 26, 2010, at A13.

26. Anne Joseph O'Connell, *Shortening Agency and Judicial Vacancies Through Filibuster Reform? An Examination of Confirmation Rates and Delays from 1981 to 2014*, 64 DUKE L. J. 1645 (2015).

27. Sunstein recalls the experience as quite surreal. *See* CASS R. SUNSTEIN, SIMPLER: THE FUTURE OF GOVERNMENT 15–24 (2013).

28. *Id.*

29. *Id.*

30. Paul Harris & Ewen MacAskill, *US Midterm Election Results Herald New Political Era as Republicans Take House*, GUARDIAN (Nov. 3, 2010), https://www.theguardian.com/world/2010/nov/03/us-midterm-election-results-tea-party.

31. U.S. Chamber of Commerce, Remarks by Thomas J. Donohue, President and CEO, Des Moines Rotary Club (Oct. 7, 2010) (on file with authors).

32. Emily Yehle, *House GOP Report Decries Obama's "Regulatory Tsunami,"* GREENWIRE (Sept. 14, 2011), https://www.eenews.net/greenwire/stories/1059953634/.

33. Randy Rabinowitz & Matt La Tronica, The Regulatory Tsunami That Wasn't (OMB Watch, Sept. 2012).

34. Mark Drajem & Catherine Dodge, *Obama Wrote 5 Percent Fewer Rules Than Bush While Costing Business*, BLOOMBERG (Oct. 25, 2011), https://www.bloomberg.com/news/articles/2011-10-25/obama-wrote-5-fewer-rules-than-bush-while-costing-business.

35. Nicole V. Crain & W. Mark Crain, Small Business Admin., The Impact of Regulatory Costs on Small Firms 18 (2010).

36. Country fixed effects were included as well. *Id*. at 22.

37. The report uses the regression coefficient for Regulatory Quality Index to derive "the estimated cost of economic regulations as reflected in lost GDP." *Id*. at 24.

38. One of the sources for the Regulator Quality Index is the Heritage Foundation Index of Economic Freedom. The Crain and Crain report points to a World Bank working paper for information on the construction of the index. *Id*. at 19 n. 21. That working paper is Daniel Kaufmann, Aart Kraay & Massimo Mastruzzi, *Governance Matters VIII: Aggregate and Individual Governance Indicators 1996–2008* (World Bank Development Research Group, Macroeconomics and Growth Team, Policy Research Working Paper 4978, 2009). That paper lists the "Heritage Foundation Index of Economic Freedom" as a source for the Regulatory Quality Index. *See* Kaufmann, Kraay & Mastruzzi at 76 tbl. B4; 56 tbl. A17.

39. Kaufmann, Kraay & Mastruzzi, *supra* note 38, at 76 tbl. B4; 53 tbl. A14. Another suite of questions asks "How problematic are [labor/tax/custom and trade] regulations for the growth of your business?" *Id*. at 76 tbl. B4; 44 tbl. A5. What a makes regulation "problematic" is open to interpretation, but it is plausible that regulation could be problematic either by being too stringent or too weak.

40. Edward E. Leamer, *Let's Take the Con Out of Econometrics*, 73 AM. ECON. REV. 31 (1983).

41. Joshua D. Angrist & Jörn-Steffen Pischke, *The Credibility Revolution in Empirical Economics: How Better Research Design Is Taking the Con Out of Econometrics*, 24 J. ECON. PERSP. 3 (2010).

42. Denise Robbins, *Experts Debunk WSJ's Favorite Report on Cost of Federal Regulations*, MEDIAMATTERS (May 18, 2015), https://www.mediamatters.org/research/2015/05/18/experts-debunk-wsjs-favorite-report-on-cost-of/203684.

43. Lou Cannon, *Reagan, Ignoring Bush, Assails Carter's Policies*, WASH. POST, May 20, 1980, at A8.

44. Inst. for Policy Integrity, Fact Sheet: Jobs and Regulation in the Media—By the Numbers (2013).

45. *See* Peter Dreier & Christopher R. Martin, "Job Killers" in the News: Allegations Without Verification 4 (June 2012) (citing WASH. POST, July 20, 2011).

46. Rep. Fred Upton, *Declaring War on the Regulatory State*, WASH. TIMES (Oct. 18, 2010), https://www.washingtontimes.com/news/2010/oct/18/declaring-war-on-the-regulatory-state/.

47. *See, e.g.*, Blue Green Alliance, Media Advisory: Blue Green Alliance to Coordinate 2009 Good Jobs, Green Jobs National Conference; National Labor Unions, Leading Environmental Organizations Join Forces to Push Green Jobs Agenda in Washington, DC (Jan. 8, 2009) (on file with authors).

48. VAN JONES, THE GREEN COLLAR ECONOMY: HOW ONE SOLUTION CAN FIX OUR TWO BIGGEST PROBLEMS 85 (2008).

49. EPA, Regulatory Impact Results for the Reconsideration Proposal for National Emission Standards for Hazardous Air Pollutants for Industrial, Commercial, and Institutional Boilers and Process Heaters at Major Sources (2012).

50. *See generally* DOES REGULATION KILL JOBS? (Cary Coglianese, Adam Finkel & Christopher Carrigan eds., 2014) (collecting views of leading experts).

51. *See* Paul Wolfson & Dale Belman, *15 Years of Research on US Employment and the Minimum Wage*, 33 LABOUR 488 (2019).

52. Office of Mgmt. and Budget, 2012 Report to Congress on the Benefits and Costs of Federal Regulations and Unfunded Mandates on State, Local, and Tribal Entities 41–42 (2012).

53. *See* Alan B. Krueger, *Teaching the Minimum Wage in Econ 101 in Light of the New Economics of the Minimum Wage*, 32 J. ECON. EDUC. 243 (2001).

54. DAVID CARD & ALAN B. KRUEGER, MYTH AND MEASUREMENT: THE NEW ECONOMICS OF THE MINIMUM WAGE (1995); David Card & Alan B. Krueger, *Minimum Wages and Employment: A Case Study of the Fast-Food Industry in New Jersey and Pennsylvania*, 84 AM. ECON. REV. 772 (1994); .

55. Wolfson & Belman, *supra* note 51.

56. Michael A. Livermore & Jason A. Schwartz, *Analysis to Inform Public Discourse on Jobs and Regulation, in* DOES REGULATION KILL JOBS?, *supra* note 50, at 239, 247.

57. For the Cross State Air Pollution Rule, the EPA estimated an annual net effect on jobs in regulated industry of between 1,000 jobs lost to 3,000 jobs gained, with a central estimate of 700 gained. For the Mercury Air Toxics Rule, the agency estimated between 15,000 jobs lost to 30,000 jobs gained, with a central estimate of 8,000 gained. *Id.* at 242–43.

58. Marc A.C. Hafstead & Roberton Williams III, *Jobs and Environmental Regulation* (Resources for the Future Working Paper 19-19, 2019).

59. THEODORE J. LOWI, THE END OF LIBERALISM: THE SECOND REPUBLIC OF THE UNITED STATES (2d. ed. 1979); DAVID SCHOENBROD, POWER WITHOUT RESPONSIBILITY: HOW CONGRESS ABUSES THE PEOPLE THROUGH DELEGATION (1993); .

60. GORDON ADAMS, THE POLITICS OF DEFENSE CONTRACTING: THE IRON TRIANGLE (1982); C. WRIGHT MILLS, THE POWER ELITE (1956); NPR Staff, *Ike's Warning of Military Expansion, 50 Years Later*, NPR (Jan. 17, 2011), https://www.npr.org/2011/01/17/132942244/ikes-warning-of-military-expansion-50-years-later.

61. R. Sam Garrett et al., *Assessing the Impact of Bureaucracy Bashing by Electoral Campaigns*, 66 PUB. ADMIN. REV. 228 (2006)

62. Karl Vick, *U.S. Suffers from Bad Timing in Request for Turkey's Help*, WASH POST, Jan. 9, 2003, at A16.

63. Jeffrey Fleishman, *A Crushing Blow for Egyptians: The Revolution's Vision of Smooth Democratic Reform Fades as Military Power Again Prevails*, L.A. TIMES, June 19, 2012, at A1 ("The country has been viewed more as a cautionary tale of how dangerous and difficult it is to unearth what many Egyptians call the 'deep state'—the vestiges of military and police power that have so far proved stronger than the voices for change arrayed against them").

64. PETER DALE SCOTT, THE ROAD TO 9/11: WEALTH, EMPIRE, AND THE FUTURE OF AMERICA xvi (2007).

65. See Ryan Gingeras, *How the Deep State Came to America: A History*, WAR ON THE ROCKS (Feb. 4, 2019), https://warontherocks.com/2019/02/how-the-deep-state-came-to-america-a-history/. War on the Rocks is a national security expert's blog that has a joint project with the University of Texas at Austin to publish the Texas National Security Review. Gingeras is an associate professor in the Department of National Security Affairs at the Naval Postgraduate School. Other Infowars affiliated commentators drew a link between Scott's views and the conspiracy theory that actors internal to the US government facilitated the September 11, 2001 terrorist attacks. *See* Saman Mohammadi, *Facing America's Shadow State*, INFORWARS (Mar. 7, 2011), https://www.infowars.com/facing-americas-shadow-state/ (quoting Scott and then asserting: "America's deep state triggered the 9/11 attacks in order to advance its interests at home and abroad").

66. William Dalrymple, *How Is Hamid Karzai Still Standing?*, N.Y. TIMES, Nov. 24, 2013, at MM45 (internal quotation marks omitted).

67. NPR, All Things Considered, transcript (July 17, 2013), https://www.npr.org/templates/transcript/ transcript.php?storyId=203032205.

68. Pat Buchanan, *Gruber: A Candid Liberal*, BUCHANAN.ORG (Dec. 13, 2014), https://buchanan.org/blog/jonathan-gruber-honest-liberal-7206.

69. For less partisan constructions, see MIKE LOFGREN, THE DEEP STATE: THE FALL OF THE CONSTITUTION AND THE RISE OF A SHADOW GOVERNMENT (2016); Michael Crowley, *The Deep State Is Real: But It Might Not Be What You Think*, POLITICO (Oct. 2017), https://www.politico.com/magazine/story/2017/09/05/deep-state-real-cia-fbi-intelligence-215537.

70. *See* Alex Matheson et al., *Study on the Political Involvement in Senior Staffing and on the Delineation of Responsibilities Between Ministers and Senior Civil Servants* 15–18 (OECD Working Papers on Public Governance 2007/6, 2007).

71. *See* Gillian E. Metzger, *1930s Redux: The Administrative State Under Siege*, 131 HARV. L. REV. 2, 11–13 (2017).

72. *But see* Jonathan H. Adler, *Placing "Reins" on Regulations: Assessing the Proposed REINS Act*, 16 LEG. & PUB. POL'Y 1 (2013) (arguing that the bill would have less of an effect on agency regulation that its proponents hope and its opponents fear).

73. Office of Senator Jim DeMint, News Release, DeMint Introduces REINS Act (Sept. 22, 2010). *See also* Metzger, *supra* note 71, at 13.

74. JOHN H. ALDRICH, WHY PARTIES? A SECOND LOOK 28–29 (2011); MARTY COHEN ET AL., THE PARTY DECIDES: PRESIDENTIAL NOMINATIONS BEFORE AND AFTER REFORM 7 (2008).

75. FRANCES E. LEE, BEYOND IDEOLOGY: POLITICS, PRINCIPLES, AND PARTISANSHIP IN THE U.S. SENATE (2009).

76. *See, e.g.,* RACHEL BITECOFER, THE UNPRECEDENTED 2016 PRESIDENTIAL ELECTION (2017).

77. *See* Trump Twitter Archive (Jun. 3, 2014 01:32:41 PM), http://www.trumptwitterarchive.com/archive.

78. *See, e.g.,* 111th Congress, 2nd Session, 155 Cong. Record No. 61, H3830 (May 26, 2010) (Congressman Hal Rogers, R-Kentucky: "This report brings to light yet another example of the EPA's war on coal that threatens our country's economic energy and security.").

79. Phillip Ricker & Robert Costa, *Bannon Vows a Daily Fight for 'Deconstruction of the Administrative State,'* WASH. POST (Feb. 23, 2017), https://www.washingtonpost.com/politics/top-wh-strategist-vows-a-daily-fight-for-deconstruction-of-the-administrative-state/2017/02/23/03f6b8da-f9ea-11e6-bf01-d47f8cf9b643_story.html.

80. Immigration & Naturalization Service v. Chadha, 462 U.S. 919 (1983).

81. Adam M. Finkel & Jason W. Sullivan, *A Cost-Benefit Interpretation of the "Substantially Similar" Hurdle in the Congressional Review Act: Can OSHA Ever Utter the E-Word (Ergonomics) Again?,* 63 ADMIN. L. REV. 707, 708 (2011).

82. There were rules within the CRA window that were unpopular with Democrats. *See* Anne Joseph O'Connell, *Agency Rulemaking and Political Transitions,* 105 Nw. U. L. REV. 471, 472 (2011); Note, *Mysteries of the Congressional Review Act,* 122 HARV. L. REV. 2162, 2175 (2009). Some of these rules were repealed through the normal administrative process, but none were addressed through the CRA. *See, e.g., id.* at 2176 (discussing repeal of late Bush-era rules during the early Obama administration).

83. Two of the disapprovals were of actions by the Consumer Financial Protection Bureau that were undertaken during the Trump administration, but under the direction of the Obama-era appointee Richard Cordray, one of which was a guidance document rather than a rule. Consumer Financial Protection Bureau, Arbitration Agreements, 82 Fed. Reg. 33210 (July 19, 2017), disapproved in H.J. Res. 111; Kris D. Kully, Christa L. Bieker & Elyse S. Moyer, *Congress Invalidates CFPB's Indirect Auto Lending Guidance,* CONSUMER FIN. SERV. REV. (May 8, 2018), https://www.cfsreview.com/2018/05/congress-invalidates-cfpbs-indirect-auto-lending-guidance/.

84. Soc. Sec. Admin., Implementation of the NICS Improvement Amendments Act of 2007, 81 Fed. Reg. 91,702 (Dec. 19, 2016) disapproved in H.J. Res. 40.

85. Dep't of Health and Human Servs., Compliance with Title X Requirements by Project Recipients in Selecting Subrecipients, 81 Fed. Reg. 91,852 (Dec. 19, 2016) disapproved in H.J. Res. 43.

86. Dep't of Labor, Federal-State Unemployment Compensation Program; Middle Class Tax Relief and Job Creation Act of 2012 Provision on Establishing Appropriate Occupations for Drug Testing of Unemployment Compensation Applicants, 81 Fed. Reg. 50,298 (Aug. 1, 2016), disapproved in H.J. Res. 42.

87. Dep't of Educ., Teacher Preparation Issues, 81 Fed. Reg. 75,494 (Oct. 31, 2016), disapproved in H.J. 58; Dep't of Educ., Elementary and Secondary Education Act of 1965, as Amended by the Every Student Succeeds Act—Accountability and State Plans, 81 Fed. Reg. 86076 (Jan. 30, 2017) disapproved in H.J. 57.

88. *See* Jon Brodkin, *How ISPs Can Sell Your Web History—And How to Stop Them*, ARS TECHNICA (Mar. 24, 2017), https://arstechnica.com/information-technology/2017/03/how-isps-can-sell-your-web-history-and-how-to-stop-them/.

89. Larry Downes, *Why Congress's Rejection of Proposed FCC Data Rules Will Not Affect Your Privacy in the Slightest*, FORBES (Mar. 30, 2017), https://www.forbes.com/sites/larrydownes/2017/03/30/why-congresss-rejection-of-proposed-fcc-data-rules-will-not-affect-your-privacy-in-the-slightest/.

90. Office of Surface Mining Reclamation and Enforcement, Stream Prot. Rule, 81 Fed. Reg. 93,066 (Dec. 20, 2016) disapproved in H.J. Res. 38.

91. *Id* at 93,069.

92. Industrial Econ. (prepared for Office of Surface Mining Reclamation and Enforcement), Regulatory Impact Analysis of the Stream Protection Rule (Nov. 2016).

93. Brad Plumer, *Why Trump Just Killed a Rule Restricting Coal Companies from Dumping Waste in Streams*, Vox (Feb. 16, 2017), https://www.vox.com/2017/2/2/14488448/stream-protection-rule.

94. Fish and Wildlife Serv., Non-Subsistence Take of Wildlife, and Public Participation and Closure Procedures, on National Wildlife Refuges in Alaska, 81 Fed. Reg. 52,247 (Aug. 5, 2016), disapproved in H.J. Res. 69.

95. Occupational Safety and Health Admin., Clarification of Employer's Continuing Obligation to Make and Maintain an Accurate Record of Each Recordable Injury and Illness, 81 Fed. Reg. 91,792 (Dec. 19, 2016), disapproved in H.J. Res. 83.

96. Dep't of Labor, Savings Arrangements Established by Qualified State Political Subdivisions for Non-Governmental Employees, 81 Fed. Reg. 92,639 (Dec. 20, 2016), disapproved in H.J. Res. 67; Dep't of Labor, Savings Arrangements Established by States for Non-Governmental Employees, 81 Fed. Reg. 59,464 (Aug. 30, 2016), disapproved in H.J. Res. 66.

97. Dep't of Def., General Servs. Admin., and Nat'l Aeronautics and Space Admin., Federal Acquisition Regulation; Fair Pay and Safe Workplaces, 81 Fed. Reg. 58,562 (Aug. 25, 2016), disapproved in H.J. Res. 37.

98. Bureau of Land Mgmt., Resource Management Planning, 81 Fed. Reg. 89,580 (Dec. 12, 2016), disapproved by H.J. Res. 44.

99. Sec. and Exch. Comm'n, Disclosure of Payments by Resource Extraction Issuers, 81 Fed. Reg. 49,359 (July 27, 2016) disapproved in H.J. Res. 41.

100. Keith B. Belton & John D. Graham, Am. Council for Capital Formation, Trump's Deregulatory Record: An Assessment at the Two-Year Mark (2019).

101. *See* Jennifer Rubin, *Here's the Case: Trump Has the Worst Cabinet Ever*, WASH. POST (Mar. 14, 2018), https://www.washingtonpost.com/blogs/right turn/wp/2018/03/14/heres-the-case-trump-has-the-worst-cabinet-ever (quoting Ornstein).

102. Joy Resmovits, *Betsy DeVos Squeaks Through as Education Secretary after Pence Casts First-Ever Tie-Breaking Vote*, L.A. TIMES (Feb. 7, 2017), https://www.latimes.com/local/education/la-na-pol-devos-senate-vote-20170207-story.html.

103. Brad Plumer, *Rick Perry Once Wanted to Abolish the Energy Department. Trump Picked Him to Run It*, Vox (Dec. 13, 2016), https://www.vox.com/energy-and-environment/2016/12/13/13936210/rick-perry-energy-department-trump.

104. Tom DiChristopher, *Energy Secretary Rick Perry Says CO2 Is Not the Main Driver of Climate Change*, CSNBC (June 19, 2017), https://www.cnbc.com/2017/06/19/energy-sec-rick-perry-says-co2-is-not-the-main-driver-of-climate-change.html.

105. Dominique Mosbergen, *Scott Pruitt Has Sued the Environmental Protection Agency 13 Times. Now He Wants to Lead It*, HUFF. POST (Jan. 17, 2017), https://www.huffpost.com/entry/scott-pruitt-environmental-protection-agency.

106. Tom DiChristopher, *EPA Chief Scott Pruitt Says Carbon Dioxide Is Not a Primary Contributor to Global Warming*, CNBC (Mar. 10, 2017), https://www.cnbc.com/2017/03/09/epa-chief-scott-pruitt.html.

107. Cameron Joseph, *House Candidate Calls Clinton "Antichrist,"* THE HILL (Jan. 31, 2014), https://thehill.com/blogs/ballot-box/197138-montana-gop-house-front-runner-calls-hillary-clinton-the-anti-christ.

108. Miranda Green, *Zinke on California Fires: "This Is Not a Debate About Climate Change,"* THE HILL (Aug. 13, 2018), https://thehill.com/policy/energy-environment/401550-zinke-on-california-fires-this-is-not-a-debate-about-climate-change. *See also* Adam K. Raymond, *Ryan Zinke Finally Admits That Climate Change Is Making Wildfires Worse*, NEW YORK MAG. (Aug. 13, 2018), http://nymag.com/intelligencer/2018/08/zinke-admits-that-climate-change-is-making-wildfires-worse.html ("There's no dispute that the climate is changing, although it has always changed," he said. "Whether man is the direct result [sic], how much that result [sic] is, that's still being disputed.").

109. Letter to FERC Commissioners from Secretary of Energy, Re: Secretary of Energy's Direction that the Federal Energy Regulatory Commission Issue Grid Resiliency Rules Pursuant to the Secretary's Authority under Section 403 of the Department of Energy Organization Act (Sept. 28, 2017).

110. FERC, Order Terminating Rulemaking Proceeding, Initiating New Proceeding, and Establishing Additional Procedures, 162 FERC ¶ 61,012 (Jan. 8, 2018).

111. David Roberts, *Trump's Crude Bailout of Dirty Power Plants Failed, But a Subtler Bailout Is Underway*, Vox (Mar. 23, 2018), https://www.vox.com/energy-and-environment/2018/3/23/17146028/ferc-coal-natural-gas-bailout-mopr. *See also* FERC, Order Rejecting Proposed Tariff Revisions, Granting in Part and Denying in Part Compliant, and Instituting Proceeding under Section 206 of the Federal Power Act, 163 FERC ¶ 61,236 (June 29, 2018); Sylwia Bialek & Burcin Unel, Inst. for Policy Integrity, Capacity Markets and Externalities: Avoiding Unnecessary and Problematic Reforms (2018).

112. Nicholas Fandos, *House Widens Inquiry with Subpoena for Perry*, N.Y. TIMES, Oct. 11, 2019, at A18.

113. *See* Richard, L. Revesz, *John Kelly Was Right to Kill EPA's "Red Team" Climate Exercise*, THE HILL (Mar. 13, 2018), https://thehill.com/opinion/energy-environment/378126-john-kelly-was-right-to-kill-epas-red-team-climate-exercise.

114. John Cook et al., *Quantifying the Consensus on Anthropogenic Global Warming in the Scientific Literature*, 8 ENVTL. RES. LETTERS 024024 (2013).

115. NAOMI ORESKES & ERIK M. CONWAY, MERCHANTS OF DOUBT: HOW A HANDFUL OF SCIENTISTS OBSCURED THE TRUTH ON ISSUES FROM TOBACCO SMOKE TO GLOBAL WARMING (2010).

116. Lisa Friedman & Julie Hirschfeld Davis, *E.P.A. Chief Wanted a Debate on Global Warming. Kelly Stopped Him*, N.Y. TIMES, Mar. 11, 2018, at A19.

117. Lisa Rein, *Where's Zinke? The Interior Secretary's Special Flag Offers Clues*, WASH. POST (Oct. 12, 2017), http://wapo.st/2i7zR4U?.

118. Michael Biesecker & Matthew Daly, *Interior Spending $139K to Fix Doors in Sec. Zinke's Office*, ASSOC. PRESS (Mar. 8, 2018), https://www.apnews.com/fe6edd739fff49d3a8e56324f7cc9721.

119. Haley Britzky, *Go Deeper: The Scandals that Led to Scott Pruitt's Resignation*, AXIOS (July 5, 2018), https://www.axios.com/go-deeper-the-scandals-that-led-to-scott-pruitts-resignation-5e7778c7-3b61-4188-92e1-5d45dc32a1fd.html; Lachlan Markay & Asawin Suebsaeng, *Scott Pruitt Personally Involved in "Ratf*cking" Ex-Aides Who He Feels Betrayed Him*, DAILY BEAST (June 28, 2018), https://www.thedailybeast.com/scott-pruitt-personally-involved-in-ratfcking-ex-aides-who-he-feels-betrayed-him?.

120. Benjamin Wittes, *Malevolence Tempered by Incompetence: Trump's Horrifying Executive Order on Refugees and Visas*, LAWFARE (Jan. 28, 2017), https://www.lawfareblog.com/malevolence-tempered-incompetence-trumps-horrifying-executive-order-refugees-and-visas.

121. *See, e.g.*, EPA, Water Quality Trading Policy (2003).

122. EPA, Rule to Reduce Interstate Transport of Fine Particulate Matter and Ozone (Clean Air Interstate Rule); Revisions to Acid Rain Program; Revisions to the NO_x SIP Call, 70 Fed. Reg. 25,162 (May 12, 2005).

123. Jo Becker & Barton Gellman, *Leaving No Tracks*, WASH. POST, June 27, 2007, at A1 (detailing conflict between Whitman and Vice President Dick Cheney over change to the New Source Review program under the Clean Air Act).

124. Institute for Policy Integrity, Roundup: Trump-Era Agency Policy in the Courts, https://policyintegrity.org/deregulation-roundup (last updated July 15, 2020).

125. Bethany A. Davis Noll & Denise A. Grab, *Deregulation: Process and Procedures That Govern Agency Decisionmaking in an Era of Rollbacks*, 38 ENERGY L. J. 269 (2017).

126. Open Communities Alliance v. Carson, 286 F. Supp. 3d 148 (D.D.C. 2017) (HUD housing); California v. Bureau of Land Mgmt., 277 F. Supp. 3d 1106 (N.D. Cal. 2017) (natural gas waste); Sierra Club v. Pruitt, 293 F. Supp. 3d 1050 (N.D. Cal. 2018) (formaldehyde).

127. 43 U.S.C. § 1701(a)(9) (2012).

128. Dep't of the Interior, Consolidated Federal Oil & Gas and Federal & Indian Coal Valuation Reform; Final Rule, 81 Fed. Reg. 43,338 (July 1, 2016); Dep't of the Interior, Consolidated Federal Oil & Gas and Federal & Indian Coal Valuation Reform; Proposed Rule, 80 Fed. Reg. 608, 616-17, 628 (Jan. 6, 2015).

129. Dep't of the Interior, Repeal of Consolidated Federal Oil & Gas and Federal & Indian Coal Valuation Reform; Final Repeal, 82 Fed. Reg. 36,934 (Aug. 7, 2017).

130. California v. Dep't of the Interior, 381 F. Supp. 3d 1153 (N.D. Cal. 2019).

131. *See, e.g.*, Fed. Aviation Admin., IFR Operations at Locations Without Weather Reporting; Final Rule 84 Fed. Reg. 35,820 (July 25, 2019) (regulation to "allow helicopter air ambulance (HAA) operators to conduct instrument flight rules departure and approach procedures at airports and heliports that do not have an approved weather reporting source").

132. Mozilla Corp. v. Fed. Commc'ns Comm'n, 940 F.3d 1 (D.C. Cir. 2019).

133. Paul Gallay, *Doing Less with Less at EPA: Environmental Enforcement Has Plummeted in the Era of Trump. Here's What We Can Do About It*, ABA, SEC. ENV'T, ENERGY, & RESOURCE TRENDS (July 9, 2019), https://www.americanbar.org/groups/environment_energy_resources/publications/trends/2018-2019/july-august-2019/doing-less-with-less/.

134. EPA & Nat'l Highway Traffic Safety Admin., The Safer Affordable Fuel-Efficient (SAFE) Vehicles Rule for Model Years 2021–2026 Passenger Cars and Light Trucks, 83 Fed. Reg. 42,986, 43,148–58 (Aug. 24, 2018).

135. *Id*. at 42,998.

136. The Institute for Policy Integrity submitted five separate sets of comments criticizing different aspects of the proposal. *See* Inst. for Policy Integrity, Comments on Proposed Weakening of Vehicle Emissions Standards (Oct. 26, 2018), https://policyintegrity.org/projects/update/comments-on-vehicle-emissions-standards. An example of a significant flaw in the analysis of the proposed rollback is the treatment of the "rebound effect," where more fuel efficient cars lead to a larger number of vehicle miles traveled. Without justification, the Trump administration ramped up the estimate of the rebound effect from prior analyses, contravening the most recent research on the subject. *See* Comments of the Institute for Policy Integrity on the Safer Affordable Fuel-Efficient (SAFE) Vehicles Rule for Model Years 2021–2026 Passenger Cars and Light Trucks (Oct. 26, 2018) at 99–125.

137. EPA, Final Rulemaking to Establish Light-Duty Vehicle Greenhouse Gas Emission Standards and Corporate Average Fuel Economy Standards, Regulatory Impact Analysis (2010).

138. Robinson Meyer, *"We Knew They Had Cooked the Books,"* ATLANTIC (Feb. 12, 2020), https://www.theatlantic.com/science/archive/2020/02/an-inside-account-of-trumps-fuel-economy-debacle/606346/.

139. Antonio M. Bento, *Flawed Analysis of U.S. Auto Fuel Economy Standards*, 362 SCIENCE 1119, 1120 (2018).

140. Half of the avoided fatalities claimed from the rule would be eliminated without the phantom car effect. *See* EPA & Nat'l Highway Traffic Safety Admin., *supra* note 134, at 43,153.

141. *See* Richard L. Revesz & Avi Zevin, *Trump's Clean Car Standards Rollback Is Based on Too Many Lies to Count*, SLATE (Apr. 1, 2020), https://slate.com/news-and-politics/2020/04/trumps-epa-clean-car-standards-rollback-lies.html. *See* EPA &

Highway Traffic Safety Admin., The Safer Affordable Fuel-Efficient (SAFE) Vehicles Rule for Model Years 2021–2026 Passenger Cars and Light Trucks, 85 Fed. Reg. 24,174 (Apr. 30, 2020); EPA & Highway Traffic Safety Admin., Final Regulatory Impact Analysis for The Safer Affordable Fuel-Efficient (SAFE) Vehicles Rule for Model Years 2021–2026 Passenger Cars and Light Trucks (2020). *See also* Letter from Thomas R. Carper to Administrator Paul Ray (January 22, 2020) (reporting that leaked draft of the final rule acknowledged over $40 billion in net costs).

142. Michael A. Livermore & Richard L. Revesz, *Regulatory Review, Capture, and Agency Inaction*, 101 GEO. L. J. 1337, 1373–75 (2013).

143. Thomas McGarty et al., Ctr. for Progressive Reformt, Trump's New 'Regulatory Czar' 12 (2017) ("In contrast to several former OIRA Administrators, Professor Rao has no apparent expertise with regard to the theory and practice of cost-benefit analysis.").

144. Neomi Rao, *Administrative Collusion: How Delegation Diminishes the Collective Congress*, 90 N.Y.U. L. REV. 1463, 1525 (2015). Notwithstanding its quasi-desuetude, the non-delegation doctrine does continue to reappear in Supreme Court opinions (generally in dissent), and a majority in favor of its more rigorous use may emerge. *See* Kristen E. Hickman, *Gundy, Nondelegation, and Never-Ending Hope*, REG. REV. (July 8, 2019), https://www.theregreview.org/2019/07/08/hickman-nondelegation/.

145. Neomi Rao, *Removal: Necessary and Sufficient for Presidential Control*, 65 ALA. L. REV. 1205, 1276 (2014).

146. Steve Eder, *Rolling Back U.S. Regulations Will Test One Scholar's Finesse*, N.Y. TIMES, July 10, 2017, at A1.

147. This center is now called the C. Boyden Gray Center for the Study of the Administrative State, and its mission is to foster "legal scholarship on new and time-less questions about the modern administrative state, in order to elevate and improve debates occurring in the courts, in Congress, in the executive branch, and in the broader public." *See* C. Boyden Gray Center, Mission, https://administrativestate. gmu.edu/about/mission/. The center's Advisory Council includes scholars representing a diverse set of perspectives concerning agencies and regulation. *See* C. Boyden Gray Center, Advisory Council, https://administrativestate.gmu.edu/ about/advisory-council/.

148. *See* Maya Earls and Manuel Quiñones, *Reading the Tea Leaves on Trump's New Regulatory Czar*, GREENWIRE (Oct. 15, 2019), https://www.eenews.net/stories/ 1061286981 ("Ray's experience stands in stark contrast with some people who have previously held the White House's top regulations job.").

149. Executive Order 13,771, 82 Fed. Reg. 9339 (Feb. 3, 2017).

150. Dep't of Labor, Tip Regulations Under the Fair Labor Standards Act, 82 Fed. Reg. 57,395, 57,408 (proposed Dec. 5, 2017) (to be codified at 29 C.F.R pt. 531).

151. *Id.* at 57404.

152. Ben Penn, *Labor Dept. Ditches Data Showing Bosses Could Skim Waiters' Tips*, BLOOMBERG L. (Feb. 1, 2018), https://bnanews.bna.com/daily-labor-report/labor-dept-ditches-data-showing-bosses-could-skim-waiters-tips.

153. Ben Penn, *Mulvaney, Acosta Override Regulatory Office to Hide Tips Rule Data*, Bloomberg L. (Mar. 21, 2018), https://news.bloomberglaw.com/daily-labor-report/mulvaney-acosta-override-regulatory-office-to-hide-tips-rule-data-1.

154. Suzy Khimm, *Trump Plan Failed to Note That It Could Jeopardize Free School Lunches for 500,000 Children, Democrats Say*, NBCNews (July 29, 2019), https://www.nbcnews.com/politics/white-house/trump-plan-failed-note-it-could-jeopardize-free-school-lunches-n1035281.

Chapter 5

1. Executive Order 13,771, 82 Fed. Reg. 9339 (Feb. 3, 2017).

2. Executive Order 12,866 § 1(b)(6), 58 Fed. Reg. 51,735, 51,736 (Oct. 4, 1993).

3. *See* Executive Order 13,771, *supra* note 1, § 2(a).

4. *See id.* §§ 2(b), 3(d). For a critical discussion of this requirement, see Richard J. Pierce, Jr., *Is a Ceiling on Regulatory Costs Reasonable*, Reg. Rev. (Sept. 30, 2019), https://www.theregreview.org/2019/09/30/pierce-ceiling-regulatory-costs/?.

5. *See* Executive Order 13,771, *supra* note 1, §2(c).

6. Admin. Conference of the U.S., Midnight Rules Appendix, Reagan Memorandum.

7. Admin. Conference of the U.S., Midnight Rules Appendix, Panetta Memorandum.

8. Memorandum for the Heads and Acting Heads of Executive Departments and Agencies, 66 Fed. Reg. 7702 (Jan. 24, 2001).

9. Memorandum for the Heads of Executive Departments and Agencies, 74 Fed. Reg. 4435 (Jan. 26, 2009).

10. *See* Kathryn A. Watts, *Regulatory Moratoria*, 61 Duke L.J. 1883, 1890–93 (2012).

11. Executive Order 13,771, *supra* note 1, § 3.

12. *Id.* § 3(d).

13. Office of Info. and Regulatory Affairs, Regulatory Reform Under Executive Order 13771: Final Accounting for Fiscal Year 2018.

14. Office of Info. and Regulatory Affairs, Regulatory Reform: Regulatory Budget for Fiscal Year 2019.

15. *See, e.g.*, *Reviewing the Office of Information and Regulatory Affairs: Hearing Before the Subcomm. on Regulatory Affairs and Fed. Mgmt. of the S. Comm. on Homeland Sec. and Governmental Affairs,* 115th Cong. (2018) (testimony of Neomi Rao, Administrator of the Office of Info. and Regulatory Affairs) [hereinafter Rao Testimony]; Neomi Rao, What's Next for Trump's Regulatory Agenda: A Conversation with OIRA Administrator Neomi Rao, Remarks at The Brookings Institution (Jan. 26, 2018) [hereinafter Rao Remarks]; Neomi Rao, Opinion, *The Trump Administration's Deregulation Efforts Are Saving Billions of Dollars*, Wash. Post (Oct. 17, 2018), https://wapo.st/2DMJlxn [hereinafter Rao Opinion]; Mick Mulvaney (@MickMulvaneyOMB), Twitter (Oct. 17, 2018, 1:50 PM), https://twitter.com/mickmulvaneyomb/status/1052617874668437504 (celebrating the administration's reduction in regulatory costs during fiscal year 2018 with an infographic with statistics from the Unified Agenda); Mick Mulvaney (@MickMulvaneyOMB), Twitter (Dec. 14, 2017, 3:12 PM), https://twitter.com/MickMulvaneyOMB/status/941400558220578816 (discussing the Trump administration's approach to regulation in a video to his followers).

16. *See, e.g.*, Rao Testimony, *supra* note 15; Rao Remarks, *supra* note 15; Rao Opinion, *supra* note 15.

17. Rao Opinion, *supra* note 15.

18. Rao Testimony, *supra* note 15.

19. Rao Opinion, *supra* note 15.

20. *See, e.g.*, Danny Vinik, *Trump's War on Regulations Is Real. But Is It Working?*, POLITICO (Jan. 20, 2018), https://www.politico.com/agenda/story/2018/01/20/trumps-regulatory-experiment-year-one-000620 (explaining that the vast majority of Trump's touted cost savings came from the repeal of a single federal contract rule, as opposed to a dramatic decrease in the number of regulations as he has claimed, while much of that deregulation was accomplished by Congress repealing Obama-era rules under the Congressional Review Act early in his term); James Pethokoukis, *What's Been the Economic Impact of Trump's Deregulation Push?*, AM. ENTERPRISE INST. (Feb. 12, 2018), http://www.aei.org/publication/whats-been-the-economic-impact-of-trumps-deregulation-push/ (highlighting a Goldman Sachs report that found that deregulation has been overshadowed by tax reform in impact on economic decision making and that there was no evidence that employment grew in sectors with higher regulatory burdens).

21. Richard L. Revesz, *Trump Rollbacks Causing Premature Deaths Should Not Be Celebrated*, THE HILL (Oct. 25, 2018), https://thehill.com/opinion/energy-environment/413157-trump-rollbacks-causing-premature-deaths-should-not-be-celebrated#bottom-s.

22. *Id.*

23. Caroline Cecot & Michael A. Livermore, *The One-In, Two-Out Executive Order Is a Zero*, 166 U. PA. L. REV. ONLINE 1, 5 (2017); *see, e.g.*, Richard J. Pierce, Jr., *The Regulatory Budget Debate*, 19 N.Y.U. J. LEGIS. & PUB. POL'Y 249, 251–52 (2016) ("It would be irrational. Any regulatory process that ignores either costs or benefits would cause great harm to society."); Sidney A. Shapiro, *Political Oversight and the Deterioration of Regulatory Policy*, 46 ADMIN. L. REV. 1, 34 (1994) (calling the imposition of an arbitrary binding constraint on an agency "incoherent").

24. Cecot & Livermore, *supra* note 23, at 9–10.

25. *Id.* at 7.

26. *See* Christopher C. DeMuth, *Constraining Regulatory Costs Part Two: The Regulatory Budget*, 4 REGULATION 29, 32 (1980) ("Benefits would indeed be taken into account—but early in the process, when the President and Congress determined the *size* of each agency's budget.").

27. John D. Graham et al., *Managing the Regulatory State: The Experience of the Bush Administration*, 33 FORDHAM URB. L.J. 953, 985 (2005).

28. Executive Order 13,771, *supra* note 1, § 3(d).

29. Richard Revesz, *E.O. 12866: 25th Anniversary Remarks*, GEO. WASH. UNIV. REG. STUD. CTR. (Oct. 9, 2018), https://regulatorystudies.columbian.gwu.edu/eo-12866-25th-anniversary-remarks.

30. Bureau of Land Mgmt., Waste Prevention, Production Subject to Royalties, and Resource Conservation; Postponement of Certain Compliance Dates, 82 Fed. Reg. 27,430 (June 15, 2017).

31. Bureau of Land Mgmt., Waste Prevention, Production Subject to Royalties, and Resource Conservation, 81 Fed. Reg. 83,008 (Nov. 18, 2016).

32. *Id.* at 83,014.

33. Bureau of Land Mgmt., *supra* note 30, at 27,431.

34. California v. Bureau of Land Mgmt., 277 F. Supp. 3d 1106, 1122 (N.D. Cal. 2017) (vacating the delay of the rule); *see also* California v. Bureau of Land Mgmt., 286 F. Supp. 3d 1054 (N.D. Cal. 2018) (enjoining the Bureau's second attempt to delay the rule).

35. California v. U.S. Bureau of Land Mgmt., 2018 WL 2735410 (Mar. 15, 2018). The Trump administration undertook a separate effort to repeal the rule, *see* Bureau of Land Management, Waste Prevention, Production Subject to Royalties, and Resource Conservation; Rescission or Revision of Certain Requirements, 83 Fed. Reg. 49,184 (Sept. 28, 2018), which has now been challenged as well.

36. EPA, Pesticides; Agricultural Worker Protection Standard; Reconsideration of Several Requirements and Notice About Compliance Dates, 82 Fed. Reg. 60,576 (Dec. 21, 2017).

37. Bethany A. Davis Noll & Alec Dawson, Inst. for Policy Integrity, Deregulation Run Amok: Trump-Era Regulatory Suspensions and the Rule of Law 9 (2018). The training materials were required by a regulation promulgated in 2015 by the Obama administration. *See* EPA, Pesticides; Agricultural Worker Protection Standard Revisions, 80 Fed. Reg. 67,495 (Nov. 2, 2015).

38. EPA, *supra* note 36, at 60,577.

39. Davis Noll & Dawson, *supra* note 37, at 9.

40. EPA, Accidental Release Prevention Requirements: Risk Management Programs Under the Clean Air Act; Further Delay of Effective Date, 82 Fed. Reg. 27,133, 27,138–39 (June 14, 2017).

41. EPA, Accidental Release Prevention Requirements: Risk Management Programs Under the Clean Air Act, 82 Fed. Reg. 4594, 4597 (Jan. 13, 2017).

42. EPA, *supra* note 40, at 27,138–39.

43. *Id.*

44. Air All. Hous. v. EPA, 906 F.3d 1049, 1069 (D.C. Cir. 2018).

45. *Id.* at 1068.

46. *Id.*

47. Food and Drug Admin., Food Labeling; Nutrition Labeling of Standard Menu Items in Restaurants and Similar Retail Food Establishments; Extension of Compliance Date; Request for Comments, 82 Fed. Reg. 20,825 (May 4, 2017).

48. *Id.* at 20,828.

49. *Id. See also* Food and Drug Admin., Interim Final Regulatory Impact Analysis for the Food Labeling; Nutrition Labeling of Standard Menu Items in Restaurants and Similar Retail Food Establishments; Extension of Compliance Date and Request for Comments 6 (2017).

50. *See* Food and Drug Admin., *supra* note 47, at 20,828.

51. Peter Lehner, *Counting Calories? New Lawsuit Will Make Restaurants Show You the Stats*, EARTHJUSTICE (Feb. 6, 2018), https://earthjustice.org/blog/2017-june/new-lawsuit-seeks-end-to-calorie-secrecy.

52. *FDA Agrees to Enforce Menu Labeling Rule in May 2018*, EARTHJUSTICE (Sept. 27, 2017), https://earthjustice.org/news/press/2017/fda-agrees-to-enforce-menu-labeling -rule-in-may-2018.

53. Executive Order 12,866, *supra* note 2, § 1(a), at 51,735.

54. Office of Mgmt. & Budget, Circular A-4, at 2 (2003).

55. KENNETH J. ARROW ET AL., BENEFIT-COST ANALYSIS IN ENVIRONMENTAL, HEALTH, AND SAFETY REGULATION: A STATEMENT OF PRINCIPLES 8 (1996).

56. Office of Mgmt. & Budget, *supra* note 54, at 2.

57. *See* Richard L. Revesz, *Quantifying Regulatory Benefits*, 102 CALIF. L. REV. 1423, 1424 (2014).

58. Executive Order 12,291 § 2(b), 46 Fed. Reg. 13,193, 13,193 (Feb. 19, 1981).

59. Bureau of Land Mgmt., Final Regulatory Impact Analysis for Regulations Governing Competitive Oil and Gas Leasing in the National Petroleum Reserve in Alaska (1982). Courts may look beyond the administrative record and take judicial notice of agencies' own records. *See* Dent v. Holder, 627 F.3d 365, 371 (9th Cir. 2010).

60. Bureau of Land Mgmt., *supra* note 59, at 33.

61. *Id.*

62. *Id.* at 31–32.

63. *Id.* at 33.

64. Bureau of Land Mgmt., Mining Claims Under the General Mining Laws; Surface Management, 65 Fed. Reg. 69,998, 70,100–02 (Nov. 21, 2000).

65. Bureau of Land Mgmt., Mining Claims Under the General Mining Laws; Surface Management, 66 Fed. Reg. 54,834, 54,844 (Oct. 30, 2001).

66. EPA, National Emissions Standards for Hazardous Air Pollutants; Benzene Emissions from Chemical Manufacturing Vents, Industrial Solvent Use, Benzene Waste Operations, Benzene Transfer Operations, and Gasoline Marketing System, 55 Fed. Reg. 8292, 8302 (Mar. 7, 1990).

67. EPA, NESHAPS: Final Standards for Hazardous Air Pollutants for Hazardous Waste Combustors, 64 Fed. Reg. 52,828, 53,023 (Sept. 30, 1999).

68. EPA, Control of Emissions of Air Pollution from Nonroad Diesel Engines and Fuel, 69 Fed. Reg. 38,958, 39,138 (June 29, 2004).

69. EPA, *supra* note 41, at 4596–98.

70. *Id.* at 4597–98.

71. *Id.* at 4597.

72. *Id.* at 4598.

73. *Id.* at 4596.

74. *Id.* at 4597.

75. *Id.*

76. *Id.* at 4598.

77. EPA, *supra* note 40, at 27,139.

78. *Id.*

79. *Speculative*, CAMBRIDGE ENGLISH DICTIONARY, https://dictionary.cambridge.org/ us/dictionary/english/speculative.

80. Pub. Citizen v. Fed. Motor Carrier Safety Admin., 374 F.3d 1209, 1219 (D.C. Cir. 2004).

81. Air All. Hous. v. EPA, *supra* note 44, at 1067.

82. EPA, Adopting Subpart Ba Requirements in Emission Guidelines for Municipal Solid Waste Landfills, 83 Fed. Reg. 54,527 (Oct. 30, 2018).

83. EPA, Emissions Guidelines and Compliance Times for Municipal Solid Waste Landfills, 81 Fed. Reg. 59,276 (Aug. 29, 2016).

84. *Id.* at 59,280.

85. *Id.* at 59,279.

86. *Id.* at 59,280.

87. *Id.*

88. *Id.*

89. *Id.*

90. *Id.*

91. EPA, *supra* note 82, at 54,531.

92. *Id.*

93. Revesz, *supra* note 57, at 1436.

94. *Id.* at 1437.

95. *Id.* at 1438–39.

96. California v. U.S. EPA, 385 F. Supp. 3d 903, 916 (N.D. Cal. 2019).

97. *Id.* at 906–07.

98. *Id.* at 908–09.

99. Bureau of Land Mgmt., Oil and Gas; Hydraulic Fracturing on Federal and Indian Lands; Rescission of a 2015 Rule, 82 Fed. Reg. 61,924 (Dec. 29, 2017).

100. Bureau of Land Mgmt., Oil and Gas; Hydraulic Fracturing on Federal and Indian Lands, 80 Fed. Reg. 16,128, 16,128 (Mar. 26, 2015).

101. *Id.* at 16,129.

102. *Id.* at 16,204.

103. *Id.*

104. *Id.* at 16,188.

105. *Id.*

106. *Id.* at 16,203.

107. *Id.* at 16,188–89.

108. *Id.* at 16,203.

109. Bureau of Land Mgmt., *supra* note 99, at 61,939 (emphasis added).

110. *Id.* at 61,942.

111. California v. Bureau of Land Mgmt., No. 18-cv-00521-HSG (N.D. Cal. Mar. 27, 2020).

112. *See* Niina H. Farah, *Groups Appeal Decision to OK Trump's Fracking Rule Rollback*, ENERGYWIRE (June 15, 2020), https://www.eenews.net/energywire/2020/06/15/stories/1063389537.

113. For example, a review of President Trump's executive orders found that "many were geared toward favored political constituencies . . . [and] few moved policy significantly." Noah Bierman, *Must Reads: What's Behind All Those Executive Orders Trump Loves to Sign? Not Much*, L.A. TIMES (Mar. 27, 2019), https://www.latimes.com/politics/la-na-pol-trump-executive-orders-ineffective-20190327-story.html.

Political scientist Kenneth Mayer, who studies presidential power, found in an empirical study that of 1,000 executive orders, only between 15 and 25 percent had substantive importance. *See* Andrew Prokop, *Why Counting Executive Orders Is an Awful Way to Measure Presidential Power*, Vox (Nov. 22, 2014), https://www.vox.com/xpress/2014/11/22/7260059/president-executive-orders-chart.

Chapter 6

1. EPA, Strengthening Transparency in Regulatory Science, 83 Fed. Reg. 18,768 (Apr. 30, 2018).
2. *Id.* at 18,768.
3. *Id.* at 18,769.
4. *See* EPA, News Release, EPA Administrator Pruitt Proposes Rule to Strengthen Science Used in EPA Regulations (Apr. 24, 2018), https://www.epa.gov/newsreleases/epa-administrator-pruitt-proposes-rule-strengthen-science-used-epa-regulations.
5. *See* David A. Savitz, *Human Studies of Human Health Hazards: Comparison of Epidemiology and Toxicology*, 3 Stat. Sci. 306, 306 (1988); Richard L. Revesz, *Trump's EPA Chooses Rodents Over People*, N.Y. Times (Sept. 26, 2019), https://www.nytimes.com/2019/09/26/opinion/epa-animal-testing.html.
6. *See* Revesz, *supra* note 5.
7. *See id.*
8. *See* W. Kip Viscusi, Pricing Lives: Guideposts for a Safer Society 27–29 (2018).
9. The reason for the confidentiality of these data has less to do with protecting personally sensitive information of the deceased in the studies than with the fear that the data will be used to identify firms that are part of the studies.
10. EPA, *supra* note 1, at 18,769.
11. *Id.*
12. *Id.* at 18,773–74.
13. *Id.* at 18,770.
14. *Id.* at 18,770 n.11.
15. *Id.* at 18,769.
16. *Id.* at 18,772.
17. H.R. 4012, 113th Cong. (2014).
18. H.R. 1030, 114th Cong. (2015).
19. H.R. 1430, 115th Cong. (2017).
20. *See* Scott Waldman & Niina Heikkinen, *Trump's EPA Wants to Stamp Out "Secret Science." Internal Emails Show It Is Harder than Expected*, Science (Apr. 20, 2018), https://www.sciencemag.org/news/2018/04/trump-s-epa-wants-stamp-out-secret-science-internal-emails-show-it-harder-expected. EPA congressional affairs staffer Aaron Ringel wrote in an email to colleagues at the EPA: "All, see below follow up from Chairman Smith's meeting with the administrator.... [T]his is in

regards to his pitch that [the] EPA internally implement the HONEST Act (no regulation can go into effect unless the scientific data is publicly available for review)." *Id.*

21. *See* Scott Waldman & Robin Bravender, *Pruitt Is Expected to Restrict Science. Here's What It Means*, CLIMATEWIRE (Mar. 16, 2018), https://www.eenews.net/climatewire/stories/1060076559/.

22. Michael Bastasch, *Andrew Wheeler Says He Will Implement Rule to Keep "Secret Science" Out of EPA*, DAILY CALLER (Mar. 5, 2019), https://dailycaller.com/2019/03/05/ANDREW-WHEELER-SECRET-SCIENCE-EPA/.

23. EPA, Strengthening Transparency in Regulatory Science, Supplemental Notice of Proposed Rulemaking; Extension of Comment Period, 85 Fed. Reg. 21,340 (Apr. 17, 2020).

24. *See* Warren Cornwall, *New Rule Could Force EPA to Ignore Major Human Health Studies*, SCIENCE (Apr. 25, 2018), https://www.sciencemag.org/news/2018/04/new-rule-could-force-epa-ignore-major-human-health-studies.

25. *See Public Health, Medical, Academic, and Scientific Groups Oppose EPA Transparency Rule*, MICHAEL J. FOX FOUND. (July 16, 2018), https://www.michaeljfox.org/publication/public-health-medical-academic-and-scientific-groups-oppose-epa-transparency-rule?category=7&id=663.

26. *See id.*

27. Michael J. Fox Found., Comment Letter on Proposed Rule for Strengthening Transparency in Regulatory Science 1 (Aug. 16, 2018).

28. Marianne Lavelle, *Science, Health Leaders Lay Out Evidence Against EPA's "Secret Science" Rule*, INSIDE CLIMATE NEWS (Aug. 15, 2018), https://insideclimatenews.org/news/15082018/epa-secret-science-rule-opposition-health-environmental-data-public-comments.

29. *See* Carolyn Kormann, *Scott Pruitt's Crusade Against "Secret Science" Could Be Disastrous for Public Health*, NEW YORKER (Apr. 26, 2018), https://www.newyorker.com/science/elements/scott-pruitts-crusade-against-secret-science-could-be-disastrous-for-public-health.

30. Heather M. Strosnider et al., *Age-Specific Associations of Ozone and Fine Particulate Matter with Respiratory Emergency Department Visits in the United States*, 199 AM. J. RESPIRATORY & CRITICAL CARE MED. 882, 887 (2018).

31. Paul English & John Balmes, *Associations Between Ozone and Fine Particulate Matter and Respiratory Illness Found to Vary Between Children and Adults. Implications for U.S. Air Quality Policy*, 199 AM. J. RESPIRATORY & CRITICAL CARE MED. 817, 818 (2019).

32. *See* Cornwall, *supra* note 24.

33. *See id.*

34. Office of Mgmt. & Budget, Guidelines for Ensuring and Maximizing the Quality, Objectivity, Utility, and Integrity of Information Disseminated by Federal Agencies; Republication, 67 Fed. Reg. 8452, 8456 (Feb. 22, 2002).

35. Letter from 985 scientists to Scott Pruitt, Administrator, EPA (Apr. 23, 2018), https://s3.amazonaws.com/ucs-documents/science-and-democracy/secret-science-letter-4-23-2018.pdf.

36. EPA, Public Hearing on Strengthening Transparency in Regulatory Science 200, 282, 372 (2018), https://yosemite.epa.gov/sab/sabproduct.nsf/C8DC97CD16CBF880852 5840B0068C228/$File/Public+comments+from+Earthjustice.pdf (attachment 2).

37. *See* Jessica Gurevitch et al., Review, *Meta-Analysis and the Science of Research Synthesis*, 555 NATURE 175 (2018).

38. Madison E. Condon, Michael A. Livermore & Jeffrey G. Shrader, *Assessing the Rationale for the U.S. EPA's Proposed "Strengthening Transparency in Regulatory Science" Rule*, 14 REV. ENVTL. ECON. & POL'Y 131 (2019).

39. *See, e.g.*, Peter Howard & Jeffrey Shrader, Inst. for Policy Integrity, An Evaluation of the Revised Definition of "Waters of the United States" 7–8 (Apr. 11, 2019).

40. Madison Condon, Oral Comments to EPA's Science Advisory Board on Planned Actions and Their Supporting Science 2–3 (June 5, 2019).

41. Howard & Shrader, *supra* note 39, at 6–7 (citing MICHAEL BORENSTEIN ET AL., INTRODUCTION TO META-ANALYSIS 280 (2009)). *See also* Condon, Livermore & Shrader, *supra* note 38, at 2.

42. EPA, Report of the EPA Work Group on VSL Meta-Analyses (2006).

43. Condon, Livermore & Shrader, *supra* note 38.

44. EPA, *supra* note 1, at 18,770.

45. *Id.* at 18,770 n.11.

46. Jeremy Berg et al., *Joint Statement on EPA Proposed Rule and Public Availability of Data*, 360 SCIENCE (May 4, 2018).

47. *Implementing TOP*, CTR. FOR OPEN SCI., https://cos.io/top/.

48. John P. A. Ioannidis, Editorial, *All Science Should Inform Policy and Regulation*, 15 PLOS MED., at 1 (May 3, 2018).

49. Shareen A. Iqbal et al., *Reproducible Research Practices and Transparency Across the Biomedical Literature*, 14 PLOS BIOLOGY (Jan. 4, 2016).

50. Ioannidis, *supra* note 48.

51. *Id.*

52. *Id.* (citing Iqbal et al., *supra* note 49).

53. *Id.* at 2.

54. *See* EPA, *supra* note 1, at 18,769–70.

55. Office of Mgmt. & Budget, *supra* note 34, at 8456.

56. *Id.* at 8455.

57. *Id.* at 8456.

58. *Id.*

59. EPA, *supra* note 1, at 18,771.

60. *See, e.g.*, Nat'l Assoc. of Mfrs., Comment Letter on Proposed Rule for Strengthening Transparency in Regulatory Science 2 (Aug. 9, 2018).

61. The Fertilizer Inst., Comment Letter on Proposed Rule for Strengthening Transparency in Regulatory Science 3 (Aug. 16, 2018). The Fertilizer Institute (TFI) wrote that "some opponents of the use of transparent data claim that use of non-public or confidentially protected data is a barrier to implementing the practices described in the proposed rule," but "arguments for using non-publicly available data are red herrings." *Id.* TFI went on to say that "many tools and methodologies exist

to mask personal information that may be sensitive." *Id.* TFI also wrote, however, that they recognize "that in some circumstances full transparency may not be achievable." *Id.* For example, "some data submissions by trade groups or TFI members is protected as confidential business information (CBI) and may present transparency challenges to the agency"; in those cases, "it may have to be considered whether to exclude such data from the analysis or determine whether a generic format may be adequate to conceal site or company-specific proprietary information." *Id.*

62. Latanya Sweeney, *Simple Demographics Often Identify People Uniquely* 2 (Carnegie Melon Univ., Data Privacy Working Paper No. 3, 2000). *See also* Latanya Sweeney, Akua Abu & Julia Winn, Identifying Participants in the Personal Genome Project by Name 1 (2013), ("We linked names and contact information to publicly available profiles in the Personal Genome Project. These profiles contain medical and genomic information, including details about medications, procedures and diseases, and demographic information, such as date of birth, gender, and postal code. By linking demographics to public records such as voter lists, and mining for names hidden in attached documents, we correctly identified 84 to 97 percent of the profiles for which we provided names").

63. *See* Alessandra Potenza & Rachel Becker, *Scott Pruitt's New "Secret Science" Proposal Is the Wrong Way to Increase Transparency*, VERGE (May 1, 2018), https://www.theverge.com/2018/5/1/17304298/epa-science-transparency-rule-scott-pruitt-data-sharing.

64. *See* Paul Ohm, *Broken Promises of Privacy: Responding to the Surprising Failure of Anonymization*, 57 UCLA L. REV. 1701, 1719–20 (2010).

65. *Id.* at 1704.

66. Luc Rocher et al., *Estimating the Success of Re-identifications in Incomplete Datasets Using Generative Models*, 10 NATURE COMM. (July 23, 2019).

67. Potenza & Becker, *supra* note 63.

68. *Id.*

69. *Id.*

70. EPA, *supra* note 1, at 18,772.

71. As discussed above, it may be impossible to adapt other studies to satisfy the rigid requirements of the rule.

72. *See* Am. Assoc. for the Advancement of Sci. (AAAS), Comment Letter on Proposed Rule for Strengthening Transparency in Regulatory Science 3 (July 16, 2018) ("Regarding prospective and retrospective application, while the proposed rule states that it will be prospectively applied to future regulations and policies, it acknowledges it will capture scientific data and models that were developed prior to this current proposal. AAAS believes that all prior studies should be exempt from this rule, as many foundational studies regarding air quality and asthma and exposure to mercury and lead were conducted decades ago. Thus, it will be difficult or impossible to make all the underlying data fully accessible").

73. *See* Lisa Friedman, *Watchdog Says E.P.A. Broke Rules in Shake-Up*, N.Y. TIMES, July 16, 2019, at A10.

74. Memorandum from Alison Cullen, Chair, SAB Work Group on EPA Planned Actions for SAB Consideration of the Underlying Science, to Members of the Chartered SAB

and SAB 3 (May 12, 2018), https://yosemite.epa.gov/sab/sabproduct.nsf/E21FFAE9 56B548258525828C00808BB7/$File/WkGrp_memo_2080-AA14_final_05132018. pdf.

75. Am. Chemistry Council, Comment Letter on Proposed Rule for Strengthening Transparency in Regulatory Science 20 (Aug. 16, 2018).

76. *Id.*

77. *See* Am. Petroleum Inst., Comment Letter on Proposed Rule for Strengthening Transparency in Regulatory Science 9 (Aug. 16, 2018) ("Regarding retrospective application, if [the] EPA does not ensure that data and models from past dose-response studies are made publicly available when reviewing a previously finalized rule or creating a new rule, [the] EPA could be giving the same weight to studies that may not have the same level of quality or veracity. This could bias the rulemaking decisions toward results which do not represent the best available science").

78. Douglas W. Dockery et al., *An Association Between Air Pollution and Mortality in Six U.S. Cities*, 329 NEW ENG. J. MED. 1753 (1993).

79. C. Arden Pope III et al., *Particulate Air Pollution as a Predictor of Mortality in a Prospective Study of U.S. Adults*, 151 AM. J. RESPIRATORY & CRITICAL CARE MED. 669 (1995).

80. *See* English & Balmes, *supra* note 31, at 818 ("If this rule is approved, then it is possible that these study findings might not be taken into consideration for any changes in the NAAQS on fine particulate matter or ozone, as they are based on personal patient data"); Renee N. Salas et al., *The U.S. Environmental Protection Agency's Proposed Transparency Rule Threatens Health*, 170 ANNALS INTERNAL MED. 197, 197 (2019) ("[The Harvard Six Cities study] was fundamental to the EPA's implementation of the Clean Air Act. . . . Although the Six Cities Study has been heralded as transparent, high-quality science, the proposed rule would have excluded it from the EPA's consideration").

81. Office of Mgmt. & Budget, 2016 Draft Report to Congress on the Benefits and Costs of Federal Regulations and Agency Compliance with the Unfunded Mandates Reform Act 2, 7–8, 11–12 (2016).

82. *Id.* at 12.

83. *See* EPA, The Benefits and Costs of the Clean Air Act from 1990 to 2020: Summary Report 14 exhibit 8 (2011). The estimates above were predicted to be achieved, annually, by the year 2020. *Id.*

84. Christopher Rowland, *House GOP Demands Harvard Study Data*, Bos. GLOBE (Sept. 6, 2013), https://www.bostonglobe.com/news/nation/2013/09/06/landmark-harvard-study-health-effects-air-pollution-target-house-gop-subpoena/2K0jhfbJsZcfXqcQHc4jzL/story.html.

85. *See* Kormann, *supra* note 29.

86. *See* Salas et al., *supra* note 80.

87. Dockery et al., *supra* note 78, at 1755 tbl.1.

88. Health Effects Inst., Reanalysis of the Harvard Six Cities Study and the American Cancer Society Study of Particulate Air Pollution and Mortality (2000).

89. *Id.* at 42.

90. *Id.* at ii.
91. *Id.*
92. *Id.* at iv.
93. George D. Thurston, *The Perils Posed by the US Environmental Protection Agency's Transparency Rule*, 6 LANCET RESPIRATORY MED. 40 (2018).
94. *See* Office of Mgmt. & Budget, *supra* note 34, at 8456.

Chapter 7

1. The absence of thresholds does not imply that all pollution must be eliminated, and federal agencies have appropriately distinguished between these two concepts, adopting no-threshold risk assessment models but, at the same time, making risk management decisions that do not totally ban the risks resulting from exposure to these substances.
2. *See* Claas Kirchhelle, *Toxic Tales—Recent Histories of Pollution, Poisoning, and Pesticides (ca. 1800–2010)*, 26 N.T.M. 213, 215 (2018).
3. The discussion throughout this chapter draws heavily from Kimberly M. Castle & Richard L. Revesz, *Environmental Standards, Thresholds, and the Next Battleground of Climate Change Regulations*, 103 MINN. L. REV. 1349 (2019).
4. *See* Niina H. Farah, *To Kill Climate Rule, Trump's EPA Wants to Redefine Danger of Soot*, E&E NEWS (Aug. 6, 2018), https://www.eenews.net/climatewire/2018/08/06/stories/1060092763 (discussing how changes in benefit calculations for particulate matter helped justify the Clean Power Plan repeal).
5. *See* NAOMI ORESKES & ERIK M. CONWAY, MERCHANTS OF DOUBT: HOW A HANDFUL OF SCIENTISTS OBSCURED THE TRUTH ON ISSUES FROM TOBACCO SMOKE TO GLOBAL WARMING (2010); RACHEL EMMA ROTHSHILD, POISONOUS SKIES: ACID RAIN AND THE GLOBALIZATION OF POLLUTION (2019).
6. *See generally* ELOF AXEL CARLSON, GENES, RADIATION AND SOCIETY: THE LIFE AND WORK OF H. J. MULLER (1981) (discussing H. J. Muller's pioneering research into how radiation causes cancer). *But see* NANCY LANGSTON, TOXIC BODIES: HORMONE DISRUPTORS AND THE LEGACY OF DES 17 (2010) (noting that early toxicological frameworks had been based on "a set of assumptions about thresholds, impermeable bodies, and purity that worked reasonably well in addressing the effects of acute poisoning" but failed to account for chronic exposures).
7. Toshihiro Higuchi, *Atmospheric Nuclear Weapons Testing and the Debate on Risk Knowledge in Cold War America, 1945–1963*, *in* ENVIRONMENTAL HISTORIES OF THE COLD WAR 301, 307 (J.R. McNeill & Corinna R. Unger eds., 2010) (examining how the 1954 "Lucky Dragon" accident in the Bikini atoll led geneticists to publicly dispute the idea that exposure to radiation below a certain threshold "would not pose a threat to human health").
8. *See* EPA, Guidelines for Carcinogen Risk Assessment 1-10 to -11 (2005) (stating that "cancer risks are assumed to conform with low dose linearity" and that such models are necessarily non-threshold); Nat'l Research Council, Science and

Decisions: Advancing Risk Assessment 8 (2009) ("For cancer, it is generally assumed that there is no dose threshold of effect"). The EPA, the FDA, and OSHA "all . . . employ a linear mathematical model for low-dose extrapolation" of carcinogenic risk assessment. Gov't Accountability Office, Chemical Risk Assessment: Selected Federal Agencies' Procedures, Assumptions, and Policies 40, 173, 197 (2001) (noting the FDA's assumption of a "linear, no-threshold approach" for low dose cancer estimation, as well as OSHA's acceptance of the "overwhelming scientific consensus . . . that genotoxins follow low-dose linear functions"); cf. Nat'l Inst. for Occupational Safety & Health, Current Intelligence Bulletin 68, NIOSH [National Institute for Occupational Safety and Health] Chemical Carcinogen Policy 19 (2017) ("For carcinogen risk assessment, the NIOSH generally treats exposure-response as low-dose linear unless a non-linear mode of action has been clearly established, in which case the NIOSH will adopt a modeling approach defined by the data (including nonlinear approaches when appropriate). In general, whether the model forms are linear or non-linear, any nonzero exposure to a carcinogen is expected to yield some excess risk of cancer").

9. See Michael A. Livermore & Richard L. Revesz, *Rethinking Health-Based Environmental Standards*, 89 N.Y.U. L. Rev. 1184, 1200–06, 1213–28 (2014) (discussing the EPA's use of threshold language for its earliest NAAQS).

10. H.R. Rep. No. 95-294, at 111 (1977). The report cites findings from the National Academy of Sciences (NAS) that it had "been unable to . . . prove[] that a threshold for nitrogen dioxide-induced injury exists" and that "ozone is a compound like carbon monoxide for which no safe threshold exists." *Id.*

11. 42 U.S.C. § 7473(b) (2012).

12. Nat'l Research Council, *supra* note 8, at 177.

13. See Al McGartland et al., *Estimating the Health Benefits of Environmental Regulations*, 357 Science 457 (2017).

14. It is interesting to note that Dr. Thomas Burke, who chaired the NAS committee that wrote *Science and Decisions* served as the deputy assistant administrator of the EPA's Office of Research and Development during the Obama administration and did not, during that time, usher in implementation of the *Science and Decisions* recommendation to eschew the threshold assumption for noncarcinogens. *See About the Deputy Assistant Administrator of EPA's Office of Research and Development, and EPA's Science Advisor*, EPA (Jan. 19, 2017), https://19january2017snapshot.epa.gov/aboutepa/about-deputy-assistant-administrator-epas-office-research-and-development-and-epas-science_.html.

15. See *Towards a Comprehensive European Union Framework on Endocrine Disruptors*, at 3, COM (2018) 734 final (July 11, 2018) (noting that "a share of scientists is of the view that a safe threshold cannot be established for endocrine disruptors").

16. See McGartland et al., *supra* note 13.

17. See, e.g., EPA, National Ambient Air Quality Standards for Particulate Matter, 78 Fed. Reg. 3086, 3104 (Jan. 15, 2013) ("There is emerging, though still limited, evidence for additional potentially at-risk populations, such as those with diabetes, people who are obese, pregnant women, and the developing fetus"); Bingheng Chen & Haidong

Kan, *Air Pollution and Population Health: A Global Challenge*, 13 ENVTL. HEALTH & PREVENTIVE MED. 94, 96 (2008) (noting that for "adverse health effects associated with exposure to air pollution . . . [h]igh-risk subgroups include young children, the elderly, persons with predisposed diseases, and persons with low socioeconomic status (SES)").

18. *See* Nat'l Research Council, *supra* note 8, at 153 ("[A study on individual thresholds] provides good physiologic plausibility of low-dose linearity on a population basis, given ubiquitous exposures that imply that a substantial number of people will be found to be at least as sensitive as the 99.9th percentile individual").

19. *See Particulate Matter (PM) Basics*, EPA, https://www.epa.gov/pm-pollution/particulate-matter-pm-basics#PM (last updated Sept. 10, 2018); *Health and Environmental Effects of Particulate Matter (PM)*, EPA, https://www.epa.gov/pm-pollution/health-and-environmental-effects-particulate-matter-pm (last updated Apr. 13, 2020) (listing the health effects linked to exposure to particulate matter).

20. Douglas W. Dockery et al., *An Association Between Air Pollution and Mortality in Six U.S. Cities*, 329 NEW ENG. J. MED. 1753, 1753 (1993).

21. C. Arden Pope III et al., *Particulate Air Pollution as a Predictor of Mortality in a Prospective Study of U.S. Adults*, 151 AM. J. RESPIRATORY & CRITICAL CARE MED. 669 (1995).

22. EPA, Regulatory Impact Analyses for the Review of Particulate Matter National Ambient Air Quality Standards 5-27 (2006).

23. *See id.* (citing the American Cancer Society's study versions from 1995, 2002, and 2004). *See also* EPA, Regulatory Impact Analyses for the Final Revisions to the National Ambient Air Quality Standards for Particulate Matter 5-7 (2012) (citing the Six Cities Study updates from 2006 and 2012).

24. *See* EPA, *supra* note 23, at 1-12 (stating that the EPA relied on the Six Cities Study for its report).

25. For instance, these studies were cited to support the Mercury Air Toxic Standards and the Clean Power Plan. *See* EPA, Regulatory Impact Analysis for the Final Mercury and Air Toxics Standards 5-27 (2011) [hereinafter MATS RIA] (relying on the analyses from the Six Cities Study and the American Cancer Society study). *See also* EPA, Regulatory Impact Analysis for the Clean Power Plan Final Rule 4-16 to -17 (2015) [hereinafter Clean Power Plan RIA] (stating that the EPA used the American Cancer Society report and the Six Cities Study to help determine "PM-related mortality").

26. In 2000, due to congressional concerns about the EPA's method of estimating health benefits from air pollution reduction, the Senate appropriated funds to the EPA and directed the agency to request a study from the NAS on the EPA's methodologies. The NAS arranged for the National Research Council's Committee on Estimating the Heath-Risk-Reduction Benefits of Proposed Air Pollution Regulations to prepare a report in 2002, which reviewed and critiqued the EPA's benefit analysis. *See* Comm. on Estimating the Health-Risk-Reduction Benefits of Proposed Air Pollution Regulations, Nat'l Research Council, Estimating the Public Health Benefits of Proposed Air Pollution Regulations 1–2 (2002) [hereinafter Health-Risk-Reduction Comm.].

27. *Id.* at 109.
28. EPA Advisory Council on Clean Air Compliance Analysis Health Effects Subcomm., Review of EPA's Draft Health Benefits of the Second Section 812 Prospective Study of the Clean Air Act 2 (2010) [hereinafter Review of EPA's Draft].
29. *Id.* at 13.
30. *See* Kevin R. Cromar et al., *American Thoracic Society and Marron Institute Report Estimated Excess Morbidity and Mortality Caused by Air Pollution Above American Thoracic Society-Recommended Standards, 2011–2013*, 13 ANNALS AM. THORACIC SOC'Y 1195, 1201 (2016) ("The ATS recommendations for . . . $PM_{2.5}$ . . . are more stringent than the current NAAQS determined by the EPA").
31. The study indicated that the marginal health risk from additional exposure at low levels is actually higher than the risk at higher levels of exposure. *See* Qian Di et al., *Air Pollution and Mortality in the Medicare Population*, 376 NEW ENG. J. MED. 2513, 2515–18 (2017).
32. World Health Org., Ambient Air Pollution: A Global Assessment of Exposure and Burden of Disease 11 (2016).
33. *See* Indus. Econ., Inc., Expanded Expert Judgment Assessment of the Concentration-Response Relationship Between $PM_{2.5}$ Exposure and Mortality i–ii (2006).
34. *See id.* at 3-26.
35. *See id.* at i–ii, iv, 3-25.
36. *See* Robert D. Brook et al., *Particulate Matter Air Pollution and Cardiovascular Disease: An Update to the Scientific Statement from the American Heart Association*, 121 CIRCULATION 2331, 2338 (2010) (finding there is an increased mortality rate for PM levels lower than the current NAAQS threshold).
37. *See id.*
38. *See id.* at 2338, 2350–51.
39. The EPA's 1984 regulatory impact analysis stated that "the data do not . . . show evidence of a clear threshold in exposed populations. Instead they suggest a continuum of response with both the likelihood (risk) of effects occurring and the magnitude of any potential effect decreasing with concentration." EPA, Regulatory Impact Analysis on the National Ambient Air Quality Standards for Particulate Matter, at VI-15 to VI-17 (1984).
40. EPA, National Ambient Air Quality Standards for Particulate Matter, 62 Fed. Reg. 38,652, 38,670 (July 18, 1997).
41. The calculations showed that there would be greater overall benefits from reductions below the level of particulate matter ultimately chosen by the agency. *See* EPA, Regulatory Impact Analyses for the Particulate Matter and Ozone National Ambient Air Quality Standards and Proposed Regional Haze Rule ES-23 tbl.ES-3 (1997).
42. EPA, National Ambient Air Quality Standards for Particulate Matter, 71 Fed. Reg. 61,144, 61,152 (Oct. 17, 2006).
43. EPA, *supra* note 22, at ES-7 tbl.ES-1 (comparing full attainment benefits with social costs through incremental attainment of the 1997 standards).
44. *See id.* at ES-8 tbl.ES-2 (estimating the reduction of adverse health and welfare effects associated with incremental attainment of alternative standards).

45. EPA, National Ambient Air Quality Standards for Particulate Matter, 78 Fed. Reg. 3086, 3148 (Jan. 15, 2013).

46. *See* EPA, *supra* note 23, at ES-2.

47. *See id.* at 5-81.

48. For an early example of this opposition, the American Chemistry Council's comments on the use of no threshold modeling for the Obama EPA's Hazardous Air Pollutants standards for the cement industry are particularly revelatory. *See* The Am. Chemistry Council, Comment Letter on Proposed Rule for National Emissions Standards for Hazardous Air Pollutants from the Portland Cement Manufacturing Industry (Sept. 9, 2009).

49. EPA, *supra* note 45, at 3119.

50. For example, state and industry challengers to the Clean Power Plan emphasized the EPA's admission that there is uncertainty about the scale of particulate matter health effects at very low exposure levels. Opening Brief of State and Industry Petitioners at 53, Murray Energy Corp. v. EPA, No. 16-1127 (D.C. Cir. Nov. 18, 2016).

51. *See* Susanne Rust, *Scientist Says Some Pollution Is Good for You—A Disputed Claim Trump's EPA Has Embraced*, L.A. Times (Feb. 19, 2019), https://www.latimes.com/local/california/la-me-secret-science-20190219-story.html.

52. EPA, Strengthening Transparency in Regulatory Science, 83 Fed. Reg. 18768, 18770 (Apr. 30, 2018).

53. Instead, scientists in the field have responded by pointing to the plethora of research on the harmful effects of pollutants at all levels of exposure. *See, e.g.*, Comment from Susan Mandel, president of the Endocrine Society, on Proposed Rule Strengthening Transparency in Regulatory Science (May 21, 2018) (citing EPA, *supra* note 8).

54. EPA, Repeal of Carbon Pollution Emission, Guidelines for Existing Stationary Sources: Electric Utility Generating, 82 Fed. Reg. 48035, 48044 (Oct. 16, 2017).

55. *See id.*

56. *See* EPA, Regulatory Impact Analysis for the Review of the Clean Power Plan: Proposal 49–50 (Oct. 2017) (noting that the Integrated Science Assessment for Particulate Matter, used to set the most recent NAAQS level in 2012, concluded there was "little evidence was observed to suggest that a threshold exists").

57. Jessica Wentz, *6 Important Points About the "Affordable Clean Energy Rule,"* St. Planet (Aug. 22, 2018), https://blogs.ei.columbia.edu/2018/08/22/affordable-clean-energy-rule/.

58. *See* Lisa Friedman, *E.P.A.'s Reckoning Is a Rosier View of Air Pollution*, N.Y. Times, May 21, 2019, at A1.

59. EPA, Emission Guidelines for Greenhouse Gas Emissions from Existing Electric Utility Generating Units; Revisions to Emission Guideline Implementing Regulations; Revisions to New Source Review Program, 83 Fed. Reg. 44746, 44790 (Aug. 31, 2018).

60. *See* EPA, Regulatory Impact Analysis for the Proposed Emission Guidelines for Greenhouse Gas Emissions from Existing Electric Utility Generating Units; Revisions to Emission Guideline Implementing Regulations; Revisions to New Source Review Program 4-25 to 4-31 (2018).

61. The final rule adopts the same approach. *See* EPA, Regulatory Impact Analysis for the Repeal of the Clean Power Plan, and the Emission Guidelines for Greenhouse Gas Emissions from Existing Electric Utility Generating Units 4-25 to 4-30 (2019).

62. *See* Dana Nuccitelli, *Pruitt Promised Polluters EPA Will Value Their Profits over American Lives*, GUARDIAN (Apr. 23, 2018), https://www.theguardian.com/environment/climate-consensus-97-per-cent/2018/apr/23/pruitt-promised-polluters-epa-will-value-their-profits-over-american-lives. *See also* Dino Grandoni, *The Energy 202: The Other Scientific Consensus the EPA Is Bucking*, WASH. POST (Oct. 11, 2017), https://wapo.st/3jnrZaW .

63. Charles Battig, *Driving Policies Through Fraud and Fear-mongering*, HEARTLAND INST. (July 10, 2015), https://www.heartland.org/news-opinion/news/driving-policies-through-fraud-and-fear-mongering?source=policybot (summarizing remarks at a Heartland Institute meeting on climate change in 2015).

64. Marlo Lewis, Jr., *Free Market Groups Call for Repeal of Clean Power Plan*, COMPETITIVE ENTERPRISE INST. (Apr. 26, 2018), https://cei.org/blog/free-market-groups-call-repeal-clean-power-plan.

65. Comments from Charles T. Discoll, PhD, et al., on the Proposal to Repeal the Carbon Pollution Emission Guidelines for Existing Stationary Sources (Apr. 26, 2018) (noting there is no evidence for a threshold of harm from particulate matter).

66. Am. Thoracic Soc'y, News Release, ATS Testifies in Opposition to Clean Power Plan Repeal (Dec. 5, 2017), https://news.thoracic.org/washington-letter/2017/ats-testifies-in-opposition-to-clean-power-plan-repeal1.php.

67. Comments from the Union of Concerned Scientists on Proposed Repeal of the Carbon Pollution Emission Guidelines for Existing Stationary Sources (Apr. 26, 2018).

68. Memorandum from Alison Cullen, Chair, Scientific Advisory Board, to Members of the Chartered Scientific Advisory Board (May 18, 2018), https://yosemite.epa.gov/sab/sabproduct.nsf/9263940BB05B89A885258291006AC017/$File/WG_Memo_Fall17_RegRevAttsABC.pdf.

69. Lisa Friedman, *Cost of E.P.A.'s Pollution Rules: Up to 1,400 More Deaths a Year*, N.Y. TIMES, Aug. 22, 2018, at A1.

70. Inst. for Energy Research, *EPA Proposes Rule to Replace Obama's Clean Power Plan*, IER COMMENT. (Aug. 24, 2018), https://www.instituteforenergyresearch.org/fossil-fuels/coal/epa-proposes-rule-to-replace-obamas-clean-power-plan/.

71. Michael Bastasch, *NYT Left Some Key Details Out of Its Claim That Ditching Obama-Era Rules Could Kill 1,400 People*, DAILY CALLER (Aug. 21, 2018), https://dailycaller.com/2018/08/21/new-york-times-energy-laws-obama/.

72. *See* DAVID MICHAELS, DOUBT IS THEIR PRODUCT: HOW INDUSTRY'S ASSAULT ON SCIENCE THREATENS YOUR HEALTH (2008).

Chapter 8

1. RISK VERSUS RISK: TRADEOFFS IN PROTECTING HEALTH AND THE ENVIRONMENT (John D. Graham & Jonathan Baert Wiener eds., 1995).

2. Graham and Wiener acknowledge the importance of counting co-benefits. *See id.* at 2 (referring to "coincident risk" reductions) but the focus of their book is on the indirect negative consequences of regulation.

3. *Id.* at 22–25.

4. *Id.* at 270.

5. *See* Kim M. Castle & Richard L. Revesz, *Environmental Standards, Thresholds, and the Next Battleground of Climate Change Regulations*, 103 MINN. L. REV. 1349 (2019).

6. In addition to Graham and Wiener, Professor Cass Sunstein, later the Obama administration's OIRA head, in the 1990s advocated broad application of risk-risk analysis. *See* Cass R. Sunstein, *Health-Health Tradeoffs*, 63 U. CHI. L. REV. 1533, 1537 (1996). W. Kip Viscusi, a prominent economist and leading proponent of cost-benefit analysis, also endorsed the use of risk trade-off analysis in the regulatory process. *See* W. Kip Viscusi, *Regulating the Regulators*, 63 U. CHI. L. REV. 1423, 1455 (1996) (arguing that "regulatory agencies should be concerned with this broader effect [ancillary costs] of regulatory policy since their mandate is to improve the health and welfare of citizens generally").

7. 531 U.S. 457, 495 (2001) (Breyer, J., concurring). The DC Circuit opinion in that case examined a different countervailing risk: less protection from harmful ultraviolet radiation as a result of reducing ozone pollution. Am. Trucking Ass'ns v. EPA, 175 F.3d 1027, 1036–37 (D.C. Cir. 1999), *rev'd on other grounds sub nom.* Whitman v. Am. Trucking Ass'ns, 531 U.S. 457 (2001).

8. *See* 531 U.S. at 495.

9. 938 F.2d 1310, 1326 (D.C. Cir. 1991) (Williams, J., concurring).

10. 938 F.2d at 1326.

11. For a detailed discussion of this criticism in our prior book, see RICHARD L. REVESZ & MICHAEL A. LIVERMORE, RETAKING RATIONALITY: HOW COST-BENEFIT ANALYSIS CAN BETTER PROTECT THE ENVIRONMENT AND OUR HEALTH 67–76 (2008), which questions the "health-wealth" effect and offers alternative explanations for both health and wealth—notably, education—as well as the potential for reverse causation (i.e., that worse health causes lower wealth).

12. Office of Mgmt. & Budget, Circular A-4 (Sept. 17, 2003).

13. *Id.* at 26.

14. *Id.*

15. EPA, Guidelines for Preparing Economic Analyses 11-2 (2010).

16. EPA, Guidelines for Preparing Economic Analyses (External Review Draft) 10-4 (2008).

17. *Id.* at 8-17.

18. EPA, Guidelines for Preparing Economic Analyses 67, 70(2000). Over time, the EPA became more precise in disaggregating the related but distinct concepts that are covered by the term "indirect" costs and benefits. The Trump administration has primarily targeted co-benefits, sometimes referred to as ancillary benefits. These are indirect in the sense that they are not the direct target of the regulation, but instead arise as a positive side effect of compliance. The 2008 Draft Guidelines and the 2010 Guidelines, adopted during the Bush and Obama administrations (respectively),

explicitly call for evaluation of co-benefits. *See* EPA, *supra* note 15; EPA, *supra* note 16.

19. EPA, supra note 18, at 114.

20. *Id.* at 59.

21. *Id.* at 70 (noting that "ecosystem services that do not directly provide some good or opportunity to individuals may be valued because they support off-site ecological resources or maintain the biological and biochemical processes required for life support"). The indirect benefits provided by ecosystems would be co-benefits (or ancillary benefits) if they were not the direct target of an agency action. For example, a rule intended to ensure the suitability of a waterbody for fishing and swimming could indirectly generate ecosystem service co-benefits of habitat protection.

22. *Id.* at 177.

23. The Senate Report accompanying the 1990 Clean Air Act amendments indicated that the EPA could take co-benefits into account when setting standards for hazardous air pollutants. S. Rep. No. 101-228, at 172 (1989) ("When establishing technology-based standards under this subsection, the Administrator may consider the benefits which result from the control of air pollutants that are not listed but the emissions of which are, nevertheless, reduced by control technologies or practices necessary to meet the prescribed limitation").

24. EPA, Costs and Benefits of Reducing Lead in Gasoline: Final Regulatory Impact Analysis, at VI-1 to -74 (1985).

25. *Id.* at E-8.

26. *See* EPA, Assessment of Municipal Waste Combustor Emissions Under the Clean Air Act, 52 Fed. Reg. 25,399, 25,406 (July 7, 1987).

27. *See* EPA, Standards of Performance for New Stationary Sources and Guidelines for Control of Existing Sources: Municipal Solid Waste Landfills, 56 Fed. Reg. 24,468, 24,469 (May 30, 1991).

28. *See id.* at 24,472.

29. *See id.*

30. *See* EPA, National Emission Standards for Hazardous Air Pollutants for Source Category: Pulp and Paper Production; Effluent Limitations Guidelines, Pretreatment Standards, and New Source Performance Standards: Pulp, Paper, and Paperboard Category, 63 Fed. Reg. 18,504, 18,504, 18,576 (Apr. 15, 1998).

31. *See id.* at 18,576.

32. *See id.* at 18,579.

33. *See* EPA, Rule to Reduce Interstate Transport of Fine Particulate Matter and Ozone (Clean Air Interstate Rule); Revisions to Acid Rain Program; Revisions to the NO_x SIP Call, 70 Fed. Reg. 25,162, 25,170 (May 12, 2005).

34. *See id.* at 25,312.

35. *See* EPA, Control of Hazardous Air Pollutants from Mobile Sources, 72 Fed. Reg. 8428, 8430, 8461 (Feb. 26, 2007).

36. *Id.* at 8461.

37. *See id.* at 8453.

38. *Id.* at 8458.

39. *See* Caroline Cecot & W. Kip Viscusi, *Judicial Review of Agency Benefit-Cost Analysis*, 22 GEO. MASON L. REV. 575, 589–603 (2015) (collecting and analyzing cases where courts reviewed agencies' cost-benefit analyses).

40. Corrosion Proof Fittings v. EPA, 947 F.2d 1201, 1229–30 (5th Cir. 1991).

41. *Id.* at 1225.

42. *Id.* at 1215 (quoting Toxic Substances Control Act, 15 U.S.C. § 2601(c) (1988)).

43. *Id.* at 1220–21, 1224.

44. *Id.* at 1207.

45. Competitive Enterprise Inst. v. Nat'l Highway Traffic Safety Admin., 956 F.2d 321, 323–25 (D.C. Cir. 1992).

46. *See id.* at 326–27.

47. *Id.* at 327.

48. Am. Dental Ass'n v. Martin, 984 F.2d 823, 823–27, 830–31 (7th Cir. 1993).

49. *See id.* at 826.

50. *Id.*

51. *See* Samuel J. Rascoff & Richard L. Revesz, *The Biases of Risk Tradeoff Analysis: Towards Parity in Environmental and Health-and-Safety Regulation*, 69 U. CHI. L. REV. 1763, 1793 (2002).

52. U.S. Sugar Corp. v. EPA, 830 F.3d 579, 591, 625 (D.C. Cir. 2016).

53. *Id.* at 624.

54. *See id.* at 625.

55. *See id.*

56. *See id.* at 624–25.

57. *Id.* at 625.

58. *See* Rascoff & Revesz, *supra* note 51, at 1793.

59. Christopher C. DeMuth & Douglas H. Ginsburg, *Rationalism in Regulation*, 108 MICH. L. REV. 877, 887 (2010).

60. *Id.* at 888.

61. EPA, Increasing Consistency and Transparency in Considering Costs and Benefits in the Rulemaking Process, 83 Fed. Reg. 27,524, 27,527 (June 13, 2018).

62. *Id.*

63. Such questions would have been futile given the extensive case law requiring that agencies take them into account. The agency may also have held the view that counting indirect costs will tend to favor less regulation. In focusing on only indirect benefits, the agency invited an irrational outcome where indirect consequences of regulation are taken into account if they are negative but ignored if they are positive. *See* Inst. for Policy Integrity, Comments to EPA on Reconsideration of Mercury and Air Toxics Standards (Apr. 17, 2019), https://policyintegrity.org/projects/update/comments-to-epa-on-reconsideration-of-mercury-and-air-toxics-standards.

64. Motion for Leave to File Amici Curiae Brief and Brief of the Chamber of Commerce of the United States, et al., as Amici Curiae in Support of Petitioners at 3, Michigan v. EPA, 135 S. Ct. 2699 (2015) (Nos. 14-46, 14-47, 14-49).

65. Brief for the Cato Institute as Amicus Curiae in Support of Petitioners at 4, Michigan v. EPA, 135 S. Ct. 2699 (2015) (Nos. 14-46, 14-47, 14-49).

66. Michael Bastasch, *Sources: Pruitt to End a Tactic Obama Used to Justify Massive EPA Rules*, DAILY CALLER (Apr. 12, 2018), https://dailycaller.com/2018/04/12/sources-pruitt-epa-obama-tactics/.

67. *See* Memorandum of Andrew R. Wheeler to Assistant Administrators, Increasing Consistency and Transparency in Considering Benefits and Costs in the Rulemaking Process (May 13, 2019).

68. Specifically, the administrator proposed that the agency proceed through separate, media-specific, analyses, based on classes of regulations that addressed, alternative, air, water, or hazardous substances. *Id.*

69. 42 U.S.C. § 7412(n)(1)(A) (2012).

70. *See* EPA, National Emission Standards for Hazardous Air Pollutants from Coal- and Oil-Fired Electric Utility Steam Generating Units and Standards of Performance for Fossil-Fuel-Fired Electric Utility, Industrial-Commercial-Institutional, and Small Industrial-Commercial-Institutional Steam Generating Units, 77 Fed. Reg. 9303 (Feb. 16, 2012).

71. Michigan v. EPA, 135 S. Ct. 2699, 2712 (2015).

72. *Id.* at 2711.

73. *Id.* (emphasis added).

74. EPA, Supplemental Finding That It Is Appropriate and Necessary to Regulate Hazardous Air Pollutants from Coal- and Oil-Fired Electric Utility Steam Generating Units, 81 Fed. Reg. 24,420, 24,420 (Apr. 25, 2016).

75. *Id.*

76. *Id.* at 24,425.

77. EPA, *supra* note 70, at 9305.

78. *Id.*

79. EPA, *supra* note 74, at 24,428.

80. EPA, National Emission Standards for Hazardous Air Pollutants: Coal- and Oil-Fired Electric Utility Steam Generating Units—Reconsideration of Supplemental Finding and Residual Risk and Technology Review, 84 Fed. Reg. 2670, 2676 (Feb. 7, 2019).

81. *Id.*

82. *Id.* The regulation was finalized in May 2020. *See* EPA, National Emission Standards for Hazardous Air Pollutants: Coal- and Oil-Fired Electric Utility Steam Generating Units—Reconsideration of Supplemental Finding and Residual Risk and Technology Review, 85 Fed. Reg. 31,286 (May 22, 2020).

83. EPA, *supra* note 75, at 24,440. Indirect costs are defined by the EPA as "those incurred in related markets or experienced by consumers or government agencies not under the direct scope of regulation." EPA, *supra* note 15, at 8-7 to 8-8.

84. Jack Lienke & Richard L. Revesz, *EPA Will Say Anything to Avoid Addressing Climate Change*, REG. REV. (July 29, 2019), https://www.theregreview.org/2019/07/29/revesz-lienke-epa-avoid-addressing-climate-change/.

85. *See* EPA, Regulatory Impact Analysis for the Repeal of the Clean Power Plan and the Emission Guidelines for Greenhouse Gas Emissions from Existing Electric Utility Generating Units 6-6 (2019).

86. Richard L. Revesz, *On Climate, the Facts and the Law Are Against Trump*, N.Y. TIMES (Dec. 4, 2018), https://www.nytimes.com/2018/12/04/opinion/climate-report-trump.html.

87. Timothy Cama & Miranda Green, *Trump Moves to Roll Back Obama Emission Standards*, THE HILL (Aug. 2, 2018), https://thehill.com/policy/energy-environment/400036-trump-submits-rule-to-weaken-iconic-obama-car-efficiency-standards.

88. *Id.*

89. *Id.*

90. 83 Fed. Reg. 42,986 (Aug. 24, 2018).

91. *See* EPA & Nat'l Highway Traffic Safety Admin., Preliminary Regulatory Impact Analysis, The Safer Affordable Fuel-Efficient (SAFE) Vehicles Rule for Model Years 2021–2026 Passenger Cars and Light Trucks 1467–68 (2018). The final rule similarly relied on co-benefits for its justification. *See* Richard L. Revesz, *Trump Shows His Cards on Environmental Protection, or Lack Thereof*, THE HILL (Apr. 30, 2020), https://thehill.com/opinion/energy-environment/495457-trump-shows-his-cards-on-environmental-protections-or-lack-thereof.

92. *See* 42 U.S.C. § 7521 (2012).

93. *See* 49 U.S.C. § 32,902 (2012).

94. The National Highway Traffic Administration, unlike the EPA, has the statutory authority to promote vehicle safety. But its safety mandate lies in other provisions of its governing statute, not in the statutory provision providing the authority for the fuel-economy standards. Thus, the agency is in the same position that the EPA was with respect to the Mercury and Air Toxics Standards. The EPA had clear statutory authority to regulate particulate matter. But the benefits from such reduction were deemed co-benefits as opposed to direct benefits because, as explained earlier in this chapter, the MATS rule was promulgated under a section of the Clean Air Act dealing with hazardous air pollutants, not with particulate matter.

Chapter 9

1. Intergovernmental Panel on Climate Change, Global Warming of 1.5° C, at 81 (Valérie Masson-Delmotte et al. eds., 2018).

2. *Id.* at 191, 196, 209, 236.

3. *Id.* at 9–10.

4. *See* U.S. Glob. Change Research Program, Fourth National Climate Assessment (2018).

5. Donald Trump (@realDonaldTrump), TWITTER (Jan. 20, 2019), https://twitter.com/realDonaldTrump/status/1086971499725160448.

6. Ctr. for Biological Diversity v. Nat'l Highway Traffic Safety Admin., 538 F.3d 1172, 1181 (9th Cir. 2008).

7. *Id.* at 1198–1200.

8. *Id.* at 1200.

9. *See* Interagency Working Group on Social Cost of Carbon, Technical Support Document:—Social Cost of Carbon for Regulatory Impact Analysis—Under Executive Order 12866 (2010) [hereinafter TSD 2010].

10. *See Scientific and Economic Background on DICE Models* (Feb. 3, 2020), https://sites. google.com/site/williamdnordhaus/dice-rice. The others were the PAGE model and the FUND model. *See* Chris Hope, *The PAGE09 Integrated Assessment Model: A Technical Description* (Cambridge Judge Bus. Sch., Working Paper No. 4, 2011); *FUND—Climate Framework for Uncertainty, Negotiation and Distribution*, http://www.fund-model.org/.

11. Inst. for Policy Integrity, Social Costs of Greenhouse Gases 2 (2017).

12. TSD 2010, *supra* note 9, at 15.

13. *Id.* at 25.

14. *Id.* at 1.

15. *Id.* at 3, 23.

16. *See id.*; Interagency Working Group on Social Cost of Greenhouse Gases, Technical Support Document:—Technical Update of the Social Cost of Carbon for Regulatory Impact Analysis Under Executive Order 12866 (2016) [hereinafter TSD 2016].

17. TSD 2016, *supra* note 16, at 4. The original estimates were given in 2007$. Using the Consumer Price Index inflation tables, the central estimate of $42 in 2007$ for year 2020 emissions equals $51.79 in 2019$.

18. *Id.* at 16. The central estimates in 2007$ are $50 (in 2030), $60 (in 2040), and $69 (in 2050).

19. *Id.*

20. *Id.*

21. *See* Zero Zone, Inc. v. Department of Energy, 832 F.3d 654 (7th Cir. 2016).

22. *Id.* at 677.

23. *Id.* at 678.

24. Richard L. Revesz et al., *Best Cost Estimate of Greenhouse Gases*, 357 SCIENCE 655 (2017).

25. TSD 2016, *supra* note 16, at 3.

26. Peter Howard, Cost of Carbon Project, Omitted Damages: What's Missing from the Social Cost of Carbon 20, 27–29, 30–31, 33–39 (2014).

27. Robinson Meyer, *California's Wildfires Are 500 Percent Larger Due to Climate Change*, ATLANTIC (July 16, 2019), https://www.theatlantic.com/science/archive/2019/07/climate-change-500-percent-increase-california-wildfires/594016/.

28. Richard L. Revesz et al, *Improve Economic Models of Climate Change*, 508 NATURE 173, 175 (2014).

29. *See* Inst. for Policy Integrity, A Lower Bound: Why the Social Cost of Carbon Does Not Capture Critical Climate Damages and What That Means for Policymakers (2019).

30. *See* Peter Howard & Derek Sylvan, Inst. for Policy Integrity, Expert Consensus on the Economics of Climate Change 2 (2015).

31. Executive Order 13,783, § 5, 82 Fed. Reg. 16,093, 16,095–96 (Mar. 31, 2017).

32. *Id.* at 16,096.

33. EPA, Regulatory Impact Analysis for the Review of the Clean Power Plan: Proposal 44 (2017).

34. *Id.* at 43.

35. Brad Plumer, *Trump Put a Low Cost on Carbon Emissions. Here's Why It Matters*, N.Y. Times, Aug. 24, 2018, at A16.

36. Michael Greenstone, *What Financial Markets Can Teach Us About Managing Climate Risks*, N.Y. Times (Apr. 4, 2017), https://www.nytimes.com/2017/04/04/upshot/what-financial-markets-can-teach-us-about-managing-climate-risks.html.

37. Laurie T. Johnson & Chris Hope, *The Social Cost of Carbon in United States Regulatory Impact Analyses: An Introduction and Critique*, 2 J. Envtl. Stud. & Sci. 205, 212 (2012).

38. EPA, Regulating Greenhouse Gas Emissions Under the Clean Air Act, 73 Fed. Reg. 44,354, 44,414 (July 30, 2008).

39. Moritz Drupp et al., *Discounting Disentangled: An Expert Survey on the Determinants of the Long-Term Social Discount Rate* 1 (Ctr. for Climate Change Econ. & Policy Working Paper No. 195, 2015).

40. Office of Mgmt. & Budget, Circular A-4, at 34 (Sept. 17, 2003).

41. EPA, *supra* note 33, at 43.

42. Office of Mgmt. & Budget, *supra* note 40, at 35–36.

43. *Id.* at 35.

44. *Id.*

45. *Id.* at 36.

46. *Id.* at 33.

47. *Id.*

48. *Id.*

49. *See id.*; Interagency Working Group on Social Cost of Carbon, Response to Comments: Social Cost of Carbon for Regulatory Analysis Under Executive Order 12866, at 21–22 (2015) [hereinafter Response to Comments].

50. TSD 2010, *supra* note 9, at 19.

51. Office of Mgmt. & Budget, *supra* note 40, at 33–34.

52. Council of Econ. Advisers, Issue Brief, Discounting for Public Policy: Theory and Recent Evidence on the Merits of Updating the Discount Rate 2, 12 (2017).

53. *See id.* at 12

54. *See id.* at 8–9.

55. *See* Martin L. Weitzman, *Why the Far Distant Future Should Be Discounted at Its Lowest Possible Rate*, 36 J. Envtl. Econ. & Mgmt. 201 (1998).

56. *See* Council of Econ. Advisers, *supra* note 52, at 9.

57. Weitzman, *supra* note 55, at 205.

58. Council of Economic Advisers, *supra* note 52, at 9.

59. Richard L. Revesz & Matthew R. Shahabian, *Climate Change and Future Generations*, 84 S. Cal. L. Rev. 1097, 1113 (2011).

60. *See* David Pearce et al., *Valuing the Future: Recent Advances in Social Discounting*, 4 World Econ. 121, 129 tbl.1 (2003) (presenting numerical example).

61. EPA, *supra* note 33, at 43.

62. TSD 2010, *supra* note 9, at 10.

63. *Id.* at 10–11.

64. Ted Gayer and W. Kip Viscusi advocate for a domestic only social cost of carbon value, but—unlike the approach of the Trump administration—explicitly account for reciprocity effects and the altruistic concern of US citizens for the well-being of people in other countries. *See* Ted Gayer & W. Kip Viscusi, *Determining the Proper Scope of Climate Change Policy Benefits in U.S. Regulatory Analyses: Domestic Versus Global Approaches*, 10 Rev. Envtl. Econ. & Pol'y 245 (2016). Acknowledging the full scope of domestic effects would be an improvement over the practice of the Trump administration.

65. TSD 2016, *supra* note 16, at 17.

66. Zero Zone, Inc. v. Department of Energy, 832 F.3d 654, 679–80 (7th Cir. 2016). In July 2020, the United States District Court for the Northern District of California went further, concluding that the global measure is consistent with the best available science, that the domestic-only approach advocated by the Trump administration "is riddled with flaws," and that the administration's reliance on this approach was "arbitrary and capricious." California v. Bernhardt, No. 4:18-cv-05712, at 34-37 (N.D. Cal. 2020).

67. TSD 2010, *supra* note 9, at 11.

68. *See* Brief of the Institute for Policy Integrity at NYU Law School as Amicus Curiae in Support of Plaintiffs' Motions for Summary Judgment at 12–13, California v. Zinke, No. 4:18-cv-05712-YGR (N.D. Cal. filed June 21, 2019). Revesz served as counsel of record in that case.

69. *See* Peter Howard & Jason Schwartz, *Think Global: International Reciprocity as Justification for a Global Social Cost of Carbon*, 42 Colum. J. Envtl. L. 203 (2017).

70. Peter Howard & Jason Schwartz, Inst. for Policy Integrity, Foreign Action, Domestic Windfall: The U.S. Economy Stands to Gain Trillions from Foreign Climate Action 11 (2015).

71. *See* Plumer, *supra* note 35.

72. Howard & Schwartz, *supra* note 69, at 229.

73. Response to Comments, *supra* note 49, at 32.

74. EPA, Regulatory Impact Analysis for the Proposed Emission Guidelines for Greenhouse Gas Emissions from Existing Electric Utility Generating Units; Revisions to Emission Guideline Implementing Regulations; Revisions to New Source Review Program 4-3 (2018).

Chapter 10

1. Office of Mgmt. & Budget, Circular A-4, at 15–16 (Sept. 17, 2003).

2. *Id.* at 18.

3. *See id.* at 7–9.

4. *Id.* at 38.

5. *Id.*

6. *Id.*

7. *Id.*

8. *See* Richard L. Revesz, *Regulation and Distribution*, 93 N.Y.U. L. Rev. 1489, 1500–11 (2018) (summarizing the "orthodox view" of distributional concerns and cost-benefit analysis).

9. *See id.* at 1500-1501; Louis Kaplow & Steven Shavell, *Why the Legal System Is Less Efficient than the Income Tax in Redistributing Income*, 23 J. Legal Stud. 667, 667 (1994). *See also* Eric Posner, *Transfer Regulations and Cost-Effectiveness Analysis*, 53 Duke L.J. 1067, 1076–78 (2003) (differentiating cost-benefit and cost-effectiveness analysis for purposes of regulations that correct market failures and those with distributional aims).

10. *See* Hila Shamir, Tsilly Dagan & Ayelet Carmeli, *Questioning Market Aversion in Gender Equality Strategies: Designing Legal Mechanisms for the Promotion of Gender Equality in the Family and the Market*, 27 Cornell J.L. & Pub. Pol'y 717, 721 (2018) ("As significant as it is, efficiency is not the only goal of desirable public policy").

11. Office of Mgmt. & Budget, Economic Analysis of Federal Regulations Under Executive Order 12866 (Jan. 11, 1996).

12. Memorandum M-00-08 from Jacob J. Lew, Director, to the Heads of Departments and Agencies 18 (Mar. 22, 2000).

13. Memorandum from Mitchell E. Daniels, Jr., Director, for the Heads of Executive Departments and Agencies (June 19, 2001) (reaffirming the use of Memorandum M-00-08).

14. *Id.* at 46.

15. *See* Office of Mgmt. & Budget, Agency Checklist: Regulatory Impact Analysis 2 ("Does the RIA provide a description/accounting of transfer payments?").

16. Executive Order 13,783, Promoting Energy Independence and Economic Growth § 5(c), 82 Fed. Reg. 16,093, 16,096 (Mar. 31, 2017).

17. Memorandum M-17-21 from Dominic J. Mancini, Acting Administrator, to Regulatory Policy Officers at Executive Departments and Agencies and Managing and Executive Directors of Certain Agencies and Commissions 6–7 (Apr. 5, 2017).

18. *See Frequently Asked Questions About the Federal Coal Leasing Program*, Bureau Land Mgmt., https://eplanning.blm.gov/epl-front-office/projects/nepa/64842/78268/88489/CoalFAQ.pdf.

19. *See generally* Jayni Foley Hein & Caroline Cecot, *Mineral Royalties: Historical Uses and Justifications*, 28 Duke Envtl. L. & Pol'y F. 1 (2017) (describing the royalty system and charting its evolution over time).

20. 30 U.S.C. § 226(b)(1)(A) (2012).

21. *See* 30 U.S.C. § 191(c)(2) (2012).

22. Headwaters Econ., An Assessment of U.S. Federal Coal Royalties: Current Royalty Structure, Effective Royalty Rates, and Reform Options (2015).

23. *See Fact Sheet: Federal Coal Royalties and Their Impact on Western States*, Bureau Land Mgmt., https://www.energy.senate.gov/public/index.cfm/files/serve?File_id=E3944689-6D71-4328-BBF2-BE7B7CDCF58D.

24. *See* Headwaters Econ., *supra* note 22, at 1.

25. *See* Council of Econ. Advisors, The Economics of Coal Leasing on Federal Lands: Ensuring a Fair Return to Taxpayers 2 (2016).

26. *See* Valuation Rule, Hearing Before the H. Subcomm. on Energy and Mineral Res. of H. Comm. on Energy & Nat. Res., 114th Cong. (2015) [hereinafter Energy Hearings] (testimony of Gregory J. Gould, Director, Office of Natural Resources Revenue).

27. *See* Gov't Accountability Office, Coal Leasing: BLM Could Enhance Appraisal Process, More Explicitly Consider Coal Exports, and Provide More Public Information 15–16 (2013).

28. *See* Energy Hearings, *supra* note 26.

29. *See id.*; *see also* Patrick Rucker, *Asia Coal Export Boom Brings No Bonus for U.S. Taxpayers*, REUTERS (Dec. 4, 2012), https://www.reuters.com/article/us-usa-coal-royalty/asia-coal-export-boom-brings-no-bonus-for-u-s-taxpayers-idUSBRE8B30IL20121204 .

30. *See* Jayni Foley Hein, Inst. for Policy Integrity, Reconsidering Coal's Fair Market Value: The Social Costs of Coal Production and the Need for Fiscal Reform 11-12 (2015).

31. *See* Cong. Research Service, U.S. Crude Oil and Natural Gas Production in Federal and Nonfederal Areas 2 (2018).

32. *See* Rucker, *supra* note 29.

33. *See id.*

34. *Id.*; *see also* Headwaters Econ., *supra* note 22, at 1.

35. *See* Gov't Accountability Office, *supra* note 27, at 48; *see also* 43 U.S.C. § 1344(a)(4) (2012) (mandating that the government collect the "fair market value").

36. *See* Letter to Ken Salazar from Sens. Lisa Murkowski and Ron Wyden (Jan. 2, 2013), https://www.wyden.senate.gov/imo/media/doc/2012-01-03%20Wyden-Murkowski%20Coal%20Royalty%20Letter.pdf.

37. *See* Dep't of the Interior, Consolidated Federal Oil & Gas and Federal & Indian Coal Valuation Reform, 81 Fed. Reg. 43,338 (July 1, 2016).

38. *See id.* at 43,359–60 ("We also estimate that industry will experience reduced annual administrative costs of $3.61 million").

39. *See id.* at 43,367.

40. *See also id.* at 43,359 ("The sum of these amendments that have cost benefits are due to administrative cost savings to industry, not a decrease in royalties due").

41. *See* Executive Order 13,783, 82 Fed. Reg. 16,093 (Mar. 31, 2017).

42. Coal companies were prominent supporters of Trump before and after the election, with the head of the country's largest coal mining company, a longtime Trump supporter, providing an "Action Plan" for the administration that was substantially followed. *See* Lisa Friedman, *How a Coal Baron's Wish List Became Trump's To-Do List*, N.Y. TIMES, Jan. 10, 2018, at B1 (discussing the leaked plan and quoting a senator discussing the "extraordinary arrogance of the fossil fuel industry based on the power they wield in Washington, D.C."). More generally, coal mining emerged as an outsized political symbol in the 2016 election, with Trump vowing to "bring back coal." Matt Egan, *Donald Trump's Energy Plan: Regulate Less, Drill More*, CNN BUS. (May 27, 2016), https://money.cnn.com/2016/05/26/investing/donald-trump-energy-plan/index.html?iid=EL.

43. Dep't of the Interior, Repeal of Consolidated Federal Oil & Gas and Federal & Indian Coal Valuation Reform, 82 Fed. Reg. 36,934 (Aug. 7, 2017).

44. *Id.* at 36, 944.

45. *Id.*

46. *See id.* at 36,946; *see also id.* at 36,944 ("We are unable to quantify that cost at this time").

47. *Id.* at 36,951–52; *see also id.* at 36,944 (giving information on the rise in administrative costs and the decrease in royalty payments).

48. *See id.* at 36,934.

49. *See* California v. U.S. Dep't of the Interior, 381 F. Supp.3d 1153, 1157–58 (N.D. Cal. 2019).

50. *See id.* at 1177–78.

51. *See id.* at 1164, 1166–69, 1177–78.

52. *Compare* FED. R. APP. P. 4(a)(1)(B)(ii) (giving sixty days to file a notice of appeal) *and* Docket, California v. U.S. Dep't of Interior, 381 F.Supp.3d (N.D. Cal. 2019) (No. 4:17-CV-05948) (noting final judgment on March 29, 2019 without such notice of appeal being filed). *See also* Charlie Passut, *Court Rejects Trump Repeal of Obama-Era Oil, NatGas Valuation Rule*, NAT. GAS INTEL. (Apr. 17, 2019), https://www.naturalgasintel.com/articles/118069-court-rejects-trump-repeal-of-obama-era-oil-natgas-valuation-rule (discussing the case from an industry perspective).

53. Note that as with coal mining companies, predatory educational lenders and institutions are similarly tied to the Trump administration. *See* Annie Waldman, *For-Profit Colleges Gain a Beachhead in Trump Administration*, PROPUBLICA (Mar. 14, 2017), https://www.propublica.org/article/for-profit-colleges-gain-beachhead-in-trump-administration. In particular, Secretary of Education Betsy DeVos, a longtime Republican donor and charter school advocate, consistently favors for-profit education. *See* David Whitman & Arne Duncan, *Betsy DeVos and Her Cone of Silence on For-Profit Colleges*, BROOKINGS (Oct. 17, 2018), https://www.brookings.edu/research/betsy-devos-for-profit-colleges-education-america/; Emma Brown, *Trump Picks Billionaire Betsy DeVos, School Voucher Advocate, as Education Secretary*, WASH. POST (Nov. 23, 2016), http://wapo.st/2g4fArJ?.

54. *See* Omnibus Budget Reconciliation Act of 1993 § 455, Pub. L. 103-66, 107 Stat 312, 346 (1993); *see also* Improving America's Schools Act of 1994, Pub. L. 103-382, 108 Stat 3518 (1994).

55. *See* Dep't of Educ., William D. Ford Federal Direct Loan Program, 59 Fed. Reg. 61,664 (Dec. 1, 1994).

56. *See* Clare McCann, New Am., The Ins and Outs of the Borrower Defense Rule 2 (2017) (describing the promulgation of the Rule from the perspective of a Department of Education staffer).

57. *See* Danielle Douglas-Gabriel, *For-Profit Corinthian Colleges Files for Bankruptcy*, WASH. POST (May 4, 2015), https://www.washingtonpost.com/news/business/wp/2015/05/04/for-profit-corinthian-colleges-files-for-bankruptcy. *See also* Anya Kamenetz & John O'Connor, *The Collapse of Corinthian Colleges*, NPR (July 8, 2014), https://www.npr.org/blogs/ed/2014/07/08/329550897/the-collapse-of-corinthian-colleges; Anya Kamenetz,

Activists Stop Paying Their Student Loans, NPR (Mar. 31, 2015), https://www.npr.org/sections/ed/2015/03/31/396585597/activists-stop-paying-their-student-loans.

58. Dep't of Educ., Student Assistance General Provisions, Federal Perkins Loan Program, Federal Family Education Loan Program, William D. Ford Federal Direct Loan Program, and Teacher Education Assistance for College and Higher Education Grant Program, 81 Fed. Reg. 75,926, 75,926 (Nov. 1, 2016) ("The current standard allows borrowers to assert a borrower defense if a cause of action would have arisen under applicable State law. In contrast, these final regulations establish a new Federal standard").

59. *See id.*; Dep't of Educ., Student Assistance General Provisions, Federal Perkins Loan Program, Federal Family Education Loan Program, William D. Ford Federal Direct Loan Program, and Teacher Education Assistance for College and Higher Education Grant Program, 81 Fed. Reg. 39,330, 39,336 (June 16, 2016).

60. McCann, *supra* note 56, at 2.

61. *See* Dep't of Educ., *supra* note 58, at 75,926.

62. *Id.*

63. Dep't of Educ., *supra* note 59, at 39,387.

64. *See id.* at 39,397 ("As required by OMB Circular A-4 . . . we have prepared an accounting statement showing the classification of the expenditures associated with the provisions of these regulations. . . . Expenditures are classified as transfers").

65. *See* Dep't of Educ., *supra* note 58, at 76,051.

66. *Id.* at 75,926.

67. *See* Dep't of Educ., *supra* note 59, at 39,391.

68. Dep't of Educ., *supra* note 58, at 76,051.

69. Jonathan Oosting, *DeVos on Mackinac: "Washington Knows Best" Is Over*, DETROIT NEWS (Sept. 22, 2017), https://www.detroitnews.com/story/news/politics/2017/09/22/mackinac-devos-romney-mcdaniel/105897636/ ("Under the previous rules, all one had to do was raise his or her hands to be entitled to so-called free money").

70. *See* Dep't of Educ., Student Assistance General Provisions, Federal Perkins Loan Program, Federal Family Education Loan Program, William D. Ford Federal Direct Loan Program, and Teacher Education Assistance for College and Higher Education Grant Program, 82 Fed. Reg. 27,621 (June 16, 2017).

71. *Id.* at 27,622.

72. *Id.*

73. Dep't of Educ., Student Assistance General Provisions, Federal Perkins Loan Program, Federal Family Education Loan Program, and William D. Ford Federal Direct Loan Program, 83 Fed. Reg. 37,242 (July 31, 2018).

74. *See* Bauer v. DeVos, 325 F. Supp. 3d 74, 78 (D.D.C. 2018).

75. *See id.* at 79.

76. *Id.* at 108.

77. *See* Andrew Kreighbaum, *Obama Student Loan Rule to Take Effect*, INSIDE HIGHER EDUC. (Oct. 17, 2018), https://www.insidehighered.com/news/2018/10/17/more-year-later-obama-student-loan-rule-takes-effect; Andrew Kreighbaum, *Missed Deadline Stalls DeVos Agenda*, INSIDE HIGHER EDUC. (Oct. 4, 2018), https://www.

insidehighered.com/news/2018/10/04/education-department-misses-deadline-its-overhaul-student-loan-rules.

78. *See* Dep't of Educ., News Release, U.S. Department of Education Finalizes Regulations to Protect Student Borrowers, Hold Higher Education Institutions Accountable and Save Taxpayers $11.1 Billion Over 10 Years (Aug. 30, 2019).

79. *See* Andrew Kreighbaum, *Raising the Bar for Loan Forgiveness*, INSIDE HIGHER EDUC. (Sept. 3, 2019), https://www.insidehighered.com/news/2019/09/03/devos-imposes-tougher-debt-relief-standards-student-borrowers-alleging-fraud (describing the removed provisions).

80. Dep't of Educ., Student Assistance General Provisions, Federal Family Education Loan Program, and William D. Ford Federal Direct Loan Program, 84 Fed. Reg. 49,788, 49,894 (Sept. 23, 2019).

81. For example, in response to a comment that alleged the proposed regulations would "save taxpayers several billions of dollars from false claims" the Department noted that it "appreciates the support." *Id.* at 49,885.

82. *See* Kreighbaum, *supra* note 79.

Chapter 11

1. *See* Arlie Russell Hochschild, *The Ecstatic Edge of Politics: Sociology and Donald Trump*, 45 CONTEMP. SOC. 683 (2016).

2. Jeff Hauser, *The Little Agency that Could (Block All Good Regulations)*, AM. PROSPECT (Sept. 25, 2019), https://prospect.org/day-one-agenda/little-federal-agency-block-regulations-oira/.

3. *Id.* ("If personnel is policy, and if OIRA is where good policy goes to either wait forever or die, then perhaps no Obama policy decision in his first term was costlier than installing his friend Cass Sunstein at OIRA").

4. Lisa Heinzerling, *Inside EPA: A Former Insider's Reflections on the Relationship Between the Obama EPA and the Obama White House*, 31 PACE ENVTL. L. REV. 325 (2014). Heinzerling's accounts differ considerably from those offered by others in the Obama administration, and specifically Cass Sunstein. *See, e.g.*, CASS R. SUNSTEIN, SIMPLER: THE FUTURE OF GOVERNMENT (2013); Cass R. Sunstein, *The Office of Information and Regulatory Affairs: Myths and Realities*, 126 HARV. L. REV. 1838 (2013).

5. Heinzerling, *supra* note 4, at 326.

6. *Id.* at 329.

7. *Id.* at 369.

8. *Id.*

9. There are many reasons that the administration declined to pursue some progressive policy goals, but concerns about cost and benefits are one. *See, e.g.*, Emily Baumgaertner, *The FDA Tried to Ban Flavors Years Before the Vaping Outbreak. Top Obama Officials Rejected the Plan*, L.A. TIMES (Oct. 1, 2019), https://www.latimes.com/politics/story/2019-10-01/vaping-flavors-obama-white-house-fda.

10. *See* Mark R. Warner, *To Revive the Economy, Pull Back the Red Tape*, WASH. POST (Dec. 13, 2010), https://www.washingtonpost.com/wp-dyn/content/article/2010/12/12/AR2010121202639.html.

11. *See* Mila Sohoni, *The Idea of Too Much Law*, 80 FORDHAM L. REV. 1585, 1594 (2012).

12. *See supra* chapters 4 and 5.

13. *See, e.g.*, Rena Steinzor, *The Case for Abolishing Centralized White House Regulatory Review*, 1 MICH. J. ENVTL. & ADMIN. L. 209 (2012).

14. *See* Rena Steinzor, *Cost-Benefit Analysis According to the Trump Administration*, REG. REV. (Jul. 23, 2019), https://www.theregreview.org/2019/07/23/steinzor-cost-benefit-analysis-according-trump-administration/.

15. Amy Sinden, *The Cost-Benefit Boomerang*, AM. PROSPECT (July 25, 2019), https://prospect.org/economy/cost-benefit-boomerang/.

16. Elena Kagan, *Presidential Administration*, 114 HARV. L. REV. 2245 (2001).

17. THOMAS J. WEKO, THE POLITICIZING PRESIDENCY: THE WHITE HOUSE PERSONNEL OFFICE, 1948–1994, at 67 (1995).

18. *Id.* at 68.

19. *Id.* at 71–73.

20. An argument along these lines is offered by James Goodwin, an advocate with the Center for Progressive Reform:

> The good news is that the demise of Executive Order 12866 is nothing to weep over. During the course of its lifetime, it did more harm than good. In fact, it would be better still if the order was officially discarded, rather than carrying on with this sad charade pretending that it's still alive. Perhaps then we might be freer to move in a more productive direction under a future, presumably more enlightened presidential administration.

James Goodwin, *Executive Order 12866 Is Basically Dead, and the Trump Administration Basically Killed It*, COALITION FOR SENSIBLE SAFEGUARDS (Oct. 1, 2018), https://sensiblesafeguards.org/executive-order-12866-is-basically-dead-and-the-trump-administration-basically-killed-it/.

21. *See* Gillian E. Metzger, *1930s Redux: The Administrative State Under Siege*, 131 HARV. L. REV. 1 (2017).

22. ROBERT AXELROD, THE EVOLUTION OF COOPERATION (1984).

23. *See* Henry Barbour et al., Growth and Opportunity Project (2013) (commonly referred to as the "RNC autopsy").

24. Keith B. Belton & John D. Graham, Am. Council for Capital Formation, Trump's Deregulatory Record: An Assessment at the Two-Year Mark 10 (2019).

25. *Id.* (internal quotation marks omitted).

26. Graham and Belton argue that Trump's libertarian concern "is closely connected to a conservative legal philosophy that is gaining favor within the Federalist Society and conservative think tanks." *Id.* Graham and Belton point in particular to a line of thinking that questions the legitimacy of the administrative state more broadly as involving an unlawful "delegation" of legislative power to the executive. For exemplars of scholars with these concerns, they cite DAVID SCHOENBROD, POWER

WITHOUT RESPONSIBILITY (1993) and PHILIP HAMBURGER, IS ADMINISTRATIVE LAW UNLAWFUL? (2014). As discussed in chapter 4, Trump's first OIRA administrator Neomi Rao has also endorsed versions of this view in her work. The link with individual freedom of the non-delegation critique is either that Congress is less likely to impose rule on private conduct, or such rules are inherently more legitimate because they arise directly via legislation, without the intervening step of agency action.

27. This symmetry is no accident. Cost-benefit analysis takes people's preferences as a starting point and essentially seeks to deliver the results that would be achieved through voluntary exchange in a perfectly operating market. Indeed, libertarians have struggled with how to incorporate pollution into their thinking, with some arguing that pollution is a form of aggression that requires (or at least justifies) state intervention because it violates people's bodily integrity. *See* MURRAY N. ROTHBARD, FOR A NEW LIBERTY: THE LIBERTARIAN MANIFESTO 319 (2006) ("Air pollution that injures others is aggression pure and simple"). Principled libertarians primarily object to policies that are paternalistic or redistributive. *See generally* ROBERT NOZICK, ANARCHY, STATE, AND UTOPIA (1974). Regulations to address classic market failures (i.e., externalities) are neither paternalistic or redistributive in nature. In addition, there are alternative autonomy-based ethical accounts, such as the "capabilities" approach offered by Amartya Sen and Martha Nussbaum. MARTHA C. NUSSBAUM, WOMEN AND HUMAN DEVELOPMENT: THE CAPABILITIES APPROACH (2000); Amartya Sen, *Well-being, Agency and Freedom: The Dewey Lectures 1984*, 82 J. PHIL. 169 (1985). These theories tend to support quite robust roles for government.

28. *See* ERIC FONER, RECONSTRUCTION, AMERICA'S UNFINISHED REVOLUTION, 1863–1877 (1988).

29. The Court has articulated its evolving views on cost-benefit analysis outside of the context of the Clean Air Act as well. There is an important intervening case, Entergy Corp. v. Riverkeeper, 556 U.S. 208 (2009), that we omit for the sake of brevity. That case concerned a George W. Bush-era EPA rule that allowed cost-benefit analysis to factor into the implementation of a provision of the Clean Water Act dealing with the regulation of cooling intake structures for power plants. As in *EME Homer*, the court found that statutory silence on the question of costs did not preclude cost consideration.

30. Whitman v. Am. Trucking Ass'ns, 531 U.S. 457 (2001).

31. 42 U.S.C. § 7409(b)(1) (2012).

32. *Whitman*, 531 U.S at 471.

33. 134 S. Ct. 1584 (2014).

34. 42 U.S.C. § 7410(a)(2)(D)(i) (2012).

35. 42 U.S.C. § 7412(n)(1)(A) (2012).

36. Michigan v. EPA, 135 S. Ct. 2699 (2015). Both the majority and dissent agreed that the EPA was required to consider costs; the difference concerned when, in the regulatory process, costs were to be taken into account.

37. *See* Jonathan Masur & Eric. A. Posner, *Cost-Benefit Analysis and the Judicial Role*, 85 U. CHI. L. REV. 935, 977–81 (2018); *see also* Caroline Cecot & W. Kip Viscusi, *Judicial*

Review of Agency Benefit-Cost Analysis, 22 GEO. MASON L. REV. 575 (2015); Cass R. Sunstein, *Cost-Benefit Default Principles,* 99 MICH. L. REV. 1651 (2001).

38. Even in the best of circumstances, courts have several important limitations as guardians of cost-benefit analysis methodology, especially compared to an institutional like OIRA. Judicial review is final and occurs after a rulemaking, whereas OIRA is able to engage in lengthy back and forth conversations with agencies over the course of the rulemaking process. Courts also, obviously, lack the type of deep familiarity with cost-benefit analysis found in OIRA, and are best positioned to identify obvious flaws rather than subtle manipulation.

Chapter 12

1. *See* Joseph E. Aldy, Admin. Conference of the U.S., Learning from Experience: An Assessment of the Retrospective Reviews of Agency Rules and the Evidence for Improving the Design and Implementation of Regulatory Policy (2014); Reeve T. Bull, *Building a Framework for Governance: Retrospective Review and Rulemaking Petitions,* 67 ADMIN. L. REV. 265, 277–86 (2015);.

2. Presidential Memorandum of January 30, 2009, Regulatory Review, 74 Fed. Reg. 5977 (Feb. 3, 2009).

3. Lisa Heinzerling, *Inside EPA: A Former Insider's Reflections on the Relationship Between the Obama EPA and the Obama White House,* 31 PACE ENVTL. L. REV. 325, 340 (2014) ("Agency personnel, buoyed by the possibility of reform of a secretive, intrusive, and time-consuming process, eagerly anticipated the new executive order. Outside groups interested in health, safety, and environmental protection cheered the prospect of changes to a system that had worked disproportionately against rules in their domain").

4. Executive Order 13,563, 76 Fed. Reg. 3821 (Jan. 21, 2011).

5. Memorandum from Cass R. Sunstein, Adm'r, Office of Info. and Regulatory Affairs, for the Heads of Executive Departments and Agencies, Disclosure and Simplifications as Regulatory Tools (June 18, 2010). President Obama also issued Executive Order 13,707, *Using Behavial Science Insights to Better Serve the American People,* which directed all agencies to "identify policies, programs, and operations where applying behavioral science insights may yield substantial improvements in public welfare, program outcomes, and program cost effectiveness . . . ." Executive Order 13,7077, 80 Fed. Reg. 56,365 (Sept. 18, 2015). This order can be understood as applying to agency rulemaking.

6. The George W. Bush administration, in keeping Clinton's order 12,866 in place and focusing on building on the existing system with its Circular A-4, took a similar approach.

7. *See generally* Kirti Datla & Richard L. Revesz, *Deconstructing Independent Agencies (and Executive Agencies),* 98 CORNELL L. REV. 769 (2013).

8. *See* Rachel E. Barkow, *Insulating Agencies: Avoiding Capture Through Institutional Design,* 89 TEX. L. REV. 15 (2010) (discussing the value of independence); Datla &

Revesz, *supra* note 7, at 827–32 (discussing and then rejecting legal arguments limiting power of the president to subject independent agencies to review).

9. Executive Order No. 13,579, 76 Fed. Reg. 41,587 (July 14, 2011).

10. Memorandum from Russell T. Vought, Acting Director, Office of Mgmt. and Budget, for the Heads of Executive Departments and Agencies, Guidance on Compliance with the Congressional Review Act (Apr. 11, 2019).

11. Pigouvian taxes, which are levied on behavior that generates externalities, are justified on the basis of their ability to correct market failures. *See* Jonathan S. Masur & Eric A. Posner, *Toward a Pigouvian State*, 164 U. PA. L. REV. 93 (2015). At least as things stand, Pigouvian taxes are not a significant portion of the US tax code, which primarily raises revenue by taxing various types of income.

12. *See, e.g.*, TAX BY DESIGN: THE MIRRLEES REVIEW 35 (James Mirrlees ed., 2011) ("We want a tax system that does not unnecessarily discourage economic activity, that achieves distributional objectives, and that is fair, transparent, and administratively straightforward").

13. *See* CHRISTOPHER HOWARD, THE HIDDEN WELFARE STATE: TAX EXPENDITURES AND SOCIAL POLICY IN THE UNITED STATES (1997); STANLEY S. SURREY & PAUL R. MCDANIEL, TAX EXPENDITURES (1985).

14. *See* Nathaniel O. Keohane, *The Technocratic and Democratic Functions of the CAIR Regulatory Analysis*, *in* REFORMING REGULATORY IMPACT ANALYSIS 33, 50 (Winston Harrington et al. eds., 2009) (suggesting that regulatory impact assessment present impacts in "natural units" (i.e., physical impacts) as well as in monetary terms).

15. U.S. Gov't Accountability Office, Reexamining Regulations: Opportunities Exist to Improve Effectiveness and Transparency of Retrospective Reviews 10 (2007) (explaining action of presidents through George W. Bush).

16. Inst. for Policy Integrity, Strengthening Regulatory Review: Recommendations for the Trump Administration from Former OIRA Leaders (2016) (report reflecting consensus of roundtable conversation among the following former OIRA administrators: Christopher C. DeMuth (1981–1984); Douglas H. Ginsburg (1984–1985); Wendy Lee Gramm (1985–1988); S. Jay Plager (1988–1989); Sally Katzen (1993–1998); John D. Graham (2001–2006); Susan E. Dudley (2007–2009); Boris Bershteyn (2012–2013, acting)).

17. Michael Mandel & Diana G. Carew, Progressive Policy Inst., Regulatory Improvement Commission: A Politically-Viable Approach to U.S. Regulatory Reform (2013); Mercatus Ctr., How Well Do Federal Regulations Actually Work? The Role of Retrospective Review (2012).

18. *See* Aldy, *supra* note 1; Bull, *supra* note 1; Cary Coglianese, *Moving Forward with Regulatory Lookback*, 30 YALE J. REG. ONLINE 57 (2013); Michael Greenstone, *Toward a Culture of Persistent Regulatory Experimentation and Evaluation*, *in* NEW PERSPECTIVES ON REGULATION 111 (David Moss & John Cisternino eds., 2009); Jonathan B. Wiener & Daniel L. Ribeiro, *Environmental Regulation Going Retro: Learning Foresight from Hindsight*, 32 J. LAND USE & ENVTL. L. 1 (2016).

19. Admin. Conference of the U.S., Recommendation 2014-5, Retrospective Review of Agency Rules, adopted December 4, 2014, 79 Fed. Reg. 75,114 (Dec. 17, 2014).

20. *See* Jonathan B. Wiener & Lori S. Bennear, Institutional Roles and Goals for Retrospective Regulatory Analysis 14 (Feb. 4, 2020) ("Despite the broad and long-standing support for retrospective review, government measures to require retrospective review have yielded only limited results, with only occasional episodes of effort to analyze past policies").

21. *See* Executive Order 13,563, § 6, *supra* note 4 (devoted to "Retrospective Analysis of Existing Rules"); Executive Order 13,579, *supra* note 9 ("independent regulatory agencies should consider how best to promote retrospective analysis of rules"); Executive Order 13,610, 77 Fed. Reg. 28,469 (May 14, 2012) (requiring agencies to periodically report on the "status of their retrospective review efforts").

22. Memorandum from Cass R. Sunstein, Adm'r, Office of Info. and Regulatory Affairs, to the Heads of Executive Departments and Agencies, Cumulative Effects of Regulations (Mar. 20, 2012); Memorandum from Cass R. Sunstein, Adm'r, Office of Info. and Regulatory Affairs, to the Heads of Executive Departments and Agencies, Retrospective Analysis of Existing Significant Regulations (Apr. 25, 2011).

23. Cass R. Sunstein, *The Regulatory Lookback*, 94 B.U. L. REV. 579 (2014).

24. U.S. Gov't Accountability Office, Reexamining Regulations: Agencies Often Made Regulatory Changes, but Could Strengthen Linkages to Performance Goals (2014).

25. Sunstein, *supra* note 23, at 588.

26. *Id.*

27. *See* Art Fraas & Alex Egorenkov, *Retrospective Analyses Are Hard: A Cautionary Tale from EPA's Air Toxics Regulation*, 9. J. BENEFIT COST ANALYSIS 247 (2018).

28. Joshua D. Angrist & Jörn-Steffen Pischke, *The Credibility Revolution in Empirical Economics: How Better Research Design Is Taking the Con out of Econometrics*, 24 J. ECON. PERSP. 3 (2010).

29. Michael Greenstone & Justin Gallagher, *Does Hazardous Waste Matter? Evidence from the Housing Market and the Superfund Program*, 123 Q. J. ECON. 951 (2008).

30. *See, e.g.*, Greenstone, *supra* note 18.

31. *See* Aldy, *supra* note 1.

32. *See* Wiener & Bennear, *supra* note 20, at 23 (calling for prioritization of "areas of regulatory learning that would improve outcomes across agencies" in regulatory review).

33. Douglas W. Dockery, *Health Effects of Particulate Air Pollution*, 14 ANNALS EPIDEMIOLOGY 257, 261 (2009).

34. President Barack Obama, Address Before a Joint Session of the Congress on the State of the Union (January 24, 2012).

35. Sunstein, *supra* note 23, at 589 ("It took a village, but I share responsibility [for the joke]").

36. *See* John Bronsteen, Christopher Buccafusco & Jonathan S. Masur, *Well-Being Analysis vs. Cost-Benefit Analysis*, 62 DUKE L. J. 1603 (2013).

37. *See* Cass R. Sunstein, *The Limits of Quantification*, 102 CALIF. L. REV. 1369 (2014).

38. Richard L. Revesz, *Quantifying Regulatory Benefits*, 102 CALIF. L. REV. 1423, 1427–30 (2014).

39. *See generally* Michael D. Bayles, *The Price of Life*, 89 ETHICS 20, 21 (1978) (ultimately arguing that "(1) it is rational and morally permissible to place a price on one's own

life, and (2) there is a morally acceptable method of using this pricing to determine some social policies").

40. E.J. Mishan, *Evaluation of Life and Limb: A Theoretical Approach*, 79 J. POL. ECON. 687, 687–90 (1971) (noting problems with this approach).

41. W. Kip Viscusi, *Monetizing the Benefits of Risk and Environmental Regulation*, 33 FORDHAM URB. L.J. 1003, 1017 (describing the view of agency officials).

42. The willingness to pay measure focuses on how people trade money, convenience, or time against mortality risk. Some jobs are riskier than others, but they also have higher wages. Some products are more expensive than others, but are also safer. It is possible to observe choices that people make about employment or purchases to infer something about the relative value that they place on mortality risk reduction.

43. Viscusi, *supra* note 41, at 1017–18.

44. *Regulatory Impact Analysis Guidance*, *in* OFFICE OF MGMT. & BUDGET, REGULATORY PROGRAM OF THE UNITED STATES GOVERNMENT, APRIL 1, 1988–MARCH 31, 1989, at 561, 569 (1988); EPA, Guidelines for Preparing Economic Analyses 7-8 (2010).

45. *See* EPA, Control of Emissions from Nonroad Large Spark-Ignition Engines, and Recreational Engines (Marine and Land-Based), 67 Fed. Reg. 68,242 (Nov. 8, 2002); EPA, Technical Addendum: Methodologies for the Benefit Analysis of the Clear Skies Act of 2003, at 38–39 (2003); Cass R. Sunstein, *Lives, Life-Years, and Willingness to Pay*, 104 COLUM. L. REV. 205, 206 (2004). Senior administration officials, notably then OIRA administrator John Graham, had been proponents of the life-years approach. *See generally* John D. Graham & Jianhui Hu, *Using Quality Adjusted Life Years in Regulatory Analysis: Definitions, Methods, Applications and Limitations* (Policy Research Initiatives, Government of Canada Working Paper Series 038, October 2008).

46. EPA, Sci. Advisory Bd., Advisory Council for Clean Air Compliance Analysis, Review of the Draft Analytical Plan for EPA's Second Prospective Analysis—Benefits and Costs of the Clean Air Act, 1990–2020, at 26 (2001); Office of Mgmt. & Budget, Circular A-4, at 30 (Sept. 17, 2003).

47. EPA, Guidelines for Preparing Economic Analyses 90 (2000).

48. W. Kip Viscusi, *Risk Guideposts for a Safer Society: Introduction and Overview*, 58 J. RISK & UNCERTAINTY 101, 112–13 tbl. 2 (2019).

49. *See, e.g.*, W. KIP VISCUSI, PRICING LIVES: GUIDEPOSTS FOR A SAFER SOCIETY (2018).

50. Office of Mgmt. & Budget, 2012 Report to Congress on the Costs and Benefits of Federal Regulations and Unfunded Mandates on State, Local, and Tribal Entities 17 n.20 (2012).

51. One important exception was the Obama administration's cost-benefit analysis of its Clean Water Rule, which assigned a value to preserving wetlands that was based on both use and non-use value. *See* EPA & Dep't of the Army, Economic Analysis of the EPA-Army Clean Water Rule 44–49 (2015).

52. *See* EPA, Economic Analysis for the Final Section 316(b) Existing Facilities Rule (2014).

53. *See generally* Shuang Liu et al., *Valuing Ecosystem Services: Theory, Practice, and the Need for a Transdisciplinary Synthesis*, 1185 ANNALS N.Y. ACAD. SCI. 54, 54 (2010).

54. Nat'l Research Council, Valuing Ecosystem Services 2–3 (2005).

55. Lynn Scarlett & James Boyd, Ecosystem Services: Quantification, Policy Applications, And Current Federal Capabilities (2011); EPA, Sci. Advisory Bd., Valuing the Protection of Ecological Systems and Services (2009).

56. *See* Michael A. Livermore, *Patience Is an Economic Virtue: Real Options, Natural Resources, and Offshore Oil*, 84 U. Colo. L. Rev. 581 (2013).

57. Of course, the economic analysis is only one component of the decision to open land for leasing. There are many other procedural and substantive considerations.

58. *See* Bureau of Ocean Energy Mgmt., 2017–2022 Outer Continental Shelf Oil and Gas Leasing Proposed Final Program 10-2 to -16 (2016).

59. EPA, Nat'l Ctr. for Envtl. Econ., Valuing Mortality Risk Reductions for Environmental Policy: A White Paper (2010).

60. Eric A. Posner & Cass R. Sunstein, *Moral Commitments in Cost-Benefit Analysis*, 103 Va. L. Rev. 1809 (2017).

61. Lisa A. Robinson, James K. Hammitt & Richard J. Zeckhauser, *Attention to Distribution in U.S. Regulatory Analyses*, 10 Rev. Envtl. Econ. & Pol'y 308 (2016).

62. Matthew D. Adler & Eric A. Posner, New Foundations of Cost-Benefit Analysis (2006).

63. *See Poverty Guidelines for 2020*, U.S. Dep't of Health & Hum. Servs., https://aspe. hhs.gov/poverty-guidelines (guidelines for family of four); Estelle Sommeiller & Mark Price, Econ. Policy Inst., The New Gilded Age: Income Inequality in the U.S. by Sate, Metropolitan Area, and County (2018). We have provided an argument from utilitarianism based on the diminishing marginal utility of consumption. There are additional reasons to have concern for the least well off. *See, e.g.*, Matthew D. Adler, Well-Being and Fair Distribution: Beyond Cost-Benefit Analysis (2012) (defending a "prioritarian" view that gives additional consideration to the least well off, entirely apart from diminishing marginal utility of consumption); John Rawls, A Theory of Justice (1971) (arguing from social contract theory that just society would be most concerned with the least well off).

64. *See* Louis Kaplow & Steven Shavell, *Fairness Versus Welfare*, 114 Harv. L. Rev. 961 (2001); Louis Kaplow & Steven Shavell, *Should Legal Rules Favor the Poor? Clarifying the Role of Legal Rules and the Income Tax in Redistributing Income*, 29 J. Legal Stud. 821 (2000); Louis Kaplow & Steven Shavell, *Why the Legal System Is Less Efficient than the Income Tax in Redistributing Income*, 23 J. Legal Stud. 667 (1994).

65. Some object to efficiency as a valid criteria—for example, because it treats all values as commensurable. *See* Elizabeth Anderson, Value in Ethics and Economics (1993). In this discussion, we seek to separate out issues of distribution from other types of questions that bear on the desirability of a regulatory policy. We therefore cabin incommensurability objections to efficiency as a criteria, along with related concerns.

66. *See* Sommeiller & Price, *supra* note 63.

67. We do not focus on libertarian objections to redistributive policy, which we find unpersuasive. *See, e.g.*, Liam Murphy & Thomas Nagel, The Myth of Ownership: Taxes and Justice (2002).

68. Memorandum of Agreement, Department of the Treasury and Office of Management and Budget Review of Tax Regulations under Executive Order 12,866 (2018).

69. There are other formulations of the basic question of the foundational good that equality matters with respect to, with philosophers weighing in for and against various alternatives. *See generally* Amartya Sen, *Equality of What?*, *in* I THE TANNER LECTURES ON HUMAN VALUES 195 (1980).

70. Richard L. Revesz, *Regulation and Distribution*, 93 N.Y.U. L. REV. 1489, 1564–65 (2018). For more detail on presidents' ability to direct resources, see JOHN HUDAK, PRESIDENTIAL PORK: WHITE HOUSE INFLUENCE OVER THE DISTRIBUTION OF FEDERAL GRANTS (2014).

71. *See* Executive Order 13,132, 64 Fed. Reg. 43,255 (Aug. 10, 1999); Catherine M. Sharkey, *Federalism Accountability: "Agency-Forcing" Measures*, 58 DUKE L. J. 2125 (2009) (documenting the failure of agencies to consider federalism impacts and suggesting reforms).

Index

For the benefit of digital users, indexed terms that span two pages (e.g., 52–53) may, on occasion, appear on only one of those pages.

Notes are indicated by n following the page number.